Family Problems and Family Violence

Heather M. Foran, PhD, is the principal investigator of a project on couple functioning and psychopathology funded by the German Research Foundation at the Technical University of Braunschweig in Germany and a part-time consultant for the Walter Reed Army Institute of Research. Her research examines intimate partner violence from a public health perspective with an emphasis on assessment, surveillance, and models of risk and protection. Dr. Foran received her doctorate in clinical psychology from Stony Brook University and is a licensed U.S. psychologist. She has numerous scholarly articles on family-related topics and psychopathology and is chair of the relational processes and ICD-11 working group.

Steven R. H. Beach, PhD, is a faculty member in the clinical psychology program at the University of Georgia and a licensed clinical psychologist with over 25 years of experience investigating the role of social relationships in the development and maintenance of psychopathology, particularly depression and substance use disorders. He currently serves as director of the William A. and Barbara R. Owens Institute for Behavioral Research, an interdisciplinary research institute. He is widely recognized as an authority on the link between marital discord and depression and the use of marital interventions in the context of depression. He is also recognized for his research on the role of genetic moderators of intervention response and other contextual variables, and the potential role of epigenetic regulation in accounting for contextual and intervention effects.

Amy M. Smith Slep, PhD, is professor of comprehensive care and cariology at New York University. Along with her collaborator Richard E. Heyman, she cofounded and codirects the Family Translational Research Group. Dr. Slep's research focuses on many different aspects of conflict and violence in families: the development of dysfunctional parenting, the connections between parenting and partner conflict, the dynamics of conflict escalation and de-escalation in productive and destructive conflicts, and what facets of exposure to violence impact children's functioning and how these impacts can be buffered. She also focuses on how to best prevent family violence. Her work on definitions of maltreatment has resulted in definitions that are now being used throughout the U.S. military. She has published nearly 100 scientific articles and book chapters and has received nearly 40 federal research grants. She is a licensed clinical psychologist.

Richard E. Heyman, PhD, is a professor at New York University. Dr. Heyman codirects the Family Translational Research Group (with Dr. Amy Slep) in the Department of Cariology and Comprehensive Care. He earned a BS from Duke University and a PhD in clinical psychology from the University of Oregon. Dr. Heyman has received 40 grants/contracts from major U.S. funding agencies on a variety of family-related topics, from anger escalation in couples to the impact of family violence on children to community-level prevention of family maltreatment, substance problems, and suicidality. Dr. Heyman has published over 100 scientific articles/chapters focused on couple dysfunction, intimate partner violence, and child maltreatment and their risk factors and consequences. Dr. Heyman is a licensed psychologist and maintains a private practice.

Marianne Z. Wamboldt, MD, is professor and vice chair of the Department of Psychiatry at the University of Colorado School of Medicine, as well as chair of Psychiatry and Behavioral Sciences at Children's Hospital Colorado. She is a board-certified child and adolescent psychiatrist, with over 25 years of clinical, teaching, and research experience. Her training included a BS magna cum laude from Marquette University, an MD as well as general psychiatry residency from the University of Wisconsin, a clinical research fellowship at NIMH, and a specialty fellowship in child and adolescent psychiatry at the University of Colorado. Her interests have focused on the role of family relationships in medical (primarily asthma) and psychological outcomes for children and teens, behavioral genetics as a tool to understanding the comorbidity of medical and psychiatric problems, and clinical interventions for children and adolescents with mood and/or anxiety disorders. She has authored over 62 scientific articles/chapters, has been involved as principal investigator or coinvestigator on over 30 grants, and is involved as president of the Board of Family Process; past chair of the Committee on the Physically Ill Child, as well as a member of the Program Committee, within the American Academy of Child and Adolescent Psychiatry; and a member of the Group for Advancement of Psychiatry's Committee on the Family.

Family Problems and Family Violence: Reliable Assessment and the ICD-11

Heather M. Foran, PhD
Steven R. H. Beach, PhD
Amy M. Smith Slep, PhD
Richard E. Heyman, PhD
Marianne Z. Wamboldt, MD
Editors

Nadine J. Kaslow, PhD, ABPP
David Reiss, MD
Associate Editors

SPRINGER PUBLISHING COMPANY
NEW YORK

Springer Publishing Company, LLC
11 West 42nd Street
New York, NY 10036
www.springerpub.com

Acquisitions Editor: Nancy S. Hale
Associate Editor: Kathryn Corasaniti
Composition: Newgen Imaging

ISBN: 978-0-8261-0910-1
e-book ISBN: 978-0-8261-0911-8

12 13 14 15 / 5 4 3 2 1

Library of Congress Cataloging-in-Publication Data

Family problems and family violence : reliable assessment and the ICD-11 / edited by Heather M. Foran ... [et al.].
p. cm.
Includes index.
ISBN 978-0-8261-0910-1
1. Family violence. 2. Spousal abuse. I. Foran, Heather M.
RC569.5.F3F34 2013
616.85'822—dc23

2012019655

Printed in the United States of America by Gasch Printing.

Contents

Contributors

Steven R. H. Beach, PhD
University of Georgia
Athens, GA

Alexander Butchart, PhD
World Health Organization
Geneva, Switzerland

Wenhong Cheng, MD
Shanghai Jiaotong University Medical Center
Shanghai, China

Anthony R. Cordaro, Jr. MD
University of Colorado School of Medicine
Aurora, CO

Ann C. Eckardt Erlanger, PsyD
New York University
New York, NY

Tamara Del Vecchio, PhD
St. John's University
Queens, NY

Yasmine Fayad, MA
American University of Beirut Medical Center
Beirut, Lebanon

Heather M. Foran, PhD
Technical University of Braunschweig
Braunschweig, Germany

Claudia García-Moreno, MD
World Health Organization
Geneva, Switzerland

Kurt Hahlweg, PhD
Technical University of Braunschweig
Braunschweig, Germany

Richard E. Heyman, PhD
New York University
New York, NY

Nadine J. Kaslow, PhD, ABPP
Emory University
Atlanta, GA

Brigitte Khoury, PhD
American University of Beirut Medical Center
Beirut, Lebanon

Jill Malik, MA
Stony Brook University
Stony Brook, NY

Christopher Mikton, PhD
World Health Organization
Geneva, Switzerland

Mokhantšo G. Makoae, PhD
Human Sciences Research Council
Cape Town, South Africa

Christina Pallitto, PhD
World Health Organization
Geneva, Switzerland

Ryan Phelps, PhD
Stephen F. Austin State University
Nacogdoches, TX

Ron Prinz, PhD, ABPP
University of South Carolina
Columbia, SC

David Reiss, MD
Yale Child Study Center
New Haven, CT

Amy M. Smith Slep, PhD
New York University
New York, NY

Jeffery D. Snarr, PhD
The College at Brockport
Brockport, NY

Douglas K. Snyder, PhD
Texas A&M University
College Station, TX

Tuula Tamminen, MD
University of Tampere Medical School
Tempere, Finland

Marianne Z. Wamboldt, MD
University of Colorado School of Medicine
Aurora, CO

Mark A. Whisman, PhD
University of Colorado at Boulder
Boulder, CO

Foreword

At its core, human life is relational. For centuries, poets, mystics, and all great spiritual traditions have testified to humanity's deep need and yearning for relationship. The African concept of *Ubuntu* bears witness to the critical importance of relationships for human flourishing. As described by Archbishop Desmond Tutu, "We believe that a person is a person through another person, that my humanity is caught up, bound up, inextricably, with yours." Or, in the words of the poet ee cummings, "I am through you so I."

As relational beings, then, we humans live in an intensely relational world. Unfortunately, not all human relationships are life-giving. Rather than nurturing our individual and collective flourishing, some relationships are devastatingly harmful. Instead of being enriching and meaningful, they can be terrifying and disabling. The magnitude of human suffering caused by unhealthy relationships can scarcely be imagined. Primary relationships—those between intimate partners or between parent and child—are particularly important. Recent scientific studies have shown that the quality of our primary relationships can have profound effects on health, wound healing, immune function, and responses to treatment for a variety of mental and physical illnesses. Given the overwhelming importance of family relationships for human health and well-being, it is surprising—and unfortunate—that in busy clinical settings, they often are not adequately considered in the assessment and treatment of individual patients. As a consequence, the tremendous healing power of relationship goes untapped and responses to treatment remain unsatisfactory.

For the past 10 years, a small group of family researchers, primarily psychologists, and psychiatrists in North America has been amassing the scientific evidence and articulating the conceptual and practical frameworks necessary to bring greater attention to relationships in clinical practice. This groundbreaking work, focused primarily on mental and relational health, is summarized in their recent book, *Relational Processes and DSM-V: Neuroscience, Assessment, Prevention, and Intervention.*

To build on this seminal effort and to explore how relational processes might be accorded greater prominence on a global scale, a meeting was held at Eranos, in Ascona, Switzerland on October 14–15, 2010. The intent of the meeting was to foster greater cross-cultural and interdisciplinary understanding of the challenges to primary relationships faced by humans around the globe. The meeting was supported by the

Eranos Foundation and the Fetzer Institute. Participants included clinical psychologists, psychiatrists, and researchers from the United States, China, South Africa, Lebanon, Finland, and Australia, as well as officials from the World Health Organization (WHO) specializing in mental health, external causes of injury, violence prevention, and reproductive health. Fields of expertise included parent–child relationships, child maltreatment, intimate partner relationships—and intimate partner violence—genetics, health systems research, and disease classification.

The timing of this meeting coincided with a major revision of the International Classification of Diseases (ICD). The ICD, published by WHO, is the global standard for classifying diseases and related health problems. Its importance for diagnosis and treatment of physical and mental illness, and for understanding global disease trends, cannot be overstated. It is used by physicians, other health workers, hospitals, ministries of health, and health information systems around the world. The 11th revision of the ICD will reflect the many scientific and conceptual advances in medicine and health since the last major revision in 1992.

Thus, the Eranos meeting provided the first opportunity for psychologists, psychiatrists, and other mental health professionals from a variety of cultural settings to explore how relational processes might be more fully incorporated into the ICD-11. Participants first reviewed the data on the massive public health and economic toll of relational problems. They then focused their attention on four specific categories of family relational problems: partner relational problems (which do not necessarily involve maltreatment or abuse), partner maltreatment, parent–child relational problems, and child maltreatment. They also developed criteria and made recommendations for greater incorporation of relational processes into the ICD-11.

The Eranos meeting marked the beginning of an expanded collaboration that has culminated in this remarkable volume, which is both conceptually robust and highly practical. For each of the four major categories of relational problems, the distinguished authors have addressed (a) definitions, prevalence, and implications for diagnosis; (b) psychological, physical, and economic impact; (c) global considerations for assessment; and (d) practical tools for clinical practice and public health. A final section describes the public health response to relational problems and outlines future directions for addressing them.

This book should be of interest to clinicians and family therapists, especially those who seek to understand the impact of family relationships from the broad perspective of global health. It will also serve as a valuable resource for public health officials involved in violence prevention, maternal–child health, and mental health, among other fields. The book promises to heighten awareness among clinicians around the world about the diagnostic and therapeutic importance of family relationships in human health and disease. It also will serve as a roadmap for the critically important work that lies ahead.

David Addiss, MD, MPH
Task Force for Global Health
Decatur, Georgia

Preface

Relational problems (intimate partner violence, partner relationship distress, child maltreatment, and parent–child relational problems) are major global concerns having vast impacts on psychological health, physical health, and economic well-being. Prevention and public health interventions for relational problems have been constrained by lack of universal definitions and assessment of these problems globally. The purpose of this book is to address this need by providing a comprehensive and concise review of the public health impact of relational problems, innovations in definitional systems for relational problems, and recommendations for improving surveillance worldwide.

THE ICD

The International Classification of Diseases (ICD) is the most widely used physical and mental health classification system. The ICD, originating as a system to classify causes of death in the 19th century, is currently used for coding of mortality and morbidity in more than 110 countries and 60% of the world's population (WHO, 2010a). The ICD is also used for national and international epidemiology, patient records, health care reimbursement and financing, referencing for treatment and research, and quality assessment of health care systems (WHO, 2010a).

It may be of surprise to many mental health professionals in the United States and Canada that the ICD is the primary system used for medical coding and health care reimbursement of both mental and physical health conditions in North America, as well. Although the *Diagnostic Statistical Manual for Mental Disorders* (*DSM-IV*; American Psychiatric Association, 1994) is used for training mental health providers, the use of ICD codes is widespread. For example, in the largest integrated health system in the United States, the Veterans Affairs medical centers, the ICD is used for all coding of mental and physical conditions within their electronic patient record system. In fact, more than 70% of the world's health expenditures are allocated using the ICD (WHO, 2010a).

The current version of the ICD, the ICD-10, was published in 1990. Revision for the next edition, the ICD-11, is underway and scheduled for full release in 2015 with the beta version available in 2012 (WHO, 2011). The ICD-11 revision steering committee has set forth priorities for the revision (WHO, 2007). Most importantly, revisions should be based on new scientific evidence, clinical utility and health system utility, and public health usefulness. In this book, we address these priorities as they apply to revisions to the relational problem categories; namely, intimate partner violence, partner relationship distress, child maltreatment, and caregiver–child relational problems.

THE ICD-11 AND RELATIONAL PROCESSES

Since the last edition of the ICD in 1992, there has been significant progress in understanding relational problems and their impact on physical and mental health (see Beach, Wamboldt, Kaslow, Heyman, & Reiss, 2006a; Schmaling & Sher, 2000). A series of studies examining immune function, cardiovascular response, and other biological processes have demonstrated that unhealthy relationships in childhood and adulthood are associated with higher morbidity and mortality (e.g., Eaker, Sullivan, Kelly-Hayes, D'Agostino, & Benjamin, 2007; Fagundes, Bennett, Derry, & Kiecolt-Glaser, 2011; Kiecolt-Glaser, Gouin, & Hantsoo, 2009; Wolf, Miller, & Chen, 2008). In addition, the importance of relational problems for treatment, clinical course, and health care utilization of a variety of physical and mental health conditions has been more thoroughly documented (e.g., Bell, 2009; Denton et al., 2010; Miklowitz, Wisniewski, Miyahara, Otto, & Sachs, 2005; Nemeroff et al., 2003; Schonbrun & Whisman, 2010; F. S. Wamboldt, M. Z. Wamboldt, Gavin, Roesler, & Brugman, 1995). Simultaneously, there has been significant innovations in assessment of key relational processes. As reviewed in this book, reliable and valid definitions for intimate partner violence, child maltreatment, relationship distress, and caregiver–child relational problems are now available and have potential to improve the surveillance and treatment of these problems by inclusion in the ICD-11.

These definitions improve existing categories used in the ICD-10 in many ways. First, there are no valid definitions for relational processes in the ICD-10. Second, the ICD-10 includes a large number of names for relational categories, but there is a lack of scientific evidence for including so many separate codes. This is illustrated below with a list of some of the codes for family problems and family violence used in the ICD-10 (WHO, 2010b):

Z60 Problems related to social environment
Z60.1 Atypical parenting situation
Z61 Problems related to negative life events in childhood
Z61.2 Altered pattern of family relationships in childhood
Z61.4 Problems related to alleged sexual abuse of child by person within primary support group
Z61.6 Problems related to alleged physical abuse of child
Z62 Other problems related to upbringing
Z62.0 Inadequate parental supervision and control
Z62.1 Parental overprotection
Z62.3 Hostility toward and scapegoating of child
Z62.4 Emotional neglect of child
Z62.5 Other problems related to neglect in upbringing
Z62.6 Inappropriate parental pressure and other abnormal qualities of upbringing
Z62.8 Other specified problems related to upbringing
Z62.9 Problems related to upbringing, unspecified
Z63 Other problems related to primary support group, including family circumstances
Z63.0 Problems in relationship with spouse or partner
Z63.1 Problems in relationship with parents and in-laws

Z63.2 Inadequate family support
Y05 Sexual assault by bodily force
Y06 Neglect and abandonment
Y06.0 By spouse or partner
Y06.1 By parent
Y07 Other maltreatment
Y07.0 By spouse or partner
Y07.1 By parent
T74 Maltreatment syndromes
T4.0 Neglect or abandonment
T74.1 Physical abuse
T74.2 Sexual abuse
T74.3 Psychological abuse
T74.8 Other maltreatment syndromes
T74.9 Maltreatment syndrome, unspecified

Third, there are no reliable tools for assessing the dozens of codes, and the complexity of the current system limits clinical utility. The large number of codes, with no definitions or tools to assess them, also makes the current system cumbersome for use in many low-resource settings. This book consolidates these codes into four scientifically based categories that have validated definitions and brief screening tools that can be easily implemented across a range of settings. Thus, it directly addresses the primary goals of the ICD-11 revisions—improvements based on science, clinical utility, and public health usefulness—and is organized accordingly.

HISTORICAL CONTEXT FOR THE CURRENT VOLUME

This book is the result of a conference attended by worldwide scholars and representatives of the World Health Organization (WHO) held October 14–15, 2010 in Ascona, Switzerland. The conference, funded by the Fetzer Institute, provided a forum to discuss specific recommendations for reliable, valid international definitions to be incorporated into the new version of the International Classification of Diseases (ICD-11).

The foundation of this book is also based on more than a decade of scholarly activities by the Relational Processes Working Group initially founded by David Reiss, Steven Beach, Nadine Kaslow, Marianne Wamboldt, and Richard Heyman in 2001. There have been two previous expert meetings on the topic of relational assessment (Relational Processes and Mental Health, Washington, DC, 2005 and Relational Processes and the *DSM-V*: Revising Current Nosology and Improving Assessment, San Diego, CA, 2007) and several other publications related to this topic (e.g., Beach et al., 2006a; Beach,Wamboldt, Kaslow, Heyman & Reiss, 2006b; Heyman et al., 2009; Wamboldt et al., 2010). Over the past decade, numerous experts from a range of fields relevant to relational processes (e.g., public health, epidemiology, clinical and social psychology, psychiatry, economics, neuroscience) have contributed to the conversation on this topic.

SUMMARY OF CHAPTER CONTENTS

The first four sections of the book each describe one relational problem: (a) partner maltreatment, (b) partner relational problems, (c) child maltreatment, and (d) caregiver–child relational problems. These four categories were selected above the smaller delineations currently found in the ICD-10, as they compose parsimonious categories with the most scientific basis for reliable and valid coding.

Each section comprises four chapters. The first chapter within each section provides definitional information, prevalences, and implications for diagnosis (see Chapters 1, 5, 9, and 13).

The second chapter within each section addresses cultural issues in the assessment of relationship problems (see Chapters 2, 6, 10, and 14). The section on partner maltreatment includes global considerations in assessment of violence against women around the world (Chapter 2, Pallitto and García-Moreno). In the section on partner relational problems, assessment issues of relational problems in the Arab world are described (Chapter 6, Khoury and Fayad). In the section on child maltreatment, issues in application of newly developing surveillance systems in South Africa, as an example, are reviewed (Chapter 10, Makoae). In the section on caregiver–child relationships, implications of the rapid development on families in China and parent–child relationships are discussed (Chapter 14, Cheng).

The third chapter in each section provides evidence for the public health importance of relational problems by reviewing the psychological, physical, and economic impacts of each relationship problem (see Chapters 3, 7, 11, and 15).

The last chapter in each section provides measures for screening each of the four relational problems and recommendations for use in applied settings (see Chapters 4, 8, 12, and 16). We expect these chapters will be of particular use to health providers seeking tools for reliable assessment and diagnosis of relational problems in hospitals, clinics, or research settings.

The aforementioned sections are supplemented by a final section that describes public health programs to address relational problems and future directions (see Chapters 17–20). Within this section, the first chapter describes the Triple P program as an example of a "success story" in terms of public health prevention to address caregiver–child relational problems (Chapter 17, Prinz). The second chapter discusses public health programming to address child and partner maltreatment from a World Health Organization perspective (Chapter 18, Mikton and Butchart).

The last two chapters provide recommendations for public health surveillance and future directions for science and public policy (Chapter 19, Reiss; Chapter 20, Beach, Kaslow et al.). The chapter by David Reiss reviews the evidence for co-occurrence of medical problems with relational problems and implications of "cross-coding" conditions for treatment and service provision. As persuasively argued in David Reiss's chapter, the value of cross-coding for diagnosis and treatment planning is apparent, but implementation has been constrained by practical issues. The ICD-11 offers a unique opportunity to overcome past constraints in cross-coding through its online format in which codes can be easily linked. Further, one of the goals of the ICD-11 is to make use of the advantages of electronic record systems in coding of mental and physical health conditions (WHO, 2007). Electronic record systems offer several advantages, including improving surveillance and monitoring, clinical care, and cost effectiveness. In particular, electronic record systems allow for programming of decision trees that have been documented to improve assessment and subsequent treatment recommendations. For example, when a child presents to a pediatrician with lacerations on the back or a woman presents with bruises to her face, maltreatment should be assessed. The use of an electronic record system could trigger the provider when entering these injury codes to assess for maltreatment. This could lead to improvements in care for victims who were previously underdetected. In addition, for disorders in which couple or family problems influence clinical course, prompting to assess for these relationship problems may help improve treatment outcomes.

A NOTE ABOUT OUR APPROACH

Clearly, there are many causes for relational problems and they may differ by region, culture, or nation. In the case of intimate partner violence and child maltreatment, prevalence of violence against women and children differ drastically from one country to another and within countries (e.g., rural and urban areas) (García-Moreno et al., 2005) and are influenced by macro-level factors such as cultural norms toward violence, availability of victim resources, and laws in a particular region or country. By providing valid definitions and tools to assess violence, our aim is explicitly not to pathologize the victim or frame these conditions as "individual disorders." Rather, our goal is to improve surveillance of family problems and family violence that are often rooted in societal or community factors mentioned above. This in turn may impact treatment, prevention, policy decisions, and resource allocation for these problems. Our perspective is thus similar to an epidemiological or public health approach adopted by the Centers for Disease Control and Prevention (CDC) and WHO in which an integrated community response is necessary for maximally effective prevention.

As the ICD is used to inform health care resource allocation decisions for 70% of expenditures (WHO, 2011), better surveillance of these types of problems can lead to changes in violence prevention efforts and resources for victims. An excellent review of some of the efforts related to child and partner maltreatment prevention globally is described in Chapter 18 (Mikton and Butchart).

WHO SHOULD READ THIS BOOK?

A Tool for Practitioners Assessing Relationship Problems

This volume includes several new state-of-the art assessment instruments. Copies of these structured diagnostic interviews and brief screening instruments for relationship problems are included in each of the "Practical Tools" chapters (see Chapters 4, 8, 12, and 16). Assessment of relational problems, such as maltreatment, is a concern that intersects with a large range of professions in diverse settings, including emergency rooms, social service agencies, primary care offices, schools, psychotherapy clinics, marital therapy clinics, psychiatry offices, and forensic settings. Hence, this volume may be a useful reference for a wide range of practitioners assessing relationship problems.

A Text for Training

We anticipate this volume will be an attractive classroom text for graduate training programs. Social workers, psychologists, marriage and family therapists, and psychiatric nurses all encounter relational problems in practice. Training in proper assessment of family maltreatment, parent–child problems, and relationship discord are components in many graduate program courses across disciplines.

A Wide Scholarly Audience

Because this volume examines a critical public health issue from a multidisciplinary perspective, we expect that it is of interest to a wide audience including clinicians, epidemiologists, prevention program developers, researchers, psychologists, physicians, cultural anthropologists, public policy makers, and advocates. Past volumes about relationship problems typically neglect global perspectives and only focus on a specific type of relationship problem (e.g., childhood dysfunctions). The focus of the current volume should be of interest to an international audience as well as readers interested in the spectrum of relational problems across childhood and adulthood.

CONCLUDING SUMMARY

The purpose of this book is to provide clinicians, scholars, students, and policy makers with (a) a comprehensive and concise review of recent innovations in defining and assessing couple and family problems and family violence; (b) global considerations of cross-cultural relationship assessment and recommendation for modifications and cross-cultural validation; (c) a review of the impact of couple and family problems and family violence on worldwide psychological health, physical health, and economic well-being; (d) an overview of practical clinical and public health tools for defining, screening, and assessing clinically significant couple and family problems and family violence; and (e) copies of the tools. In this book, we have provided an up-to-date review of the public health impacts of relational problems and scientifically based tools for improving surveillance of these problems; we hope this will help move the field toward universal definitions and assessment of these problems and lead to improvements in treatment, prevention, and public health decisions.

REFERENCES

American Psychiatric Association. (1994). Diagnostic and statistical manual for mental disorders (4th ed.). Washington, DC: Author.

Beach, S. R. H., Wamboldt, M., Kaslow, N. J., Heyman, R. E., & Reiss, D. (2006a). Relational processes and mental health: A bench to bedside dialogue to guide the *DSM-V*. In S. R. H. Beach, M. Wamboldt, N. Kaslow, R. E. Heyman, M. First, L. G. Underwood, & D. Reiss (Eds.) *Relational processes and* DSM-V*: Neuroscience, assessment, prevention, and treatment* (pp. 1–20). Washington, DC: American Psychiatric Press.

Beach, S. R. H., Wamboldt, M., Kaslow, N. J., Heyman, R. E., & Reiss, D. (2006b). Describing relationship problems in *DSM-V*: Toward better guidance for research and clinical practice. *Journal of Family Psychology, 20*, 359–368.

Bell, N. S. (2009). Health and occupational consequences of spouse abuse victimization among male U.S. Army soldiers. *Journal of Interpersonal Violence, 24*, 751–769.

Denton, W. H., Carmody, T. J., Rush, A. J., Thase, M. E., Trivedi, M. H., Arnow, B. A., . . . Keller, M. B. (2010). Dyadic discord at baseline is associated with lack of remission in the acute treatment of chronic depression. *Psychological Medicine, 40*, 415–424.

García-Moreno, C., Jansen, H. A, Ellsberg, M., Heise, L., Watts, C. (2005). *WHO multi-country study on women's health and domestic violence against women*. Geneva, World Health Organization.

Eaker, E. D., Sullivan, L. M., Kelly-Hayes, M., D'Agostino, R. B., & Benjamin, E. J. (2007). Marital status, marital strain, and risk of coronary heart disease or total mortality: The Framingham offspring study. *Psychosomatic Medicine, 69*(6), 509–513.

Fagundes, C. P., Bennett, J. M., Derry, H. M., & Kiecolt-Glaser, J. K. (2011). Relationships and inflammation across the lifespan: Social developmental pathways to disease. *Social and Personality Psychology Compass, 5*, 891–903.

Heyman R. E., Slep, A. M. S., Beach, S. R. H., Wamboldt, M., Kaslow, N. J., & Reiss, D. (2009). Relationship problems and the *DSM*: Needed improvements and suggested solutions. *World Psychiatry, 8*, 7–14.

Kiecolt-Glaser, J. K., Gouin, J. -P., & Hantsoo, L. (2009). Close relationships, inflammation, and health. *Neuroscience and Biobehavioral Reviews, 35*, 33–38.

Miklowitz, D. J., Wisniewski, S. R., Miyahara, S., Otto, M. W., & Sachs, G. S. (2005). Perceived criticism from family members as a predictor of the 1-year course of bipolar disorder. *Psychiatry Research, 136*, 101–111.

Nemeroff, C. B., Heim, C. M., Thase, M. E., Klein, D. N., Rush, A. J., Schatzberg, A. F., . . . Keller, M. B. (2003). Differential responses to psychotherapy versus pharmacotherapy in patients with

chronic forms of major depression and childhood trauma. *Proceedings of the National Academy of Sciences of the United States of America, 100,* 14293–14296.
Schmaling, K. B., & Sher, T. G. (2000). *The Psychology of Couples and Illness: Theory, Research, and Practice.* Washington, DC: American Psychological Association.
Schonbrun, Y. C., & Whisman, M. A. (2010). Marital distress and mental health care service utilization among married adults. *Journal of Consulting and Clinical Psychology, 78,* 732–736.
Wamboldt, F. S., Wamboldt, M. Z., Gavin, L. A., Roesler, T. A., & Brugman, S. M. (1995). Parental criticism and treatment outcome in adolescents hospitalized for severe, chronic asthma. *Journal of Psychosomatic Research, 39,* 995–1005.
Wamboldt, M. Z., Beach, S. R. H., Kaslow, N. J., Heyman, R. E., First, M. B. & Reiss, D. (2010). Describing relationship patterns in *DSM-V*: A preliminary proposal. In T. Millon, R. R. Krueger, & E. Simonsen (Eds.), *Contemporary Directions in Psychopathology: Scientific Foundations of the* DSM-V *and ICD-11* (pp. 565–576). New York, NY: Guilford Press.
Wolf, J., Miller, G., & Chen, E. (2008). Parent psychological states predict changes in inflammatory markers in children with asthma and healthy children. *Brain, Behavior, and Immunity, 22,* 433–441.
World Health Organization (WHO). (2007). *Production of the ICD-11.* Geneva, Switzerland: Author.
World Health Organization (WHO). (2010a). *ICD-11 revision project plan—Draft 2.0.* Geneva, Switzerland: Author.
World Health Organization (WHO). (2010b). *ICD-10 Version: 2010.* Geneva, Switzerland: Author. Retrieved from www.who.int/classifications/icd/en
World Health Organization (WHO). (2011). *Classifications: ICD revision timelines.* Retrieved December, 2011, from www.who.int/classifications/icd/revision/en/index.html

Acknowledgments

We would like to thank the many contributors without whom this volume would not have been possible. First and foremost, much credit is owed to the joint efforts of the relational processes working group assembled in 2001 by David Reiss, including (in alphabetical order) Steven Beach, Richard Heyman, Nadine Kaslow, and Marianne Wamboldt, and later joined by Heather Foran and Amy M. Smith Slep. Three past conferences on assessment of relational processes (in 2005, 2007, and 2010) and several publications on the topic (e.g., Beach, Wamboldt, Kaslow, Heyman, First, Underwood, & Reiss, 2006) serve as foundational building blocks for the current volume.The perseverance of the group—along with the network of experts on relationship processes from psychology, psychiatry, public health, epidemiology, and neuroscience—laid the necessary scientific groundwork.

We are grateful to the Fetzer Institute for their generous support over the years, including funding of the very fruitful 2010 conference on relational processes and the ICD-11 in Ascona, Switzerland, on which this book was based. Notably, we are thankful to Heidi Ihrig for her indispensable assistance in the organization of the Ascona conference and the Ascona Foundation for hosting us in such a beautiful location. We are also deeply indebted to the efforts of David Addiss, former Fetzer Institute program manager. His engagement and hard work stimulated international discussions and collaborations necessary for this project to be a success.

There are many individuals from the World Health Organization who deserve recognition for their contributions as well. They include Claudia García-Moreno, Christopher Mikton, James Harrison, Alexander Butchart, and Geoffrey Reed, who have provided critical insights into relational processes from a global perspective and how these problems are handled in the ICD. We owe a special thanks to Geoffrey Reed for his guidance on the ICD-11 revision process and continued assistance along the way.

Finally, we would like to thank the many experts from Africa, Europe, North America, South America, and Asia who contributed to this volume and the development of the proposals for revisions to the ICD-11. We are grateful to William Bernet and the parental alienation group for the helpful feedback provided on the proposal forms for child maltreatment and caregiver–child relational problems. We are also grateful to all the Ascona conference participants who were instrumental in formulating the current revision proposals for the ICD-11: David Addiss, Wenhong Cheng, Claudia García-Moreno, Kurt Hahlweg, James Harrison, Nadine Kaslow, Brigitte Khoury, Christopher Mikton,

Mokhantso Makoae, Ron Prinz, Geoffrey Reed, David Reiss, Tuula Tamminen, Mark Whisman, and Frederick Wamboldt.

In recognition of the long-term contributions of the relational processes working group members instrumental to development of this book, the citation for this book should include all editors and associate editors: Foran, H. M., Beach, S. R. H., Slep, A. M. S., Heyman, R. E., Wamboldt, M. Z., Kaslow, N. J., & Reiss D., Eds (2012). *Family violence and family problems: Reliable assessment and the ICD-11*. New York, NY: Springer Publishing.

PART I: PARTNER MALTREATMENT

1

Intimate Partner Maltreatment: Definitions, Prevalence, and Implications for Diagnosis

Richard E. Heyman, Amy M. Smith Slep, Ann C. Eckardt Erlanger, and Heather M. Foran

DEFINITIONS OF INTIMATE PARTNER MALTREATMENT

Intimate partner maltreatment (IPV)—comprising physical abuse, emotional abuse, and sexual abuse—has been a concern of advocates, clinicians, public policy makers, and public health officials worldwide since at least the early 1970s (Ellsberg & Heise, 2005). Despite the 40 years of research, however, there is still no agreed-upon criteria for what constitutes intimate partner maltreatment, let alone one that can be used reliably and validly in both clinical and research settings.

As noted first by Straus (1990) and Johnson (1995), there has been controversy about what constitutes partner maltreatment largely because of the existence of two distinct subfields. One subfield studies individuals or couples from the general population; the other studies women who have been highly victimized (e.g., women in shelters) and men who have faced legal adjudication (e.g., men in court-mandated treatment programs). These vastly different perspectives have shaped, often quite bitterly, views of what maltreatment is, what causes it, what its course is, and what the proper societal response should be.

PROBLEM WITH DEFINING PHYSICAL AND EMOTIONAL ABUSE WITH SINGLE BEHAVIORAL ACT

The most influential measures of physical and emotional abuse—the Conflicts Tactics Scale (CTS; Straus, 1979) and the Revised Conflict Tactics Scale (CTS2; Straus, Hamby, Boney-McCoy, & Sugarman, 1996)—provided the key operationalization for what constituted abuse. The CTS is an 18-item list—arranged roughly in order of severity—of nonaggressive constructive conflict behaviors, putatively emotionally aggressive tactics, and physically aggressive tactics. The 39-item CTS2 was updated by including randomly ordered items (i.e., not in increasing severity and not grouped by type of IPV), expanding emotional and physical aggression items, and adding of sexual coercion/assault and physical impact questions.

Most general population studies (e.g., Ellsberg & Heise, 2005; Straus & Gelles, 1990; Tjaden & Thoennes, 2000) solely report or emphasize prevalences of a single act of physical assault or purported emotionally aggressive behavior (even when impact was measured). Defining either physical or emotional abuse as a "single aggressive act in the last year" is of questionable validity for two reasons. First, despite near-universal expert belief that "true" abuse—that which significantly harms the victim or evokes fear substantial enough to control the victim or to constrict her culturally expected freedoms—is largely a male-perpetrated phenomenon, women in high-income countries are equally or more physically and emotionally partner aggressive than are men in all age groups (Archer, 2000). The high prevalence of female-to-male aggression cannot be due to self-defense, as women attribute their actions to self-defense less than one fourth of the time (Cascardi & Vivian, 1995) and a substantial proportion of reported female-to-male aggression occurs in the absence of male-to-female aggression. Second, again running counter to expert beliefs about "true abuse," reported instances of physical aggression typically are not severe (e.g., Caetano, Cunradi, Clark, & Schafer, 2000), are infrequent (Straus & Gelles, 1990), and often desist spontaneously (e.g., Quigley & Leonard, 1996); victims typically are uninjured (e.g., Stets & Straus, 1990) and report minimal psychological impact (Ehrensaft & Vivian, 1996).

EMERGING CONSENSUS FOR DEFINING INTIMATE PARTNER MALTREATMENT

Because most prevention, intervention, and public policy efforts are targeted at partner maltreatment that either directly harms victims or prevents victims from living freely without fear of harm, several recent conceptualizations have gone beyond using only reporting acts of physical or emotional aggression to define intimate partner maltreatment. Research definitions by the World Health Organization (WHO) (Heise & García-Moreno, 2002; Jewkes, Sen, & García-Moreno, 2002), U.S. Centers for Disease Control and Prevention (Saltzman, Fanslow, McMahon, & Shelley, 1999), and a growing number of researchers (e.g., Coker et al. 2002; Graham-Kevan & Archer, 2003; Heyman, Feldbau-Kohn, Ehrensaft, Langhinrichsen-Rohling, & O'Leary, 2001; Johnson & Leone, 2005; Smith, Thornton, DeVellis, Earp, & Coker, 2002) have made clearer distinctions between impactful assaults (i.e., those that cause or have a high potential to cause, injury, harm, or death) and nonimpactful assaults.

The *World Report on Violence and Health* (Heise & García-Moreno, 2002; Jewkes et al., 2002) defined intimate partner maltreatment as "behavior within an intimate relationship that causes physical, sexual or psychological harm, including acts of physical aggression, sexual coercion, psychological abuse and controlling behaviors." The Centers for Disease Control and Prevention (Saltzman et al., 1999) uses a similar definition but (a) includes potential for harm as an element of the physical abuse definition and (b) restricts psychological abuse to relationships in which there has been prior actual or threatened physical or sexual abuse.

In our program of research, which produced the proposed criteria for intimate partner maltreatment, we used the following definitions:

- Intimate partner maltreatment: Physical, verbal/symbolic, or sexual acts (or, in the case of neglect, omissions) that cause—or have reasonable potential to cause—harm to an intimate partner.
- Physical abuse: Nonaccidental acts of physical force that result, or have reasonable potential to result, in physical harm to an intimate partner or that evoke significant fear in the partner.
- Emotional abuse: Nonaccidental verbal or symbolic acts of that result in significant psychological harm to an intimate partner.
- Sexual abuse: Forced or coerced sexual acts with an intimate partner or sexual acts with an intimate partner who is unable to consent.
- Neglect: Acts or omissions that result, or have reasonable potential to result, in physical harm to an intimate partner who is incapable of self-care.

DEVELOPMENT AND TESTING OF CRITERIA FOR INTIMATE PARTNER MALTREATMENT

The proposed intimate partner maltreatment criteria were developed in a multistage process described in depth elsewhere (Heyman & Slep, 2006a, 2006b, 2009; Heyman, Collins, Slep, & Knickerbocker, 2009; Slep & Heyman, 2006). The steps are (a) examining the content validity and field usability of a set of maltreatment criteria already in use; (b) creating a unifying conceptualization for what constituted an above-threshold problem; (c) reviewing and adapting (where appropriate) existing operationalizations; (d) field testing and refining criteria, assessments, and decision-making process; (e) testing criteria's use in wide-scale dissemination; (f) creating criteria-informed screeners and structured clinical interviews; and (g) examining the content validity of the final criteria. All assessments were made by credentialed providers (typically master's-level social workers), although the decisions regarding whether an incident met criteria for maltreatment were made by small committees, typically with only one member with a clinical services background.

In developing these criteria, we adopted, wherever possible, extant legal, research, or clinical definitions/operationalizations that were specific enough to promote reliable use in clinical and research settings. By adapting specific elements that had already been used, the new maltreatment criteria would putatively have more content and clinical validity than novel criteria. Dozens of civilian and military definitions and operationalizations were reviewed, including the following: (a) Centers for Disease Control intimate partner violence definitions (Saltzman et al., 1999), (b) state laws (National Clearinghouse on Child Abuse and Neglect Information, 2003a), and (c) Department of Defense definitions and proposed modifications (Office of the Under Secretary of Defense, 1997, 1999, 2000, 2002) and Defense Task Force on Domestic Violence (2001) recommended definitions.

RELIABILITY AND VALIDITY OF DEFINITIONAL SYSTEMS

Field Tests of Reliability

Heyman and Slep (2006, 2009) reported on three field tests of the proposed definitions. In the pilot trial (Heyman & Slep, 2006, Study 3), operationalizations were iteratively improved for clarity and to improve agreement between local sites and master reviewers. Prior to the first field test, agreement between site decisions and master reviewers was approximately 50% (Heyman & Slep, 2006). During the pilot trial, agreement between sites and master reviewers was 76% ($\kappa = 0.50$, $n = 103$) for intimate partner physical abuse and 70% ($\kappa = 0.33$, $n = 40$) for intimate partner emotional abuse. (There were no allegations of sexual abuse received during the pilot.)

For the second field trial (Heyman & Slep, 2006, Study 4), several changes were made. Most notably, a structured clinical interview that paralleled the diagnostic criteria for each form of maltreatment was developed and disseminated and votes were cast for each criterion separately, aided by a computer-guided decision matrix that presented the criteria. In the second field trial, agreement between sites and master reviewers was 91% ($\kappa = 0.82$, $n = 233$) for intimate partner physical abuse, 89% ($\kappa = 0.76$, $n = 79$) for intimate partner emotional abuse, and 88% ($\kappa = 0.75$, $n = 8$) for intimate partner sexual abuse. This exceptional level of reliability suggested that the refinement of the criteria had been successful.

Although the second trial involved field-generated decisions under real-world conditions, it was clearly an effectiveness trial with a small number of volunteer sites and did not speak to the performance of the criteria when used broadly and under typical circumstances. A dissemination trial of the diagnostic system's use under typical conditions at many sites was necessary.

In the third (dissemination) trial (Heyman & Slep, 2009), 41 sites of our partner organization—located in the United States, Europe, and Asia but staffed entirely by Americans—participated. Agreement between the field decisions and those of master reviewers remained high (partner physical abuse: 92%, $\kappa = 0.84$, $n = 435$; partner emotional abuse: 93%, $\kappa = 0.83$, $n = 109$; partner sexual abuse: 80%, $\kappa = 0.62$, $n = 5$). The maintenance of high agreement is especially noteworthy given (a) the relative lack of expertise and training among the majority of those on the determination committees and (b) the nature of standard operating procedure of the participating sites (i.e., they were not volunteer test sites as in the earlier field trials). During the second and third field trials, users were anonymously surveyed (including among others, 73 clinical social workers who used the criteria). In both studies (Heyman et al., 2009; Slep & Heyman, 2006), over 90% of users rated the criteria and decision process as fair or somewhat fair to alleged offenders and victims. About half rated the determinations as easy or very easy to make, with most of the rest rating "neither easy nor difficult."

Notably, the Heyman and Slep (2006, 2009) studies compared field versus expert decisions. Although not conclusive, the few studies in mental health that have tested the concordance of field clinicians' diagnoses and "criterion standard" diagnoses found problematic levels of agreement (First, 2007). Basco et al. (2000) and Shear et al. (2000) reported poor match (κ = 0.13–0.45) between field clinicians' diagnoses and those by master reviewers (using structured interviews, sometimes supplemented with other data sources). Kashner et al. (2003) reported comparable concordance between clinicians and diagnoses from structured interviews (κ = 0.20–0.30), except for diagnoses for severe mental illness (κ = 0.52–0.60). Similarly, a study of psychotic first-time inpatients (Fenning et al., 1994) reported decent clinician-versus-master reviewer agreement (κ = 0.51–0.73), but only for academic and community hospitals; agreement between clinicians at public hospitals and master reviewers was poor (κ = 0.13–0.34). Thus, the maltreatment criteria compare favorably to psychiatric criteria for other mental health problems in terms of agreement between typical clinicians and master reviewers.

Validity

Content validity of the proposed criteria can be inferred given the reasonably high concordance (see the Appendix at the end of this chapter) between the proposed criteria and that of (a) the Centers for Disease Control and Prevention, which were approved by expert researchers, representatives from U.S. and international governments and nongovernmental organizations, U.S. state health department representatives, professional associations, and medical organizations, advocacy coalitions) and (b) the *WHO Multi-Country Study on Women's Health and Domestic Violence Against Women* (García-Moreno et al., 2006).

Convergent validity for the criteria was established through relations of physical abuse and emotional abuse to a variety of hypothesized outcomes, such as relationship satisfaction, depressive symptoms, and alcohol problems (Foran, Heyman, Slep, & Linkh, 2012; Slep, Foran, Heyman, Snarr, & Linkh, 2010).

THRESHOLD CONSIDERATIONS

Each form of partner maltreatment has different criteria and thus different threshold considerations. In each case, the act defines the type of maltreatment (physical, emotional, sexual, or neglect). It is possible that these types are unnecessary; however, they are widely used and provide clarity for both the types of acts under consideration and the types of harm that can result from each form of maltreatment.

Similar to diagnoses for psychopathology, we adopted a "symptom/behavior + impact" strategy. Just as having a depressed mood or consuming alcohol is not sufficient to receive a diagnosis of a depressive disorder or alcohol dependence, we too have relied on evidence of substantial impact as a marker of crossing a clinically significant boundary. For intimate partner maltreatment, these boundaries are as follows:

- Partner physical abuse: Overtly injuring partner; engaging in physically aggressive acts with a reasonable potential for significant injury (e.g., strangling partner without leaving bruises; attempting to shoot, stab, or run partner over with an automobile [but missing]); engaging in physically aggressive acts that evoke significantly fear and anxiety.
- Partner emotional abuse: Acts that evoke significant (a) fear and anxiety, (b) psychological distress at or near diagnostic thresholds, (c) somatic symptoms, or (d) fear that causes the victim to preemptively restrict engagement in major life activities (i.e., work, education, religion, necessary medical or mental health services, or contact with family/friends).

- Partner neglect: Egregious acts or omissions that cause significant injury or have the potential to do so.
- Partner sexual abuse: (Due to the nature of sexual interactions, this has clearer natural boundaries.): A sex act that is nonconsensual (i.e., forced, coerced, or with someone who is unable at the time to consent).

For each type of maltreatment, the acts are inclusive of all behaviors that are nonaccidental and fit for that kind of action (physical, sexual, verbal/symbolic, and neglectful). The impacts are the smallest number of natural consequences of that kind of action. For physical acts, the natural consequences are injury (actual, potential, or feared); for verbal/symbolic acts, the natural consequences are psychological (fear of harm that the symbolic act conveyed [e.g., self or child will be physically harmed in the future], actual psychological or somatic symptoms evoked or exacerbated by the behavior, pre-emptive significant life limitations to avoid the future physical, or psychological harm implied by the verbal/symbolic acts); for neglect, the natural consequences are injury (actual or potential). Again, the boundaries of nonconsensual sex acts made it unnecessary to require impact, although the vast majority of such intimate acts will have physical and psychological consequences similar to those of other types of maltreatment.

Although many intimate partner maltreatment advocates and scholars (e.g., Pence & Paymar, 1993) believe that a pattern of such behavior is a necessary element of maltreatment, we have chosen not to include pattern as a criterion. First, it is unclear what the appropriate threshold would be, since a pattern would minimally require two instances but could be set to require more. Second, it did not seem sensible to put the threshold at two when some acts may only require a single instance to be highly traumatic (e.g., a woman presents complaining of extreme fear and anxiety after her husband angrily puts a gun to her head and says he will kill her, even though he had never been aggressive before).

Likewise, although many intimate partner maltreatment advocates and scholars believe that an intention to control the partner is a necessary element of maltreatment (e.g., Pence & Paymar, 1993) we have chosen not to include that either as a criterion. First, it is difficult to judge intent—does one believe the alleged perpetrator's (often minimized) descriptions of intent or the alleged victim's inferences about the other's intent? Second, there are many situations in which injury or other noteworthy harm is inflicted but in which there is no intent to control. Thus, power/control seemed to be neither a necessary nor sufficient element and would make reliable assessment exceedingly difficult.

GLOBAL PREVALENCE RATES

Tracking intimate partner maltreatment across countries—or agreeing how to measure prevalences at all—is a challenge due to variability in methodology, design, and presentation of findings. The WHO collated studies from over 50 countries, resulting in approximately 80 population-based projects. Regions assessed included Africa, Latin America and the Caribbean, North America, Asia and the Western Pacific, Europe, and the Eastern Mediterranean. (Due to space limitations, we will present examples of prevalence data from one country in each region.) Nationally representative studies in South Africa (Marco International, South Africa Department of Health, 1998) and Peru (Dávila, Ramos, & Mattei, 1998) reported that women's lifetime prevalence of physical aggression victimization was 13%; a somewhat higher lifetime prevalence was found in India (19%; Kishor & Johnson, 2004). Rates for women's lifetime intimate partner physical aggression victimization were even higher in nationally representative studies in Germany (23%; Federal Ministry for Family Affairs, Senior Citizens, Women and Youth, 2004), Canada (29%, also including intimate partner sexual victimization; Johnson, 1996), and Egypt (34%; El-Zanaty, Hussein, Shawky, Way, & Kishor, 1996).

To enhance comparability, the WHO joined with 15 sites in 10 countries for the *WHO Multi-Country Study on Women's Health and Domestic Violence Against Women.* This study examined intimate partner physical aggression and intimate partner sexual aggression using standardized measures and procedures in combination with assessor training. Lifetime reports of intimate partner physical aggression ranged from 13% in urban Japan to 27% in urban Brazil to over 40% in urban and rural Bangladesh, rural Tanzania, and rural Ethiopia.

Finally, the WHO study also confirmed that sexual abuse almost always occurs in relationships that also experience physical abuse. The majority of sites supported this, with exceptions: in Bangladesh, Ethiopia, and two sites in Thailand, a substantial proportion of women reported partner sexual abuse but no partner physical aggression.

CURRENT LIMITATIONS IN GLOBAL SURVEILLANCE SYSTEMS

The lack of accepted operationalized criteria of what constitutes partner maltreatment has vast implications for public health surveillance and response. First, because partner maltreatment is not defined in a consistent way, data on incidence, prevalence, trends, and cultural and geographic differences are hard to compare (e.g., Ellsberg & Heise, 2005). Second, a reliable and valid operationalization of a problem is a necessary precursor to studies of its causes and consequences and to the development and testing of effective interventions to treat and prevent it (e.g., Mrazek & Haggerty, 1994). Finally, a lack of clear operationalization of partner maltreatment muddies attempts to form community consensus on what behavior is unacceptable and undermines informal community processes that discourage antisocial behavior. After adopting the maltreatment criteria, communities in the earlier described trial evidenced a strong tertiary preventive effect. Being labeled as having crossed the partner maltreatment threshold (with the new, clear criteria and a perceived fair process) resulted in a 50% decrease in recidivism compared with the earlier, highly unreliable criteria/process, likely due to informal community sanctions (Snarr, Heyman, Slep, & Malik, 2010).

CLINICAL UTILITY AND THE IMPLICATIONS OF IMPROVED CRITERIA FOR DIAGNOSIS

As discussed in greater detail in the partner maltreatment impact chapter, intimate partner maltreatment is associated with (a) symptoms at or near diagnostic thresholds for major depressive disorder (e.g., Magdol, Moffitt, Caspi, Fagan, & Silva, 1997), posttraumatic stress disorder (e.g., Jones, Hughes, & Unterstaller, 2001), generalized anxiety disorder (e.g., Magdol et al., 1997), alcohol abuse (e.g., Magdol et al., 1997) and alcohol dependence (e.g., Danielson, Moffitt, Caspi, & Silva, 1998) and (b) a vast array of acute and chronic health problems (Coker et al., 2002; Gelles & Straus, 1990).

In many relationships marked by partner maltreatment, intimate partner maltreatment is either the primary or a key causal factor in the clinical physical or psychological diagnosis. Thus, it would be clinically useful to be able to reliably assess, establish the prevalences of, know the etiology of, and efficaciously prevent and treat partner maltreatment. Given the variety of operationalizations that are likely of marginal clinical utility (partner maltreatment involves a single act of aggression; partner maltreatment only involves situations marked by exerting power and control over the partner).

CONCLUSIONS AND RECOMMENDATIONS

The research results indicate that the proposed diagnostic criteria support an exceptionally high level of reliability and are demonstrating signs of validity. The high level of reliability (over 90%) between site decisions and those of master reviewers is particularly noteworthy given the relative lack of clinical training and expertise that characterized nearly all of those voting at local sites. These results suggest several implications. First, nuanced, multifaceted, diagnostic criteria, such as those proposed, can be used reliably and validly in both interview and self-report formats. Using definitions such as these would likely lead to more reliable decision making in the field and more consistency across studies. Second, when applying complex diagnostic criteria in real-world settings, tools such as the computer-guided decision tree used in the second and third trials may be particularly effective in promoting consistent decision making.

This series of studies, however, represents only the first step in developing reliable and valid diagnostic criteria for family maltreatment. Several caveats are noteworthy. First, although the diagnostic criteria were used reliably and have initial signs of validity, additional work must be conducted to further establish the convergent, discriminant, discriminative, and predictive validity of the definitions. Second, neither the criteria overall nor the elements should be reified. Each element and the thresholds set still need additional study to validate our a priori decisions. This is no different than almost all of psychiatric nosology, but it should not be overlooked. Third, the diagnosis reliability studies used committee majority votes to determine outcomes; replication with individual evaluators (the more typical clinical use) is necessary. Fourth, reliability and validity research in a variety of settings and cultures is needed. Finally, taxometric methods should be used to investigate whether making qualitative distinctions between "maltreatment" and "not maltreatment" is empirically supportable.

ACKNOWLEDGMENT

Preparation of this chapter was supported by a grant U49CE00124602 from the Centers for Disease Control and Prevention. We are grateful for Jamie Kissee's assistance in creating the tables.

REFERENCES

Archer, J. (2000). Sex differences in aggression between heterosexual partners: A meta-analytic review. *Psychological Bulletin, 126*, 651–680.

Basco, M. R., Bostic, J. Q., Davies, D., Rush, A. J., Witte, B., Hendrickse, W., & Barnett, V. (2000). Methods to improve diagnostic accuracy in a community mental health setting. *American Journal of Psychiatry, 157*, 1599–1605.

Caetano, R., Cundradi. C. B., Clark, C.L., & Schafer, J. (2000). Intimate partner violence and drinking patterns among white, black, and Hispanic couples in the U.S. *Journal of Substance Abuse, 11*, 123–138.

Cascardi, M., & Vivian, D. (1995). Context for specific episodes of marital violence: Gender and severity of violence differences. *Journal of Family Violence, 10*, 265–293.

Coker, A. L., Davis, K. E., Arias, I., Desai, S., Sanderson, M., Brandt, H. M., & Smith, P. H. (2002). Physical and mental health effects of intimate partner violence for men and women. *American Journal of Preventive Medicine, 23*, 260–268.

Danielson, K. K., Moffitt, T. E., Caspi, A., & Silva, P. A. (1998). Comorbidity between abuse of an adult and DSM-III-R mental disorders: Evidence from an epidemiological study. *American Journal of Psychiatry, 155*, 131–133.

Dávila, A. L., Ramos, G., & Mattei, H. (1998). *Encuesta de salud reproductiva: Puerto Rico, 1995–96*. San Juan, Puerto Rico: CDC.

Defense Task Force on Domestic Violence. (2001). *Initial report of the Defense Task Force on Domestic Violence*. Retrieved January 11, 2005, from http://www.dtic.mil/domesticviolence/reports/dv_rpt1.pdf

Ehrensaft, M. K., & Vivian, D. (1996). Spouses' reasons for not reporting existing marital aggression as a marital problem. *Journal of Family Psychology, 10*, 443–453.

Ellsberg, M., & Heise, L. (2005). *Researching violence against women: A practical guide for researchers and activists*. Washington, DC: World Health Organization and Program for Appropriate Technology in Health.

El-Zanaty, F., Hussein, E. M., Shawky, G. A., Way, A. A., & Kishor, S. (1996). *Egypt demographic and health survey 1995*. Calverton, MD: Macro International.

Federal Ministry for Family Affairs, Senior Citizens, Women and Youth, BMFSFJ. (2004). *Health, well-being and personal safety of women in Germany: A representative study of women in Germany*. Bonn, Germany: BMFSFJ.

Fennig, S., Craig, T., Tanenberg-Karant, M., & Bromet, E. (1994). Comparison of facility and research diagnoses in first-admission psychotic patients. *American Journal of Psychiatry, 151*, 1423–1429.

First, M. B. (2007). The reliability of psychiatric diagnoses: Counterpoint—there isn't enough evidence available to speculate on the reliability of diagnoses in clinical settings. *Psychiatry, 4*, 22–25.

Foran, H. M., Heyman, R. E., Slep, A. M. S., & Linkh, D. J. (2012). A population study of risk factors for clinically significant emotional intimate partner violence. Manuscript submitted for publication.

García-Moreno, C., Jansen, H., Ellsberg, M., Heise, L., & Watts, C. H. (2006). Prevalence of intimate partner violence: Findings from the *WHO multi-country study on women's health and domestic violence. The Lancet, 368*, 1260–1269.

Gelles, R. J., & Straus, M. A. (1990). The medical and psychological costs of family violence. In M. A. Straus & R. J. Gelles (Eds.), *Physical violence in American families: Risk factors and adaptation to violence in 8,145 families* (pp. 425–430). New Brunswick, NJ: Transaction Publishing.

Graham-Kevan, N., & Archer, J. (2003). Physical aggression and control in heterosexual relationships: The effect of sampling. *Violence & Victims, 18*, 181–196.

Haynes, S. N., Richard, D. C. S., & Kubany, E. S. (1995). Content validity in psychological assessment: A functional approach to concepts and methods. *Psychological Assessment, 7*, 238–247.

Heise, L., & García-Moreno, C. (2002). Violence by intimate partners. In E. Krug, L. L. Dahlberg, J. A. Mercy, A. B. Zwi, & R. Lozano (Eds.), *World report on violence and health* (pp. 87-121). Geneva, Switzerland: World Health Organization.

Heyman, R. E., Feldbau-Kohn, S. R., Ehrensaft, M. K., Langhinrichsen-Rohling, J., & O'Leary, K. D. (2001). Can questionnaire reports correctly classify relationship distress and partner physical abuse? *Journal of Family Psychology, 15*, 334–346.

Heyman, R. E., Collins, P. S., Slep, A. M. S., & Knickerbocker, L. (2010). Evidence-based substantiation criteria: improving the reliability of field decisions of child maltreatment and partner abuse. *Protecting Children, 25*, 35–46.

Heyman, R. E., & Slep, A. M. S. (2006a). Creating and field-testing diagnostic criteria for partner and child maltreatment. *Journal of Family Psychology, 20*, 397–408.

Heyman, R. E., & Slep, A. M. S. (2006b). Relational diagnoses: From reliable rationally-derived criteria to testable taxonic hypotheses. In S. R. H. Beach, M. Wamboldt, N. Kaslow, R. E. Heyman, M. First, L. G. Underwood, & D. Reiss (Eds.), *Relational processes and DSM-V: Neuroscience, assessment, prevention, and treatment* (pp. 139–156). Washington, DC: American Psychiatric Press.

Heyman, R. E., & Slep, A. M. S. (2009). Reliability of family maltreatment diagnostic criteria: 41 site dissemination field trial. *Journal of Family Psychology, 23*, 905–910.

Jewkes, R., Sen, P., & García-Moreno, C. (2002). Sexual violence. In E. Krug, L. Dahlberg, J. A. Mercy, A. B. Zwi, & R. Lozano (Eds.), *World report of violence and health* (pp. 147–181). Geneva, Switzerland: The World Health Organization.

Johnson, H. (1996). *Dangerous domains: Violence against women in Canada.* Ontario, Canada: International Thomson Publishing.

Johnson, M. P. (1995). Patriarchal terrorism and common couple violence: Two forms of violence against women. *Journal of Marriage and the Family, 57*, 283–294.

Johnson, M. P., & Leone. J. (2005). The differential effects of intimate terrorism and situational couple violence: Findings from the National Violence Against Women Survey. *Journal of Family Issues, 26*(3), 322–349.

Jones, L., Hughes, M., & Unterstaller, U. (2001). Post-traumatic stress disorder (PTSD) in victims of domestic violence: A review of the research. *Trauma,Violence, and Abuse, 2*, 99–119.

Kashner, T., Rush, A., Suris, A., Biggs, M. M., Gajewski, V. L., Hooker, D. J.,..., Altshuler, K. Z. (2003). Impact of structured clinical interviews on physicians' practices in community mental health settings. *Psychiatric Services, 54*, 712–718.

Macro International, South Africa Department of Health. (1998). *South Africa Demographic and Health Survey 1998: Preliminary Report.* DHS survey. Calverton, MD: Macro International.

Magdol, L., Moffitt, T. E., Caspi, A., Newman, D. L., Fagan, J., & Silva, P. A. (1997). Gender differences in partner violence in a birth cohort of 21-year olds: Bridging the gap between clinical and epidemiological approaches. *Journal of Consulting and Clinical Psychology, 65*, 68–78.

Mrazek, P. J., & Haggerty, R. J., (Eds.). (1994). *Reducing risks for mental disorders: frontiers for preventive intervention research.* Washington, DC: National Academy Press.

National Clearinghouse on Child Abuse and Neglect. (2003). *Compendium of laws, definitions of domestic violence.* Retrieved from http://dx.doi.org/10.1037/a0017011.supp

Office of the Under Secretary of Defense. (1997). *DoD Instruction 6400.2, 1-Aug-97.* Washington, DC: Office of the Under Secretary of Defense for Personnel and Readiness.

Office of the Under Secretary of Defense. (1999). *Proposed DoD Instruction 6400.2, 25-May-99 draft.* Unpublished manuscript.

Office of the Under Secretary of Defense. (2000) *Proposed DoD Instruction 6400.2, 25-Dec-00 draft.* Unpublished manuscript.

Office of the Under Secretary of Defense. (2002) *Proposed DoD Instruction 6400.2,* 22-Feb-02 *draft.* Unpublished manuscript.

Pence, E., & Paymar, M. (1993). *Education groups for men who batter: The Duluth model.* New York, NY: Springer Publishing.

Quigley, B. M., & Leonard, K. E. (1996). Desistance of husband aggression in the early years of marriage. *Violence & Victims, 11*, 355–370.

Saltzman, L. E., Fanslow, J. L., McMahon, P. M., & Shelley, G. A. (1999). *Intimate partner violence surveillance: Uniform definitions and recommended data elements (Ver. 1.0).* Atlanta, GA: Centers for Disease Control and Prevention.

Shear, M., Greeno, C., Kang, J., Ludewig, D., Frank, E., Swartz, H. A., & Hanekamp, M. (2000). Diagnosis of nonpsychotic patients in community clinics. *American Journal of Psychiatry, 157*, 581–587.

Slep, A. M. S., Foran, H. M., Heyman, R. E., Snarr, J. D., & USAF Family Advocacy Program. (2012). Ecological risk factors for intimate partner violence and clinically significant intimate partner violence. Manuscript submitted for publication.

Slep, A. M. S., Foran, H. M., Heyman, R. E., Snarr, J. D., & Linkh, D. J. (2010). *An ecological model of intimate partner violence at different levels of severity.* Manuscript submitted for publication.

Slep, A. M. S., & Heyman, R. E. (2006). Creating and field-testing child maltreatment definitions: Improving the reliability of substantiation determinations. *Child Maltreatment, 11*, 397–408.

Smith, P. H., Thornton, G. E., & DeVellis, R. (2002). A population-based study of the prevalence and distinctiveness of battering, physical assault, and sexual assault in intimate relationships. *Violence Against Women, 8*, 1208–1232.

Snarr, J. D., Heyman, R. E., Slep, A. M. S., & Malik, J. (2011). Preventive impacts of reliable family maltreatment criteria. *Journal of Consulting and Clinical Psychology, 79*, 826–833.

Stets, J. E., & Straus, M. A. (1990). Gender differences in reporting marital violence and its medical and psychological consequences. In M. A. Straus & R. J. Gelles (Eds.), *Physical violence in American families: Risk factors and adaptation to violence in 8,145 families* (pp. 151–165). New Brunswick, NJ: Transaction Publishing.

Straus, M.A. (1979). Measuring intrafamily conflict and violence: The Conflict Tactics (CT) Scale. *Journal of Marriage and the Family, 41*, 75–78.

Straus, M. A. (1990). The Conflict Tactics Scales and its critics: An evaluation and new data on validity and reliability. In M. A. Straus & R. J. Gelles (Eds.), *Physical violence in American families: Risk factors and adaptation to violence in 8,145 families* (pp. 3–16). New Brunswick, NJ: Transaction Publishing.

Straus, M. A., & Gelles, R. J. (1990). *Physical violence in American families: Risk factors and adaptations to violence in 8,145 families.* New Brunswick, NJ: Transaction.

Straus, M. A., Hamby, S. L., Boney-McCoy, S., & Sugarman, D. B. (1996). The revised Conflict Tactics Scales (CTS2): Development and preliminary psychometric data. *Journal of Family Issues, 17*, 283–316.

Tjaden, P., & Thoennes, N. (2000). Prevalence and consequences of male-to-female and female-to-male intimate partner violence as measured by the National Violence Against Women Survey. *Violence Against Women, 6*, 141–162.

APPENDIX: COMPARISON OF PROPOSED INTIMATE PARTNER MALTREATMENT DEFINITIONS AND OTHER COMMONLY USED DEFINITIONS

TABLE 1.1 Comparison of Intimate Partner Physical Abuse Definitions: Proposed Criteria, CDC Uniform Definitions, and WHO Operationalizations

	Proposed Criteria	CDC	WHO
Act	The nonaccidental use of physical force. Physical force includes, but is not limited to, pushing, shoving, slapping, grabbing, poking, hair-pulling, scratching, pinching, restraining, shaking, throwing, biting, kicking, hitting with fist, hitting with a stick, strap, or other object, scalding, burning, poisoning, stabbing, applying force to throat, cutting off air supply, holding under water, using a weapon.	The intentional use of physical force includes, but is not limited to, scratching, pushing, shoving, throwing, grabbing, biting, choking, shaking, poking, hair-pulling, slapping, punching, hitting, burning, use of a weapon (gun, knife, or other object), and use of restraints or one's body, size, or strength against another person	Behavior within an intimate relationship that causes physical harm, including acts of physical aggression. *Moderate violence:* Was slapped or had something thrown at partner that could hurt Was pushed or shoved Had hair pulled *Severe violence:* Was hit with fist or something else that could hurt Was kicked, dragged, or beaten up Was choked or burned on purpose Perpetrator threatened to use or actually used a gun, knife, or other weapon against partner
Impact	Significant impact on the intimate partner involving any of the following: 1. *Any* physical injury (including, but not limited to, pain that lasts at least four hours, bruises, cuts, sprains, broken bones, loss of consciousness) 2. Reasonable potential for more than inconsequential physical injury[1] given the degree of force used and the physical environment in which acts occurred; 3. More than inconsequential fear reaction.[2]	The potential for causing death, disability, injury, or harm	None

Source: World Report on Violence and *WHO Multi-Country Study on Women's Health and Domestic Violence Against Women.*

TABLE 1.2 Comparison of Intimate Partner Sexual Abuse Definitions: Proposed Criteria, CDC Uniform Definitions, WHO Operationalizations

	Proposed Criteria	CDC	WHO
Act	1. The use of physical force to compel the intimate partner to engage in a sex act against his or her will, whether or not the act is completed • A sex act is defined as contact between the penis and the vulva or the penis and the anus involving penetration, however slight; contact between the mouth and the penis, vulva, or anus; or penetration of the anal or genital opening by a hand, finger, or other object 2. The use of a physically or emotionally aggressive act to coerce a sex act (attempted or completed) 3. An attempted or completed sex act involving an intimate partner who is unable to provide consent. That is, the victim is unable to understand the nature or conditions of the act, to decline participation, or to communicate unwillingness to engage in the sexual act (including, but not limited to, victim's illness, disability, being asleep, or under the influence of alcohol or other drugs). 4. Physical contact of a sexual nature (including, but not limited to, kissing, groping, rubbing, fondling—directly or through clothing) not meeting the above criteria but that (a) is against the expressed wishes of the intimate partner and (b) causes considerable distress to the intimate partner that is more than transient. "Considerable distress" involves anguish that does not necessarily meet diagnostic thresholds for psychiatric disorders but exceeds distress incurred in normal, day-to-day activities.	1. Use of physical force to compel a person to engage in a sexual act against his or her will, whether or not the act is completed • A sex act is defined as contact between the penis and the vulva or the penis and the anus involving penetration, however slight; contact between the mouth and the penis, vulva, or anus; or penetration of the anal or genital opening by a hand, finger, or other object 2. An attempted or completed sex act involving a person who is unable to understand the nature or condition of the act, to decline participation, or to communicate unwillingness to engage in the sexual act (e.g., because of illness, disability, or the influence of alcohol or other drugs, or due to intimidation or pressure) 3. Intentional touching directly, or through the clothing, of the genitalia, anus, groin, breast, inner thigh, or buttocks of any person against his or her will, or of any person who is unable to understand the nature or condition of the act, to decline participation, or to communicate unwillingness to be touched (e.g., because of illness, disability, or the influence of alcohol or other drugs, or due to intimidation or pressure)	1. Any sexual act, attempt to obtain a sexual act, unwanted sexual comments or advances, or acts to traffic, or otherwise directed, against a person's sexuality using coercion • Was physically forced to have sexual intercourse when did not want to • Had sexual intercourse when did not want to because he or she was afraid of what partner might do • Was forced to do something sexual that he or she found degrading or humiliating
Impact	None required	None required	

Source: World Report on Violence and *WHO Multi-Country Study on Women's Health and Domestic Violence Against Women*

TABLE 1.3 Comparison of Intimate Partner Emotional Abuse Definitions: Proposed Criteria, CDC Uniform Definitions, and WHO Operationalizations

	Proposed Criteria	CDC	WHO

Act	Nonaccidental verbal or symbolic act(s) (excluding physical and sexual abusive acts) such as those listed below. Acts not listed, but of similar severity, are also eligible
	• Berating, disparaging, degrading, humiliating victim (or other similar behavior)
	• Interrogating victim
	• Stalking victim
	• Threatening to harm victim directly or indirectly (including, but not limited to, threatening to hurt people/things victim cares about, such as children, self, other people, pets, property)
	• Harming people/things victim cares about, such as children, self, other people, pets, property
	• Restricting victim's access to or use of economic resources (only when unwarranted)
	• Restricting victim's access to or use of military services (including, but not limited to, taking away dependent's ID)
	• Isolating victim from family, friends, or social support resources
	• Obstructing victim from receiving medical services
	• Trying to make victim think that she or he was crazy (or make others think that intimate partner is crazy)
		1. There has also been prior:
		• Physical violence (see definition in Table 1.1)
		• Sexual violence (see definition in Table 1.2)
		• Threat of physical or sexual violence
		2. Acts, threats of acts, or coercive tactics, such as those on the following list:
		• Humiliating the victim
		• Controlling what the victim can and cannot do
		• Withholding information from the victim
		• Getting annoyed if the victim disagrees
		• Deliberately doing something to make the victim feel diminished (e.g., less smart, less attractive)
		• Deliberately doing something that makes the victim feel embarrassed
		• Using money that is the victim's
		• Taking advantage of the victim
		• Disregarding what the victim wants
		• Isolating the victim from friends or family
		• Prohibiting access to transportation or telephone
		• Getting the victim to engage in illegal activities
		• Using the victim's children to control victim's behavior
		• Threatening loss of custody of children
		• Smashing objects or destroying property
		• Denying the victim access to money or other basic resources
		• Disclosing information that would tarnish the victim's reputation
			Behavior within an intimate relationship that causes…psychological harm, including acts of…coercion, psychological abuse and controlling behaviors
			• Was insulted or made to feel bad about self
			• Was belittled or humiliated in front of other people
			• Perpetrator had done things to scare or intimidate partner on purpose (e.g., by the way he looked at her, by yelling or smashing things)
			• Perpetrator threatened to hurt someone partner cared about
			• Controlling behaviors
			  • Tried to keep from seeing friends
			  • Tried to restrict contact with family of birth
			  • Insisted on knowing where partner was at all times
			  • Ignored partner and treated her indifferently
			  • Got angry if partner spoke with person of the opposite sex
			  • Was often suspicious that partner was unfaithful
			  • Expected partner to ask permission before seeking health care for self

Impact	Significant impact on the intimate partner involving any of the following: 1. Psychological harm, including any of the following • More than inconsequential fear reaction[2] • Significant psychological distress (major depressive disorder, posttraumatic stress disorder, acute stress disorder, or a constellation of symptoms similar to other psychiatric disorders) related to, or exacerbated by, the act(s) • Fear of emotionally abusive act(s) that significantly interferes with the ability to carry out any of these five major life activities: work, education, religion, necessary medical or mental health services, or contact with family/friends 2. Stress-related somatic symptoms (related to or exacerbated by the acts) that significantly interfere with normal functioning	Trauma (undefined) to the victim caused by acts

Source: World Report on Violence and *Multi-Country Study on Women's Health and Domestic Violence Against Women.*

TABLE 1.4 Intimate Partner Neglect Proposed Criteria

	Proposed Criteria
Act	Egregious act(s) or omission(s) on the part of the caregiving partner when one intimate partner is incapable of self care due to substantial limitations in one or more of the following areas: 1. Physical (including, but not limited to, quadriplegia) 2. Psychological/Intellectual (including, but not limited to, vegetative depression, very low IQ, psychosis) 3. Cultural (including, but not limited to, inability to communicate, inability to manage activities of rudimentary daily living due to foreign culture)
Impact	Significant deprivation-related impact involving any of the following: 1. More than inconsequential physical injury[1]; 2. Reasonable potential for more than inconsequential physical injury[1]

Notes:
Expanded operationalization of terms used.

1. More than inconsequential physical injury involving any of the following:
   - Any injury to the face or head
   - A more than superficial bruise: The bruise was a color other than very light red or had a total area exceeding that of the victim's hand or was tender to light touch.
   - More than superficial cut or scratch: The cut or scratch was bleeding and required pressure to stop the bleeding.
   - Bleeding internally or from mouth or ears
   - A welt (a bump or ridge raised on the skin)
   - Loss of consciousness
   - A burn
   - Heat exhaustion or heat stroke
   - Loss of functioning (including, but not limited to, sprains, broken bones, detached retina, a loose or chipped tooth)
   - Damage to internal organs
   - Disfigurement (including, but not limited to scarring)
   - Swelling lasting at least 24 hours
   - Pain felt in the course of normal activities and at least 24 hours after the physical injury was suffered. (Note: At times, the victim is (a) unable to report verbally about pain or (b) inaccessible for assessment. In such cases, the criterion is met if the nature of the injuries would typically result in pain as defined above.)
   - Death

2. More than inconsequential fear reaction:

(a) Fear (verbalized or displayed) of bodily injury to self or others *AND*
(b) At least one of the following signs of fear or anxiety lasting at least 48 hours:

i. Persistent intrusive recollections of the incident,
ii. Marked negative reactions to cues *related to incident*, as evidenced by (a) avoidance of cues, (b) subjective or overt distress to cues, or (c) physiological hyperarousal to cues (Note: Perpetrator can be a cue.)
iii. Acting or feeling as if incident is recurring
iv. Marked symptoms of anxiety (any of the following):

- Difficulty falling or staying asleep
- Irritability or outbursts of anger
- Difficulty concentrating
- Hypervigilance (i.e., acting overly sensitive to sounds and sights in the environment; scanning the environment expecting danger; feeling keyed up and on edge)
- Exaggerated startle response

2

Intimate Partner Violence and Its Measurement: Global Considerations

Christina Pallitto and Claudia García-Moreno

Violence against women may take different forms in different settings, but it occurs throughout the world and harms women's health, violates their human rights, and limits their full participation in society. In addition, it negatively affects their children and families and exacts a tremendous economic cost on societies and countries, as well as a toll on human suffering.

The movement to stop violence against women globally has been steadily gaining momentum and has highlighted the universality of this phenomenon as a result of efforts by individuals and organizations from around the world in all sectors and levels of society—from community-based to international organizations. Measurement of violence against women across cultures must take into account this universality, while also determining the context-specific nature of violence and the factors that contribute to its occurrence.

There are many forms of violence against women inflicted within the public and private spheres; however, this chapter, in keeping with the theme of the book, focuses on intimate partner violence (IPV). IPV refers to behavior in an intimate relationship that causes physical, sexual, or psychological harm, including physical aggression, sexual coercion, psychological abuse, and controlling behaviors (WHO, 2011; Heise & García-Moreno, 2002). It differs from other forms of violence because of the private nature of the violence and the fact that it is inflicted by persons who are married, cohabitating, or in an intimate relationship with the person who is abused. It is usually perpetrated by men against women, although men can also suffer partner violence and it also occurs between same sex partners. Although private, and often hidden, this type of violence exists within a wider sociocultural context that must also be understood.

This chapter first briefly describes the key milestones in acknowledging violence against women as a public health and an international human rights problem. It identifies how human rights instruments have introduced a level of accountability and action that previously did not exist, as well as a new international standard that is not subject to the laws of individual countries. In addition, a public health approach provides a systematic framework for investigating and addressing violence against women. An ecological framework helps research as well as programs consider the interconnected yet distinct layers of factors that influence the perpetuation of violence against women—including at the societal level, community level, relationship level, and individual level. In turn, each of these layers of factors will be described, showing that studying violence against women in general, and IPV in particular, requires an understanding of how the risk and protective factors operate at and across various levels. Developing a public health response to violence against women requires not only proper measurement strategies, but also appropriate framing of the issue within sociocultural context. These issues are presented, followed by a discussion of the typologies of IPV that have been proposed and a set of recommendations for future directions of violence research internationally.

VIOLENCE AGAINST WOMEN AS AN INTERNATIONAL HUMAN RIGHTS AND PUBLIC HEALTH ISSUE

The UN Declaration on the Elimination of Violence Against Women states that violence against women includes "any act of gender-based violence that results in, or is likely to result in, physical, sexual or psychological harm or suffering to women, including threats of such acts, coercion or arbitrary deprivation of liberty, whether occurring in public or in private life" (UN, 1993). This Declaration was an important milestone in recognizing violence against women as a global human rights problem and in making governments responsible for action. In addition, the Convention on Elimination of All Forms of Discrimination Against Women, and the Beijing Declaration and Platform of Action at the Fourth World Conference on Women in 1995 also call on states to categorize violence against women as a form of discrimination against women and to take actions to eliminate it. Following these declarations and noting the lack of sufficient progress, in 2008 the United Nations Secretary General Ban Ki-Moon launched his UNiTE Campaign to End Violence Against Women (http://endviolence.un.org), renewing the call to action for governments, civil society, and other sectors of society to join forces to end violence against women. An important aspect of the UN Secretary General's campaign, in addition to the development of national laws and national plans of action, is institutionalizing data collection on many forms of violence against women for monitoring and advocacy purposes, as will be discussed later in the chapter.

These key international milestones highlight that violence against women in its many forms is not a series of disconnected acts, but rather is a cross-cultural phenomenon in which violent acts are inflicted on a group of people because they belong to a particular group (in this case, being a woman or girl). They also recognize that much of the violence that women and girls experience across the world is related to their lower status in society vis-à-vis men, which often leads to discrimination, some of which is even codified in laws. Hence, regardless of cultural norms and state laws, violence against women requires international and state action.

Changes in societal norms around violence against women do not automatically follow changes in international norms and even in national laws, which is why a public health approach is useful in addressing violence and understanding its determinants. The public health approach recognizes the context in which problems occur and applies a multisectoral systematic approach to problem solving that includes four stages: (a) a problem is identified and its magnitude determined; (b) its causes and correlates are analyzed; (c) programs and policies for preventing and addressing the problem at a population level are implemented; and (d) results are evaluated and the tested interventions are adapted and scaled up.

As a first step, greater understanding of the nature and meaning of IPV in low- and middle-income settings with high gender inequality is needed to provide culturally relevant solutions that address not only the current manifestations of violence but also the underlying factors. The dominance of North American and European researchers in the study of partner violence has resulted in more data emerging from these settings and less from low- and middle-income countries in other parts of the world, although this is increasingly changing. The development of frameworks and typologies of different forms of IPV, which we will discuss later in the chapter, has been largely based on context-specific data from North America. It cannot be assumed that these models are globally applicable and that the experience of violence is the same across countries/settings, especially given the drastic differences in sociocultural norms and even laws that place women in a secondary and often dependent situation. Furthermore, the prevalence of IPV in other regions is much higher than in North America and Western Europe, and these differences must be understood better and incorporated into the public health models and the responses to this violence.

UNDERSTANDING RISK FACTORS THROUGH AN ECOLOGICAL FRAMEWORK

Applying an ecological framework to understanding the risk factors that lead to violence can focus research as well as program efforts on the interconnected yet distinct layers of factors that influence the experience and perpetration of violence against women. One can envision these factors as falling within a set of concentric circles in which the different layers of factors nest within each other, starting from the largest circle, which represents the *societal level*—the laws, policies and cultural norms, and belief systems that influence dynamics between men and women and dictate women's role in society—moving to the *community level*—which describes how communities and extended kin networks and availability of services may influence women's participation and status in society, the acceptability of violence, and the options women have to leave abusive relationships—to the *relationship level*—the dynamics between partners and the characteristics of the partner, where notions of male control may influence the dynamics—and finally the *individual level*—the personal experiences, history, or characteristics that influence one's risk for experiencing violence or of perpetrating it.

Much of the research on IPV focuses on individual characteristics and risk factors, yet it is also necessary to study the community and societal-level factors. The next section describes some of the research showing how violence against women and gender equality have been studied cross-culturally and how these factors can explain some of the variation in levels of violence observed (Figure 2.1).

Societal- and Community-Level Factors in Violence Research

Although abusing a female partner might be a socially deviant behavior in some settings, it is a socially acceptable behavior in many others, and in a few even legally acceptable. Whether it happens depends, among other things, on the acceptability of such violence, which is also linked to the level of gender inequality (i.e., the norms that grant men power and the right to control women) in a particular setting and how these sociocultural norms are reinforced by legal, political, and cultural institutions and customs. Some examples of how tolerance for structural inequality between men and women can contribute to violence against women include lack of political will for preventing violence against women and punishing the perpetrators; social practices that prevent female members of society from having equal opportunities for education, employment, land and property, and social participation, which fosters dependence on male family members; power structures, such as inheritance systems and contractual norms that favor male members of society as property holders, which make it more difficult for women to leave abusive relationships; media messages that reinforce traditional gender roles between the sexes; and religious and cultural values that fail to recognize divorce, reproductive choice, or contraceptive use, which keeps women closely tied to more traditional and domestic roles in society.

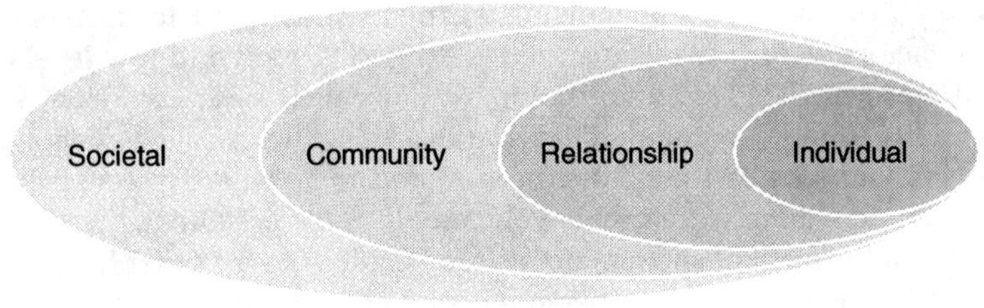

FIGURE 2.1 Ecological model for violence research.
Source: Heise (1998).

While these examples of gender inequalities play out at the societal level, they provide a backdrop for individual norms and beliefs that foster a tolerance for violence against women and create structural barriers for overcoming it. An important question to consider in the discussion of measurement and meaning of violence against women is whether it is considered a normative or deviant behavior in a given society, as this also influences the types of interventions that are needed. Different conceptual frameworks and strategies need to be developed and tested in settings where gender inequality is normative as opposed to deviant or depending on where on the spectrum it falls.

Measuring Whether Violence Against Women Is Normative in Some Societies

Several empirical approaches can be applied in determining whether violence against women is normative in a given society. One approach is to look at data from international population-based surveys, such as the Demographic and Health Survey (DHS) and the World Health Organization (WHO) *WHO Multi-Country Study on Women's Health and Domestic Violence,* which are important sources of data on violence against women and gender norms in low- and middle-income countries. A quick glance at these data reveals prevalence rates of ever experiencing physical and/or sexual partner violence as high as 71% in rural Ethiopia, 69% in rural Peru, 61% in rural Bangladesh, 56% in rural Tanzania, 46% in Samoa, and 41% in rural Thailand. Between 50% and 80% of the physical violence in each of these sites was considered severe based on the type of acts perpetrated (García-Moreno et al., 2005). When considering physical and/or sexual partner violence in the past 12 months, the figures range from 22% to 54% in these sites (García-Moreno et al., 2005) in contrast to 1.5% to 3% in North American prevalence studies (Heise, Ellsberg, & Gottemoeller, 1999; Statistics Canada, 2006; Tjaden & Thoennes, 2000).

When posed with the question of whether a husband would be justified in beating his wife under a set of hypothetical circumstances (going out without telling him, neglecting the children, arguing with him, answering him back, refusing to have sex with him, not preparing food, talking to other men), the following rates were reported in DHS data: 50% of abused women in Zambia, 40% of abused women in Egypt, 32% of abused women in Nicaragua, and 31% of abused women in Haiti believed that husbands were justified in beating their wives for one or more of the reasons mentioned (Kishor & Johnson, 2004). Data from the WHO survey found even higher percentages of women agreeing that male violence against their female partners was justified, and women who had experienced violence reported higher agreement in all sites (García-Moreno et al., 2005). In fact, 94% of abused women in rural Ethiopia, 86% in rural Bangladesh, 84% in rural Peru, 76% in Samoa, and 74% in rural Thailand believed that violence against female partners was justified under at least one of the hypothetical circumstances mentioned. These numbers speak for themselves in demonstrating the normative nature of IPV against women in a range of settings, both in terms of actual prevalence of IPV and in attitudes of acceptance of IPV.

Another approach in exploring whether violence against women is a normative behavior in some cultures is to review ethnographic data on different cultures and classify them as exhibiting high or low levels of violence against women and to determine what risk and protective factors were present in societies exhibiting high and low levels of violence, respectively (Campbell, 1999; Counts, Brown, & Campbell, 1992; Levinson, 1989; Sanday, 1981). These studies found that among the societies studied, women in low violence societies tended to have power outside the home; there tended to be an active community response to violence (sanctions); there were exclusively female work or solidarity groups; and there were sanctuaries in the form of shelters, friends, or family. On the other hand, high violence societies tended to favor violent interpersonal conflict resolution; there were higher levels of economic inequality between men and women; there was an ideal of masculinity that favored male dominance/toughness/honor; and males tended to have greater economic and decision-making authority in the family (Counts et al., 1992).

Another researcher highlighted the importance of applying a cross-cultural rather than a culturally specific framework for comparison on violence against women (Rozée, 1993). This framework, which is specific to sexual violence, is based on female consent rather than social norms as the defining aspect of sexual violence. It emphasizes the fact that some societies might tolerate acts that are harmful to women in the name of sociocultural norms rather than applying a cross-cultural standard. Accordingly, some societies might consider nonconsensual acts as legal and normative (e.g., marital rape), while other consensual acts might be considered illegal or non-normative (e.g., homosexual relations). Measurement of violence, therefore, must enquire about specific acts of violence applying a universal standard, rather than allowing cultural norms to dictate abuse status. Results that are based on social norms alone will underestimate actual prevalence. As a result, act-based instruments for measuring violence against women internationally are preferable, although the meaning and context of specific acts is subject to interpretation.

While the chapter focuses on IPV, evidence on the normative nature of other forms of violence against women, such as sexual violence among partners and nonpartners, can show the cultural acceptability of violence against women and highlight the challenges in ending it. Emerging research among young men in Bangladesh, South Africa, and China shows that social norms around gender and sexual violence provide justification for men to commit these acts. In all of these settings, men who raped claimed sexual entitlement as the key motivating factor, and female consent was overridden by the belief in sexual entitlement (Fulu, 2011). In Bangladesh, up to 81% of men who raped reported that they felt entitled to have sex with the woman they raped, and 66% stated that they enjoyed the violent act (Naved, Huque, & Farah, 2011). Similarly, in China, 86% of men who raped claimed sexual entitlement as the motivating factor, and 58% claimed they did it for fun or boredom (Wang, 2011). In South Africa, 28% of adult men admitted to raping a woman or girl (partners and nonpartners). Among them almost 70% felt they were entitled to the forced sex, even when the girl was under 15 years old. More than half of the men who gang raped a woman or girl claimed that they were motivated by fun and sexual entitlement (Jewkes, Sikweyiya, Morrell, & Dunkle, 2011a, 2011b). These disturbing findings show that rape in many settings is justified by the men who commit it and that it is so widespread as to be normative, or at least acceptable among many men, in some settings.

The case study from Nepal on marital rape described in Box 2.1 shows the deeply rooted cultural beliefs and practices present in this setting. Similar challenges are faced in other settings that are also marked by high gender inequality and high prevalence of violence against women.

Another means of exploring the effect of societal-level variables related to gender equality is the use of standardized survey instruments to quantify different forms of gender equality—such as women's status, women's autonomy, attitudes toward gender norms, and male patriarchal norms—in relation to violence experience and reproductive health outcomes by using either individual or community-level measures of gender inequality in statistical models. Women's individual responses to questions on status, autonomy, or gender attitudes can be analyzed in relation to individual reproductive decision making and outcomes (Dyson & Moore, 1983; Hindin, 2000) or individual experiences of violence (Uthman, Lawoko, & Moradi, 2009). These measures can also be aggregated at the community level to analyze how variation in community-level gender norms can influence IPV experience (Ackerson, Kawachi, Barbeau, & Subramanian, 2008; Hindin & Adair, 2002; Koenig et al., 2003; Pallitto O'Campo, 2005; Schuler, Hashemi, Riley, & Akhter, 1996; Yllo, 1983).

Multilevel models can be used to measure variation in social norms at the community level and explore their effect on violence and health outcomes. For example, research in Bangladesh on female autonomy and economic participation showed that in areas with less rigid gender roles women's ability to generate income was associated with lower levels of IPV, while in areas with more conservative gender roles, women's income generation and economic control was associated with higher levels of IPV (Koenig, Saifuddin, Mian Bazle, & Khorshed Alam Mozumder, 2003). Research from Colombia showed that not only

In 2006, Nepal passed a law on marital rape. It was not being enforced, however, and researchers visited 387 households, interviewing male and female respondents to understand how sexual violence in marriage is perceived and the reasons it occurs.

The respondents considered double standards in gender roles, traditional cultural norms, lack of family and legal support, use of alcohol, and women's economic dependence on men to be the major underlying causes of sexual violence. Victims tended to be blamed rather than supported. Quotes from participants in the study provide insight into the community perceptions of sexual violence in marriage and its causes:

"Our society is male dominated so women cannot express their views openly. That is why sexual violence takes place within marriage. If a woman expresses her sexual desires to her husband she would be considered indecent."

–Community leaders, Brahmin/Chhetri community

"I got married at the age of 14 years. I did not know anything about sex before my marriage. So when I had sex for the first time, my husband convinced me to have sex even though I did not want to. But he did it (sex) forcibly and I bled and screamed and cried but he did not stop".

–Woman, Brahmin/Chhetri community, 22 years

"It is natural that I take alcohol, and I return home late. In such a situation, she doesn't let me have sex. But I have desire, so we fight. So when I hold her hands firmly she, being a woman, can't do anything, and then I have sex with her forcibly".

–Man, Tharu community, 22 years

Source: World Health Organization. 2009. *Perspectives on Sexual Violence During Early Years of Marriage in Nepal: Findings from a Qualitative Study.* Social Science Research Policy Brief: WHO/RHR/HRP/09.01

BOX 2.1 Marital rape in Nepal: A qualitative study.

experiencing IPV oneself but also living in a community with high levels of IPV or with high levels of gender inequality was significantly associated with having an unintended pregnancy (Pallitto & O'Campo, 2005). Studies from the United States also found that patriarchal norms were highly correlated with wife abuse (Smith, 1990), and that living in a state in the United States with higher gender inequality was associated with a higher risk of IPV (Yllo, 1983).

Each of these studies shows the importance of recognizing gender inequality within the larger societal- or community-level structure as a contributing factor for adverse reproductive outcomes and IPV. In summary, lower levels of female education, autonomy, and women's status; higher tolerance for gender inequality and violence; and higher rates of actual violence at the community level were all found to be predictive of women's risk of violence and other health outcomes (Ackerson et al., 2008; Hindin, 2000; Koenig, 1999; Pallitto & O'Campo, 2005).

Family and Partnership Factors

Relationship factors and family dynamics, such as relationship quality, can also be important predictors of violence. As will be described shortly, there is debate about the nature of conflict in violent relationships and the appropriate responses to those conflicts, depending on whether the violence is reciprocal in nature or whether it is based on power and control by one partner. Regardless of the type of violence, relationships with violence are more likely to be marked by low satisfaction, high conflict, and high disagreement as compared with relationships without violence (Aldarondo & Sugarman, 1996; Stith, Smith, Penn, Ward, & Tritt, 2004). Whether the disagreements are a precursor to violence or violent relationships are by nature conflict-ridden, at least some violence could potentially be prevented by intervening in relationships where it is possible that dissatisfaction and discord are present and by improving communication between couples (Derrington, Johnson, Menard, Ooms, & Stanley, 2010). However, caution is needed in assuming that patterns of conflict within couples that are found in one setting marked by lower prevalence of IPV and greater female autonomy will apply to settings with higher prevalence of IPV and lower female autonomy.

Sources of conflict vary among couples, but research has shown that dissonance in beliefs around gender roles, educational status, age, and desired fertility between partners can lead to conflict that can escalate to violence (Ackerson et al., 2008; Hindin & Adair, 2002; Koenig et al., 2003; Schuler et al., 1996). The same beliefs and attitudes about gender roles that were discussed in the section on societal-level factors as being indicative of unequal status and power between men and women can cause problems within relationships when the partners hold different beliefs or individual women's autonomy is greater than social norms dictate (Boyle, Georgiades, Cullen, & Racine, 2009; Hindin & Adair, 2002; Koenig et al., 2003; Schuler et al., 1996). Whether the dissonance leads to mild discord or is used as a means to justify abuse and maintain control through violent means depends on other factors, but dissonance can be an important risk factor in understanding why IPV occurs. Dissonance in educational status can be a remnant of societal-level attitudes about female education and economic participation, so that women with lower educational status vis-à-vis male partners have fewer skills and alternatives to enact a change in relationship status, have lower power or autonomy within the relationship, or have lower self-esteem (Abramsky et al., 2011; Jejeebhoy & Cook, 1997; Kishor & Johnson, 2004). However, women with higher educational status or greater autonomy and decision making than their partners may also be at an increased risk of IPV, possibly due to the desire of male partners to assert control over the female partner with higher status (Hindin & Adair, 2002; Schuler et al., 1996; Uthman et al., 2009; Yllo, 1983). Sometimes differences in fertility preferences can lead to reproductive control, in which the male partner uses pregnancy promotion efforts (birth control sabotage, forced sex, failure to use condoms, prevention of abortion) or exerts other influences on fertility control (Clark et al., 2008; Moore, Frohwirth, & Miller, 2010). Regardless of the source of conflict, strategies for primary and secondary prevention of violence include improving communication, fostering respect, and promoting conflict resolution among couples.

Individual Factors

Some of the societal- and community-level factors discussed previously can be measured in an aggregated manner to show their influence as societal or community-level risk factors (e.g., How does living in a community with high gender inequality affect risk of experiencing IPV or adverse reproductive health outcomes?) (Koenig et al., 2003; Pallitto & O'Campo, 2005; Schuler et al., 1996), but they can also be measured at the individual level to show their influence as individual-level risk factors (e.g., How do women's education level and level of autonomy affect their own risk of IPV?) (Dyson & Moore, 1983; Gage, 1998; Hindin, 2000). It is important to recognize this interrelationship between the different levels in the ecological framework (Heise, 1998). For example, if women's economic participation and educational attainment is not valued in a society, the levels of female literacy and education will be lower at the societal level, affecting whether individual women are educated or not (Heward, 1999). So, while it is consistently found that women's lower education level is related to risk of IPV (Abramsky et al., 2011; Kishor & Johnson, 2004), is this higher risk of IPV related more to her own education level or to the lack of opportunities for education and participation in society that is rooted in societal-level norms of gender inequality (WHO, 2005)? Both types of research contribute to the knowledge we have about risk, but it is important to keep in mind how these various interrelated factors affect one another, and the relative importance of one level as compared with another is not known.

Research on individual risk and protective factors has found that some factors are consistently predictive in understanding women's risk of IPV and male perpetration of IPV, even across diverse settings. A recent analysis of data from 15 sites participating in the WHO multi-country study showed that childhood factors, educational and socioeconomic status, alcohol use, and attitudes about wife abuse were highly predictive of risk (Abramsky et al., 2011). These findings are supported by other research as well, and researchers consistently find that experiencing child abuse or witnessing parental violence during childhood increases men's risk of perpetrating IPV and women's risk of being victimized (Abramsky et al., 2011; Hotaling & Sugarman, 1986; Kishor & Johnson, 2004; McKinney, Caetano, Ramisetty-Mikler, & Nelson, 2009). Often these perpetration and victimization experiences *further* increase one's risk for subsequent events because men who have a history of violent behavior are more likely to be violent with partners, and women who have a history of victimization, whether in childhood or in a partner or nonpartner relationship, have a heightened risk of subsequent victimization (Hotaling & Sugarman, 1986). These findings suggest the need for responses that aim to short-circuit patterns of abuse and violence that are rooted in childhood and other early stages in the life cycle. Preventing childhood experiences from becoming lifelong patterns of violence and victimization is an important primary and secondary prevention strategy (WHO, 2010).

Other socioeconomic and demographic factors predictive of risk include young age, lower educational attainment, and low socioeconomic status (Abramksy et al., 2011; Kishor & Johnson, 2004). Although some factors can be altered more easily than others, identifying high-risk groups is important in preventing violence and providing care for those who experience it. For example, knowing that younger couples are more vulnerable to violence can help focus efforts to build self-esteem and improve communication and relationship dynamics among younger populations (Jewkes et al., 2010b; Kim et al., 2009). Likewise, subgroups that are socially marginalized because of their socioeconomic status, race, or ethnicity can be more vulnerable to many forms of abuse and may need special targeted efforts that are sensitive to their particular risks (Sen & Ostlin, 2008). Similarly, certain stages in the life cycle or in a relationship may be indicative of greater vulnerability, including violence during pregnancy and the postpartum period (Gazmararian et al., 1996; Gelles, 1988), as well as initial separation periods among women who decide to leave their partners after a history of violence (Johnson, 2006).

Some research and intervention efforts have focused on the role of mediating factors, such as alcohol and drug use, in perpetration and victimization. Consumption by perpetrators and victims is associated with increased levels of violence, but since alcohol itself is not the sole causal factor and since it is generally associated with other risk behaviors as well, removal of alcohol is not sufficient for eliminating IPV. It may lessen IPV occurrence and/or severity, however, by creating a less favorable context for violence to occur even when other risk factors are present.

TYPOLOGIES OF IPV IN THE GLOBAL CONTEXT

It is important to position this chapter within the larger debate that surrounds IPV research. Some researchers frame the issue of IPV as an extreme form of relationship/family conflict, in which couples resort to violence when they are unable to resolve conflict successfully (Straus, 1979). These conflict-ridden relationships are considered part of a pattern of family violence that includes child abuse as well. This dichotomy between the family violence paradigm and the gender-based violence paradigm that considers IPV as being about women's control and based in unequal power dynamics between the sexes has created divergent fields of research, with the family violence researchers emphasizing relationship conflict issues rather than underlying sociocultural factors.

Straus and Gelles created the widely used instrument for measuring relationship violence—the Conflict Tactics Scale (CTS)—which measures specific acts of violence between partners in the context of relationship conflict. Although this instrument is widely used, it has also been widely criticized because of its failure to consider inequalities in power between men and women (Shepard & Campbell, 1992; Swan & Snow, 2006), to recognize the context in which abuse occurs, and to account for differences in fear and control that tend to be more prevalent in relationships where men abuse their female partners (Dobash, Dobash, Wilson, & Daly, 1992). Some of these criticisms have been addressed in the revised version, which includes more questions on psychological aggression and more specific questions about different forms of physical and sexual abuse (Straus, Hamby, Boney-McCoy, & Sugarman, 1996), and other researchers have expanded the debate by applying other instruments in conjunction with the CTS to understand the context of violence (Dutton, Goodman, & Schmidt, 2006; Johnson 2006).

While the CTS is designed to capture acts of violence committed by women as well as men in the context of conflict, further research of couples in which reciprocal violence occurs has shown that female partners were more likely to be victims of sexual violence, and suffer injury and coercive control, by their male partners (Ansara & Hindin, 2010; Swan & Snow, 2002); they were more likely to consider their actions as being in self-defense rather than initiating violence (Bair-Merritt et al., 2010; Downs, Rindels, & Atkinson, 2007; Swan et al., 2008); and they tended to experience more adverse health effects than men (Ansara & Hindin, 2010; Swan, Gambone, Caldwell, Sullivan, & Snow, 2008). These findings are supported by data from the British Crime Survey, in which women were much more likely to state that they lived in fear of their partner, had been threatened by their partner, and injured more by their partner than men experiencing violence by their female partners, even though the prevalence of reported acts was similar (Mirrlees-Black, 1999).

Johnson and colleagues (Johnson, 2006; Johnson & Ferraro, 2000; Kelly & Johnson, 2008) rightly argue that we need to move beyond the dichotomy of whether or not violence occurs between partners and move toward a greater understanding of the nuances and patterns underlying these actions. Johnson's typology differentiates types of IPV into several distinct patterns—*coercive controlling violence* describes violence that is committed in the context of control and intimidation and emotional abuse in which one partner (generally the male partner) exerts power through violence and the threat of violence; *violent resistance* describes the violent response to a violent and coercively controlling partner either in direct response as self-defense or in response during a prolonged violent relationship; *situational couple violence* describes the conflict-escalation type of violence that is committed by either partner as a response to disagreement and discord; and *separation-instigated violence* describes violence that begins at the moment of separation as opposed to violence that might continue or even escalate at the moment of separation.

Johnson's violence typology can enable researchers and service providers to understand the patterns and dynamics in a relationship so that appropriate interventions can be provided. He acknowledges that certain populations—generally those linked to the social service or judicial systems—tend to have experienced the coercive controlling type of violence, therefore studies focused on these populations are more likely to identify violence that falls into that category, whereas other study designs, such as population-based studies using the CTS, tend to identify reciprocal or situational violence, particularly where prevalence is low. Some forms of violence (coercive controlling) are more likely to be inflicted by men and others by women (violent resistance), and others more reciprocally (situational couple violence). Although he presents data to support these typologies, it is important to note that his research is context-specific, and it should not be generalized beyond the contexts in which it was studied (the United States and Canada). The context of the populations he studied differs greatly from that of women in countries marked by high gender inequality. In settings where honor killing, child marriage, or physical/sexual abuse by partners and extended family is culturally acceptable, or where the prevalence of IPV is extremely high (between 30% and 70% ever and 22% to 54% in the last 12 months; García-Moreno et al., 2005; Kishor & Johnson, 2004) and where violence against women is so culturally acceptable that between 46% and 94% of women state that wife beating is justifiable under certain conditions (Kishor & Johnson, 2004), such a typology of partner violence and conflict may not be relevant because it does not take into account the severely restrained context in which women in these settings live. In these settings, coercive control of women tends to be normative. The WHO multi-country study collected information on a range of controlling behaviors by a women's intimate partner and found that between 50% and 90% of ever-partnered women from low- and middle-income countries reported one or more controlling behaviors (e.g., partner kept her from seeing friends or contacting family, insisted on knowing where she was at all times, was suspicious she was unfaithful, or got angry if she spoke with others). Even in settings where controlling behavior was normative, men who were violent also tended to be more controlling (García-Moreno et al., 2005).

In addition, ongoing analyses of the WHO study data also show that there are different patterns of partner violence as defined by the intensity (frequency and severity of acts) as well as combinations of physical, sexual, and emotional partner violence experienced by women. Preliminary findings from latent class analysis of these elements in selected sites suggest that the most severe violence, defined by higher frequency and more forms of violence, was most closely correlated with severe health outcomes (Heise, 2012). These findings will be explored further, but the available evidence suggests that the typologies of violence in low- and middle-income countries may be different than those suggested by Johnson.

The DHS data shed light on the issue of perpetration of violence by women against their male partners, indicating different patterns in the countries with available data. In four DHS countries, women were asked whether they had ever physically abused their partner. Among ever married women, 3.5% in Cambodia, 5% in Haiti, and 13% in the Dominican Republic had ever physically abused their partner. In Cambodia, this figure was validated through a survey with men, in which 3% of men reported violence by their female partners, a slightly lower but similar rate to that reported by the women themselves (Kishor & Johnson, 2004). The data on female and male perpetrated violence are depicted in Figure 2.2. These results from low- and middle-income countries indicate a different pattern of IPV as compared with the United States, where researchers have documented rates of physical violence by women of 15% in a military population, although only 3.5% was clinically significant in that study (Foran, Slep, & Heyman, 2011), and 54% in the general population, although this captured all types of violence (Johnson, 2006).

Population-based surveys asking men about perpetration confirm the high rates of partner violence reported by women. For example, in urban Bangladesh, 60% of men reported having committed physical and/or sexual violence against their wives (Sambisa, Angeles, Lance, Naved, & Curtis, 2010), which is similar to the 62% reported by women in the same urban area in the WHO multi-country study (García-Moreno et al., 2005). In South Africa 30% of men in a household survey reported having committed a rape of a partner or non-partner and 31% reported physical violence against a partner (Jewkes, Sikweyiya, Morrell, & Dunkle, 2011c).

Given the normative nature and high prevalence of partner violence against women in low- and middle-income countries, and the fact that much of this violence occurs when women deviate from accepted cultural norms as opposed to when there is overt conflict between partners, it is important to study the patterns of violence and their meaning in such high prevalence settings and develop new typologies that are relevant to these settings. In particular, there is a need to understand better the different patterns and levels of severity as this is likely to have direct implications for services and other responses.

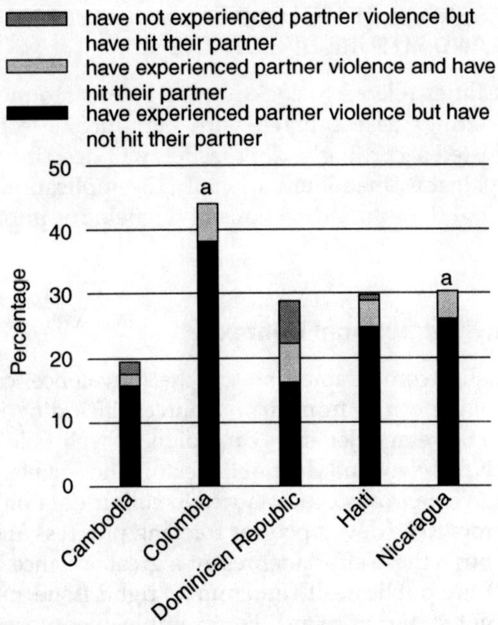

Note: [a]In Colombia and Nicaragua, the percentage of women who hit their partners but had not experienced partner violence was not assessed.

FIGURE 2.2 Percentages of ever-married women who have hit their partner under different circumstances of male violence.
Source: Adapted from Kishor and Johnson (2004) as printed in García-Moreno et al. (2005).

VIOLENCE AGAINST WOMEN AS A RISK FACTOR FOR ILL HEALTH

Regardless of the meaning of an act of violence in a given typology, violent acts can cause injuries and are associated with many other physical and mental health consequences. These health consequences impact women across many spheres, including sexual and reproductive health. Violence has particular effects when it occurs during and around the time of pregnancy, leading to pregnancy complications, adverse birth outcomes, and in some settings, lingering effects on infant and child mortality (Asling-Monemi, Tabassum, & Persson, 2008; Boy & Salihu, 2004). Violence has been closely linked with depression in general, which can have additional adverse effects on maternal health during pregnancy and the postpartum period, as well as infant and child health and development when depressed mothers have difficulty bonding and caring for their infants (Bacchus, Mezey, & Bewley, 2004; Beydoun Al-Sahab, Beydoun, & Tamim, 2010; Leung, Wong, & Leung, 2004). These patterns can increase the risk for a cycle of violence by which children exposed to interparental violence grow up to form relationships marked also by intimate partner and other forms of violence.

IPV can be used to control reproductive decisions and outcomes in a variety of forms, including pregnancy promotion (birth control sabotage, unprotected or forced sex, and threats) or influencing pregnancy outcomes (through either forced pregnancy, forced abortions, or actively preventing abortion as well as violence during pregnancy; Moore et al., 2010), and has been closely associated with unintended pregnancy, sexually transmitted infections (STIs), HIV, unsafe abortion, and other negative reproductive health outcomes (Alio, Daley, Nana, Duan, & Salihu, 2009; Emenike, Lawoko, & Dalal, 2008; Jewkes, Dunkle, Nduna, & Shai, 2010; Pallitto & O'Campo, 2004; Pallitto et al., forthcoming; Weiss et al., 2008).

INTERNATIONAL RESEARCH OF VIOLENCE AGAINST WOMEN: CURRENT EFFORTS AND FUTURE DIRECTIONS

Given the different realities related to sociocultural norms around gender equality in low- and middle-income settings as compared with high-income settings, measurement and response must be adjusted accordingly. This section will describe some of the key issues in measuring violence against women internationally, the application of existing knowledge in public health efforts, and the future directions of the field for improving measurement and response to violence.

Measurement in the International Context

Demand for good quality comparable data on the prevalence, causes, and consequences of violence against women comes from many sources, including internationally mandated efforts, such as the UN Secretary General's campaign, as well as local, national, and international pressure from civil society and the public sector. The Secretary General's Campaign to End Violence Against Women calls on countries to collect data on violence against women and for a set of indicators to be developed for tracking progress and quantifying prevalence by the year 2015. Although these efforts represent a great advance in recognition of violence against women (VAW) as a public health and human rights issue, measuring violence against women accurately is not straightforward. For example, incorporating violence modules in census data collection or in other nonhealth-related surveys will not allow for the same level of support that specialized surveys allow and could potentially yield underreporting and falsely low prevalence rates. In addition, there are safety concerns for participants upon disclosure if mechanisms of support are not in place. Dedicated surveys at the population level, such as the WHO multi-country study, the DHS, and the Centers for Disease Control's Reproductive Health Surveys remain the gold standard for data collection on IPV and other forms of violence against women because of the importance of having interviewers well trained in violence research and able to provide adequate support and referral where necessary, while also ensuring privacy and safety in data collection (e.g., not in the presence of male partners).

To collect high-quality data that can be compared across settings and over time requires the following: a well-validated instrument—based on behavioral acts to avoid cultural bias in interpretation—that accurately captures the relevant domains of IPV and other forms of violence against women (García-Moreno, Jansen, Ellsberg, Heise, & Watts, 2006); use of the same instrument and measurement in different settings to enable comparison; sampling strategies that provide robust population-level estimates from representative samples (García-Moreno et al., 2006); interviewers who are well trained in violence research so that adequate measures are taken to protect participants and researchers from harm and to ensure that participants feel safe to disclose their violence experience (WHO, 2001); inclusion of questions related to the context in which the violence occurred and on gender norms and attitudes; and adherence to ethical and safety guidelines related to confidentiality, referral, support, and protection of participants (Jansen, Watts, Ellsberg, Heise, & García-Moreno, 2004). In addition, political will and support is needed to disseminate and use the data to address violence against women, as is an international commitment to provide the necessary financial and technical support for action.

Public Health Response to Violence Against Women Internationally

In keeping with a public health approach, the ultimate purpose of understanding the magnitude, the prevalence, the risk factors, and the consequences of violence against women is to inform the development of practical responses to address VAW in all sectors, and especially within the health sector. All of the surveys and analyses at the national, regional, and global levels contribute to developing primary prevention interventions, as well as parameters for the thresholds of clinical significance to develop appropriate strategies for assessment and care of women suffering from violence. The development of typologies, such as those outlined by Johnson, are a good starting point for disentangling different types of violence in certain settings. Practitioners in these settings can benefit from the knowledge gained from this research, and counselors working with individual women or couples can appropriately intervene in some cases by tailoring their approach to the type of violence experienced (Derrington et al., 2010). However, in cases of more severe violence and in settings where underlying sociocultural issues justify violence and where social services are lacking, other strategies are required and marriage and relationship education are likely to be a less appropriate solution.

While the field of IPV research has advanced considerably in many high-income countries, it still lags behind in other countries. Conducting a population-based study in countries where no data exist represents an enormous advance in making violence against women visible and highlighting its public health and social significance. Prevalence data have provided the impetus to implement multisectoral activities in coordination with civil society and the public sector, to develop or modify legislation or to invest in programs to address violence against women. Prevalence data can also raise public awareness and help link violence survivors with appropriate services (Ellsberg & Heise, 2005). Below we describe some examples of countries that have used national prevalence data to take action for change. In Nicaragua, qualitative and quantitative data from a prevalence study led to a multisectoral effort that resulted in passage of a domestic violence bill in the National Assembly and important public awareness raising (Ellsberg, Liljestrand, & Winkvist, 1997); researchers in Thailand were able to use the prevalence data from the first study on violence against women in the country to advocate successfully for inclusion of "marital rape" in a domestic violence bill under discussion in 2007 (personal communication with Churnrurtai Kanchanachitra, study coordinator), which was subsequently passed by the National Assembly (BBC, 2007; Immigration and Refugee Board of Canada, 2007). In many other countries, including Tanzania, Uganda, Liberia, Kenya, South Africa, among others, innovative campaigns, such as community theater, murals and art projects, development of communication materials, establishment of hotlines and social service networks, and incorporation of messages into radio and television dramas, have been carried out using national prevalence data to show the magnitude of the problem and to raise awareness to reduce its occurrence (Ellsberg & Heise, 2005). In the Maldives, following a prevalence study using the WHO multicountry study methodology, the data were used for a nationwide awareness-raising campaign in which 27,000 handprints, which were both a pledge to not commit violence and also a representation of each woman in the country who had experienced partner violence, were displayed around the capital (personal communication with Emma Fulu, study coordinator; Maldives Ministry of Gender and Family, 2006).

In addition to prevalence data, data on the patterns and consequences of violence against women can demonstrate whether a dose–response relationship exists between violence and certain health outcomes, to establish thresholds of clinical significance important for assessment by health providers, and also to look at the impact of different forms of violence (physical, sexual, and emotional or combinations thereof) on health outcomes (Ellsberg et al., 2008; García-Moreno et al., 2005). Likewise, understanding risk and protective factors is crucial in targeting high-risk groups and developing prevention strategies, whether through community-based or health center–based programs (WHO, 2010).

Beyond recognition of the magnitude of the problem, it is important to gain support of the health sector in building the capacity of health providers to recognize partner violence as a "risk factor" underlying a vast array of medical problems/conditions. At the same time it is important not to medicalize the problem by turning it into a diagnosis for women, which may lead to stigmatization and put the blame on them and not the perpetrator. Rather, violence against women should be seen as a risk factor for other medical conditions that require attention. Implementation of health sector–based interventions and evaluation of results has added to the knowledge about how to address violence against women in the health sector. WHO is developing global guidance on best practices for assessment and implementation of health sector responses, as well as interventions for primary prevention (WHO, 2010). However, much remains to be developed, particularly in terms of psychological and mental health support services for victims of violence.

The amount of capacity and resources available to address violence in the health sector varies greatly throughout the world. Recommendations must therefore be sensitive to these differing realities so that routine enquiry, which is recommended in the United States, for example, is not imposed on low-resource, high-prevalence settings where this approach is not only impractical but also potentially damaging if no referral or follow-up possibilities are available and if the safety of a woman could be jeopardized upon disclosure. In settings where routine enquiry is not possible, it becomes more crucial to understand the clinical significance of certain acts and conditions. For example, some acts of violence may raise concern because of the severity of the act. Research has shown that violence during pregnancy, threats with weapons, injuries involving weapons, threats against children, and other life-threatening injuries from violence (e.g., strangulation or head injuries) are such that urgent intervention is needed among women experiencing these acts. However, women might not readily admit the cause of their injuries or might not disclose violence, even when asked. There are, however, clinically significant points of contact with the health system where providers can make further inquiry, assuming that some level of support and care could be provided in the event of disclosure. Likewise, some conditions raise concern because of the severity of the condition. These include mental health disorders/conditions, such as depression, suicidality, and post-traumatic stress and other anxiety disorders; HIV infection or related risk behaviors; alcohol or substance abuse; and severe injuries or injuries to the genitals, head, or abdomen (if pregnant). Presentation with these conditions would require further enquiry and intervention.

Future Directions for Measurement and Response to VAW Internationally

There has been much progress in the past decade in researching IPV, particularly its prevalence and risk and protective factors, in low- and middle-income countries. While there are still geographical gaps, we know much more about partner violence from low- and middle-income countries than we did before 2005. There is a need, however, for more longitudinal studies to understand better the associations between different forms of violence and health outcomes, and to capture better the different levels of severity and their consequences. We also need to improve our understanding of the causal pathways between exposure to violence and disease, including the biological pathways, and also of protective factors and resilience.

Interventions research is urgently needed to test different approaches both to prevent violence from happening in the first place (primary prevention) and to respond to the health and other needs of survivors and mitigate the consequences of such violence (secondary and tertiary prevention). Globally, many small- and large-scale projects are carried out, but only a small percentage of these are evaluated in any way. The results are often not consolidated or disseminated, and there is little knowledge gained from these efforts. More capacity building is needed around evaluation so evidence can be generated on smaller-scale projects and programs, especially those in low-resource settings, and the findings can inform future programs, scale up of effective interventions, and further research of promising interventions.

In terms of primary prevention, research is needed on strategies and interventions to change social and cultural norms that condone or support partner violence against women, as discussed previously. Research on other early childhood interventions, including parenting and home visiting to prevent child abuse and maltreatment should also contribute to a reduction in subsequent violence, including partner violence, in the long term. Research should also include looking at school-based interventions not only to address violence, but also more broadly to build emotional and social skills in children and adolescents. All of this will require adaptation and innovation, taking into account the specific needs of resource-poor settings since much of the existing research has been conducted in high-income settings. In addition to replication of existing models, it is necessary to identify the specific elements that make these models work to adapt them to new modes of delivery in new settings.

To improve health care and health services response, more research is needed to understand the types, content, and duration of health care provider trainings for IPV that are most useful; what forms of health system changes are needed to provide care effectively to survivors of IPV; and what specific interventions are most helpful for survivors. For the latter, a better understanding of the types and levels of severity of IPV is needed. This can inform tools to identify types of violence that may benefit from different sets of interventions and help to refine our responses.

For all of this research, having standardized and universally agreed definitions will be extremely useful. This book is a contribution in this regard, although care must be taken when translating standards and definitions from North America to other settings.

ACKNOWLEDGMENT

This chapter has been reproduced with permission from the WHO. The authors are staff members of the WHO. The authors alone are responsible for the views expressed in this chapter and they do not necessarily represent the decisions, policy, or views of the WHO.

REFERENCES

Abramsky, T., Watts, C. H., García-Moreno, C., Devries, K., Kiss, L., Ellsberg, M.,…, Heise, L. (2011). What factors are associated with recent intimate partner violence? Findings from the WHO multi-country study on women's health and domestic violence. *BMC Public Health, 11*, 109–126.

Ackerson, L. K., Kawachi, I., Barbeau, E. M., & Subramanian, S. V. (2008). Effects of individual and proximate educational context on intimate partner violence: A population-based study of women in India. *American Journal of Public Health, 98*, 507–514.

Aldarondo, E., & Sugarman, D. B. (1996). Risk marker analysis of the cessation and persistence of wife assault. *Journal of Consulting and Clinical Psychology, 64*, 1010–1019.

Alio, A. P., Daley, E. M., Nana, P. N., Duan, J., & Salihu, H. M. (2009). Intimate partner violence and contraception use among women in Sub-Saharan Africa. *International Journal of Gynecology and Obstetrics, 107*, 35–38.

Ansara, D. L., & Hindin, M. J. (2010). Exploring gender differences in the patterns of intimate partner violence in Canada: A latent class approach. *Journal of Community Health, 6*, 849–854.

Asling-Monemi, K., Tabassum, N. R., & Persson, L. A. (2008). Violence against women and the risk of under-five mortality: Analysis of community-based data from rural Bangladesh. *Acta Paediatrica, 97*, 226–232.

Bacchus, L., Mezey, G., & Bewley, S. (2004). Domestic violence: Prevalence in pregnant women and associations with physical and psychological health. *European Journal of Obstetrics, Gynecology and Reproductive Biology, 113*, 6–11.

Bair-Merritt, M. H., Crowne, S. S., Thompson, D. A., Sibinga, E., Trent, M., & Campbell, J. (2010). Why do women use intimate partner violence? A systematic review of women's motivations. *Trauma Violence Abuse, 11*, 178–189.

Beydoun, H. A., Al-Sahab, B., Beydoun, M. A., & Tamim, H. (2010). Intimate partner violence as a risk factor for postpartum depression among Canadian women in the Maternity Experience Survey. *Annals of Epidemiology, 20*, 575–583.

Boy, A., & Salihu, H. M. (2004). Intimate partner violence and birth outcomes: A systematic review. *International Journal of Fertility and Women's Medicine, 49*, 159–164.

Boyle, M. H., Georgiades, K., Cullen, J., & Racine, Y. (2009). Community influences on intimate partner violence in India: Women's education, attitudes towards mistreatment and standards of living. *Social Science and Medicine, 69*, 691–697.

British Broadcasting Corporation (BBC). (2007, June 21). *Thailand passes marital rape bill.* Retrieved February 20, 2012, from http://news.bbc.co.uk/2/hi/asia-pacific/6225872.stm

Campbell, J. C. (1999). Sanctions and sanctuary, wife battering within cultural contexts. In D. Counts, J. Brown, & J. Campbell (Eds.), *To have and to hit, anthropological perspectives on wife beating* (pp. 261–285). Urbana: University of Illinois Press.

Clark, C. J., Silverman, J., Khalaf, I. A., Ra'ad, A. B., Al Sha'ar, Z. A., Al Ata, A. A., & Batieha, A. (2008). Intimate partner violence and interference with women's efforts to avoid pregnancy in Jordan. *Studies in Family Planning, 39*,123–132.

Counts, D. A., Brown, J., & Campbell, J. (1992). *Sanctions and sanctuary: Cultural perspectives on the beating of wives.* Boulder, CO: Westview Press.

Derrington, R., Johnson, M., Menard, A., Ooms, T., & Stanley, S. (2010). *Making distinctions among different types of intimate partner violence: A preliminary guide.* National Health Marriage Resource Center and the National Resource Center on Domestic Violence.

Dobash, R. P., Dobash, R. E., Wilson, M., & Daly, M. (1992). The myth of sexual symmetry in marital violence. *Social Problems, 39,* 71–91.

Downs, W., Rindels, B., & Atkinson, C. (2007). Women's use of physical and nonphysical self-defense strategies during incidents of partner violence. *Violence Against Women, 13,* 28–45.

Dutton, M. A., Goodman, L., & Schmidt, J. (2006). *Development and validation of a coercive control measure for intimate partner violence: Final technical report.* Washington, DC: National Institute of Justice.

Dyson, T., & Moore, M. (1983). On kinship structure, female autonomy, and demographic behavior in India. *Population and Development Review, 9,* 35–60.

Ellsberg, M., & Heise, L. (2005). *Researching violence against women: A practical guide for researchers and activists.* Washington, DC: WHO and PATH.

Ellsberg, M., Jansen, H. A. F. M., Heise, L., Watts, C. H., García-Moreno, C., on behalf of the WHO multi-country study on women's health and domestic violence against women study team. (2008). Intimate partner violence and women's physical and mental health in the WHO multi-country study on women's health and domestic violence: an observational study. *The Lancet, 37,* 1165–1172.

Ellsberg, M., Liljestrand, J., & Winkvist, A. (1997). The Nicaraguan network of women against violence: Using research and action for change. *Reproductive Health Matters, 10,* 82–92.

Emenike, E., Lawoko, S., & Dalal, K. (2008). Intimate partner violence and reproductive health of women in Kenya. *International Nursing Review, 55,* 97–102.

Foran, H. M., Slep, A. M. S., & Heyman, R. E. (2011). Prevalences of intimate partner violence in a representative US Air Force Sample. *Journal of Consulting and Clinical Psychology, 79,* 391–397.

Fulu, E. (2011). *Overview of gender-based violence prevention and masculinities regional research project: Building an evidence base for violence prevention.* Presentation at SVRI Forum, Cape Town, South Africa, October 12, 2011. Retrieved February 24, 2012, from www.svri.org/forum2011/Overview.pdf

Gage, A. J. (1998). Premarital childbearing, unwanted fertility and maternity care in Kenya and Namibia. *Population Studies, 52,* 21–34.

García-Moreno, C., Jansen, H. A. F. M., Ellsberg, M., Heise, L., & Watts, C. (2005). *WHO multi-country study on women's health and domestic violence against women: Initial results on prevalence, health outcomes, and women's responses.* Geneva, Switzerland: World Health Organization.

García-Moreno, C., Jansen, H., Ellsberg, M., Heise, L., & Watts, C. H. (2006). Prevalence of intimate partner violence: Findings from the *WHO multi-country study on women's health and domestic violence. The Lancet, 368,* 1260–1269.

Gazmararian, J. A., Lazorick, S., Spitz, A. M., Ballard, T. J., Saltzman, L. E., & Marks, J. S. (1996). Prevalence of violence against pregnant women. *JAMA, 275,* 1915–1920.

Gelles, R. (1988). Violence and pregnancy: Are pregnant women at greater risk? *Journal of Marriage and Family, 50,* 841–847.

Heise, L. (1998). Violence against women: an integrated, ecological framework. *Violence Against Women, 4,* 262–290.

Heise, L. Determinants of individual and population level risk of partner violence in low and middle income countries. Dissertation submitted in partial fulfilment of a PhD in social epidemiology, Department of Global Health and Development, LSHTM, 2012.

Heise, L., Ellsberg, M., & Gottemoeller, M. (1999). Ending violence against women. *Population reports,* Series L, No. 11. Baltimore: Johns Hopkins University School of Public Health, Population Information Program.

Heise, L., & García-Moreno, C. (2002). Violence by intimate partners. In E. Krug, L. L. Dahlberg, J. A. Mercy, et al. (Eds.), *World report on violence and health (pp. 87– 121).* Geneva: World Health Organization. Retrieved from www.who.int/violence_injury_prevention/violence/world_report/chapters/en/index.html

Heward, C. (1999). Introduction: The new discourses of gender, education and development. In C. Heward & S. Bunwaree (Eds.), *Gender, education and development: Beyond access to empowerment.* London, UK: Zed Books.

Hindin, M. J. (2000). Women's autonomy, women's status and fertility-related behavior in Zimbabwe. *Population Research and Policy Review, 19,* 255–282.

Hindin, M. J., & Adair, L. S. (2002). Who's at risk? Factors associated with intimate partner violence in the Philippines. *Social Science & Medicine, 55,* 1385–1399.

Hotaling, G. T., & Sugarman, D. B. (1986). An analysis of risk markers in husband and wife violence: The current state of knowledge. *Violence and Victims, 1,* 101–124.

Immigration and Refugee Board of Canada. (2007, December 20). *Thailand: Domestic violence; state protection and resources available to victims of domestic abuse,* THA102669.E. Retrieved February 20, 2012, from www.unhcr.org/refworld/docid/47d6547b23.html

Jansen, H. A., Watts, C. H., Ellsberg, M., Heise, L., & García-Moreno, C. (2004). Interviewer training for cross-cultural research on domestic violence: Experience from the WHO multi-country study on women's health and domestic violence. *Violence Against Women, 10,* 831–849.

Jejeebhoy, S. J., & Cook, R. J. (1997). State accountability for wife-beating: The Indian challenge. *The Lancet, 349*, S110–S112.

Jewkes, R., Dunkle, K., Nduna, M., & Shai, N. (2010). Intimate partner violence, relationship power inequity, and incidence of HIV infection in young women in South Africa: A cohort study. *The Lancet, 376*, 41–48.

Jewkes, R., Sikweyiya, Y., Morrell, R., & Dunkle, K. (2011a, October 12). Gender inequitable masculinity and sexual entitlement in rape perpetration in South Africa: Findings of a cross-sectional study. Presentation at SVRI Forum, Cape Town, South Africa. Retrieved February 24, 2012, from www.svri.org/forum2011/Crosssectionalstudy.pdf

Jewkes, R., Sikweyiya, Y., Morrell, R., & Dunkle, K. (2011b). Gender inequitable masculinity and sexual entitlement in rape perpetration South Africa: Findings of a cross-sectional study. *PLoS One, 6*, e29590.

Jewkes, R., Sikweyiya, Y., Morrell, R., & Dunkle, K. (2011c). The relationship between intimate partner violence, rape and HIV amongst South African men: A cross-sectional study. *PLoS One, 6*, e24256.

Johnson, M. P. (2006). Conflict and control: Gender symmetry and asymmetry in domestic violence. *Violence Against Women, 12*, 1003–1018.

Johnson, M. P., & Ferraro, K. J. (2000). Research on domestic violence in the 1990s: Making distinctions. *Journal of Marriage and the Family, 62*, 948–963.

Kelly, J. B., & Johnson, M. P. (2008). Differentiation among types of intimate partner violence: Research update and implications for interventions. *Family Court Review, 46*, 476–499.

Kim, J., Ferrari, G., Abramsky, T., Watts, C., Hargreaves, J., Morison, L.,..., Pronyk, P. (2009). Assessing the incremental effects of combining economic and health interventions: The IMAGE study in South Africa. *Bulletin of the World Health Organization, 87*, 824–832.

Kishor, S., & Johnson, K. (2004). *Profiling domestic violence – A multi-country study.* Calverton, MD: ORC Macro.

Koenig, M. A., Saifuddin, A., Mian Bazle, H., & Khorshed Alam Mozumder, A. B. M. (2003). Women's status and domestic violence in rural Bangladesh: Individual- and community-level effects. *Demography, 40*, 269–288.

Leung, W. C., Wong, T. W., & Leung, P. C. H. (2004). Domestic violence and postnatal depression in a Chinese community. *International Journal of Gynecology and Obstetrics, 79*, 159–166.

Levinson, D. (1989). *Family violence in cross-cultural perspective.* Thousand Oaks, CA: Sage.

Maldives Ministry of Gender and Family. (2006). "Violence against women... That doesn't happen in the Maldives. Retrieved February 20, 2011, from www.mgf.gov.mv/downloads/news%20supliment%20on%20the%20survey%20on%20Women's%20Health%20and%20Life%20Experiences(english).pdf

McKinney, C. M., Caetano, R., Ramisetty-Mikler, S., & Nelson, S. (2009). Childhood family violence and perpetration and victimization of intimate partner violence: Findings from a national population-based study of couples. *Annals of Epidemiology, 19*, 25–32.

Mirrlees-Black, C. (1999). *Domestic violence: Findings from a new British Crime Survey self-completion questionnaire.* Home Office Research Study 191. London, Home Office. Retrieved from www.homeoffice.gov.uk/rds/pdfs/hors191.pdf

Moore, A. M., Frohwirth, L., & Miller, E. (2010). Male reproductive control of women who have experienced intimate partner violence in the United States. *Social Science and Medicine, 70*, 1737–1744.

Naved, R. T., Huque, H., & Farah, S. (2011, October 12). Men's perpetration of sexual violence against women in Bangladesh: Magnitude, correlates, motivations and men's reactions. Presentation at SVRI Forum: Cape Town, South Africa. February 24, 2012, from www.svri.org/forum2011/Bangladesh.pdf

Pallitto, C. C., García-Moreno, C. M., Jansen, H. A. F. M., Heise, L., Ellsberg, M., & Watts, C. (forthcoming). Intimate partner violence, abortion and unintended pregnancy: Results from the WHO multi-country study on women's health and domestic violence. Unpublished manuscript.

Pallitto, C. C., & O'Campo, P. (2004). The relationship between intimate partner violence and unintended pregnancy: Analysis of a national sample from Colombia. *International Family Planning Perspectives, 30*, 165–173.

Pallitto, C. C., & O'Campo, P. (2005). Community level effects of gender inequality on intimate partner violence and unintended pregnancy in Colombia: Testing the feminist perspective. *Social Science and Medicine, 60*, 2205–2216.

Rozée, P. D. (1993). Forbidden or forgiven. *Psychology of Women Quarterly, 17*, 499–514.

Sambisa, W., Angeles, G., Lance, P. M., Naved, R. T., & Curtis, S. L. (2010). Physical and sexual abuse of wives in urban Bangladesh: husbands' reports. *Studies in Family Planning, 41*, 165–178.

Sanday, P. R. (1981). The socio-cultural context of rape. *Journal of Social Issues, 37*, 5–27.

Schuler, S. R., Hashemi, S. M., Riley, A. P., & Akhter, S. (1996). Credit programs, patriarchy and men's violence against women in rural Bangladesh. *Social Science and Medicine, 43*, 1729–1742.

Sen, G., & Ostlin, P. (2008). Gender inequity in health: Why it exists and how we can change it. *Global Public Health, 3*, 1–12.

Shepard, M., & Campbell, J. (1992). The abusive behavior inventory: A measure of psychological and physical abuse. *Journal of Interpersonal Violence, 7*, 291–305.

Smith, M. D. (1990). Patriarchal ideology and wife beating: A test of a feminist hypothesis. *Violence and Victims, 5*, 257–273.

Statistics Canada. (2006). *Measuring violence against women: Statistical trends 2006.* Catalogue no. 85–570-XIE. Ottawa, Ontario: Canadian Centre for Justice Statistics.

Stith, S. M., Smith, D. B., Penn, C. E., Ward, D. B., & Tritt, D. (2004). Intimate partner physical abuse perpetration and victimization risk factors: A meta-analytic review. *Aggression and Violent Behavior, 10*, 65–98.

Straus, M. A. (1979). Measuring intrafamily conflict and violence: The Conflict Tactics Scales. *Journal of Marriage and the Family, 41*, 75–88.

Straus, M. A., Hamby, S. L., Boney-McCoy, S., & Sugarman, D. B. (1996). The revised Conflict Tactics Scale (CTS2): Development and preliminary psychometric data. *Journal of Family Issues, 17*, 283–316.

Swan, S. C., Gambone, L. J., Caldwell, J. E., Sullivan, T. P., & Snow, D. L. (2008). A review of research on women's use of violence with male intimate partners. *Violence & Victims, 23*, 301–314.

Swan, S. C., & Snow, D. L. (2002). A typology of women's use of violence in intimate relationships. *Violence Against Women, 8*, 286–319.

Swan, S. C., & Snow, D. L. (2006). The development of a theory of women's use of violence in intimate relationships. *Violence Against Women, 12*, 1026–1045.

Tjaden, P., & Thoennes, N. (2000, November). *Full report of the prevalence, incidence, and consequences of violence against women: Findings from the National Violence Against Women Survey.* Research Report. Washington, DC, and Atlanta, GA: U.S. Department of Justice, National Institute of Justice, and U.S. Department of Health and Human Services, Centers for Disease Control and Prevention, NCJ 183781.

United Nations General Assembly. (1993, December 20). Declaration on the Elimination of Violence Against Women, A/RES/48/104.

Uthman, O. A., Lawoko, S., & Moradi, T. (2009). Factors associated with attitudes towards intimate partner violence against women: A comparative analysis of 17 sub-Saharan countries. *BMC International Health and Human Rights, 9*, 14–29.

Wang, X. (2011, October 12). GBV prevention and masculinities project: Preliminary findings on sexual violence against women from China. Presentation at SVRI Forum, Cape Town, South Africa. Retrieved February 24, 2012, from www.svri.org/forum2011/China.pdf

Weiss, H. A., Patel, V., West, B., Peeling, R. W., Kirkwood, B. R., & Mabey, D. (2008). Spousal sexual violence and poverty are risk factors for sexually transmitted infections in women: A longitudinal study of women in Goa, India. *Sexually Transmitted Infections, 84*, 133–139.

World Health Organization. (2001). *Putting women first: Ethical and safety recommendations for research on domestic violence against women.* Geneva, Switzerland: Author.

World Health Organization. (2005). *Addressing violence against women and achieving the Millennium Development Goals.* Geneva, Switzerland: Author.

World Health Organization. (2009). *Perspectives on sexual violence during early years of marriage in Nepal: Findings from a qualitative study.* Social Science Research Policy Brief: WHO/RHR/HRP/09.01.

World Health Organization. (2010). *Preventing intimate partner and sexual violence against women: Taking action and generating evidence.* Geneva, Switzerland: Author.

World Health Organization. (2011). Violence against women: Intimate partner and sexual violence against women. Fact sheet no. 239. Geneva, Switzerland: Author. Retrieved February 24, 2012, from www.who.int/mediacentre/factsheets/fs239/en/index.html

Yllo, K. (1983). Sexual equality and violence against wives in American states. *Journal of Comparative Family Studies, 14*, 676–686.

3

Psychological, Physical, and Economic Consequences of Intimate Partner Violence

Heather M. Foran and Ryan Phelps

In this chapter, the evidence for psychological health, physical health, and economic impacts of intimate partner violence (IPV) is reviewed. IPV includes three types—sexual, physical, and emotional (see Chapter 1 in this volume). Although, not completely overlapping, they often co-occur. Emotional abuse is a strong predictor of risk for physical abuse and nearly all women who report physical abuse also report emotional abuse (e.g., Ellsberg, Pena, Herrera, Liljestrand, & Winkvist, 2000; Tjaden & Thoennes, 2000). The co-occurrence between physical and sexual violence varies by country (García-Moreno, Jansen, Ellsberg, Heise, & Watts, 2005). They tend to co-occur in studies of North America (Ellsberg & Heise, 2005) but are less likely to occur in countries such as Thailand (García-Moreno et al., 2005). Although there is some variation among types of IPV, there are many similarities in impacts of IPV and many studies assess types of IPV aggregated. Hence, this review largely focuses on IPV across sexual, physical, and emotional types.

LITERATURE REVIEW SOURCES

Efforts are made through this review to reflect the impact of IPV worldwide. Differences in (a) what is known about IPV across countries/cultures, (b) prevalence, severity, and types of IPV across countries, (c) public health response to IPV, and (d) cultural attitudes toward IPV across countries are notable and lead to wide variation across studies. Most of the research on IPV has been conducted in North America and Europe (see the World Health Organization [WHO] multi-country study—García-Moreno et al., 2005, for an exception). Results from high-income countries are not necessarily generalizable to other countries where rates of IPV may be higher and fewer resources are available for IPV victims. However, for severe violence (see Chapter 1, this volume, for definitions) impacts are likely to share similarities across countries (e.g., depression, physical health).

Most of the studies reviewed herein focus on female victims due to research showing higher risk for severe forms of violence across samples among women (Caetano, McGrath, Ramisetty-Mikler, & Field, 2005; Foran, Slep, Heyman, & U.S. Air Force Family Advocacy Program, 2011; Schafer, Caetano, & Clark, 1998). Although the prevalence rates are lower, men are also at risk for negative consequences of IPV and relevant research on male victimization is noted, when available and applicable.

PSYCHOLOGICAL IMPACTS OF IPV

The impact of IPV on mental health is extensive with a wide range of potential consequences. In a review of the literature, Heise and García-Moreno (2002; see p. 101, Table 4.6), identify the following psychological and behavioral consequences of IPV: depression, anxiety, phobias, panic disorder, poor self-esteem, posttraumatic stress disorder (PTSD), smoking, alcohol and drug abuse, eating disorders, sleep disorders, psychosomatic disorders, suicidal behavior, self-harm, and physical inactivity. Furthermore, there is increased risk for psychiatric disorders among IPV victims, even after controlling for psychiatric history prior to the abuse (Ehrensaft, Moffit, & Caspi, 2006).

Depression, Anxiety, and Substance Abuse

Of the psychological impacts noted above, depression, anxiety/fear, and substance abuse are some of the most prevalent psychological impacts of IPV and have received the most research attention. In a meta-analytical review of nine psychological and demographic victim risk factors, depression was the second largest correlate of IPV (r =.28, n = 899, 6 studies), fear was the third largest correlate of IPV (r =.27, n = 4,388, 5 studies), and alcohol use/abuse was the fourth largest correlate (r =.13, n = 7,084, 11 studies; Stith, Smith, Penn, Ward, & Tritt, 2004). The effect sizes were larger for these risk factors than all demographic variables examined and only smaller than the effect size for bidirectional violence.

IPV may lead to increased risk for depression, anxiety/fear, and substance abuse through several mechanisms. Victims of IPV may abuse substances as a method to cope with the abuse (Wingood, DiClemente, & Raj, 2000) and abuse of substances may place them at further risk for IPV (Lipsky, Caetano, & Field, 2005). Depression and anxiety (e.g., PTSD symptoms) may be reactions to the IPV trauma. In the month following IPV experiences, women are at increased risk for depressive and anxiety symptoms (Cano & O'Leary, 2000; Gleason, 1993). Further, the psychological impacts of IPV are long-lasting. History of IPV in the past year also predicts elevated depressive symptoms compared to women without an IPV history (e.g., Stets & Straus, 1990). Long-lasting effects may be due the impact of IPV on ability to carry out daily activities. In the WHO multi-country study of IPV, lifetime history of sexual or physical abuse was associated with increased likelihood of problems with walking and carrying out daily activities (García-Moreno et al., 2005). This may be due to comorbid mental health problems or alternatively, IPV may increase risk for development of mental health problems through low levels of environmental reinforcement and impacts on self-esteem and perceived control.

Suicide

Furthermore, suicidal behaviors are possible sequelae of mental health problems among victims (Abbott, Johnson, Koziol-McLain, & Lowenstein, 1995; Amaro, Fried, Cabral, & Zuckerman, 1990; Bailey et al., 1997; Bergman & Brismar, 1991; Kaslow et al., 1998). In the WHO study of IPV, women with history of sexual or physical abuse were more likely to have made a suicide attempt or have thoughts of suicide than nonvictimized women (García-Moreno et al., 2005). For example, 20% of women with no history of victimization in a Brazil urban region reported suicidal thoughts compared to 47% of women with a history of physical or sexual victimization. Across the 15 regions examined, the average percentage of those reporting suicidal thoughts among ever-victimized women was 2.48 greater than nonvictimized women.

Male Victims

Studies have also supported psychological impacts for male victims, although the range of mental health impacts may be narrower than they are for women (e.g., Afifi et al., 2009; Coker et al., 2002), and there may be specific impacts that are more likely to occur among male victims (e.g., substance abuse, antisocial personality disorder symptoms; Magdol et al., 1997). Similar to women, effects of severe victimization for men are likely to be long-lasting and lead to increased likelihood of hospitalization for substance abuse and mental health treatment for many years following the abuse than nonvictims (Bell, 2009).

The Impact on Children

Studies have found that children in families with IPV are at increased risk for injury themselves (Appel & Holden, 1998; Asling-Monemi, Tabassum & Persson, 2008; Edleson, 1999; Holt, Buckley & Whelan, 2008; Kitzmann, Gaylord, Holt, & Kenny, 2003; McGuigan & Pratt, 2001; Parkinson, Adams, & Emerling, 2001; Silverman et al., 2009; Wolfe, Crooks, Lee, McIntyre-Smith, & Jaffe, 2003). Approximately one-third to two-thirds of children in families with IPV are also victims of abuse (Herrenkohl, Sousa, Tajima, & Herrenkohl, 2008). Additionally, children living with a victimized mother are 12 to 14 times more likely to be sexually abused compared to children living with nonvictimized mothers (McCloskey, Figuerdo, & Koss, 1995).

PHYSICAL IMPACTS OF IPV

Similar to the psychological impacts, the evidence for the link between IPV and physical health is extensive. For example in Australia, Vos et al. (2006) found that IPV was associated with 7% of overall burden of disease among women aged 18 to 44 (more so than other factors such as blood pressure, tobacco use, and body weight). Below the evidence for the direct and indirect physical impacts of IPV is reviewed.

Injury

Those victimized by their partners are at high risk for incurring injury at some point in their lives. In a review of population-based studies of IPV, approximately 40% to 72% of women who reported victimization had a lifetime history of physical injury (Heise & García-Moreno, 2002). In the National Violence Against Women Study (NVAWS) conducted in the United States, 36.2% of women sexually victimized by their partner, and 41.5% of women physically victimized by their partner, sustained injury (Tjaden & Thoennes, 2000).

Furthermore, studies of emergency rooms indicate that IPV is a common cause of injury among women seeking services (Kyriacou et al., 1999). However, rates of injury due to IPV in emergency room settings are likely underestimated because of reluctance to report the IPV and lack of appropriate screening procedures and training in ERs and primary care offices (Petridou et al., 2002).

Homicide

At the most severe end, IPV can lead to injuries resulting in death. In the United States, nearly one third of female homicides are caused by an intimate partner (Federal Bureau of Investigation, 2001). In 2007, murder by intimate partners resulted in over 1,600 female and 700 male murders in the United States alone (Bureau of Justice Statistics, 2007). Homicide rates by intimate partners are even higher in other countries where violence against partners is more socially accepted and there are less resources and protections available for victims. In some countries up to 70% of female murders are by partners with a history of IPV (Bailey et al., 1997; Dannenberg et al., 1995; Harper & Parsons, 1997; Heise & García-Moreno, 2002).

Other Negative Physical Health Outcomes

In WHO multi-country study, women in most countries surveyed were significantly more likely to report *poor* or *very poor health* if they had a lifetime history of sexual or physical victimization by a partner than nonvictimized women (García-Moreno et al., 2005). This suggests that the physical effects of violence may be long-lasting (García-Moreno et al., 2005). Additionally, history of sexual or physical abuse was associated with pain, memory loss, and dizziness, in the month prior to the interview. These women were also more likely to report miscarriages than nonvictimized women.

In a population survey of U.S. adult men ($N = 27{,}590$) and women ($N = 42{,}566$) conducted in 2005 across 18 states (BRFSS; Black & Breiding, 2008), a lifetime history of sexual or physical violence, after adjusting for demographic covariates, was associated with high blood cholesterol, cardiovascular disease, joint diseases, asthma, smoking, heavy or binge drinking, and risky sexual behaviors for women. It was also associated with diabetes and being overweight (body mass index [BMI] > 25). For men, a history of victimization was associated with joint disease (e.g., arthritis), asthma, smoking, heavy or binge drinking, and risky sexual behavior (Black & Breiding, 2008). The largest adjusted odds ratio was with risky sexual behaviors (e.g., behaviors that place one at risk for sexually transmitted diseases [STDs] or HIV infection) for both men (odds ratio [OR] = 2.6) and women (OR = 3.1). Several other studies also support the link between IPV and risky sexual behaviors and HIV/AIDS (e.g., Campbell et al., 2008; Decker et al., 2009; Dunkle et al., 2004; García-Moreno & Watts, 2000; Jewkes, Sikweyiya, Morrell, & Dunkle, 2009; Maman, Campbell, Sweat, & Gielen, 2000; Maman et al., 2002). IPV may interfere with victims' use of condoms or other contraceptives that place them at risk for STDs such as HIV/AIDS (Heise, Moore, & Toubia, 1995; Quigley et al., 2000).

As the studies above suggest, the type of diseases linked with IPV is considerable. One potential mechanism for the wide-ranging physical problems associated with IPV is through its effect on chronic stress, leading to decreased immune and endocrine system functioning (Breiding, Black, & Ryan, 2008; Crofford, 2007; Leserman & Drossman, 2007). Other conditions associated with IPV include fibromyalgia, irritable bowel syndrome, other gastrointestinal problems, pregnancy complications, sexual dysfunction, central nervous system disorders, gynecological disorders, infertility, and reduced overall physical functioning (Bullock & McFarlane, 1989; Campbell, 1995, 2002; CDC, 2010; Curry, Perin, & Wall, 1998; Heise & García-Moreno, 2002; Leserman et al., 1996; Murphy, Schei, Myhr, & Du Mont, 2001; Newberger et al., 1992; Parker, McFarlane, & Soeken, 1994; Petersen et al., 1997; Valdez-Santiago & Sanin-Aguirre, 1996; Valladares, Ellsberg, Peña, Högberg, & Persson, 2002; Walker, Katon, Roy-Byrne, Jemelka, & Russo, 1993; Walker et al., 1997). Although most of this research has focused on female victims there is also some evidence that males experience negative health outcomes. In a study of substantiated cases of male victims of IPV and nonvictims in the U.S. Army between 1991 and 2000 ($n = 87{,}426$), male victims were more likely than nonvictims to be hospitalized in the years following the abuse for a variety of reasons even after controlling for demographic and occupational risk factors (Bell, 2009).

ECONOMIC IMPACTS OF IPV

The economic impact of IPV has been established across many studies (e.g., see Duvvury, Grown, & Redner, 2004, for a review). Studies generally break down costs into two categories—direct and indirect (Butchart et al., 2008). Direct costs can include two subcategories—medical (e.g., hospital visits, mental health services) and nonmedical (e.g., criminal justice system costs). Indirect costs include tangible costs (loss of days working and work productivity) or intangible (reduced access to services, job opportunities). Most of the studies of economic impact have been conducted in high-income countries (Duvvury et al., 2004) and estimates are based on only a fraction of direct and indirect costs due to limitations in the available data. Thus, these estimates are by nature seriously incomplete but of course very valuable and helpful toward informing the magnitude of the issue.

Overall Costs

In the United States, the annual cost of IPV based on available data was estimated to be $5.8 billion in 1995 (National Center for Injury Prevention and Control [NCIPC], 2003).[1] This was largely due to direct costs from medical services (45%) and mental health services (25%).

This estimate did not include direct nonmedical costs related to the criminal justice system, and is thus, an underestimation of total direct costs. The largest percentage of cost (73%) was due to IPV physical assault because it is the highest frequency form of IPV. However, this estimate captures only a fraction of the value lost as result of IPV physical assault. One sixth of the $5.8 billion cost represents lost wages for victims of IPV homicide during 1995. While the idea of placing a dollar amount on an individual's life is grotesque, it is certain that more has been lost than just the wages that would have been earned had the event not happened. Calculating the value of a statistical life (VSL) is one method used to derive a more complete estimate of the value lost in the case of a fatality. VSL estimates are obtained by examining the compensation that people accept in exchange for facing a higher probability of death. If the VSL estimates based on age group provided in Aldy and Viscusi (2008) were used here instead of projected lost earnings, then this figure alone would be in excess of $5.8 billion. As a result of this change, a more complete estimate of the monetary value of the affects of IPV can be restated as 10.75 billion in 1995 (nearly twice the NCIPC estimate of economic impact).[2]

Direct Costs

The link between IPV and direct medical costs is clear—IPV can lead to physical and psychological injuries that necessitate treatment. Several studies in the United States have found that victims of IPV use more health care services than nonabused women (Bonomi, Anderson, Rivara, & Thompson, 2009; Miller, Cohen, & Wiersema, 1996) and this continues for years after the abuse has ceased (Rivara et al., 2007). Health care utilization among the abused was still 20% higher 5 years after the abuse had ceased than among nonabused women (using the BRFSS U.S. sample), even after adjusting for demographic differences (Rivara et al., 2007).

Indirect Costs

IPV is also linked with high indirect costs (e.g., lost days of work, lost household productivity, lower employment rates and salaries). IPV may include deliberate undermining of employment of women (e.g., failing to provide child care, beating before job interviews, depriving transportation, harassing them at work, or forbidding them to work; Brandwein, 1998; Lloyd & Taluc, 1999). IPV may also indirectly impact employment through psychological and physical consequences of abuse impairing self-esteem about work abilities, increasing absenteeism, and decreasing work quality or productivity (Johnson & Ferraro, 2000; Reeves & O'Leary-Kelly, 2007; Rodgers, 1994). Based on data from the National Violence Against Women Survey (NVAWS), IPV victims lose an estimated 8 million days of paid work or 32,114 full-time jobs and ~5.6 million days of household productivity (NCIPC, 2003). Notably, IPV may be more likely to impact frequency of job change, salary, and productivity than employment status, although some studies have found a link between employment status and IPV in a randomly selected subsample of low-income households in Chicago. Lloyd and Taluc (1999) found no differences in employment status, but victimized women were more likely to have a history of unemployment and were more likely to be welfare recipients. In a 1-year longitudinal study of low-income women, Browne, Salomon, and Bassuk (1999) found that women experiencing IPV were significantly less likely (one third the odds) of being employed in the year following the IPV.

As noted above, most of the studies have examined women victims. One study of male Army substantiated victims of IPV found that they were more likely to be discharged from active duty service earlier than nonvictims even after controlling for relevant demographic and occupational characteristics (Bell, 2009). However, using data from the NVAWS, women and male victimization costs were compared and women victimization costs were about twice those of men's victimization due to higher utilization rates of emergency rooms, inpatient hospital services, physician services, and mental health services, and a higher likelihood of time off work (Arias & Corso, 2005), indicative of the increased economic impact for women compared to men.

Economic Impacts in Other Countries

Butchart et al. (2008) presented economic estimates of IPV based on the International Statistical Classification of Diseases and Related Health Problems (ICD-10) injury codes (X85 to Y09) for Brazil in 2004, Jamaica in 2006, and Thailand in 2005; these results are reviewed below as further examples of the economic impacts of IPV. Direct medical costs in Brazil were 356 million Brazilian reis and indirect costs (lost days work, productivity) were 13.7 Brazilian reis (1.4% of total gross domestic product [GDP]). Direct medical costs in Jamaica were 2.1 billion Jamaican dollars (12% of Jamaicans total health expenditure in 2006). Indirect costs were 27.5 billion Jamaican dollars. The lost work productivity accounted for 4% of their GDP. In Thailand, direct medical costs were 1.3 billion Thai baht for injuries due to IPV, which was 4% of Thailand's total health budget. Indirect costs were 14.4 billion Thai baht or 0.4% of the total Thai GDP.

Other studies have found similar results. IPV costs approximately 2% of the 1996 GDP (1.6 billion) in Chile and 2% of the estimated 1996 GDP in Nicaragua (30 million; Morrison & Orlando, 1999). Taken together, these studies indicate that IPV has substantial economic impacts for many different countries (Duvvury et al., 2004).

SUMMARY

As discussed, there is substantial evidence that IPV has vast physical, psychological, and economic impacts. A summary of the key impacts reviewed can be found in Table 3.1. IPV leads to both direct consequences (e.g., emergency room visit costs, physical injuries, homicides) and indirect consequences (e.g., increased risk for physical diseases, lost work days, mental health disorders). Rates of IPV are high across low-, middle-, and high-income countries and no country is immune to the significant impacts of IPV. Improvements in definitions, surveillance, and public health response across and within countries are needed.

NOTES

1. In 2004, Max et al. reanalyzed the NCIPC 1995 data to estimate rates for 2003. They found the cost to be 8.3 billion U.S. dollars.
2. While this estimate does not take into account the fact that most of the victims were women, it also does not include adjusted figures for 101 homicide victims whose age precluded an estimate based on the tables provided in Aldy and Viscusi (2008).

REFERENCES

Abbott, J., Johnson, R., Koziol-McLain, J., & Lowenstein, S. R. (1995). Domestic violence against women: Incidence and prevalence in an emergency department population. *Journal of the American Medical Association, 27,* 1763–1767.

Afifi, T. O., MacMillian, H., Cox, B. J., Asmundson, G. J. G., Stein, M. B., & Sareen, J. (2009). Mental health correlates of intimate partner violence in marital relationships in a nationally representative sample of males and females. *Journal of Interpersonal Violence, 24,* 1398–1417.

Aldy, J., & Viscusi, K. (2008). Adjusting the value of a statistical life for age and cohort effects. *The Review of Economics and Statistics, 90*(3), 573–581.

Amaro, H., Fried, L. E., Cabral, H., & Zuckerman, B. (1990). Violence during pregnancy and substance use. *American Journal of Public Health, 80,* 575–579.

Appel, A. E., & Holden, G. W. (1998). The co-occurrence of spouse and physical child abuse: A review and appraisal. *Journal of Family Psychology, 12,* 578–599.

Arias, I., & Corso, P. (2005). Average cost per person victimized by an intimate partner of the opposite gender: A comparison of men and women. *Violence and Victims, 20,* 379–391.

Asling-Monemi, K., Tabassum, N. R., & Persson, L. A. (2008). Violence against women and the risk of under-five mortality: Analysis of community-based data from rural Bangladesh. *Acta Paediatrica, 97,* 226–232.

Bailey, J. E., Kellerman, A. L., Somes, G. W., Banton, J. G., Rivara, F. P., & Rushforth, N. P. (1997). Risk factors for violent death of women in the home. *Archives of Internal Medicine, 157,* 777–782.

Bell, N. S. (2009). Health and occupational consequences of spouse abuse victimization among male U.S. Army soldiers. *Journal of Interpersonal Violence, 24,* 751–769.

Bergman, B., & Brismar, B. (1991). Suicide attempts by battered wives. *Acta Psychiatrica Scandinavica, 83,* 380–384.

Black, M. C., & Breiding, M. J. (2008). Adverse health conditions and health risk behaviors associated with intimate partner violence United States, 2005. *Journal of American Medical Association, 300,* 646–649.

Bonomi, A. E., Anderson, M. L., Rivara, F. P., & Thompson, R. S. (2009). Health care utilization and costs associated with physical and non-physical-only intimate partner violence. *Health Research and Educational Trust, 44,* 1052–1067.

Brandwein, R. A. (1998). *Battered women, children, and welfare reform: The ties that bind.* Thousand Oaks, CA: Sage.

Breiding, M. J., Black, M. C., & Ryan, G. W. (2008). Chronic disease and health risk behaviors associated with intimate partner violence—18 U.S. states/territories, 2005. *Annuals of Epidemiology, 18,* 538–544.

Browne, A., Salomon, A., & Bassuk, S. S. (1999). The impact of recent partner violence on poor women's capacity to maintain work. *Violence Against Women, 5,* 393–426.

Bullock, L. F., & McFarlane, J. (1989). The birth-weight/battering connection. *American Journal of Nursing, 89,* 1153–1155.

Bureau of Justice Statistics. (2007). Intimate partner violence [online]. Retrieved September 3, 2011, from http://bjs.ojp.usdoj.gov/index.cfm?ty=tp&tid=971#summary

Butchart, A., Brown, D., Khanh-Huynh, A., Corso, P., Florquin, N., & Muggah, R. (2008). *Manual for estimating the economic costs of injuries due to interpersonal and self-directed violence.* World Health Organization and Center for Disease Control and Prevention.

Caetano, R., McGrath, C., Ramisetty-Mikler, S., & Field, C. A. (2005). Drinking, alcohol problems and the five-year recurrence and incidence of male to female and female to male partner violence. *Alcoholism, Clinical and Experimental Research, 29,* 98–106.

Campbell, J. C. (1995). Addressing battering during pregnancy: Reducing low birth weight and ongoing abuse. *Seminars in Perinatology, 19,* 301–306.

Campbell, J. C. (2002). Health consequences of intimate partner violence. *The Lancet, 359,* 1331–1336.

Campbell, J. C., Baty, M. L., Ghandour, R. M., Stockman, J. K., Francisco, L., & Wagman, J. (2008). The intersection of intimate partner violence against women and HIV/AIDS: A review. *International Journal of Injury Control and Safety Promotion, 15,* 221–231.

Cano, A., & O'Leary, K. D. (2000). Infidelity and separations precipitate major depressive episodes and symptoms of nonspecific depression and anxiety. *Journal of Consulting and Clinical Psychology, 68,* 774–781.

Centers for Disease Control and Prevention (CDC). (2010). Retrieved from www.cdc.gov/ViolencePrevention/intimatepartnerviolence/consequences.html

Coker, A. L., Davis, K. E., Arias, I., Desai, S., Sanderson, M., Brandt, H. M., & Smith, P. H. (2002). Physical and mental health effects of intimate partner violence for men and women. *American Journal of Preventive Medicine, 23,* 260–268.

Crofford, L. J. (2007). Violence, stress, and somatic syndromes. *Trauma Violence Abuse, 8,* 299–313.

Curry, M. A., Perrin, N., & Wall, E. (1998). Effects of abuse on maternal complications and birth weight in adult and adolescent women. *Obstetrics and Gynecology, 92,* 530–534.

Dannenberg, A. L., Carter, D. M., Lawson, H. W., Ashton, D. M., Dorfman, S. F., & Graham, E. H. (1995). Homicide and other injuries as causes of maternal death in New York City, 1987 through 1991. *American Journal of Obstetrics and Gynecology, 172,* 1557–1564.

Decker, M. R. Seage, G. R. 3rd, Hemenway, D., Raj, A., Saggurti, N., Balaiah, D., & Silverman, J. G. (2009). Intimate partner violence functions as both a risk marker and risk factor for women's HIV infection: Findings from Indian husband–wife dyads. *Journal of Acquired Immune Deficiency Syndrome, 51,* 593–600.

Dunkle, K. L., Jewkes, R. K., Brown, H. C., Gray, G. E., McIntryre, J. A., & Harlow, S. D. (2004). Gender-based violence, relationship power, and risk of HIV infection in women attending antenatal clinics in South Africa. *The Lancet, 363,* 1415–1421.

Duvvury, N., Grown, C., & Redner, J. (2004). *Costs of intimate partner violence at the household and community levels: An operational framework for developing countries.* Washington, DC: International Center for Research on Women (ICRW).

Edleson, J. (1999). Children's witnessing of adult domestic violence. *Journal of Interpersonal Violence, 14,* 839–870.

Ehrensaft, M., Moffit, T., & Caspi, A. (2006). Is domestic violence followed by an increased risk for psychiatric disorders among women but not among men? A longitudinal cohort study. *American Journal of Psychiatry, 163,* 885–892.

Ellsberg, M., & Heise, L. (2005). *Researching violence against women: A practical guide for researchers and activists.* Washington, DC: World Health Organization, PATH.

Ellsberg, M. C., Pena, R., Herrera, A., Liljestrand, J., & Winkvist, A. (2000). Candies in hell: Women's experience of violence in Nicaragua. *Social Science and Medicine, 51*, 1595–1610.
Federal Bureau of Investigation. Crime in the United States 2000. (2001). *Uniform crime reports*. Washington, DC: U.S. Department of Justice.
Foran, H., Slep, A. M. S., Heyman, R. E., & U.S. Air Force Family Advocacy Program (2011). Prevalences of intimate partner violence in a representative U.S. Air Force sample. *Journal of Consulting and Clinical Psychology, 79*, 391–397.
García-Moreno, C., Jansen, H. E. F., Ellsberg, M., Heise, L., & Watts, C. H. (2005). *WHO multi-country study on women's health and domestic violence against women*. Geneva, Switzerland. World Health Organization.
García-Moreno, C., & Watts, C. (2000). Violence against women: Its importance for HIV/AIDS. *AIDS, 14*(3), S253–S265.
Gleason, W. J. (1993). Mental disorders in battered women: An empirical study. *Violence and Victims, 8*, 53–68.
Harper, M., & Parsons, L. (1997). Maternal deaths due to homicide and other injuries in North Carolina: 1992–1994. *Obstetrics and Gynecology, 90*, 920–923.
Heise, L., & García-Moreno, C. (2002). Violence by intimate partners. In E. G. Krug, et al. (Eds.), *World report on violence and health* (pp. 87–121). Geneva: World Health Organization.
Heise, L., Moore, K., & Toubia, N. (1995). *Sexual coercion and women's reproductive health: A focus on research*. New York, NY: Population Council.
Herrenkohl, T. I., Sousa, C. Tajima, E. A., & Herrenkohl, R. C. (2008). Intersection of child abuse and children's exposure to domestic violence. *Trauma, Violence, and Abuse, 9*, 84–99.
Holt, S., Buckley, H., & Whelan, S. (2008). The impact of exposure to domestic violence on children and young people. *Child Abuse & Neglect, 32*, 797–810.
Jewkes, R., Sikweyiya, Y., Morrell, R., & Dunkle, K. (2009) *Understanding men's health and use of violence: Interface of rape and HIV in South Africa*. Medical Research Council Technical Report. Pretoria, South Africa: Medical Research Council.
Johnson, M. P., & Ferraro, K. J. (2000). Research on domestic violence in the 1990s: Making distinctions. *Journal of Marriage and the Family, 62*, 948–963.
Kaslow, N. J., Thompson, M. P., Meadows, L. A., Jacobs, D., Chance, S., Gibb, B.,..., Phillips, K. (1998). Factors that mediate and moderate the link between partner abuse and suicidal behavior in African-American women. *Journal of Consulting and Clinical Psychology, 66*, 533–540.
Kitzmann, K. M., Gaylord, N. K., Holt, A. R., & Kenny, E. D. (2003). Child witnesses to domestic violence: A meta-analytic review. *Journal of Consultative Clinical Psychology, 71*, 339–352.
Kyriacou, D. N., Anglin, D., Taliaferro, E., Stone, S., Tubb, T., Linden, J. A.,..., Kraus, J. F. (1999). Risk factors for injury to women from domestic violence against women. *New England Journal of Medicine, 341*, 1892–1898.
Leserman, J., & Drossman, D. A. (2007). Relationship of abuse history to functional gastrointestinal disorders and symptoms. *Trauma Violence Abuse, 8*, 331–343.
Leserman, J., Drossman, D. A., Li, Z., Toomey, T. C., Nachman, G., & Glogau, L. (1996). Sexual and physical abuse history in gastroenterology practice: How types of abuse impact health status. *Psychosomatic Medicine, 58*, 4–15.
Lipsky, S., Caetano, R., & Field, C. A. (2005). Is there a relationship between victim and partner alcohol use during an intimate partner violence event? Findings from an urban emergency department study of abused women. *Journal of Studies on Alcohol, 66*, 407–412.
Lloyd, S., & Taluc, N. (1999). The effects of male violence on female employment. *Violence Against Women, 5*, 370–392.
Magdol, L., Moffitt, T. E., Caspi, A., Newman, D. L., Fagan, J., & Silva, P. A. (1997). Gender differences in partner violence in a birth cohort of 21-year olds: Bridging the gap between clinical and epidemiological approaches. *Journal of Consulting and Clinical Psychology, 65*, 68–78.
Maman, S., Campbell, J., Sweat, M. D., & Gielen, A. C. (2000). The intersection of HIV and violence: Directions for future research and interventions. *Social Science and Medicine, 50*, 459–478.
Maman, S., Mbwambo, J. K., Hogan, N. M., Kilonzo, G. P., Campbell, J. C., Weiss, E., & Sweat, M. D. (2002). HIV positive women report more lifetime partner violence: Findings from a voluntary counseling and testing clinic in Dares Salaam, Tanzania. *American Journal of Public Health, 92*, 1331–1337.
Max, W., Rice, D. P., Finkelstein, E., Bardwell, R. A., & Leadbetter S. (2004). The economic toll of intimate partner violence against women in the United States. *Violence and Victims*, 19, 259–72.
McCloskey, L. A., Figueredo, A. J., & Koss, M. P. (1995). The effects of systemic family violence on children's mental health. *Child Development, 66*, 1239–1261.
McGuigan, W. M., & Pratt, C. C. (2001). The predictive impact of domestic violence on three types of child maltreatment. *Child Abuse & Neglect, 25*, 869–883.
Miller, T. R., Cohen, M. A., & Wiersema, B. (1996). *Victim costs and consequences: A new look*. National Institute of Justice Research Report. Washington, DC: National Institute of Justice, U.S. Department of Justice, NCJ 155282.
Morrison, A., & Orlando, M. B. (1999). Social and economic costs of domestic violence: Chile and Nicaragua. In A. Morrison & M. L. Beihl (Eds.), *Too close to home* (pp. 51–80). Washington, DC: Inter-American Development Bank.

Murphy, D., Schei, B., Myhr, T., & Du Mont, J. (2001). Abuse: A risk factor for low birth weight? A systematic review and meta-analysis. *Canadian Medical Association Journal, 164,* 1567–1572.

National Center for Injury Prevention and Control (NCIPC). (2003). *Costs of intimate partner violence against women in the United States.* Atlanta, GA: Centers for Disease Control and Prevention.

Newberger, E. H., Barkan, S. E., Lieberman, E. S., McCormick, M. C., Yllo, K., Gary, L. T., & Schechter, S. (1992). Abuse of pregnant women and adverse birth outcome: Current knowledge and implications for practice. *Journal of the American Medical Association, 267,* 2370–2372.

Parker, B., McFarlane, J., & Soeken, K. (1994). Abuse during pregnancy: Effects on maternal complications and birth weight in adult and teenage women. *Obstetrics and Gynecology, 84,* 323–328.

Parkinson, G. W., Adams, R. C., & Emerling, F. G. (2001). Maternal domestic violence screening in an office-based pediatric practice. *Pediatrics, 108,* E43.

Petersen, R., Gazmararian, J. A., Spitz, A. M., Rowley, D. L., Goodwin, M. M., Saltzman, L. E., & Marks, J. S. (1997). Violence and adverse pregnancy outcomes: A review of the literature and directions for future research. *American Journal of Preventive Medicine, 13,* 366–373.

Petridou, E., Browne, A., Lichter, E., Dedoukou, X., Alexe, D., & Dessypris, N. (2002). What distinguishes unintentional injuries from injuries due to intimate partner violence: A study of Greek ambulatory care settings. *Injury Prevention, 8,* 197–201.

Quigley, M., Morgan, D., Malamba, S. S., Mayanja, B., Okongo, M. J., Carpenter, L. M., & Whitworth, J. A. (2000). Case–control study of risk factors for incident HIV infection in rural Uganda. *Journal of Acquired Immune Deficiency Syndrome, 23,* 418–425.

Reeves, C., & O'Leary-Kelly, A. M. (2007). The effects and costs of intimate partner violence for work organizations. *Journal of Interpersonal Violence, 22,* 327–344.

Rivara, F. P., Anderson, M. L., Fishman, P., Bonomi, A. E., Reid, R. J., Carrell, D., & Thompson, R. S. (2007). Healthcare utilization and costs for women with a history of intimate partner violence. *American Journal of Preventive Medicine, 32,* 89–96.

Rodgers, K. (1994). Wife assault: The findings of a national survey. *Juristat Service Bulletin, 14,* 1–22.

Schafer, J., Caetano, R., & Clark, C. L. (1998). Rates of intimate partner violence in the United States. *American Journal of Public Health, 88,* 1702–1704.

Silverman, J. G., Decker, M. R., Gupta, J., Kapur, N., Raj, A., & Naved, R. T. (2009). Maternal experiences of intimate partner violence and child morbidity in Bangladesh: Evidence from a national Bangladeshi sample. *Archives of Pediatrics & Adolescent Medicine, 163,* 768–770.

Stets, J., & Straus, M. A. (1990). Gender differences in reporting marital violence and its medical and psychological consequences. In M. A. Straus & R. J. Gelles (Eds.), *Physical violence in American families: Risk factors and adaptations in 8,145 American families* (pp. 151–165). New Brunswick, NJ: Transactional Books.

Stith, S. M., Smith, D. B., Penn, C., Ward, D., & Tritt, D. (2004). Intimate partner physical abuse perpetration and victimization risk factors: A meta-analytic review. *Aggression and Violent Behavior, 10,* 65–98.

Tjaden, P., & Thoennes, N. (2000). *Full report of the prevalence, incidence, and consequences of violence against women: Findings from the National Violence Against Women Survey.* Washington, DC: National Institute of Justice, Office of Justice Programs, United States Department of Justice and Centers for Disease Control and Prevention, NCJ 183781.

Valdez-Santiago, R., & Sanin-Aguirre, L. H. (1996). Domestic violence during pregnancy and its relationship with birth weight. *Salud Publica Mexicana, 38,* 352–362.

Valladares, E., Ellsberg, M., Peña, R., Högberg, U., & Persson, L. A. (2002). Physical partner abuse during pregnancy: A risk factor for low birth weight in Nicaragua. *Obstetrics and Gynecology, 100,* 100–105.

Vos, T., Astbury, J., Piers, L. S., Magnus, A., Heenan, M., Stanley, L.,..., Webster, K. (2006). Measuring the impact of intimate partner violence on the health of women in Victoria, Australia. *Bulletin of the World Health Organization, 84,* 739– 744.

Walker, E. A., Katon, W. J., Roy-Byrne, P. P., Jemelka, R. P., & Russo, J. (1993). Histories of sexual victimization in patients with irritable bowel syndrome or inflammatory bowel disease. *American Journal of Psychiatry, 150,* 1502–1506.

Walker, E. A., Keegan, D., Gardner, G., Sullivan, M., Bernstein, D., & Katon, W. J. (1997). Psychosocial factors in fibromyalgia compared with rheumatoid arthritis: II. Sexual, physical, and emotional abuse and neglect. *Psychosomatic Medicine, 59,* 572–577.

Wingood, G. M., DiClemente, R. J., & Raj, A. (2000). Adverse consequences of intimate partner abuse among women in non-urban domestic shelters. *American Journal of Preventive Medicine, 19,* 270–275.

Wolfe, D. A., Crooks, C. V., Lee, V., McIntyre-Smith, A., & Jaffe, P. G. (2003). The effects of children's exposure to domestic violence: A metaanalysis and critique. *Clinical Child and Family Psychology Review, 6,* 171–187.

APPENDIX

TABLE 3.1 Summary of Key Impacts of Intimate Partner Violence

Economic
Missed days of work
Missed days of household productivity
Difficulty maintaining employment and potential of lower salary
Increased medical costs and health care utilization
Physical Health
Injury
Mortality (homicide, maternal mortality)
Sexually transmitted diseases
Poor overall health
Functional impairment
Permanent disability
Chronic pain syndromes, fibromyalgia
Gastrointestinal disorders, irritable bowel syndrome
Psychosomatic disorders
Gynecological disorders
Pregnancy problems (miscarriages, unsafe abortions, complications, low birth weight)
Psychological Health
Depression
Anxiety disorders
Eating disorders
Sexual dysfunctions
Substance abuse disorders
Suicide
Sexually risky behaviors
Self-esteem
Sleep disturbances
Physical inactivity and poor self-care behaviors
Child behavior problems
Poor child academic performance

4

Practical Tools for Assessing Partner Maltreatment in Clinical Practice and Public Health Settings

Richard E. Heyman, Amy M. Smith Slep, Jeffery D. Snarr, and Heather M. Foran

Given the high prevalence of physically and psychologically aggressive acts among intimate partners, with relatively few of these incidents meeting the threshold of clinical significance (see Chapter 1, this volume; see also Foran, Slep, Heyman, & U.S. Air Force Family Advocacy Program, 2012), a screener with high sensitivity and high specificity is badly needed. High sensitivity would mean that those flagged by the screener as a "yes" would nearly always meet criteria for clinically significant abuse (i.e., high proportion of true positives/all positives). High specificity would mean that those flagged as a "no" would nearly always not meet criteria for maltreatment (high proportion of true negatives/all negatives).

In this chapter, we summarize recent development of a screener that was developed in a large population sample, has high sensitivity and specificity, and was developed to predict clinically significant partner physical abuse as defined by the International Statistical Classification of Diseases and Related Health Problems (ICD) criteria proposed in this volume. Although other screening measures for partner abuse exist (e.g., Hurts, Insults, Threatens, and Screams: Sherin, Sinacore, Li, Zitter, & Shakil, 1998; Partner Violence Screen: Feldhaus, Koziol-McLain, Amsbury, Norton, Lowenstain, & Abbott, 1997; Abuse Assessment Screen: McFarlane, Parker, Soaken, & Bullock, 1992; Ongoing Abuse Screen: Ernst, Weiss, Cham, & Marquez, 2002), none meet even two of these three criteria.

BRIEF SCREENING INSTRUMENT FOR PARTNER MALTREATMENT: INSTRUMENT PSYCHOMETRICS AND RECOMMENDATIONS FOR USE

As described in more detail by Heyman et al. (2012), we used two large population surveys (2006 survey, $N = 69{,}228$; 2008 survey, $N = 76{,}518$) to develop and cross-validate a short screening test for partner physical abuse and partner emotional abuse. For both types of maltreatment, the questions operationalized the criteria presented by Heyman, Slep, Erlanger, and Foran in Chapter 1 of this volume. That is, partner physical abuse comprises nonaccidental acts of physical force that result, or have reasonable potential to result, in physical harm to an intimate partner or which evoke significant fear in the partner; emotional abuse comprises nonaccidental verbal or symbolic acts of that result in significant psychological harm to an intimate partner. Thus, the questions presented inquired about acts and their impacts.

Both years' surveys included a measure of family maltreatment that was developed, refined, and tested over a several-year period to operationalize the criteria in this volume (see Heyman, Snarr, Slep, & U.S. Air Force Family Advocacy Program, 2012). The partner physical abuse module comprised 14 items assessing the frequencies of various aggressive acts in the previous year engaged in by respondents and their partners (e.g., "I pushed or shoved my partner," "My partner punched or hit me"). Follow-up questions asked about injuries and fear resulting from acts endorsed. Partner physical abuse was operationalized as reporting at least one act of physical aggression and at least one significant impact (i.e., victim injury or fear, or an exceptionally dangerous act that was likely to result in victim impact, such as "choked"). The partner emotional abuse module assessed for victimization only (because these acts are ubiquitous and the impacts are often either not known to or not recognized by the instigator). Impacts were assessed first, in that all participants with partners were asked whether they had experienced significant depression, stress, and/or fear as a result of their partners' behavior in the past 12 months. Those who answered in the affirmative were then presented with a list of nine specific acts and asked how often in the past 12 months their partners had committed them (e.g., "put me down or humiliated me," "stalked me," "grilled or interrogated me about where I had been, what I had done, etc."). If at least one act was reported, participants were presented with a list of all endorsed acts and asked whether the acts had caused or contributed to the depression, stress, and/or fear they had reported earlier. Partner emotional abuse was operationalized as (a) at least one reported emotionally aggressive act that caused (b) significant stress, depression, or fear that impaired functioning.

To derive the screener, we used the 2006 sample and dichotomized all acts as either endorsed or not (1 or 0). We then computed a dichotomous summary variable for every possible combination of up to 10 items; the summary variable indicated whether any one of the items in the combination had been endorsed. For each summary variable, we then calculated its sensitivity (i.e., abuse identified by those screener items/all cases of that type of abuse) and specificity (i.e., abuse not indicated by those screener items/all noncases). The optimally predictive combination of as few items as possible was then selected for both types of abuse. All analyses were conducted separately for men and women reporters and for male-to-female and female-to-male abuse. Finally, after deriving the screeners, we cross-validated them by calculating their sensitivity and specificity in the 2008 sample.

Sensitivity and Specificity

Partner Physical Abuse

For male-to-female partner physical abuse, four items were needed for a screener with high sensitivity and specificity: push/shove, grab, bite, punch (see Appendix—Conflict Screener Forms A and B). Sensitivity was 93% and specificity was 97% (92% and 97%, respectively, in the cross-validation). For female-to-male partner physical abuse, six items were needed: Push/shove, scratch, slap, throw something that could hurt, punch, bite (see Appendix—Conflict Screener Form C). Sensitivity was 97% and specificity was 94% (96%–98% and 94%, respectively, in the cross-validation). The male-to-female and female-to-male measures have three items in common, producing a measure for both forms of abuse with seven items (see Appendix—Conflict Screener Form D).

Partner Emotional Abuse

For partner emotional abuse, only one act was necessary for high sensitivity (96%–98%) and specificity (92%–95%)—insult or swore at. As shown in Appendix—Conflict Screener Form E, partner emotional abuse is coded as "yes" if the respondent (a) answers "a little" or greater to relationship-induced depression or stress or "rarely" or above for partner-induced fear and (b) reports that the partner insulted or swore at him or her in the past 12 months. In the cross-validation, sensitivity was 96% to 98% and specificity was 93% to 96%.

Partner Sexual Abuse

Although comparable work has not been conducted for sexual abuse, two items adapted from the *WHO Multi-Country Study on Women's Health and Domestic Violence* (García-Moreno, Jansen, Ellsberg, Heise, & Watts, 2006) fit the proposed ICD definitions and thus at least have face and content validity. The items can be found in Appendix—Conflict Screener Form F.

Composite measures of physical, emotional, and sexual abuse are provided in Appendix G to assess victimization and Appendix H to assess both victimization and perpetration.

Administration

Procedure

Like all measures of sensitive health information, participants should complete the abuse screener privately (i.e., away from the partner). When this is assured, respondents are not at increased risk for violence due to disclosure (Houry et al., 2008). Computerized and written screening appear to result in similar amount of reporting (MacMillan et al., 2006), and both result in tremendously higher reporting than does haphazard asking and reporting in clinical contacts (e.g., Ahmad et al., 2009; Rhodes, Lauderdale, He, Howes, & Levinson, 2002). Several studies have found a preference for computerized or written, over face-to-face, screening (Glass, Dearwater, & Campbell, 2001; McCord-Duncan, Floyd, Kemp, Bailey, & Lang, 2006; Mears & Visher, 2005).

Time to Complete

All forms of the screener take very little time to complete. For example, the version to assess the greatest public health threat (women's victimization by men via physical, emotional, and/or sexual abuse) is only nine items, and thus could be completed in a couple of minutes.

Settings

Private screening for abuse does not put respondents at risk, even in emergency department settings (e.g., Houry et al., 2008). Given the connection between abuse and physical and mental health (e.g., Coker et al., 2002), screening in all physical and mental health care settings is warranted.

Scoring

Scoring is straightforward. For physical and sexual abuse items (Appendix Forms A, B, C, D, F, G, and H), a single act in the past 12 months is a sensitive and specific indicator of abuse. For emotional abuse (Appendix Forms E, G, and H), both impacts and acts are assessed. A respondent would indicate some impact on question 1 (depressed/stressed—"a little" or above) or question 2 (fear—"rarely" or above) *and* a single act of insulting or swearing on question 3 to be considered a "yes" on the screen for partner emotional abuse.

Follow-Up to a Positive Screen

The screener, despite the high sensitivity and specificity, is not a perfect predictor of actual abuse. Participants can misunderstand questions, can mistakenly choose responses, or can be describing a situation that would not be considered abuse (e.g., a scratch during a fun pillow fight). Assessors should follow-up (privately and confidentially) and ask respondents to describe more about the positive responses. For example, "I see that you put that your partner has grabbed and has punched you in the past 12 months. Can you tell me a bit about that?" After hearing the respondent's description, the assessor can follow up by saying, "I'd like you to think about the most serious incident in the past year. I'd like you to tell me exactly what happened in the incident. You can tell me like you were watching a video screen and describe for me everything that you see, from the beginning to the end." The assessor should then ask questions to flesh out his or her understanding of the incident (e.g., "Where were you when this happened?" "How hard was [act] on a scale of 1–10, with 1 being feather-light and 10 being as hard as possible?").

In clinical care settings, disclosure on a screener implies that some professional will follow up. Liebschutz, Battaglia, Finley, and Averbuch (2008, p. 235) conducted a qualitative study of disclosure in medical settings and concluded: "In all specialties, participants were more likely to disclose IPV and find disclosure beneficial if clinicians respectfully addressed the abuse, ensured participants' physical safety after an assault, assured participants of confidentiality regarding disclosed information, gave patient choices for action and demonstrated emotional support. Indeed, our study demonstrates that inquiry and discussion of IPV in the right setting can be a powerful tool for change." Conversely, similar to other past research (e.g., Gerbert, Abercrombie, Caspers, Love, & Bronstone, 1999) found that if the assessor acted paternalistically, advocating action being the respondent's comfort level, or failed to make an emotional connection with the respondent, the disclosure was perceived as unhelpful and may reduce the likelihood of health care seeking or future disclosure.

Detailed recommendations for assessor responses are beyond the scope of this chapter (see Campbell, 2001; McFarlane, Parker, Soeken, Silva, & Reel, 1998; Warshaw, Ganley, & Salber, 1998). At a minimum, assessors should be prepared to discuss safety planning and make referrals to community resources and hotlines. Safety planning involves a conversation with the victim about the particulars of her or his situation and to allow the respondent to get information, assess the dangers and resources in her or his home and environment, and to discuss possible action strategies to take. As summarized by one of the leaders in this field (Campbell, 2001, p. 130), the areas most in need of discussion with the respondent during a safety planning discussion are: "(a) the potential lethality or dangerousness from her partner; (b) whether she is planning to stay, is in the process of leaving, or has left; (c) her emotional status; (d) resources offered by her family, job, and community; and (e) her children."

Of particular promise is a computerized safety planning tool that has preliminary empirical support (Glass, Eden, Bloom, & Perrin, 2010). Although it was tested on women already self-identified as abused, it seems like a promising adjunctive for women screened-in as possibly abused, although further work in health care and general mental health settings is needed.

Documentation

After determination that physical, emotional, and/or sexual abuse has occurred, this should be documented using ICD codes for maltreatment. In the current version, the ICD-10, these codes are found in the injury and external causes of morbidity and mortality chapters of the classification system (Chapter 19, T74.1 Physical abuse, T74.2 Sexual abuse, T74.3 Psychological abuse; Chapter 20, Y05 Sexual assault, Y07.0 Other maltreatment by spouse or partner including mental cruelty, physical abuse, sexual abuse, and torture). Codes in the ICD Chapter 21, "Factors influencing health status and contact with health services," may also be applicable to document and facilitate appropriate treatment planning and follow-up care.

STRUCTURED CLINICAL DIAGNOSTIC INTERVIEW FOR PARTNER MALTREATMENT

In research settings, multimethod assessment for abuse is strongly recommended (e.g., O'Leary, Vivian, & Malone, 1992). A detailed, structured interview for partner physical, sexual, and emotional abuse and partner neglect (for both perpetration and victimization) is provided at the end of this chapter (see Appendix). The questions parallel the specific criteria proposed of each type of maltreatment. For ease of administration, the structured interview was patterned after the Structured Clinical Interview for the *Diagnostic and Statistical Manual of Mental Disorders* (*DSM-IV*; First, Spitzer, Gibbon, & Williams, 1996). As with all such interviews, the detailed assessment matching the diagnostic criteria make it the "gold standard" to which questionnaires are compared. However, its length and requirements for trained assessors make its use practically limited to research settings. Finally, the structured interview in the Appendix only covers current abuse and neglect; it can be modified slightly to also inquire about past abuse and neglect.

ACKNOWLEDGMENT

Preparation of this chapter was supported by a grant U49CE00124602 from the Centers for Disease Control and Prevention.

REFERENCES

Ahmad, F., Hogg-Johnson, S., Stewart, D. E., Skinner, H. A., Glazier, R. H., & Levinson, W. (2009). Computer-assisted screening for intimate partner violence and control. *Annals of Internal Medicine, 151*, 93–102.

Campbell, J. (2001). Safety planning based on lethality assessment for partner of batterers in intervention programs. *Journal of Aggression, Maltreatment & Trauma, 5*, 129–143.

Coker, A., Davis, K., Arias, I., Desai, S., Sanderson, M., Brandt, H., & Smith, P. (2002). Physical and mental health effects of intimate partner violence for men and women. *American Journal of Preventive Medicine, 23*, 260–268.

Ernst, A. A., Weiss, S. J., Cham, E., & Marquez, M. (2002). Comparison of three instruments for assessing ongoing intimate partner violence. *Medical Science Monitor, 8*, 197–201.

Feldhaus, K. M., Koziol-McLain, J., Amsbury, H. L., Norton, I. M., Lowenstein, S. R., & Abbott, J. T. (1997). Accuracy of 3 Brief Screening Questions for detecting partner violence in the emergency department. *Journal of the American Medical Association, 277*, 1357–1361.

First, M. B., Spitzer, R. L., Gibbon, M., and Williams, J. B. W. (1996). *Structured Clinical Interview for DSM-IV Axis I Disorders, Clinician Version (SCID-CV)*. Washington, DC: American Psychiatric Press, Inc..

Foran, H. M., Slep, A. M. S., Heyman, R. E., & U.S. Air Force Family Advocacy Program (2011). Prevalences of intimate partner violence in a representative U.S. Air Force sample. *Journal of Consulting and Clinical Psychology, 79*, 391–397.

García-Moreno, C., Jansen, H. A., Ellsberg, M., Heise, L., & Watts, C. H. (2006). Prevalence of intimate partner violence: Findings from the WHO multi-country study on women's health and domestic violence. *The Lancet, 368*, 1260–1269. doi:10.1016/S0140–6736(06)69523–8

Gerbert, B., Abercrombie, P., Caspers, N., Love, C., & Bronstone, A. (1999). How health care providers help battered women: The survivor's perspective. *Women and Health, 29*, 115–135.

Glass, N., Dearwater, S., & Campbell, J. C. (2001). Intimate partner violence screening and intervention: Data from eleven Pennsylvania and California community hospital emergency departments. *Journal of Emergency Nursing, 27*, 141–149.

Glass, N., Eden, K. B., Bloom, T., & Perrin, N. (2010). Computerized aid improves safety decision process for survivors of intimate partner violence. *Journal of Interpersonal Violence, 25*, 1947–1964. doi:10.1177/0886260509354508

Heyman, R. E., Snarr, J. D., Foran, H. M., Makin-Byrd, K., Slep, A. M. S., & U.S. Air Force Family Advocacy Program (2012). *High sensitivity and specificity screening for clinically significant intimate partner violence*. Manuscript submitted for publication.

Heyman, R. E., Snarr, J. D., Slep, A. M. S., & U.S. Air Force Family Advocacy Program. (2012). *Validity of a measure of clinical significant intimate partner violence and child abuse*. Manuscript submitted for publication.

Houry, D., Kaslow, N. J., Kemball, R. S., McNutt, L. A., Cerulli, C., Straus, H.,..., Rhodes, K. V. (2008). Does screening in the emergency department hurt or help victims of intimate partner violence. *Annals of Emergency Medicine, 51*, 433–442. doi:10.1016/j.annemergmed.2007.11.019

Liebschutz, J., Battaglia, T., Finley, E., & Averbuch, T. (2008). Disclosing intimate partner violence to health care clinicians—What a difference the setting makes: A qualitative study. *BMC Public Health, 8*, 229–237. doi:10.1186/1471–2458-8–229

MacMillan, H. L., Wathen, C. N., Jamieson, E., Boyle, M., McNutt, L. A., Worster, A.,..., Webb, M. (2006). Approaches to screening for intimate partner violence in health care settings. *JAMA: The Journal of the American Medical Association, 296*, 530–536.

McCord-Duncan, E., Floyd, M., Kemp, E., Bailey, B., & Lang, F. (2006). Detecting potential intimate partner violence: Which approach do women want? *Family Medicine, 38*, 416–422.

McFarlane, J., Parker, B., Soeken, K., & Bullock, L. (1992). Assessing for abuse during pregnancy: Severity and frequency of injuries and associated entry into prenatal care. *Journal of American Medical Association, 267*, 3176–3178.

McFarlane, J., Parker, B., Soeken, K., Silva, C. and Reel, S. (1998), Safety Behaviors of Abused Women After an Intervention During Pregnancy. *Journal of Obstetric, Gynecologic, & Neonatal Nursing, 27*, 64–69. doi: 10.1111/j.1552-6909.1998.tb02592.x

Mears, D., & Visher, C. (2005). Trends in understanding and addressing domestic violence. *Journal of Interpersonal Violence, 20*, 204–211.

O'Leary, K.D., Vivian, D., & Malone, J. (1992). Assessment of physical aggression in marriage: The need for a multimodal method. *Behavioral Assessment, 14*, 5–14.

Rhodes, K. V., Lauderdale, D. S., He, T., Howes, D. S., & Levinson, W. (2002). Between me and the computer: Increased detection of intimate partner violence using a computer questionnaire. *Annals of Emergency Medicine, 40*, 476–484.

Sherin, K. M., Sinacore, J. M., Li, X., Zitter, R. E., & Shakil, A. (1998). HITS: A short domestic violence screening tool for use in a family practice setting. *Family Medicine, 30*, 508–512.

Warshaw C., Ganley A.L., Salber P.R. (1998). *Improving the health care response to domestic violence: A resource manual for health care providers*. (2nd ed.). San Francisco, CA: Family Violence Prevention Fund.

APPENDIX: CONFLICT SCREENERS

FORM A. SCREENER: MALE-TO-FEMALE PARTNER PHYSICAL ABUSE

- Conflicts between partners are very common.
  - The majority of partners report that, at some point in their lives, their conflicts have included physical behaviors such as pushing, grabbing, or slapping.
- The following is a list of behaviors that partners often use during conflicts.
- Please indicate how often these have happened IN THE PAST 12 MONTHS.

How many times IN THE PAST 12 MONTHS:	1 time	2 times	3-5 times	6-10 times	11-20 times	More than 20 times	Never	Not this year, but has happened in the past
1. Have you pushed or shoved your partner?	1	2	3	4	5	6	0	☐
2. Has your partner pushed or shoved you?	1	2	3	4	5	6	0	☐
3. Have you grabbed your partner?	1	2	3	4	5	6	0	☐
4. Has your partner grabbed you?	1	2	3	4	5	6	0	☐
5. Have you bitten your partner?	1	2	3	4	5	6	0	☐
6. Has your partner bitten you?	1	2	3	4	5	6	0	☐
7. Have you punched your partner?	1	2	3	4	5	6	0	☐
8. Has your partner punched you?	1	2	3	4	5	6	0	☐

FORM B. SCREENER: MALE-TO-FEMALE PARTNER PHYSICAL ABUSE VICTIMIZATION

- Conflicts between partners are very common.
  - The majority of partners report that, at some point in their lives, their conflicts have included physical behaviors such as pushing, grabbing, or slapping.
- The following is a list of behaviors that partners often use during conflicts.
- Please indicate how often these have happened IN THE PAST 12 MONTHS.

How many times IN THE PAST 12 MONTHS:	1 time	2 times	3-5 times	6-10 times	11-20 times	More than 20 times	Never	Not this year, but has happened in the past
1. Has your partner pushed or shoved you?	1	2	3	4	5	6	0	☐
2. Has your partner grabbed you?	1	2	3	4	5	6	0	☐
3. Has your partner bitten you?	1	2	3	4	5	6	0	☐
4. Has your partner punched you?	1	2	3	4	5	6	0	☐

FORM C. SCREENER: FEMALE-TO-MALE PARTNER PHYSICAL ABUSE

- Conflicts between partners are very common.
  - The majority of partners report that, at some point in their lives, their conflicts have included physical behaviors such as pushing, grabbing, or slapping.
- The following is a list of behaviors that partners often use during conflicts.
- Please indicate how often these have happened IN THE PAST 12 MONTHS.

How many times IN THE PAST 12 MONTHS:	*1 time*	*2 times*	*3-5 times*	*6-10 times*	*11-20 times*	*More than 20 times*	*Never*	*Not this year, but has happened in the past*
1. Have you pushed or shoved your partner?	1	2	3	4	5	6	0	☐
2. Has your partner pushed or shoved you?	1	2	3	4	5	6	0	☐
3. Have you scratched your partner?	1	2	3	4	5	6	0	☐
4. Has your partner scratched you?	1	2	3	4	5	6	0	☐
5. Have you slapped your partner?	1	2	3	4	5	6	0	☐
6. Has your partner slapped you?	1	2	3	4	5	6	0	☐
7. Have you thrown something at your partner that could hurt?	1	2	3	4	5	6	0	☐
8. Has your partner thrown something at you that could hurt?	1	2	3	4	5	6	0	☐
9. Have you punched your partner?	1	2	3	4	5	6	0	☐
10. Has your partner punched you?	1	2	3	4	5	6	0	☐
11. Have you bitten your partner?	1	2	3	4	5	6	0	☐
12. Has your partner bitten you?	1	2	3	4	5	6	0	☐

FORM D. SCREENER: COMBINED PARTNER PHYSICAL ABUSE

- Conflicts between partners are very common.
  - The majority of partners report that, at some point in their lives, their conflicts have included physical behaviors such as pushing, grabbing, or slapping.
- The following is a list of behaviors that partners often use during conflicts.
- Please indicate how often these have happened IN THE PAST 12 MONTHS.

How many times IN THE PAST 12 MONTHS:	1 time	2 times	3-5 times	6-10 times	11-20 times	More than 20 times	Never	Not this year, but has happened in the past
1. Have you pushed or shoved your partner?	1	2	3	4	5	6	0	☐
2. Has your partner pushed or shoved you?	1	2	3	4	5	6	0	☐
3. Have you grabbed your partner?	1	2	3	4	5	6	0	☐
4. Has your partner grabbed you?	1	2	3	4	5	6	0	☐
5. Have you scratched your partner?	1	2	3	4	5	6	0	☐
6. Has your partner scratched you?	1	2	3	4	5	6	0	☐
7. Have you slapped your partner?	1	2	3	4	5	6	0	☐
8. Has your partner slapped you?	1	2	3	4	5	6	0	☐
9. Have you thrown something at your partner that could hurt?	1	2	3	4	5	6	0	☐
10. Has your partner thrown something at you that could hurt?	1	2	3	4	5	6	0	☐
11. Have you bitten your partner?	1	2	3	4	5	6	0	☐
12. Has your partner bitten you?	1	2	3	4	5	6	0	☐
13. Have you punched your partner?	1	2	3	4	5	6	0	☐
14. Has your partner punched you?	1	2	3	4	5	6	0	☐

FORM E. SCREENER: PARTNER EMOTIONAL ABUSE VICTIMIZATION

- Conflicts between partners are very common.
  - The majority of partners report that, at some point in their lives, their conflicts have included physical behaviors such as pushing, grabbing, or slapping.
- The following is a list of behaviors that partners often use during conflicts.
- Please indicate how often these have happened IN THE PAST 12 MONTHS.

1. During the past 12 months, were you ever so depressed or stressed that it affected you almost every day for 2 weeks?
   ❍ No
   ❍ Yes ➡ (If yes) How much of your sadness/depression or stress was related to things your partner said or did?

   ❍ Almost all
   ❍ Most
   ❍ Some
   ❍ A little
   ❍ Almost none

2. During the past 12 months, how often did you fear your partner might physically hurt (not by accident) you or someone that you cared about (family member, friend, pet)?
   ❍ Almost always
   ❍ Often
   ❍ Sometimes
   ❍ Rarely
   ❍ Never

3. During the past 12 months, how often did your partner insult or swear at you?
   ❍ More than 10 times
   ❍ 6–10 times
   ❍ 3–5 times
   ❍ Twice
   ❍ Once
   ❍ Never

FORM F. SCREENER: PARTNER SEXUAL ABUSE VICTIMIZATION

- The following behaviors commonly happen in relationships.
- Please indicate how often these have happened IN THE PAST 12 MONTHS.

How many times IN THE PAST 12 MONTHS:	1 time	2 times	3-5 times	6-10 times	11-20 times	More than 20 times	Never	Not this year, but has happened in the past
1. Has your partner physically forced you to do something sexually when you didn't want to?	1	2	3	4	5	6	0	☐
2. Have you done something sexually because you were afraid of what your partner might do?	1	2	3	4	5	6	0	☐

FORM G. SCREENER: MALE-TO-FEMALE PARTNER PHYSICAL, EMOTIONAL, AND SEXUAL ABUSE VICTIMIZATION

- Conflicts between partners are very common.
  - The majority of partners report that, at some point in their lives, their conflicts have included physical behaviors such as pushing, grabbing, or slapping.
- The following is a list of behaviors that partners often use during conflicts.
- Please indicate how often these have happened IN THE PAST 12 MONTHS.

1. During the past 12 months, were you ever so depressed or stressed that it affected you almost every day for 2 weeks?
   ❍ No
   ❍ Yes ➡ (If yes) How much of your sadness/depression or stress was related to things your partner said or did? ❍ Almost all ❍ Most ❍ Some ❍ A little ❍ Almost none
2. During the past 12 months, how often did you fear your partner might physically hurt (not by accident) you or someone that you cared about (family member, friend, pet)?
   ❍ Almost always
   ❍ Often
   ❍ Sometimes
   ❍ Rarely
   ❍ Never
3. During the past 12 months, how often did your partner insult or swear at you?
   ❍ More than 10 times
   ❍ 6–10 times
   ❍ 3–5 times
   ❍ Twice
   ❍ Once
   ❍ Never

How many times IN THE PAST 12 MONTHS:	*1 time*	*2 times*	*3-5 times*	*6-10 times*	*11-20 times*	*More than 20 times*	*Never*	*Not this year, but has happened in the past*
1. Has your partner pushed or shoved you?	1	2	3	4	5	6	0	☐
2. Has your partner grabbed you?	1	2	3	4	5	6	0	☐
3. Has your partner bitten you?	1	2	3	4	5	6	0	☐
4. Has your partner punched you?	1	2	3	4	5	6	0	☐
5. Has your partner physically forced you to do something sexually when you didn't want to?	1	2	3	4	5	6	0	☐
6. Have you done something sexually because you were afraid of what your partner might do?	1	2	3	4	5	6	0	☐

FORM H. SCREENER: COMBINED PARTNER PHYSICAL, EMOTIONAL, AND SEXUAL ABUSE

- Conflicts between partners are very common.
  - The majority of partners report that, at some point in their lives, their conflicts have included physical behaviors such as pushing, grabbing, or slapping.
- The following is a list of behaviors that partners often use during conflicts.
- Please indicate how often these have happened IN THE PAST 12 MONTHS.

1. During the past 12 months, were you ever so depressed or stressed that it affected you almost every day for 2 weeks?

   ❍ No

   ❍ Yes ➠ (If yes) How much of your sadness/depression or stress was related to things your partner said or did? ❍ Almost all ❍ Most ❍ Some ❍ A little ❍ Almost none

2. During the past 12 months, how often did you fear your partner might physically hurt (not by accident) you or someone that you cared about (family member, friend, pet)?

   ❍ Almost always

   ❍ Often

   ❍ Sometimes

   ❍ Rarely

   ❍ Never

3. During the past 12 months, how often did your partner insult or swear at you?

   ❍ More than 10 times

   ❍ 6–10 times

   ❍ 3–5 times

   ❍ Twice

   ❍ Once

   ❍ Never

(continued)

How many times IN THE PAST 12 MONTHS:	1 time	2 times	3-5 times	6-10 times	11-20 times	More than 20 times	Never	Not this year, but has happened in the past
1. Have you pushed or shoved your partner?	1	2	3	4	5	6	0	☐
2. Has your partner pushed or shoved you?	1	2	3	4	5	6	0	☐
3. Have you grabbed your partner?	1	2	3	4	5	6	0	☐
4. Has your partner grabbed you?	1	2	3	4	5	6	0	☐
5. Have you scratched your partner?	1	2	3	4	5	6	0	☐
6. Has your partner scratched you?	1	2	3	4	5	6	0	☐
7. Have you slapped your partner?	1	2	3	4	5	6	0	☐
8. Has your partner slapped you?	1	2	3	4	5	6	0	☐
9. Have you thrown something at your partner that could hurt?	1	2	3	4	5	6	0	☐
10. Has your partner thrown something at you that could hurt?	1	2	3	4	5	6	0	☐
11. Have you bitten your partner?	1	2	3	4	5	6	0	☐
12. Has your partner bitten you?	1	2	3	4	5	6	0	☐
13. Have you punched your partner?	1	2	3	4	5	6	0	☐
14. Has your partner punched you?	1	2	3	4	5	6	0	☐
15. Has your partner physically forced you to do something sexually when you didn't want to?	1	2	3	4	5	6	0	☐
16. Have you done something sexually because you were afraid of what your partner might do?	1	2	3	4	5	6	0	☐

STRUCTURED INTERVIEW FOR RELATIONAL PROBLEMS, VERSION 1.0 (AUGUST 2011)

Partner Physical Abuse (Victimization)

Partner Physical Abuse (Victimization)	Partner Physical Abuse (Victimization) Criteria				
Now I'm going to ask you some questions about things that go on in the majority of relationships at some time or another. First I'm going to ask about what your partner has done, then I'll ask about what you've done.					
In the past year…					
…has your partner done any of these things to you? (show category-1 physical force list to interviewee)	A. Nonaccidental use of physical force: pushing, shoving, slapping, grabbing, throwing, poking, hair-pulling, scratching, pinching, restraining, shaking, throwing object at	?	1	2	3
Okay, how about any of these? (show category-2 physical force list to interviewee)	Biting, kicking, hitting with fist, hitting with a stick, strap, or other object, scalding, burning, poisoning, stabbing, applying force to throat, cutting off air supply, holding under water, using a weapon	?	1	2	3
What about anything similar but not listed here?	Any other nonaccidental use of physical force	?	1	2	3

IF NONE ARE CODED "3," SKIP TO THE NEXT MODULE

(*continued*)

Partner Physical Abuse (Victimization) *(continued)*

Partner Physical Abuse (Victimization)	Partner Physical Abuse (Victimization) Criteria				
Think about what you would consider to be the most serious incident during the past year. Okay, do you have one in mind?	B. Significant impact on the victim as evidenced by any of the following:				
Sometimes when things get physical, people notice marks, bruises, or cuts. Did you notice any? If NO: What about pain? (How long did that last?) If NO: What about any other injury?	(1) Any physical injury (including, but not limited to, pain that lasts at least four hours, bruises, cuts, sprains, broken bones, loss of consciousness)	?	1	2	3
"Were you afraid, either during or after the incident? (What were you afraid of?) (How long did it last?)"	(2) More Than Inconsequential Fear Reaction a. Fear (verbalized or displayed) of bodily injury to self or others AND	?	1	2	3
If YES to fear: "I'm going to ask you some questions about specific ways that the(se) incident(s) may have affected you	b. At least one of the following signs of fear or anxiety lasting at least 48 hours				
"Have you thought about the incident(s) when you don't want to? Have thoughts about the incident come to you suddenly when you don't want them to? (Tell me about that...)"	(1) Persistent intrusive recollections of the incident	?	1	2	3
"Have you gone out of your way to avoid people, places, or things related to the incident? (Tell me about that...)"	(2) Marked negative reactions to cues related to incident, as evidenced by any of the following: a. Avoidance of cues	?	1	2	3
"What about getting very upset when something reminded you of the incident(s)?"	b. Subjective or overt distress to cues	?	1	2	3
"What about physical symptoms—like breaking out in a sweat, breathing heavily or irregularly, or your heart pounding or racing?"	c. Physiological hyperarousal to cues	?	1	2	3
"What about finding yourself acting or feeling as if you were back in the incident?"	(3) Acting or feeling as if incident is recurring	?	1	2	3
Since the incident(s)...	(4) Persistent symptoms of increased arousal, as evidenced by any of the following				
...have you had trouble sleeping?	a. Difficulty falling or staying asleep	?	1	2	3
...have you been unusually irritable? What about outbursts of anger?	b. Irritability or outbursts of anger	?	1	2	3
...have you had trouble concentrating?	c. Difficulty concentrating	?	1	2	3
...have you been watchful or on guard even when there was no reason to be?	d. Hypervigilance	?	1	2	3
...have you been jumpy or easily startled, like by sudden noises?	e. Exaggerated startle response	?	1	2	3
	B1 IS CODED 3 OR (B2a IS CODED "3" AND AT LEAST ONE OF B2b (1–4) IS CODED "3")		1		3

(continued)

Partner Physical Abuse (Victimization) *(continued)*

Partner Physical Abuse (Victimization)	Partner Physical Abuse (Victimization) Criteria	
"Again, I'd like you to think about the most serious physical incident in the past year. I'd like you to tell me exactly what happened in the incident. Please be as detailed as if you were watching it on a video screen and describe for me everything that you see, from the beginning to the end." ("Where were you when this happened") ("How hard was [act] on a scale of 1–10, with 1 being feather-light and 10 being as hard as possible?")	(3) Given the inherent dangerousness of the act, the degree of force used, and the physical environment in which the acts occurred, there was *reasonable potential* for a *more than inconsequential physical injury*, defined as follows: a. Any injury to the face or head b. More than superficial bruise(s) c. More than superficial cut(s)/scratch(es) (i.e., requiring pressure to stop bleeding) d. Bleeding e. Welts f. Loss of consciousness g. Loss of functioning (including, but not limited to, sprains, broken bones, detached retina, loose or chipped teeth) h. Heat exhaustion or heat stroke i. Damage to internal organs j. Disfigurement (including, but not limited to, scarring) k. Swelling lasting at least 24 hours l. Pain felt (a) in the course of normal activities and (b) at least 24 hours after the physical injury was suffered.	? 1 2 3
	AT LEAST ONE A SX IS CODED "3" AND AT LEAST ONE OF B1, B2, OR B3 CODED "3"	1 3
	C. The acts of physical force were NOT committed for any of the following reasons:	
"You said that your partner has [ACTS] and that, as a result, you had [IMPACTS].	(1) PARTNER'S act(s) DID NOT OCCUR ONLY to protect partner from imminent physical harm because interviewee was in the act of physical force	
In any of these incidents, did his/her [ACTS] come after you had already used physical force? (If YES, "In what percentage of the incidents had you used force first?")	a. There was an incident when the interviewee DID NOT use force first or WAS NOT still in the act of using force when partner's act(s) occurred	1 3
If 100% - "In what percentage of the incidents were you still in the act of using force when s/he [ACT]?)	b. Partner's act(s) was/were NOT SOLELY to stop interviewee's use of physical force	1 3
(If 100%, "Was your force the ONLY reason your partner was using force?") (If YES, "Did s/he ever use more force than was necessary to stop you?")	c. Partner's act(s) used MORE THAN minimally sufficient force to stop interviewee's use of physical force	1 3 IF 1a, b, and c ALL ARE CODED "1," CODE C1 "1" AND SKIP TO C2
	C1. Act(s) DID NOT OCCUR ONLY to protect self from imminent physical harm from partner's use of physical force	1 3 PHYSICAL AGGRESSION DUE TO SELF-PROTECTION

(continued)

Partner Physical Abuse (Victimization) *(continued)*

Partner Physical Abuse (Victimization)	Partner Physical Abuse (Victimization) Criteria	
"During any of the times that your partner has [ACTS] and, as a result, you had [IMPACTS], did his/her [ACTS] come after you threatened him/her? (IF YES) "In what percentage of the incidents did you threaten him/her?" (If 100%) "How did you threaten him/her?" "What did you threaten to do?") ("Did your partner ever [ACTS] at a time when you had NOT threatened to harm him/her?") (If YES) Had you ever hurt your partner previously? (If YES, "I'd like you to think about the most serious physical incident in which you hurt your partner. I'd like you to tell me exactly what happened in the incident.")	(2) Act(s) by partner DID NOT OCCUR ONLY to protect him/herself from imminent harm because of interviewee's threat and a history of more than inconsequential physical injury	
	a. There exists an incident when the partner's act DID NOT follow interviewee's threat (verbal or nonverbal) to imminently inflict more than inconsequential physical injury	1 3 IF 1a, b, and c ALL ARE CODED "1," CODE C1 "1" AND SKIP TO C3
	b. There is NO previous incident of interviewee inflicting more than inconsequential physical injury.	1 3
	C2. Act(s) by partner DID NOT OCCUR ONLY to protect him/herself from imminent harm because of interviewee's threat accompanied by a history of more than inconsequential physical injury	1 3 PHYSICAL AGGRESSION TO PROTECT FROM THREAT OF PHYSICAL HARM
(If not clear from prior questions) "During any of the times your partner has [ACTS] and, as a result, you had [IMPACTS], were the two of you playing? (If YES, "In what percentage of the incidents did your partner's [ACTS] happen during play?)	C3. Act(s) by partner DID NOT ALWAYS occur in play	1 3 PHYSICAL AGGRESSION IN PLAY
(If not clear from prior questions) During any of the times your partner has [ACTS] and that, as a result, you had [IMPACTS], did your partner [ACTS] to protect you or someone else from physical harm? (If YES, "Tell me about such a time.") ("In what percentage of the incidents did your partner's [ACTS] happen to protect you or someone else?")	C4. Act(s) by partner WERE NOT ALWAYS to directly protect interviewee or another person from imminent physical harm (including, but not limited to, pushing interviewee out of the way of a car, taking weapon away from interviewee if suicidal, stopping interviewee from inflicting injury on child)	1 3 PHYSICAL AGGRESSION TO PROTECT OTHERS

Note: ?=inadequate information, 1 = absent or false, 2 = subthreshold, 3 = threshold or true.

Partner Physical Abuse (Perpetration)

Partner Physical Abuse (Perpetration)	Partner Physical Abuse (Perpetration) Criteria	
Okay. This time I'm going to ask you some questions about what you've done.		
In the past year...		
...have you done any of these things to your partner? (show category-1 physical force list to interviewee)	A. Nonaccidental use of physical force: pushing, shoving, slapping, grabbing, throwing, poking, hair-pulling, scratching, pinching, restraining, shaking, throwing object at	? 1 2 3

(continued)

Partner Physical Abuse (Perpetration) *(continued)*

Partner Physical Abuse (Perpetration)	Partner Physical Abuse (Perpetration) Criteria				
Okay, how about any of these? (show category-2 physical force list to interviewee)	Biting; kicking; hitting with fist; hitting with a stick, strap, or other object; scalding; burning; poisoning; stabbing; applying force to throat; cutting off air supply; holding under water; using a weapon	?	1	2	3
What about anything similar but not listed here?	Any other nonaccidental use of physical force	?	1	2	3
Think about what you would consider to be the most serious incident. I'm going to ask you some questions about your partner. You may not know some of these details, but just answer the best you can.	B. Significant impact on the partner as evidenced by any of the following:	IF NONE ARE CODED "3," SKIP TO THE NEXT MODULE			
Sometimes when things get physical, people notice marks, bruises, or cuts. Did your partner have any? If NO: What about pain? (How long did that last?) If NO: What about any other injury?	(1) Any physical injury (including, but not limited to, pain that lasts at least four hours, bruises, cuts, sprains, broken bones, loss of consciousness)	?	1	2	3
"Was your partner afraid, either during or after the incident? (What was s/he afraid of?) (How long did it last?)"	(2) More than inconsequential fear reaction a. Partner's fear (verbalized or displayed) of bodily injury to self or others AND	?	1	2	3
If YES to fear: "I'm going to ask you some questions about specific ways that the(se) incident(s) may have affected your partner.	b. At least one of the following signs of fear or anxiety lasting at least 48 hours				
"Has your partner thought about the incident(s) when s/he didn't want to or did thoughts about it come to him/her suddenly when s/he didn't want them to? (Tell me about that...)"	(1) Persistent intrusive recollections of the incident	?	1	2	3
"Has s/he go out of his/her way to avoid people, places, or things related to the incident? (Tell me about that...)"	(2) Marked negative reactions to cues related to incident, as evidenced by any of the following: a. Avoidance of cues	?	1	2	3
"What about getting very upset when something reminded him/her of the incident(s)?"	b. Subjective or overt distress to cues	?	1	2	3
"What about physical symptoms—like breaking out in a sweat, breathing heavily or irregularly, or his/her heart pounding or racing?"	c. Physiological hyperarousal to cues	?	1	2	3
"What about finding him/herself acting or feeling as if s/he were back in the incident?"	(3) Acting or feeling as if incident is recurring	?	1	2	3
Since the incident(s)...	(4) Persistent symptoms of increased arousal, as evidenced by any of the following				
...has your partner had trouble sleeping?	a. Difficulty falling or staying asleep	?	1	2	3

(continued)

Partner Physical Abuse (Perpetration) (*continued*)

Partner Physical Abuse (Perpetration)	Partner Physical Abuse (Perpetration) Criteria				
…has your partner been unusually irritable? What about outbursts of anger?	b. Irritability or outbursts of anger	?	1	2	3
…has your partner had trouble concentrating?	c. Difficulty concentrating	?	1	2	3
…has your partner been watchful or on guard even when there was no reason to be?	d. Hypervigilance	?	1	2	3
…has your partner been jumpy or easily startled, like by sudden noises?	e. Exaggerated startle response	?	1	2	3
	B1 IS CODED 3 OR (B2a IS CODED "3" AND AT LEAST ONE OF B2b (1–4) IS CODED "3")		1 IF CODED "1" AND B1 IS CODED "1" CONTINUE TO B3.		3
"Again, I'd like you to think about the most serious physical incident in the past year in which you were physical toward your partner. I'd like you to tell me exactly what happened in the incident. Please be as detailed as if you were watching it on a video screen and describe for me everything that you see, from the beginning to the end." ("Where were you when this happened") "How hard was [ADDITIONAL ACT] on a scale of 1–10, with 1 being feather-light and 10 being as hard as possible?"	(3) Given the inherent dangerousness of the act, the degree of force used and the physical environment in which the acts occurred, there was *reasonable potential* for more than inconsequential physical injury, defined as follows: a. Any injury to the face or head b. More than superficial bruise(s) c. More than superficial cut(s) / scratch(es) (i.e., requires pressure to stop bleeding) d. Bleeding e. Welts f. Loss of consciousness g. Loss of functioning (including, but not limited to, sprains, broken bones, detached retina, loose or chipped teeth) h. Heat exhaustion or heat stroke i. Damage to internal organs j. Disfigurement (including, but not limited to, scarring) k. Swelling lasting at least 24 hours l. Pain felt (a) in the course of normal activities and (b) at least 24 hours after the physical injury was suffered.	?	1	2	3
	AT LEAST ONE A SX ARE CODED "3" AND AT LEAST ONE OF B1, B2, OR B3 CODED		1		3
	C. The acts of physical force were not committed for any of the following reasons:				

(*continued*)

Partner Physical Abuse (Perpetration) (*continued*)

Partner Physical Abuse (Perpetration)	Partner Physical Abuse (Perpetration) Criteria	
You said that you have [ACTS] and that, as a result, your partner had [IMPACTS]. In any of these incidents, did your [ACTS] come after s/he had already used physical force? (If YES, "In what percentage of the incidents had s/he used force first?") (If 100%, "In what percentage of the incidents was s/he still in the act of using force when you [ACT]?) (If 100%, "Was there ever a time that your [ACTS] occurred for some reason other than to stop your partner's use of force?") (If NO, "Did you ever do more than was necessary to stop your partner from using force?")	(1) Act(s) by self DID NOT OCCUR ONLY to protect self from imminent physical harm because partner was in the act of physical force a. There exists an incident when the partner DID NOT use force first or WAS NOT still in the act of using force when self's act(s) occurred b. Interviewee's act(s) was/were NOT SOLELY to stop partner's use of physical force c. Interviewee's act(s) used MORE THAN minimally sufficient force to stop partner's use of physical force	 a. 1 3 b. 1 3 c. 1 3 PHYSICAL AGGRESSION TO DEFEND AGAINST PHYSICAL ACT
In any of the times you [ACTS] and that, as a result, your partner had [IMPACTS], did your [ACTS] come after s/he threatened to harm you? (If YES, "How did s/he threaten you? What did s/he threaten to do?) ("Did you ever [ACTS] at a time when your partner had NOT threatened to harm you?") Had your partner ever harmed you previously? (If YES, "I'd like you to think about the most serious physical incident in which your partner harmed you. I'd like you to tell me exactly what happened in the incident.")	(2) Act(s) by self DID NOT OCCUR ONLY to protect him/herself from imminent harm because of partner's threat and a history of more than inconsequential physical injury a. There exists an incident when the self's act DID NOT follow partner's threat (verbal or nonverbal) to imminently inflict more than inconsequential physical injury b. There is no previous incident of partner inflicting more than inconsequential physical injury	 a. 1 3 b. 1 3 PHYSICAL AGGRESSION DUE TO SELF-DEFENSE OF VIABLE THREAT OF PHYSICAL ACT 1 3
(If not clear from prior questions) In any of the times you have [ACTS] and that, as a result, your partner had [IMPACTS], were your [ACTS] happening in play? (If YES, "In what percentage of the incidents did your [ACTS] happen in play?)	(3) Act(s) by self DID NOT ALWAYS occur in play	1 3 PHYSICAL AGGRESSION IN PLAY
(If not clear from prior questions) In any of the times you have [ACTS] and that, as a result, your partner had [IMPACTS], did you [ACTS] to protect your partner or someone else from physical harm? (If YES, "Tell me about such a time.) ("In what percentage of the incidents did your [ACTS] happen to protect your partner or someone else?")	(4) Act(s) by self WERE NOT ALWAYS to directly protect partner or another person from imminent physical harm (including, but not limited to, pushing partner out of the way of a car, taking weapon away from suicidal partner, stopping partner from inflicting injury on child)	1 3 PHYSICAL AGGRESSION TO PROTECT OTHERS

Note: ? = inadequate information, 1 = absent or false, 2 = subthreshold, 3 = threshold or true.

Partner Emotional Abuse (Victimization)

Partner Emotional Abuse (Victimization)	Partner Emotional Abuse (Victimization) Criteria	
Now I'm going to ask you about other kinds of things that happen in the majority of relationships at some time or another. Again, first I'll ask about what your partner has done, and then I'll ask about what you have done. In the past year…	A. Verbal or symbolic acts (excluding physically aggressive acts and sexual abuse) with the potential to cause psychological harm to the victim. Such acts include, but are not limited to:	
Has your partner scolded, criticized, or humiliated you?	(1) Berating, disparaging, degrading, humiliating partner	? 1 2 3
Has your partner interrogated or grilled you?	(2) Interrogating partner	? 1 2 3
Has your partner stopped you from being able to come and go freely?	(3) Restricting partner's ability to come and go freely (when unwarranted)	? 1 2 3
Has your partner stopped you from getting some kind of help (like police, legal help, or seeing a doctor)?	(4) Obstructing partner's access to assistance, including, but not limited to, law enforcement, legal resources protective resources, medical resources	
Has your partner threatened you?	(5) Threatening partner	? 1 2 3
Has your partner harmed someone or thing you care about? What about threatening to do that?	(6) Harming, or threatening to harm, people/things that partner cares about, such as children, self, other people, pets, property	? 1 2 3
Has your partner stopped you from accessing money or economic resources?	(7) Restricting partner's access to or use of economic resources (when unwarranted)	? 1 2 3
Has your partner isolated you from family, friends, or support from people?	(8) Isolating partner from family, friends, or social support resources	? 1 2 3
Has your partner stalked you?	(9) Stalking partner	? 1 2 3
Has your partner tried to make you think you were crazy, or tried to make others think you were crazy?	(10) Trying to make partner think that s/he is crazy (or make others think that partner is crazy)	? 1 2 3
What about anything similar?	(11) Any other psychologically harmful acts	? 1 2 3
	B. At least one of the following features:	IF NO ITEMS 1-11 ARE CODED "3", SKIP TO THE NEXT MODULE
	(1) Psychological harm, including any of the following	
Think about what you would consider to be the most serious incident of [ACTS].	a. More than inconsequential fear reaction	
"Were you afraid, either during or after the incident? (What were you afraid of?) (How long did it last?)"	i. Fear (verbalized or displayed) of bodily injury to self or others AND	? 1 2 3
If YES to fear: "I'm going to ask you some questions about specific ways that the(se) incident(s) may have affected you	ii. At least one of the following signs of fear or anxiety lasting at least 48 hours	
"Have you thought about the incident(s) when you didn't want to or did thoughts about it come to you suddenly when you didn't want them to? (Tell me about that…)"	(a) Persistent intrusive recollections of the incident	? 1 2 3

(continued)

Partner Emotional Abuse (Victimization) *(continued)*

Partner Emotional Abuse (Victimization)	Partner Emotional Abuse (Victimization) Criteria				
	(b) Marked negative reactions to cues related to incident, as evidenced by any of the following:				
"Do you go out of your way to avoid people, places, or things related to the incident? (Tell me about that…)"	1. Avoidance of cues	?	1	2	3
"What about getting very upset when something reminded you of the incident(s)?"	2. Subjective or overt distress to cues	?	1	2	3
"What about physical symptoms — like breaking out in a sweat, breathing heavily or irregularly, or your heart pounding or racing?"	3. Physiological hyperarousal to cues	?	1	2	3
"What about finding yourself acting or feeling as if you were back in the incident?"	(c) Acting or feeling as if incident is recurring	?	1	2	3
Since the incident(s)…	(d) Persistent symptoms of increased arousal, as evidenced by any of the following:	?	1	2	3
…have you had trouble sleeping?	1. Difficulty falling or staying asleep	?	1	2	3
…have you been unusually irritable? What about outbursts of anger?	2. Irritability or outbursts of anger	?	1	2	3
…have you had trouble concentrating?	3. Difficulty concentrating	?	1	2	3
…have you been watchful or on guard even when there was no reason to be?	4. Hypervigilance	?	1	2	3
…have you been jumpy or easily startled, like by sudden noises?	5. Exaggerated startle response	?	1	2	3
	B-1-a-i IS CODED "3" AND AT LEAST 1 ITEM FROM B-1-a-ii IS CODED "3"		1		3
How did [ACTS] affect you? (If needed: "As a result of [ACTS], did you feel depressed? Anxious? Like you might be having a nervous breakdown?" If YES: "Tell me what that was like"	b. Significant psychological distress (i.e., psychiatric disorders at or near diagnostic thresholds)	?	1	2	3
	c. Fear of emotionally abusive act(s) that significantly interfere(s) with the victim's ability to carry out any of these five major life activities:				
Did being afraid of your partner's [ACTS] make things difficult for you at work? [Describe]	i. Work	?	1	2	3
How about at school? [Describe]	ii. Education	?	1	2	3
Did it interfere with your religious practices? [Describe]	iii. Religion	?	1	2	3
Did being afraid of your partner's [ACTS] interfere with you getting medical or mental health care that you needed? [Describe]	iv. Necessary medical or mental health services	?	1	2	3

(continued)

Partner Emotional Abuse (Victimization) *(continued)*

Partner Emotional Abuse (Victimization)	Partner Emotional Abuse (Victimization) Criteria	?	1	2	3
Did it interfere with your contact with family or friends? [Describe]	v. Contact with family/friends	?	1	2	3
After the [ACTS], how was your physical health? Did you feel sick a lot? What kinds of problems were you experiencing? (If YES, "How did [feeling sick] affect your everyday life?")	(2) Stress-related somatic symptoms (related to or exacerbated by the acts) that significantly interfere with normal functioning	?	1	2	3
	AT LEAST 1 ITEM FROM B1 (a–c) OR B2 IS CODED "3"		1		3

Note: ? = inadequate information, 1 = absent or false, 2 = subthreshold, 3 = threshold or true.

Partner Emotional Abuse (Perpetration)

Partner Emotional Abuse (Perpetration)	Partner Emotional Abuse (Perpetration) Criteria	?	1	2	3
Now I'm going to ask you again about things that happen in the majority of relationships at some time or another. This time I'll ask about what you have done In the past year…	A. Verbal or symbolic acts (excluding physically aggressive acts and sexual abuse) with the potential to cause psychological harm to the victim. Such acts include, but are not limited to:				
Have you scolded, criticized, or humiliated your partner?	(1) Berating, disparaging, degrading, humiliating partner	?	1	2	3
Have you interrogated your partner, or persistently asked your partner lots of personal questions or grilled him/her?	(2) Interrogating partner	?	1	2	3
Have you stopped your partner from being able to come and go freely?	(3) Restricting partner's ability to come and go freely (when unwarranted)	?	1	2	3
Have you stopped your partner from getting some kind of help (like police, legal help, or medical care)?	(4) Obstructing partner's access to assistance, including, but not limited to, law enforcement, legal resources protective resources, medical resources				
Have you threatened your partner?	(5) Threatening partner	?	1	2	3
Have you harmed or threatened to harm someone or thing your partner cares about?	(6) Harming, or threatening to harm, people/things that partner cares about, such as children, self, other people, pets, property	?	1	2	3
Have you stopped your partner from accessing money or economic resources?	(7) Restricting partner's access to or use of economic resources (when unwarranted)	?	1	2	3
Have you isolated your partner from family, friends, or social support?	(8) Isolating partner from family, friends, or social support resources	?	1	2	3
Have you stalked your partner?	(9) Stalking partner	?	1	2	3
Have you tried to make your partner think s/he was crazy, or tried to make others think s/he was crazy?	(10) Trying to make partner think that s/he is crazy (or make others think that partner is crazy)	?	1	2	3
What about anything similar?	(11) Any other psychologically harmful acts	?	1	2	3
	B. At least one of the following features:	IF NO ITEMS 1–11 ARE CODED "3", SKIP TO THE NEXT MODULE			

(continued)

Partner Emotional Abuse (Perpetration) *(continued)*

Partner Emotional Abuse (Perpetration)	Partner Emotional Abuse (Perpetration) Criteria				
	(1) Psychological harm, including any of the following:				
Think about what you would consider to be the most serious incident of [ACTS]. "Was your partner afraid, either during or after the incident? (What was s/he afraid of?) (How long did it last?)"	a. More than inconsequential fear reaction i. Fear (verbalized or displayed) of bodily injury to self or others AND	?	1	2	3
If YES to fear: "I'm going to ask you some questions about specific ways that the(se) incident(s) may have affected your partner.	ii. At least one of the following signs of fear or anxiety lasting at least 48 hours				
"Did your partner think about the incident(s) when s/he didn't want to or did thoughts about it come to him/her suddenly when s/he didn't want them to? (Tell me about that...)"	a. Persistent intrusive recollections of the incident	?	1	2	3
	b. Marked negative reactions to cues related to incident, as evidenced by any of the following:				
"Does your partner go out of his/her way to avoid people, places, or things related to the incident? (Tell me about that...)"	1. Avoidance of cues	?	1	2	3
"What about getting very upset when something reminded him/her of the incident(s)?"	2. Subjective or overt distress to cues	?	1	2	3
"What about physical symptoms — like breaking out in a sweat, breathing heavily or irregularly, or his/her heart pounding or racing?"	3. Physiological hyperarousal to cues	?	1	2	3
"What about acting or feeling as if s/he were back in the incident?"	c. Acting or feeling as if incident is recurring	?	1	2	3
Since the incident(s)...	d. Persistent symptoms of increased arousal, as evidenced by any of the following:	?	1	2	3
...has your partner had trouble sleeping?	1. Difficulty falling or staying asleep	?	1	2	3
...has s/he been unusually irritable? What about outbursts of anger?	2. Irritability or outbursts of anger	?	1	2	3
...has s/he had trouble concentrating?	3. Difficulty concentrating	?	1	2	3
...has s/he been watchful or on guard even when there was no reason to be?	4. Hypervigilance	?	1	2	3
...has s/he been jumpy or easily startled, like by sudden noises?	5. Exaggerated startle response	?	1	2	3
	B-1-a-i IS CODED "3" AND AT LEAST 1 ITEM FROM B-1-a-ii IS CODED "3"		1		3
How did [ACTS] affect your partner? (If needed: "As a result of [ACTS], did your partner feel depressed? Sad? Lonely? Did s/he have crying spells?"	(2) Significant psychological distress (i.e., psychiatric disorders at or near diagnostic thresholds)	?	1	2	3
	(3) Fear of emotionally abusive act(s) that significantly interfere(s) with the victim's ability to carry out any of these five major life activities:				
Did being afraid of your [ACTS] make things difficult for your partner at work? [Describe]	a. Work	?	1	2	3
How about at school? [Describe]	b. Education	?	1	2	3

(continued)

Partner Emotional Abuse (Perpetration) (*continued*)

Partner Emotional Abuse (Perpetration)	Partner Emotional Abuse (Perpetration) Criteria				
Did it interfere with his/her religious practices? [Describe]	c. Religion	?	1	2	3
Did being afraid of your [ACTS] interfere with him/her getting medical or mental health care that s/he needed? [Describe]	d. Necessary medical or mental health services	?	1	2	3
Did it interfere with your partner's contact with family or friends? [Describe]	e. Contact with family/friends	?	1	2	3
After the [ACTS], how was your partner's physical health? Did your partner feel sick a lot? What kinds of problems was s/he experiencing? (If YES, "How did [feeling sick] affect your partner's everyday life?")	(4) Stress-related somatic symptoms (related to or exacerbated by the acts) that significantly interfere with normal functioning	?	1	2	3
	AT LEAST 1 ITEM FROM B1, B2, B3, OR B4 IS CODED "3"		1		3

Note: ? = inadequate information, 1 = absent or false, 2 = subthreshold, 3 = threshold or true.

Partner Sexual Abuse (Victimization)

Partner Sexual Abuse (Victimization)	Partner Sexual Abuse (Victimization) Criteria				
Now I'm going to ask you about other things that sometimes happen in relationships. First I'll ask you about what your partner has done, and then I'll ask you about what you have done. In the past year…	A. Any of the following acts committed by partners in a current or former romantic relationship				
Has your partner used physical force to try to make you have vaginal sex, anal sex, oral sex, or another sexual activity? (Tell me about it.)	(1) The use of physical force to compel participation in a sex act against the interviewee's will, whether or not the act is completed. Sex act is defined as: a. Contact between the penis and the vulva or the penis and the anus involving penetration, however slight. b. Contact between the mouth and the penis, vulva, or anus. c. Penetration of the anal or genital opening by a hand, finger, or other object	?	1	2	3
Before, I asked you about your partner doing things like scolding, criticizing, or humiliating you, stopping you from being able to come and go freely, threatening you, harming or threatening to harm someone or thing you care about, stopping you from accessing money or economic resources, and other things like that. Has your partner ever done anything like those things to try to make you have vaginal sex, anal sex, oral sex, or another sexual activity? (If YES: "Tell me about that.")	(2) The use of a physical force or an emotionally aggressive act to coerce the victim to participate in a sex act. Emotionally aggressive act is defined as: a. Berating, disparaging, degrading, humiliating interviewee b. Interrogating interviewee c. Restricting interviewee's ability to come and go freely (when unwarranted) d. Obstructing interviewee's access to assistance (including, but not limited to, law enforcement, legal, protective, or medical resources) e. Threatening interviewee (including, but not limited to, indicating/implying future physical harm, sexual assault)	?	1	2	3

(*continued*)

Partner Sexual Abuse (Victimization) *(continued)*

Partner Sexual Abuse (Victimization)	Partner Sexual Abuse (Victimization) Criteria				
	f. Harming, or threatening to harm, people/things that interviewee cares about, such as children, self, other people, pets, property g. Restricting partner's access to or use of economic resources (when unwarranted). Warranted restrictions involve obstructing interviewee from behaviors that may injure self or others (e.g., taking an intoxicated partner's car keys) or obstructing a recklessly spending interviewee from incurring debts despite an obviously grave economic situation (e.g., impending bankruptcy). Restrictions not meeting these rare circumstances would be considered unwarranted. h. Isolating interviewee from family, friends, or social support resources i. Stalking interviewee j. Trying to make interviewee think that s/he is crazy (or make others think that partner is crazy)				
	(3) An attempted or completed sex act when the interviewee was unable to provide consent for the following reasons:				
	a. Interviewee was unable to understand the nature or conditions of the act or to decline participation	?	1	2	3
Has your partner ever tried to make you have vaginal sex, anal sex, oral sex, or another sexual activity when you were too ill to refuse? When you were asleep? When you were intoxicated or using drugs? When you were unable to refuse for any other reason?	b. Interviewee could not communicate unwillingness to engage in the sexual act (e.g., due to illness; disability; being asleep or under the influence of alcohol or other drugs)	?	1	2	3
	(4) Physical contact of a sexual nature (including, but not limited to, kissing, groping, rubbing, fondling — directly or through clothing) that meets both of the following:				
Has your partner initiated some kind of physical contact like kissing, groping, rubbing, or fondling, when you said or showed that you didn't want to?	a. The contact was against the expressed wishes of the interviewee	?	1	2	3
(If YES) How did [ACTS] affect you? (If needed: "As a result of [ACTS], did you feel depressed? Sad? Lonely? Did you have crying spells?"	b. The contact caused considerable distress to the interviewee that lasts for more than 24 hours. "Considerable distress" involves anguish that does not necessarily meet diagnostic thresholds for psychiatric disorders but exceeds distress incurred in normal, day-to-day activities.	?	1	2	3
	BOTH 4a AND 4b ARE CODED 3		1		3
	A1, A2, A3, OR A4 IS CODED 3.		1		3

(continued)

Partner Sexual Abuse (Perpetration) *(continued)*

Partner Sexual Abuse (Perpetration)	Partner Sexual Abuse (Perpetration) Criteria				
Now I'm going to ask you again about things that sometimes happen in relationships, but this time I'll ask you about what you have done. In the past year…	A. Any of the following acts committed by partners in a current or former romantic relationship				
Have you used physical force to try to make your partner have vaginal sex, anal sex, oral sex, or another sexual activity? (Tell me about it.)	(1) The use of physical force to compel participation in a sex act against the partner's will, whether or not the act is completed.Sex act is defined as: a. Contact between the penis and the vulva or the penis and the anus involving penetration, however slight b. Contact between the mouth and the penis, vulva, or anus c. Penetration of the anal or genital opening by a hand, finger, or other object	?	1	2	3
Before, I asked you about you doing things like scolding, criticizing, or humiliating your partner, stopping your partner from being able to come and go freely, threatening your partner, harming or threatening to harm someone or thing your partner cared about, stopping your partner from accessing money or economic resources, and other things like that. Have you ever done anything like those things to try to make your partner have vaginal sex, anal sex, oral sex, or another sexual activity? (Tell me about it.)	(2) The use of a physical force or an emotionally aggressive act to coerce the partner to participate in a sex act. Emotionally aggressive act is defined as: a. Berating, disparaging, degrading, humiliating partner b. Interrogating partner c. Restricting partner's ability to come and go freely (when unwarranted) d. Obstructing partner's access to assistance (including, but not limited to, law enforcement, legal, protective, or medical resources) e. Threatening partner (including, but not limited to, indicating/implying future physical harm, sexual assault) f. Harming, or threatening to harm, people/things that partner cares about, such as children, self, other people, pets, property g. Restricting partner's access to or use of economic resources (when unwarranted). Warranted restrictions involve obstructing a partner from behaviors that may injure partner or others (e.g., taking an intoxicated partner's car keys) or obstructing a recklessly spending partner from incurring debts despite an obviously grave economic situation (e.g., impending bankruptcy). Restrictions not meeting these rare circumstances would be considered unwarranted. h. Isolating partner from family, friends, or social support resources i. Stalking partner j. Trying to make partner think that s/he is crazy (or make others think that partner is crazy)	?	1	2	3

(continued)

Partner Emotional Abuse (Perpetration) *(continued)*

Partner Sexual Abuse (Perpetration)	Partner Sexual Abuse (Perpetration) Criteria				
	(3) An attempted or completed sex act when the partner was unable to provide consent for the following reasons:				
	a. Partner was unable to understand the nature or conditions of the act or to decline participation	?	1	2	3
Have you ever tried to make your partner have vaginal sex, anal sex, oral sex, or another sexual activity when your partner was too ill to refuse? When your partner was asleep? When your partner was intoxicated or using drugs? When your partner was unable to refuse for any other reason?	b. Partner could not communicate unwillingness to engage in the sexual act (e.g., due to illness; disability; being asleep or under the influence of alcohol or other drugs)	?	1	2	3
	(4) Physical contact of a sexual nature (including, but not limited to, kissing, groping, rubbing, fondling—directly or through clothing) that meets both of the following:				
Have you initiated some kind of physical contact like kissing, groping, rubbing, or fondling, when your partner said or showed that s/he didn't want to?	a. The contact is against the expressed wishes of the partner	?	1	2	3
(If YES) How did [ACTS] affect your partner? (If needed: "As a result of [ACTS], did your partner feel depressed? Sad? Lonely? Did your partner have crying spells?"	b. The contact causes considerable distress to the partner that lasts for more than 24 hours. "Considerable distress" involves anguish that does not necessarily meet diagnostic thresholds for psychiatric disorders but exceeds distress incurred in normal, day-to-day activities.	?	1	2	3
	BOTH 4a AND 4b ARE CODED 3		1		3
	A1, A2, A3, OR A4 IS CODED 3.		1		3

Note: ? = inadequate information, 1 = absent or false, 2 = subthreshold, 3 = threshold or true.

Partner Neglect (Victimization)

Partner Neglect (Victimization)	Partner Neglect (Victimization) Criteria
Now I'm going to ask you some questions about your partner's and your ability to care for yourselves. First I'll ask about you and then I'll ask about your partner.	

(continued)

Partner Neglect (Victimization) *(continued)*

Partner Neglect (Victimization)	Partner Neglect (Victimization) Criteria	?	1	2	3
How capable are you in caring for yourself? How capable are you in getting yourself food, shelter, medical attention, and keeping yourself clean? Is there currently any reason you cannot perform these duties for yourself? Has there ever been a time in the past 12 months when you could not do these things for yourself? (Tell me about that.)	A. One partner is incapable of self care due to substantial limitations in one or more of the following areas:				
	(1) Physical (including, but not limited to, quadriplegia)	?	1	2	3
	(2) Psychological/intellectual (including, but not limited to, vegetative depression, very low IQ, psychosis)	?	1	2	3
	(3) Cultural (including, but not limited to, inability to communicate, inability to manage activities of rudimentary daily living due to foreign culture)	?	1	2	3
	A1, A2, OR A3 IS CODED 3.		1		3 (IF NOT CODED 3, SKIP TO NEXT MODULE.)
When one person cannot take care of him/herself, it often falls on the partner to make sure the person has certain needs taken care of.	B. Deprivation-related significant impact on the incapable partner via act(s) or omission(s)				
(When you were [DISABLED].../In the past 12 months...), what percentage of the time did your partner make sure you had access to enough food? What about shelter? What percentage of the time did your partner make sure you were clean enough? What percentage of the time did your partner make sure you had the necessary medical or mental health care? What about making sure you were safe? [IF ANY LESS THAN 100%] Tell me about the most serious time when your partner didn't make sure you had [FOOD/SHELTER/HYGIENE/MEDICAL CARE/SAFETY].	(1) Deprivation involves the withholding of, or withholding access to, adequate food, shelter, hygiene, or necessary medical/psychiatric services and/or gross negligence regarding the safety needs of the incapable partner	?	1	2	3 (IF NOT CODED 3, SKIP TO NEXT MODULE.)
As a result of times like that, when your partner didn't make sure you had [FOOD/SHELTER/HYGIENE/MEDICAL CARE/SAFETY], what happened to you?	(2) Deprivation-related significant impact involves any of the following:				
	a. More than inconsequential physical injury resulting from capable partner's acts or omissions	?	1	2	3
(IF UNCLEAR) What do you think the worst thing is that could have happened to you at a time like that?	b. Reasonable potential for more than inconsequential physical injury	?	1	2	3
	B(1) IS CODED 3 AND B(2)a OR B(2)b IS CODED 3.	?	1	2	3

Note: ? = inadequate information, 1 = absent or false, 2 = subthreshold, 3 = threshold or true.

Partner Neglect (Perpetration)

Partner Neglect (Perpetration)	Partner Neglect (Perpetration) Criteria	
Now I'm going to ask you some questions about your partner's ability to care for him/herself.		
How capable is your partner in caring for him/herself? How capable is s/he in getting him/herself food, shelter, medical attention, and keeping him/herself clean? Is there currently any reason your partner cannot perform these duties for him/herself? Has there ever been a time in the past 12 months when your partner could not do these things for him/herself? (Tell me about that.)	A. One partner is incapable of self care due to substantial limitations in one or more of the following areas:	
	(1) Physical (including, but not limited to, quadriplegia)	? 1 2 3
	(2) Psychological/intellectual (including, but not limited to, vegetative depression, very low IQ, psychosis)	? 1 2 3
	(3) Cultural (including, but not limited to, inability to communicate, inability to manage activities of rudimentary daily living due to foreign culture)	? 1 2 3
	A1, A2, OR A3 IS CODED 3.	? 1 2 3 IF NOT CODED 3, SKIP TO NEXT MODULE.
When one person cannot take care of him/herself it often falls on the partner to make sure the person has certain needs taken care of.	B. Deprivation-related significant impact on the incapable partner via act(s) or omission(s).	
(When your partner was [DISABLED].../ In the past 12 months...), what percentage of the time did you make sure s/he had access to enough food? What about shelter? What percentage of the time did you make sure s/he was clean enough? What percentage of the time did you make sure s/he had the necessary medical or mental health care? What about making sure s/he was safe? [If ANY LESS THAN 100%] Tell me about the most serious time when you didn't make sure your partner had [FOOD/SHELTER/HYGIENE/ MEDICAL CARE/SAFETY].	(1) Deprivation involves the withholding of, or withholding access to, adequate food, shelter, hygiene, or necessary medical/psychiatric services and/or gross negligence regarding the safety needs of the incapable partner.	? 1 2 3 IF NOT CODED 3, SKIP TO NEXT MODULE.
As a result of times like that, when you didn't make sure your partner had [FOOD/SHELTER/HYGIENE/ MEDICAL CARE/SAFETY], what happened to your partner?	(2) Deprivation-related significant impact involves any of the following: a. More than inconsequential physical injury resulting from capable partner's acts or omissions	? 1 2 3
(If UNCLEAR) What do you think the worst thing is that could have happened to your partner at a time like that?	b. Reasonable potential for more than inconsequential physical injury	? 1 2 3
	B(1) IS CODED 3 AND B(2)a. OR B(2)b. IS CODED 3.	? 1 2 3

Note: ? = inadequate information, 1 = absent or false, 2 = subthreshold, 3 = threshold or true.

PART II: PARTNER RELATIONAL PROBLEMS

5

Relationship Distress: Assessment, Definition, and Implications for Mental Health Diagnosis

Mark A. Whisman and Steven R. H. Beach

Social relationships play an integral role in individual health and well-being. For example, a recent meta-analysis of 148 studies on the influence of social relationships on risk for mortality indicated a 50% increased likelihood of survival for people with stronger relationships: the magnitude of this effect is comparable to quitting smoking and exceeds many well-known risk factors for mortality, such as obesity and physical inactivity (Holt-Lunstad, Smith, & Layton, 2010). For many people, the relationship they have with their spouse or partner is one of the most, if not the most, important social relationships in their lives.

Relationship distress has been shown to predict a variety of important outcomes, including the mental and physical health of adults and children, as well as family economics (for a review, see Chapter 7 in this volume). There is also an emerging body of evidence about the effect of couple functioning on treatment outcome for people with mental health problems (for a review, see Whisman, 2006). For example, poorer marital functioning at posttreatment predicted poorer outcome across individually oriented treatment conditions for depression (Kung & Elkin, 2000; Whisman, 2001) and the same pattern was observed if degree of marital improvement over treatment was used to predict outcomes (Kung & Elkin, 2000). Poor marital functioning has also been shown to predict increased likelihood of relapse, percent days abstinent, and time to relapse among people with substance use problems in treatment (e.g., Fals-Stewart, O'Farrell, & Hooley, 2001), and relationship tension and friction predicts poorer improvement for individuals with generalized anxiety disorder (Durham, Allan, & Hackett, 1997). Furthermore, individual-based treatments for mental health problems generally do not significantly improve relationship problems (e.g., Beach & O'Leary, 1992; Fals-Stewart, Birchler, & O'Farrell, 1996).

In this chapter, we review (a) measures for the assessment of problems in relationships with spouse or partner (i.e., relationship distress), (b) evidence that supports a categorical definition of relationship distress, (c) screening methods for detecting relationship distress, and (d) implications of this research for mental health diagnosis.

ASSESSMENT OF RELATIONSHIP DISTRESS

In the tenth edition of the International Statistical Classification of Diseases and Related Health Problems (ICD-10; World Health Organization [WHO], 1992), relationship problems are included among the Z categories, which refer to "Factors influencing health status and contact with health services." The Z categories are to be used for occasions when problems other than a disease, injury, or external cause are recorded as "diagnoses" or "problems," such as when a person who may or may not be sick encounters health services of a specific purpose or when a problem is present that influences a person's health but is not itself an illness or injury. Included among the Z categories is Z63, "Other problems related to primary support group, including family circumstance," which includes category Z63.0, "Problems in relationship with spouse or partner." Specifically, Z63.0 is defined as "Discord between partners resulting in severe or prolonged loss of control, in generalization of hostile or critical feelings or in a persisting atmosphere of severe interpersonal violence (hitting or striking)."

The Z categories can also be used as part of the ICD-10 multiaxial system, which consists of Axis I—Clinical diagnoses, Axis II—Disabilities, and Axis III—Contextual factors (WHO, 1997). The multiaxial system was designed as a tool for clinicians to aid in promoting a multifaceted assessment and comprehensive formulation of clients in adult psychiatry. Specifically, Axis III "provides an opportunity for the clinician to assess contextual factors that are considered to contribute significantly to the occurrence, presentation, course, outcomes or treatment of the present mental and physical disorders recorded on Axis I or to be of clear relevance for the clinical care of the present illness episode" (WHO, 1997, pp. 19–20). The WHO conducted a field trial of the multiaxial system between 1993 and 1995, to evaluate the reliability and cross-cultural applicability of the ICD-10 multiaxial system (WHO, 1997). This field trial included 274 clinicians from 63 centers located in 20 different countries spanning all the regions of the world. Assessments were made for local patients and case vignettes. In the field trials, Z63.0 was the most frequently recorded specific contextual factor, found in 5.6% of the patient group.

Based on existing data, problems in relationships with spouses or partners are common and important problems. However, the descriptions of such problems are overly vague and general. Moreover, they provide minimal guidance for clinical assessment and no guidance for deciding whether a treatable problem is present. In the WHO field trials, the kappa value for the agreement between the rates on the absence and presence of Z63.0 was 0.64 (WHO, 1997). However, the description of Z63.0 includes severe interpersonal violence, which is more behaviorally descriptive and which may be more reliably assessed than the other two aspects of this code (severe or prolonged loss of control, generalization of hostile or critical feelings). Therefore, the reliability for assessing problems in relationship with spouse or partner that does not include the assessment of violence may be expected to be lower.

Given the importance of relationship problems for morbidity and mortality, are there ways for improving the assessment of such problems? It may be useful first to consider the existing measures that have been used to assess marriage or other close romantic relationships. Measures of *adjustment* typically combine objective characteristic of the relationship (e.g., processes that are believed to be necessary to achieve a functional relationship) and subjective evaluations or attitudes toward the partner and the relationship, whereas measures of *satisfaction* (or *quality*) typically assess only subjective evaluations (Fincham & Rogge, 2010; Sabatelli, 1988). Most of these measures are scored on a continuum, and most are scored to yield a global measure of relationship adjustment or satisfaction, with low scores labeled "distress" or "discord." The most commonly used measures are the 32-item Dyadic Adjustment Scale (DAS; Spanier, 1989) and the 15-item Marital Adjustment Test (MAT; Locke & Wallace, 1959); other commonly used measures include the 6-item Quality of Marital Index (QMI; Norton, 1983), the 7-item Relationship Assessment Scale (RAS; Hendrick, 1988), and the 3-item Kansas Marital Satisfaction Scale (KMS; Schumm, Nichols, Schectman, & Grigsby, 1983). These scales correlate highly with one another (e.g., Funk & Rogge, 2007), supporting the convergent validity of the measures and suggesting that the scales are measuring a similar theoretical construct. Recently, Funk and Rogge (2007) created an item pool from existing relationship adjustment measures, as well as additional items that they wrote, and used principal-components analysis and item response theory (IRT) on data collected from over 5,300 participants to develop a new measure, which they called the Couples Satisfaction Index (CSI). Specifically, they developed a 32-item, a 16-item, and a 4-item version of the CSI. The new measure demonstrated excellent convergent and construct validity, and results from IRT analysis indicated it was more powerful and precise (i.e., contained less "noise") than existing measures, suggesting it may be a particularly strong instrument for global assessment of relationships.

Multidimensional measures of relationship adjustment have also been developed. For example, the Marital Satisfaction Inventory–Revised (MSI–R; Snyder, 1997) consists of 150 True–False items that assess the nature and extent of conflict across distinct areas of interaction within a marriage or close romantic relationship. It consists of 2 validity scales, 1 global scale, and 10 scales assessing relationship adjustment across such areas as affective and problem-solving communication, aggression, leisure time together, finances, sexual relationship, role orientation, family of origin, and interaction regarding children.

CATEGORICAL DEFINITION OF RELATIONSHIP DISTRESS

Given the large number of individuals with mental health problems that also experience problems in their relationship with their spouse or partner, and further given that the likelihood that such difficulties are distressing in their own right, unlikely to respond to standard (i.e., individually based) interventions, and consequential for long-term outcomes, it is important that referring arrangements be facilitated for those offering primary treatment. This requires attention to the determination of guidelines or defining cut scores for identifying clinically significant levels of relationship distress, the presence of which would suggest the need for intervention.

One commonly used strategy for defining relationship distress has been to dichotomize a continuous measure of relationship adjustment or satisfaction. If a continuous measure is to be dichotomized, how does one go about selecting a threshold or cut score? In some cases, the basis for existing cut scores for defining relationship distress is not specified. For example, a cut score of 100 on the MAT (Locke & Wallace, 1959) is commonly used to define relationship distress; Locke and Wallace (1959) reported the percentages of "well-adjusted" and "maladjusted" groups that scored above this cut score, but did not provide a discussion of how they selected this score. In comparison, the bases of other cut scores for defining relationship distress have been specified. For example, one of the most commonly used cut scores for defining relationship distress is a score of 97 or below on the DAS (Spanier, 1989). This cut score was established by Jacobson et al. (1984) as the score that is halfway between the mean of the functional population and the mean of the dysfunctional population, where the functional population was defined in terms of Spanier's (1976) married sample of 218 persons and the dysfunctional population was defined in terms of Spanier's (1976) divorced sample of 94 persons. Thus, a cut score of ≤97 on the DAS was advanced as a threshold for defining relationship distress based on the relative likelihood of a particular score ending up in the functional or dysfunctional population distributions.

Because a cut score of ≤97 on the DAS is widely used for defining relationship distress, it may be useful to develop comparable cut scores for other continuous measures of relationship adjustment or satisfaction. One method for creating comparable cut scores for other measures is to use linear regression analyses to predict participants' scores on another measure from their DAS scores, and using the resulting regression coefficient and intercept values to determine the score on the new measure that corresponds to the score of ≤97 on the DAS. For example, Heyman, Sayers, and Bellack (1994) used linear regression analyses to predict scores on the QMI from the DAS and then used this formula and derived a cut score of 29 for the QMI that corresponds to the cut score of ≤97 on the DAS. Another method for creating comparable cut scores for other measures of relationship distress is to categorize individuals as distressed using the cut score of ≤97 on the DAS, and then use receiver operating characteristic (ROC) analysis (Swets, Dawes, & Monahan, 2000) to identify the corresponding cut score on the other measure that maximizes sensitivity and specificity for the measure. For example, Funk and Rogge (2007) conducted ROC analyses in a sample of over 5,300 participants who had been classified as distressed based on a cut score of ≤97.5 on the DAS and created comparable cut scores for the MAT (95.5), QMI (24.5), RAS (23.5), and KMS (12.5).

An alternative strategy for measuring and diagnosing relationship distress was proposed by Heyman, Feldbau-Kohn, Ehrensaft, Langhinrichsen-Rohling, and O'Leary (2001), who developed a structured interview modeled after the Structured Clinical Interview for the *DSM* (SCID; First, Spitzer, Gibbon, & Williams, 1997). The interview was designed to be a face valid and content valid relationship diagnosis instrument. Participants were asked questions about their relationships for the month preceding the interview, and individuals were diagnosed as distressed if they met at least one criterion for overall dissatisfaction (i.e., perceived unhappiness, pervasive thoughts of divorce, or perceived need for professional help) and at least one criterion for key symptoms (i.e., symptoms of significant behavioral, cognitive, or affective impairment). The interview demonstrated good inter-rater reliability (kappa of 0.92), and discriminant validity for the interview was evidenced by significant differences between individuals diagnosed as distressed and nondistressed on (a) self-report measures of marital functioning, and (b) observer coding of problem-solving discussions. However, there was only fair agreement (kappas of 0.63 for men and 0.49 for women) between the interviewer-based distress diagnosis and distress classification on the DAS using a cut score of ≤97; compared to classification based on the DAS, the diagnostic interview resulted in lower rates of classification of distress for both women (49% vs. 40%, respectively) and men (43% vs. 32%, respectively). Thus, there was limited evidence that the interview yielded similar diagnosis as those obtained from cut scores for self-report measures of relationship distress. However, because there are no established criteria for relationship distress, there is no evidence that one measure is more valid than the other at identifying relationship distress.

Determining the boundaries and cut scores for identifying when relationship problems with a spouse or partner become clinically meaningful may be aided by a recent set of statistical methods labeled the *taxometric method*, which now makes it possible to evaluate whether dimensional scales are reflective of an underlying discrete entity or *taxon* (Waller & Meehl, 1998). In short, taxometric procedures examine the covariation among indicators (e.g., test scores), seeking patterns that are diagnostic of either latent categories (i.e., taxa) or dimensions. As such, a taxon is a nonarbitrary latent category whose members differ qualitatively from nonmembers.

Various taxometric procedures have been developed to test for the presence of a latent categorical structure (for detailed descriptions of these procedures, see Ruscio, Haslam, & Ruscio, 2006; Schmidt, Kotov, & Joiner, 2004; Waller & Meehl, 1998). Specifically, a set of analytic strategies referred to in the aggregate as *coherent cut kinetics* have been developed to distinguish between latent taxa and latent dimensions. Because each approach is based on different statistical considerations, each has different statistical vulnerabilities. Therefore, using several of the coherent cut kinetic procedures allows an investigator to check the consistency of the results among procedures; such consistency tests are required to confirm apparently taxonic results. That way, if a particular distributional abnormality is responsible for the appearance of taxonicity using one procedure, it will likely become apparent in subsequent analyses using other taxometric procedures. Taxometric analyses have been widely studied with respect to mental disorders, and the results of these analyses suggest that some disorders seem to be best represented as discreet categories, whereas others seem to be best represented as dimensional continua (for a review, see Haslam, 2007).

Beach, Fincham, Amir, and Leonard (2005) examined the taxometric structure of marital distress in a sample of newlywed couples ($N = 447$). They created Wife × Husband product terms for 13 items from the MAT (Locke & Wallace, 1959), and these dyadic indicators were examined using taxometric methods. Results from the study suggested the presence of a marital distress taxon with a base rate of approximately 0.20. Furthermore, Beach et al. (2005) found evidence for the validity of the taxon: compared to couples assigned to the complement, couples assigned to the taxon scored significantly lower on shared leisure activities, higher on negative partner behavior, and lower on an alternative measure of marital adjustment.

More recently, Whisman, Beach, and Snyder (2008) created Wife × Husband product terms for five subscales from the MSI–R (Snyder, 1997): the Global Distress (GDS), Time Together (TTO), Sexual Dissatisfaction (SEX), Affective Communication (AFC), and Problem-Solving

Communication (PSC) scales. These scales were selected as indicators in the taxometric analyses because they are applicable to most types of couples and they focus primarily on current relationship functioning, broadly conceived. Whisman et al. (2008) evaluated the taxonic structure of these indicators in a sample of 1,020 couples that was representative of the U.S. population with respect to race and ethnicity, educational level, and occupation. Results indicated that marital distress was taxonic, with an overall base rate of approximately 0.31, with approximately 0.20 of those married a relatively short time categorized as distressed, similar to the results obtained by Beach et al.'s (2005) estimated base rate for the taxon in their newlywed sample. Whisman et al. (2008) also evaluated the short-term (i.e., 6-week) test–retest reliability of the taxon classification in a community sample of 105 couples, and the resulting kappa for taxon classification at baseline and follow-up was 0.75, thereby supporting the short-term stability of taxon classification. Furthermore, validity of the taxon classification was supported by (a) differences in the base rate of the taxon between clinical and community samples, and (b) significant correlations between the taxon classification and therapists' ratings of couple functioning for couples in treatment. Finally, they created a user friendly method for classifying couples as members of the taxon based on the mean of husbands' and wives' scores on the five MSI–R scales (GDS, TTO, SEX, AFC, and PSC). ROC analyses (Swets et al., 2000) were conducted using this composite, and a score of 54*T* was identified as the point that maximized sensitivity and specificity. Consequently, researchers and clinicians interested in diagnosing the relationship distress taxon could administer these five scales to couples, compute the mean score, and use this score to classify a couple as belonging to the relationship distress taxon (i.e., distressed) if they scored ≥54*T* or as belonging to the complement (i.e., nondistressed) if they scored <54*T*.

Combined, the results from the Beach et al. (2005) and Whisman et al. (2008) studies suggest that couples in distressed relationships differ qualitatively, and not just quantitatively, from couples in nondistressed relationships. Furthermore, findings from these studies suggest that the base rate of the taxon differs depending on the sample composition in terms of years married. These results provide a nonarbitrary boundary or threshold for defining the presence or absence of problems in relationships with spouses or partners.

SCREENING METHODS FOR DETECTING RELATIONSHIP DISTRESS

Many individuals presenting for treatment of "individual" problems also have serious marital or relationship difficulties, but they are rarely referred for treatment of any sort. Because arranging referrals from individually oriented mental health practitioners can be challenging, it may be useful for couple- and family-based clinicians to be able to recommend user-friendly screening tools that can help prompt referrals from interested practitioners. This may be particularly important in working with individually oriented practitioners who may not be sophisticated about relationship functioning and who may not want to conduct extensive relationship assessments themselves—but who recognize its importance for physical and mental health outcomes.

Whisman, Snyder, and Beach (2009) developed a simple screening tool to identify couples who are members of the taxon (i.e., who were "distressed") that could be useful in identifying people who are members of the relationship distress taxon and so may be in need of referral for more detailed relationship assessment or treatment. They first computed item-total correlations in the representative sample of 1,020 couples for the five MSI–R scales (GDS, TTO, SEX, AFC, and PSC) used by Whisman et al. (2008) to define the marital distress taxon, and selected the two items from each scale that had the highest item-total correlation. The original MSI–R item numbers for the 10 selected items were #58, #124, #43, #39, #81, #95, #54, #80, #76, and #127. The resulting 10-item scale was then scored by counting the number of coded (i.e., distressed) responses; half of the items are coded as distressed if answered true and half are coded as distressed if answered false, which is an ideal distribution of keyed responses for countering "all true" or "all false" response sets. Scores on the 10-item scale can range from 0 to 10, with higher scores indicating greater relationship distress. The mean score in the normative sample was 3.20 (*SD* = 2.81) for wives and 3.08 (*SD* = 2.68) for husbands. Coefficient alpha for the 10-item scale was 0.82 for wives and 0.81 for husbands; the mean interitem correlation was 0.32 for wives and 0.30 for husbands. To identify a cut score for defining distress using the 10-item screen, couples were first classified as distressed or nondistressed using the methods reported by Whisman et al. (2008). An ROC analysis was then conducted, and a score of 4 was identified as the point that maximized sensitivity and specificity on the 10-item screen. Therefore, individuals who scored ≥4 on the 10-item screen were classified as belonging to the taxon (i.e., they were classified as distressed) and individuals who scored <4 were classified as belonging to the complement (i.e., they were classified as nondistressed). The kappa for the 6-week test–retest reliability of the taxon classification based on the 10-item screen was 0.70 for husbands and 0.68 for wives, indicating good short-term stability. Finally, to optimize the utility of the 10-item screen in diverse clinical and research settings, both self-report and interview-based measures were presented; the self-report version of the screening measure (called the MSI–B) is available from Western Psychological Services.

The 10-item measure may be useful for screening and monitoring the presence of relationship distress. Administration and scoring of the screen is straightforward, rendering it easy for nonfamily clinicians to determine whether someone is a member of the relationship distress taxon and so may be in need of referral for more detailed relationship assessment. It is estimated that the entire administration, scoring, and classification process should require less than 5 minutes. Of course, when the screening instrument leads to referral for further evaluation or clinical intervention, we recommend a more extensive multimodal assessment (see, e.g., Snyder et al., 2004) incorporating multidimensional self-report measures differentiating among sources of relationship distress; behavioral samples of partners' interactions involving problem-solving and support-providing communication; and clinical interviews delineating the functional relations among specific indicators of relationship distress, individual and relationship functioning, and sources of support or stress in the couple's broader environment.

Furthermore, because the 10-item screen is highly structured and requires little judgment by interviewers for making decisions whether the item is present or absent, the interview version of the screen may be administered by lay interviewers, making the screen an appropriate measure for epidemiologic studies and field research on problems in relationship with spouse or partner. Furthermore, because there already exist Spanish, German, and Korean adaptations of the MSI–R (Snyder et al., 2004), the 10-item screen could be used in cross-cultural and cross-national clinical and research settings.

IMPLICATIONS OF RELATIONSHIP DISTRESS FOR MENTAL HEALTH DIAGNOSIS

Because relationship functioning is so strongly associated with physical and mental health of adults and children, as well as with family economics (for a review, see Chapter 7, this volume), problems in relationship with spouse or partner may have important implications for mental health diagnosis. Beach, Wamboldt, Kaslow, Heyman, and Reiss (2006) proposed several recommendations for how social functioning could be better addressed in classification systems such as the ICD. In particular, Beach et al. suggested the use of disorder-specific relational processes using relational specifiers. In the context of the revised ICD, this would take the form of encouragement to indicate the relational context of clinical diagnoses by using the appropriate Z categories as part of a comprehensive formulation of a person's clinical condition. This could then influence both assessment and treatment planning.

Because there are a number of treatments for marital and relationship distress that have been shown to be effective in controlled clinical trials (for a review, see Snyder, Castellani, & Whisman, 2006) there are many opportunities for intervention and prevention of problems in relationship with spouse or partner. There may also be conditions under which analogous techniques can be used for violent couples (O'Leary & Vega, 2005), particularly in the context of drug or alcohol abuse (Fals-Stewart, O'Farrell, Birchler, Cordova, & Kelley, 2005). Likewise, meta-analytic studies have provided evidence for the effectiveness of couple-based interventions in the treatment of depression (Barbato & D'Avanzo, 2008) and alcohol and drug use disorders (Powers, Vedel, & Emmelkamp, 2008). Accordingly, a revised ICD that encouraged use of appropriate Z categories, provided better guidance regarding when to refer for services in these areas and when to utilize relationship-oriented interventions to enhance outcomes, would have great clinical benefit.

CONCLUSIONS

In this chapter, we (a) reviewed existing measures for assessing relationship distress; (b) provided evidence that distressed and nondistressed couples may differ in kind as well as in degree (i.e., that relationship distress appears to be taxonic), thereby suggesting a nonarbitrary definition for relationship distress; (c) introduced a brief measure that may be useful for screening for relationship distress; and (d) offered some recommendations for how relationship distress may impact mental health diagnosis. Given the importance of relationship functioning for well-being, we hope that developments in defining and measuring relationship distress will help guide decision making regarding treatment and inform research on the onset and course of physical and mental health problems.

REFERENCES

Barbato, A., & D'Avanzo, B. (2008). Efficacy of couple therapy as a treatment for depression: A meta-analysis. *Psychiatric Quarterly, 79*, 121–132.

Beach, S. R. H., Fincham, F. D., Amir, N., & Leonard, K. E. (2005). The taxometrics of marriage: Is marital discord categorical? *Journal of Family Psychology, 19*, 276–285.

Beach, S. R., & O'Leary, K. D. (1992). Treating depression in the context of marital discord: Outcome and predictors of response of marital therapy versus cognitive therapy. *Behavior Therapy, 23*, 507–528.

Beach, S. R. H., Wamboldt, M. Z., Kaslow, N. J., Heyman, R. E., & Reiss, D. (2006). Describing relationship problems in *DSM-V*: Toward better guidance for research and clinical practice. *Journal of Family Psychology, 20*, 359–368.

Durham, R. C., Allan, T., & Hackett, C. A. (1997). On predicting improvement and relapse in generalized anxiety disorder following psychotherapy. *British Journal of Clinical Psychology, 36*, 101–119.

Fals-Stewart, W., Birchler, G. R., & O'Farrell, T. J. (1996). Behavioral couples therapy for male substance-abusing patients: Effects on relationship adjustment and drug-using behavior. *Journal of Consulting and Clinical Psychology, 64*, 959–972.

Fals-Stewart, W., O'Farrell, T. J., Birchler, G. R., Cordova, J., & Kelley, M. L. (2005). Behavioral couples therapy for alcoholism and drug abuse: Where we've been, where we are, and where we're going. *Journal of Cognitive Psychotherapy, 19*, 229–246.

Fals-Stewart, W., O'Farrell, T. J., & Hooley, J. M. (2001). Relapse among married or cohabiting substance-abusing patients: The role of perceived criticism. *Behavior Therapy, 32*, 787–801.

Fincham, F. D., & Rogge, R. (2010). Understanding relationship quality: Theoretical challenges and new tools for assessment. *Journal of Family Theory and Review, 2*, 227–242.

First, M. B., Spitzer, R. L., Gibbon, M., & Williams, J. B. W. (1997). *Structured Clinical Interview for DSM-IV Axis I Disorders—Clinician Version (SCID-CV)*. New York, NY: Biometrics Research Department, New York State Psychiatric Institute.

Funk, J. L., & Rogge, R. D. (2007). Testing the ruler with item response theory: Increasing precision of measurement for relationship satisfaction with the Couples Satisfaction Index. *Journal of Family Psychology, 21*, 572–583.

Haslam, N. (2007). The latent structure of mental disorders: A taxometric update on the categorical vs dimensional debate. *Current Psychiatry Reviews, 3*, 172–177.

Hendrick, S. S. (1988). A generic measure of relationship satisfaction. *Journal of Marriage and the Family, 50*, 93–98.

Heyman, R. E., Feldbau-Kohn, S. R., Ehrensaft, M. K., Langhinrichsen-Rohling, J., & O'Leary, K. D. (2001). Can questionnaire reports correctly classify relationship distress and partner physical abuse? *Journal of Family Psychology, 15*, 334–346.

Heyman, R. E., Sayers, S. L., & Bellack, A. S. (1994). Global marital satisfaction versus marital adjustment: An empirical comparison of three measures. *Journal of Family Psychology, 8,* 432–446.

Holt-Lunstad, J., Smith, T. B., & Layton, J. B. (2010). Social relationships and mortality risk: A meta-analytic review. *PLoS Medicine, 7,* e1000316.

Jacobson, N. S., Follette, W. C., Revenstorf, D., Baucom, D. H., Hahlweg, K., & Margolin, G. (1984). Variability in outcome and clinical significance of behavioral marital therapy: A reanalysis of outcome data. *Journal of Consulting and Clinical Psychology, 52,* 497–504.

Kung, W. W., & Elkin, I. (2000). Marital adjustment as a predictor of outcome in individual treatment of depression. *Psychotherapy Research, 10,* 267–278.

Locke, H. J., & Wallace, K. M. (1959). Short marital adjustment and prediction tests: Their reliability and validity. *Marriage and Family Living, 21,* 251–255.

Norton, R. (1983). Measuring marital quality: A critical look at the dependent variable. *Journal of Marriage and the Family, 45,* 141–151.

O'Leary, K. D., & Vega, E. M. (2005). Can partner aggression be stopped with psychosocial interventions? In W. M. Pinsof & J. L. Lebow (Eds.), *Family psychology: The art of the science* (pp. 243–263). New York: Oxford University Press.

Powers, M. B., Vedel, E., & Emmelkamp, P. M. (2008). Behavioral couples therapy (BCT) for alcohol and drug use disorders: A meta-analysis. *Clinical Psychology Review, 28,* 952–962.

Ruscio, J., Haslam, N., & Ruscio, A. M. (2006). *Introduction to the taxometric method: A practical guide.* Mahwah, NJ: Lawrence Erlbaum Associates Publishers.

Sabatelli, R. M. (1988). Measurement issues in marital research: A review and critique of contemporary survey instruments. *Journal of Marriage and the Family, 50,* 891–915.

Schmidt, N. B., Kotov, R., & Joiner, T. E. (2004). *Taxometrics: Toward a new diagnostic scheme for psychopathology.* Washington, DC: American Psychological Association.

Schumm, W. R., Nichols, C. W., Schectman, K. L., & Grigsby, C. C. (1983). Characteristics of responses to the Kansas Marital Satisfaction Scale by a sample of 84 married mothers. *Psychological Reports, 53,* 567–572.

Snyder, D. K. (1997). *Manual for the Marital Satisfaction Inventory–Revised.* Los Angeles, CA: Western Psychological Services.

Snyder, D. K., Castellani, A. M., & Whisman, M. A. (2006). Current status and future directions in couple therapy. *Annual Review of Psychology, 57,* 317–344.

Snyder, D. K., Cepeda-Benito, A., Abbott, B. V., Gleaves, D. H., Negy, C., Hahlweg, K., & Laurenceau, J. P. (2004). Cross-cultural applications of the Marital Satisfaction Inventory–Revised (MSI–R). In M. E. Maruish (Ed.), *Use of psychological testing for treatment planning and outcomes assessment* (3rd ed., pp. 603–623). Mahwah, NJ: Erlbaum.

Spanier, G. B. (1976). Measuring dyadic adjustment: New scales for assessing the quality of marriage and similar dyads. *Journal of Marriage and the Family, 38,* 15–28.

Spanier, G. B. (1989). *Dyadic Adjustment Scale manual.* North Tonawanda, NY: Multi-Health Systems, Inc.

Swets, J. A., Dawes, R. M., & Monahan, J. (2000). Psychological science can improve diagnostic decisions. *Psychological Science in the Public Interest, 1,* 1–26.

Waller, N. G., & Meehl, P. E. (1998). *Multivariate taxometric procedures: Distinguishing types from continua.* Thousand Oaks, CA: Sage Publications.

Whisman, M. A. (2001). Marital adjustment and outcome following treatments for depression. *Journal of Consulting and Clinical Psychology, 69,* 125–129.

Whisman, M. A. (2006). Role of couples relationships in understanding and treating mental disorders. In S. R. H. Beach, M. Z. Wamboldt, N. J. Kaslow, R. E. Heyman, M. B. First, L. G. Underwood, & D. Reiss (Eds.), *Relational processes and DSM-V: Neuroscience, assessment, prevention, and intervention* (pp. 225–238). Washington, DC: American Psychiatric Publishing, Inc.

Whisman, M. A., Beach, S. R. H., & Snyder, D. K. (2008). Is marital discord taxonic and can taxonic status be assessed reliably? Results from a national representative sample of married couples. *Journal of Consulting and Clinical Psychology, 76,* 745–755.

Whisman, M. A., Snyder, D. K., & Beach, S. R. H. (2009). Screening for marital and relationship discord. *Journal of Family Psychology, 23,* 247–254.

World Health Organization. (1992). *International Statistical Classification of Diseases and Related Health Problems, tenth revision (ICD-10).* Geneva, Switzerland: Author.

World Health Organization. (1997). *Multiaxial presentation of the ICD-10 for use in adult psychiatry.* Cambridge: Cambridge University Press.

6

Defining Partner Relational Problems in the Arab Region

Brigitte Khoury and Yasmine Fayad

CURRENT DEFINITIONS OF A PARTNER RELATIONAL PROBLEM

The tenth edition of the International Classification of Diseases (ICD-10; World Health Organization, 1992) and the fourth edition of the *Diagnostic and Statistical Manual of Mental Disorders* (*DSM-IV-TR*; American Psychiatric Association, 2000) briefly address couple relationship problems.

ICD-10 defines "problems in relationship with spouse or partner" (ICD-10 code Z63.0) as "discord between partners resulting in severe or prolonged loss of control, in generalization of hostile or critical feelings or in a persisting atmosphere of severe interpersonal violence (hitting or striking)" (World Health Organization, 2007). These problems are addressed as an Axis III contextual stressor when they significantly affect the current status of the patient or are of relevance to the treatment of the existing mental illness (World Health Organization, 1997).

DSM-IV-TR describes "a partner relational problem" (*DSM-IV-TR* code V61.1) as "a pattern of interaction between spouses or partners characterized by negative communication (e.g., criticisms), distorted communication (e.g., unrealistic expectations), or noncommunication (e.g., withdrawal) that is associated with clinically significant impairment in individual or family functioning or the development of symptoms in one or both partners" (p. 737).When this problem is the main focus of clinical attention, it should be listed on Axis I. Otherwise it may be addressed as an Axis IV psychosocial stressor.

The *DSM-IV* conceptualization has been extensively criticized and represents a marginal improvement over previous *DSM* versions. First, it is based on the assumption that communication plays an exclusive role in the etiology of partner relational problems. Nevertheless, to date, this assumption has not been supported by adequate empirical evidence (Snyder, Heyman, & Haynes, 2009). Second, the provided criteria describing couple interactions are very general and lack specificity (Beach, Wamboldt, Kaslow, Heyman, & Reiss, 2006). Third, this conceptualization is focused on pathological patterns of couple interactions (e.g., negative communication, distorted communication, and noncommunication) and excludes nonsymptomatic deficits such as lack of positive emotions and experiences that usually characterize increasing intimacy in relationships (Snyder et al., 2009).

In response to the lack of empirically driven, clear, and specific diagnostic criteria for partner relational problem, Heyman et al. (2009) suggested the following criteria: Criterion A, which refers to a subjective sense of relationship dissatisfaction experienced by one or both partners over the past month and Criterion B, which refers to the significant impact of relational dissatisfaction as indicated by the presence of at least one of the behavioral, cognitive, or affective symptoms listed in Table 6.1 (Snyder et al., 2009).

The definitions of partner relational problems in the *DSM-IV* and those proposed for *DSM-V* were developed from a Western perspective that may limit applicability of these definitions to Arab couples due to significant cultural differences existing between Western and Arab cultures. Western individuals tend to perceive themselves as well-differentiated, unique,

TABLE 6.1 Proposed Criteria for Partner Relational Discord Syndrome in *DSM-V*

During the past month, a subjective sense of relationship dissatisfaction (Criterion A) was noted by one or both partners and was accompanied by at least one significant symptom in the interactional, cognitive, or affective domains (Criteria B–D).

A. Relationship dissatisfaction
   1. Pervasive sense of unhappiness with the relationship
   2. Thoughts of divorce/separation that are more than transitory
   3. Perceived need for professional help for the relationship

B. Interactional symptoms
   1. Conflict resolutions difficulties
      a. Marked escalation of negative behavior or affect (e.g., "little" disputes quickly and frequently evolve into heated arguments)
      b. Pervasive withdrawal of interaction so that resolution is impeded. Withdrawal can be either through leaving a discussion before it is resolved or through more pervasive disconnectedness that impedes bringing up or resolving problems
   2. Other coercive exchanges:
      a. Widespread withholding of vital relationship behaviors (e.g., contributing to childcare, household responsibilities, affection)
      b. Engaging in frequent nonverbal negative behaviors not including physical aggression (e.g., "cold shoulder," angry looks)
   3. Notable lack of positive exchanges
      a. Notable lack of sharing thoughts and feelings
      b. Notable lack of sexual and nonsexual physical intimacy
      c. Notable lack of positive shared activities
      d. Notable lack of emotional and tangible social support

C. Cognitive symptoms
   1. Perceived negative intentions
      a. Negative behaviors of the partner are pervasively attributed to negative personality traits or are perceived to be done voluntarily, intentionally, or with negative intent
      b. Positive behaviors of the partner are pervasively attributed to temporary states or are perceived to be done accidentally, unintentionally, or with hidden negative intentions.
   2. Low relationship efficacy
      Low sense of efficacy that the relationship can improve (without professional help)

D. Affective symptoms. Interactions with or thoughts about the partner are frequently marked by intense and persistent levels of
   1. Anger or contempt
   2. Apathy
   3. Sadness

and independent selves (Harb & Smith, 2008; Markus & Kitayama, 1991). Individuation, independence, autonomy, self-actualization, and self-efficacy are considered markers of healthy development and functioning in the West. However, these Western ideals may mislead rather than inform assessment when applied to Arab culture, where individuals tend to construe their selves in relation to significant others and conform to larger in-groups (through political and religious memberships; Harb & Smith, 2008; Markus & Kitayama, 1991).

THE ARAB FAMILY

Individual–family interdependence is predominant in the Arab world due to ancestral tribal heritage and is maintained by religious, sociopolitical, and economic factors (Dwairy, 2006).

Religious ideology, which greatly influences the everyday life of Arabs, encourages interdependence with the family-of-origin (Abu-Baker, 2003). The monotheist religions consider respecting and obeying parents as a religious duty. Islam, which is the most prevalent religion in the Arab world, urges parents to help their sons financially for marriage at a young age to prevent sexual exploration and ensure a virtuous lifestyle.

Moreover, due to sociopolitical and economic factors, Arab states do not provide their citizens with basic governmental services, maintaining individual-family interdependence (Dwairy, 2006). The family is responsible for the survival of its members and is the main source of social and economic support, securing education, jobs, housing, and financial assistance in times of crisis. Financial dependency fosters psychological dependency. Individuals choose to submit to the family's will, norms, values, and aspirations so as not to lose vital economic and social familial support. A gender and generational hierarchy exists within the family unit according to which females and younger members should submit to the authority of males and older members (Dwairy, 2006).

ARAB PERSONALITY

Within this interdependent system, the boundary between the individual and the family or social group is blurred (Dwairy, 2006). Personality in the Arab world is best conceptualized as a collective construct that entails external social factors (such as social norms, values, aspirations, roles and expectations, and family authority) as well as intrapsychic factors. External cultural factors dominate intrapsychic factors and determine the behavior of individuals in the Arab world. External cultural factors are the main source of pressure in the lives of Arab individuals. Thus, individuals often suffer from interpsychic (intrafamilial) rather than intrapsychic conflicts. Given that authentic self-expression may lead to the loss of familial support and alienation, Arabs mainly use three social mechanisms to cope with these external demands: *mosayara*, *istighaba*, and identification with the oppressor. *Istighaba* and *mosayara*, are complementary in that one does what the other prohibits. *Istighaba* allows for the ventilation of emotions to nonjudgmental sources of support. *Mosayara* entails hiding one's true feelings and expressing what others would want to hear. Identification with the oppressor occurs when the individual justifies the family's oppressive act (Dwairy, 2006).

In addition to the lack of clear boundary between the individual and the family/the collective social group, the inner world of Arabs is fused with no distinction between intrapsychic constructs such as ego, id, superego, thoughts, emotions, attitudes, and values (Dwairy, 2006). The main distinction that exists within the inner world of Arabs is between the social layer and private layer of personality. The social layer maintains interdependent relationships with the family and social approval using the social coping mechanisms of *mosayara* and identification with the oppressor. The private layer allows for authentic self-expression and the ventilation of emotions using the coping mechanism of *istighaba* (Dwairy, 2006).

THE ARAB COUPLE

Celibacy until marriage is the rule in the Arab world because premarital sex is considered a sin and a dishonorable act, especially for women (Abu-Baker, 2005; Douki, Zineb, Nacef, & Halbreich, 2007; Dwairy, 2006). However, Arab society is more lenient with men and much more concerned with the chastity of women (Abu-Baker, 2005). A woman's virginity is highly valued and considered as an indicator of her virtuousness and good upbringing. When women engage in romantic and/or sexual relationships before they get married, they run the risk of damaging their reputation and their prospects for marriage (Khoury, 2003). Some very conservative Arab families may even kill their daughters for dishonoring them in that way, which is known as honor-killing (Abu-Baker, 2005; Douki et al., 2007). In addition to being socially ostracized, these women experience a lot of guilt, dissonance, and interfamilial conflicts over dating and having sex and are at a greater risk of committing suicide (Al-Krenawi & Graham, 2006b; Douki et al., 2007; Dwairy, 2006). In traditional settings, gender segregation and early marriages have been ways to ensure celibacy and preserve women's virginity (Abu-Baker, 2003; Barakat, 1993; Bebbington, Ghubash, & Hamdi, 1993). In other less traditional settings, where romantic relationships are allowed outside marriage, close supervision of the couple by the family is undertaken to prevent sexual activity

(Abu-Baker, 2003). Thus, most of the time, emotional, sexual, and relational maturity is only achieved within marriage, especially for women. The younger the age and the lower the socioeconomic status of individuals, the greater the influence of the family-of-origin on the choice of marital partner, the age of marriage, wedding, and housing arrangements (Abu-Baker, 2003). In some traditional settings, interference of the extended family can go as far as traditionally arranging or forcing a marital union between two relatives to preserve wealth and property within the same clan (Barakat, 1993; Bebbington et al., 1993: Douki et al., 2007). Marriage in the Arab world is seen as a union of two individuals and their extended families (Abu-Baker, 2003). Sometimes, the nuclear family and the extended family live in close proximity (Abu-Baker, 2003; Bebbington et al., 1993). Privacy is nonexistent and the extended family interferes with many aspects of the couple's life, such as housing issues, family size, child-bearing, childrearing, marital problems, and divorce (Abu-Baker, 2003; Dwairy, 2006). Within the Arab couple, a gender hierarchy exists where the wife has a lower status than the husband and is dominated by him. Moreover, different marital roles are ascribed to men and women. The wife is responsible for running the household and childrearing while the husband is responsible for supporting the family financially (Abu-Baker, 2005; Dwairy, 2006). With respect to emotional and sexual intimacy, these aspects are not usually characteristic of traditional marriages. Given that discussing sexual and intimate issues is a social taboo, couples in such marriages construe love as friendship, companionship, mutual respect, and trust (Bebbington et al., 1993; Dwairy, 2006).

However, a recent study conducted by Khoury (2011) and exploring perceptions and practices of sexuality among Arab youth, has shown a slight shift in attitudes as well as behaviors in sexuality. Among a largely Lebanese sample, results showed that around 51% of young women as compared to 37% of young men perceived the issue of virginity as unimportant. In addition 33% of the females in the sample reported not being virgins anymore and having engaged in sexual intercourse. These figures seem to indicate a more liberal trend in sexuality whether in attitudes or in practices with Lebanese youth. Of course this trend cannot be generalized to the rest of the Arab world.

External Social Factors and the Well-Being of the Arab Couple

Societal structure and the system of values underlying it greatly influence the functioning and the well-being of the Arab couple (Dwairy, 2006). In the Arab culture, the boundary between the individual and the family is blurred and the impact of the extended family on the well-being of the Arab couple is considerable. Marriage is a family rather than an individual matter. The extended family interferes with the choice of marital partner and may go as far as arranging or forcing a marriage between two individuals (relatives, nonrelatives, or complete strangers). However, arranged or forced marriages are less likely to succeed. Marital conflict and domestic violence were more frequently reported in the context of consanguineous marriages or arranged marriages between two strangers (Chaleby, 1988).The extended family also plays a pivotal role in the resolution of marital difficulties (Abu-Baker, 2003). When marital problems arise, the extended family is the first to know. It intervenes immediately and tries to resolve the problem by suggesting solutions and pressuring the couple to apply them. In the case of forced or arranged marriages, the involvement of the extended family is even greater as the wife completely relies on her family to find a solution to the situation at hand. In the case of severe marital difficulties, the upset wife goes back to her parents' house and relies on her extended family to take action, especially the male figures in the family (such as the father, brothers, uncles, or cousins). However, heavy involvement of the extended family in marital affairs may be stressful, especially when the wife is not related to the family or does not have similar views concerning marriage. Moreover, the treatment of marital problems by the extended families may aggravate the situation because it is biased and does not provide the couple with the professional help needed to address deeply rooted relational dysfunction (Abu-Baker, 2003, 2005).

Family structure has been linked to psychopathology within individuals and in the relationships of Arab couples. The impact of polygamous family structure on the well-being of family members has been extensively researched during the past decade (Beitin, Allen, & Bekheet, 2010). Findings showed that polygamy is associated with poor psychosocial outcomes among women in polygamous marriages, especially among the first wives of the marriage. Al-Krenawi (1999) compared the well-being of Bedouin-Arab senior and junior wives from polygamous marriages living in Negev, Israel. Senior wives had lower self-esteem and marital satisfaction than junior wives. Usually, second marriages are not traditional or forced marriages and are based on love. This contributes to the senior wives' low self-esteem and poor relationships with their husbands. Moreover, many studies examined the psychological, marital, and family functioning of Bedouin-Arab wives in the context of polygamous and monogamous marriages from Negev, Israel. Women in polygamous marriages reported greater levels of loneliness, somatization, depression, phobia, anxiety, hostility, paranoid ideation, and impaired family functioning compared to the wives in monogamous marriages (Al-Krenawi, 2001; Al-Krenawi & Graham, 2006a; Al-Krenawi & Vered, 2008). Polygamous respondents also reported lower levels of self-esteem, life satisfaction, and marital satisfaction compared to their monogamous counterparts (Al-Krenawi, 2001; Al-Krenawi & Graham, 2006a; Al-Krenawi & Vered, 2008). Findings also revealed that polygamy is associated with poor mental health and adjustment among husbands. Al-Krenawi, Slonim-Nevo, and Graham (2006) examined Bedouin-Arab men from polygamous and monogamous families. Men in polygamous marriages were at higher risk of being unemployed. They also reported greater levels of mental health symptomatology (such as anxiety, depression, somatization, and psychotic symptoms), impairment in family functioning, marital dissatisfaction, and relational difficulties with children.

Various psychosocial trends characterizing Arab communities affect the well-being of the Arab couple and its members, especially women (Abu-Baker, 2005). First, Arab society and Arab families evaluate people's emotional expressions differently depending on their gender. Men are only allowed to express feelings that lead to actions while women are limited to the expression of emotions that reflect weakness and elicit support. Based on these gender-dependent social standards regarding emotional expression, the provision of social support differs depending on the person seeking it. Women obtain sympathy at best and end up being silenced, whereas men receive support and an immediate solution to their problems. This differential attitude toward emotional expression may generate more distress in women (Abu-Baker, 2005). Second, Arab society and the Arab family are more tolerant with men's deviant behavior than that of women. For instance, men can explore sexual relationships outside marriage without being punished, whereas women would suffer harsh consequences if they do so (such as social ostracism, honor-killing, etc.). Moreover, the husbands' transgressions are tolerated and considered normal by Arab society, whereas the wives' deviances can lead to divorce. These gender-dependent norms force women into a weaker, inferior, and helpless position compared to men and may lead to the development of gender-dependent psychological problems (Abu-Baker, 2003, 2005; Douki et al., 2007). Third, married Arab women holding multiple roles (housewife, working woman, mother) are torn between modern and traditional lifestyles (Abu-Baker, 2005; Douki et al., 2007). Although the call for gender equality in the Arab world encourages women to work and share the financial burden of the family, men are still not urged to help women in running the household and childrearing. This hypocritical adoption of modern values by the Arab society according to what is best for the collective and not the individual put women under a great deal of pressure, confusion, and psychological strain (Abu-Baker, 2005). In fact, husbands' involvement in running the household has been associated with better psychosocial health outcomes (less psychosocial distress, less marital dissatisfaction, and less overall unhappiness) among wives (Khawaja & Habib, 2007). Fourth, Arab society and Islam praise women who are submissive and obedient to their husbands. However, assuming such a subordinate position and repressing their own authority put these wives at a greater risk of developing mental illnesses and being abused (Douki et al., 2007). Indeed, increasingly liberal gender role attitudes have been associated with greater well-being and healthier spousal relations. More egalitarian gender role attitudes positively predicted psychological well-being among wives and husbands from educated Arab Israeli dual-earner families (Kulik & Rayyan, 2003). A liberal gender role orientation was also found to be associated with greater levels of provided and received spousal support or reciprocity in spousal support (Kulik & Rayyan, 2003). Haj-Yehia and Edleson (1994) investigated conflict resolution tactics among engaged Arab Palestinian men. Those, who resorted to reasoning during conflicts, were more likely to adopt egalitarian gender role attitudes. Those, who were verbally and physically abusive, were more likely to have a traditional gender role orientation toward marriage. Fifth, Arab society glorifies women who suffer in silence ("mastoura" women) and consider them as psychologically stable and mature (Abu-Baker, 2005). However, silent suffering usually preserves the nature of marital problems and even aggravates them. Marital problems become more and more complicated and chronic over the years. Enduring undesirable sexual relations adds further stress to the lives of these women. Somatic complaints are common among these women because they constitute a socially acceptable way of expressing distress and eliciting support (Abu-Baker, 2005; Douki et al., 2007). Sixth, women's social duty to be fertile and give birth to male offspring put wives under a great deal of pressure and may lead to divorce in case of infertility. Seventh, women's religious and social duty to remain a virgin before marriage and repress their sexual needs, as well as the lack of proper sexual education and female genital mutilation, increase the risk of developing sexual disorders (such as orgasmic disorders, vaginismus, and sexual desire disorder [Douki et al., 2007; Dwairy, 2006]).

Marital Problems and Divorce

The societal structure, norms, and values subject Arab wives to a great deal of pressure and contribute to the development of gender-dependent psychological problems and marital difficulties in Arab couples. Abu-Baker (2005) content analyzed reports of 90 Arab couples and divided marital problems into five categories. Marital difficulties were mainly related to various aspects of the Arab patriarchic society that strives to control women and empower men. The first category consisted of immature marriages mainly involving young couples lacking proper sexual education. Such marriages are primarily characterized by sexual problems and coercion or abuse of the young wife by the husband's extended family. The second category consisted of depressed wives who remained silent about their marital difficulties and expressed their psychological distress through somatic complaints (such as "pains in the heart," "headaches," "nerve pains," "backaches," "overall fatigue," and "an inability to stand on their feet"). The third category consisted of educated women who were unsatisfied with their marriage due to the discrepancy between their expectations of marital relationships and those of their husbands. Mismatched expectations occur in marriages where the wife's success threatens the husband's self-confidence. Clashing expectations also characterize marriages in which the wife is deeply disappointed with her husband's lack of authority, yet forced to repress her own authority. The fourth category consisted of wives who decided to break the silence after enduring marital problems for a long time in secrecy. These women are deeply disappointed with the result of being silent for so long and want a divorce or a solution to the problem. The fifth category consisted of career women and wives who were aware of their social condition and psychological suffering and wanted to improve their lives. These women struggled with the lack of independence and gender equality. They often felt misunderstood by their husbands and unfairly treated by society (Abu-Baker, 2005).

Despite the fact that marital problems can become chronic and complex throughout the years, Arab women prefer to stay in bad marriages than divorce (Dwairy, 2006). Divorce lowers the social status of Arab women and threatens their reputation given that, once divorced, they are considered looser or less inhibited and more likely to provide sexual favors. Divorced women may never marry. Moreover, in some very traditional settings, they may be forced to get married to protect their reputation, which increases their risk of ending up in another stressful marriage (Dwairy, 2006). Sometimes divorce creates a lot of hostility and animosity between the extended families of the couple, and this is very destructive when the husband and wife belong to the same family unit (Abu-Baker, 2003). Unlike Western wives who tend to divorce due to emotional and psychological reasons (such as communication problems and lack of self-fulfillment or freedom, lack of compatibility, disagreement over division of roles, no love or satisfying sex), divorce in the Arab world occurs only when the marital conflicts are unbearable and after years of suffering by the couple (Abu-Baker, 2003, 2005). Cohen and Savaya (1997) conducted an exploratory qualitative study on divorce as viewed by Israeli-Arab divorced women. Divorce was caused by severe reasons such as the spouse's substance abuse, mental illness, and/or physical abuse. Following the dissolution of the marriage, divorced women had to throw themselves into housework and childrearing as well as hide their femininity to protect their reputation. Savaya and Cohen (1998) also examined the reasons for marital breakups among Muslim Israeli Arab female divorcees. These women divorced only when marital conflicts had become overwhelmingly stressful (physical, psychological, sexual abuse, and/or mental illness of their husbands) and when the in-laws actively interfered to end the marriage. Moreover, Kulik and Klein (2010) compared Israeli Muslim-Arab women who divorced with those who remained in stressful marriages. The major marital problem reported by divorced women was domestic violence, whereas the main difficulty experienced by those who remained in bad marriages was the husband's alcoholism and addiction problem. Finally, Savaya and Cohen (2003) compared the reasons for divorce of regular divorcees and contract divorcees. Regular divorcees are those who divorced after living together and contract divorcees are those who divorced after signing the marital contract but before the actualization of the marriage (cohabitation). The reasons of contract divorces (incompatibility, poor communication, and lifestyle differences) were more emotional and psychological and less drastic than those of the regular divorces (abuse, poor commitment to the marriage and family, alcoholism, mental illness, and interference by the in-laws).

BARRIERS TO THE USE OF MENTAL HEALTH SERVICES

Despite the considerable need for professional help, Arab individuals rarely seek marital counseling or couples therapy. They primarily rely on the family or certain figures in the community (religious leaders, palm readers, and fortune tellers) to resolve their marital issues. Underutilization of mental health services in the Arab world is due to shame and stigma, financial reasons, ignorance, confidentiality issues and fear of self-disclosure, lack of mental health specialists, and the social value attached with the silent suffering of women (Abu-Baker, 2003, 2005; Al-Krenawi & Graham, 2006b; Bebbington et al., 1993). Moreover, Arab families respond to the mental health needs of men immediately while they neglect those of women. Women also conceal their needs and rarely seek therapy to avoid shame and stigma. Only when the mental illness is a significant threat to the reputation of the entire extended family, do Arab families consider therapy as a necessity (Dwairy, 2006). When Arab wives seek counseling or couples therapy, they may do it alone and fully assume the responsibility of resolving marital problems without the husbands' involvement in the process of therapy (Abu-Baker, 2005). Based on clinical experience with Arab couples, it is quite common that the therapist/counselor personally asks the husband to attend therapy sessions and even tries to persuade him to do so. Savaya (1995) examined the attitudes of Arab Israeli wives toward marital and family counseling. The wives reported more accepting attitudes toward seeking counseling for issues related to the children than for those related to their husbands. Community interventions aimed at raising awareness about the importance of marital/family therapy and its advantages over traditional folk methods of dealing with marital problems are needed (Abu-Baker, 2003). Stigma may be avoided or reduced by integrating mental health services into primary care.

WESTERN DEFINITION OF PARTNER RELATIONAL PROBLEM AND ARAB CULTURE

Given that the Arab couple is a union of two individuals highly enmeshed with each other and with their extended families, various conclusions can be drawn regarding the validity of the current definitions of a partner relational problem in Arab culture.

With respect to ICD-10 definition of "problems in relationship with spouse or partner" as "discord between partners resulting in severe or prolonged loss of control, in generalization of hostile or critical feelings or in a persisting atmosphere of severe interpersonal violence (hitting or striking)," two important cultural issues need to be taken into account. First, this definition is a description of couple relationship difficulties that may not typically occur in Arab couples. A discord resulting "in severe or prolonged loss of control" or "in generalization of hostile or critical feelings" may not be characteristic of Arab marriages in traditional contexts, where wives are expected to be submissive and obedient (Douki et al., 2007). Second, "severe interpersonal violence (hitting or striking)" is common among Arab couples and wife beating is even considered legitimate in this culture (Douki et al., 2007; Douki, Nacef, Belhadj, Bouasker, & Ghachem, 2003). Therefore, Arab wives may conceal or underreport being physically abused. They may justify their husbands' abusive behavior and blame themselves using the social mechanism of identification with the aggressor (Dwairy, 2006). Other reasons may be related to financial dependence on the husband, not wanting to abandon their children, or not wanting to face the social shame of possibly being divorced (Abu-Baker, 2005; Dwairy, 2006).

The most recently suggested diagnostic criteria for a partner relational problem to be incorporated in *DSM-5* and ICD-10 are listed in Tables 6.1 (Snyder et al., 2009) and 6.2 (Chapter 8, Beach et al., this volume), respectively. Again, there are potential problems in applying the suggested *DSM-5* criteria to Arab couples, and where possible the improvements in the proposed ICD-11 criteria over *DSM-5* criteria are discussed (see Chapter 8, Beach et al., this volume).

With respect to the first manifestation of relationship dissatisfaction under Criterion A ("pervasive sense of unhappiness with the relationship") in the *DSM-5* criteria, two cultural considerations are worth mentioning. First, the Arab family and society may greatly affect a person's subjective experience of the relationship. Given that the individual in the Arab world is enmeshed with the family and the collective social net (Dwairy, 2006), a person's satisfaction with a romantic or marital relationship may be highly affected by external social factors. For instance, the family's disapproval of a potential marital partner may greatly influence the person's experience of the relationship and may lead to a breakup. Moreover, given that Arab wives tend to suppress their pain and suffer in silence (Abu-Baker, 2005), their subjective experience may be biased and may not constitute an accurate indicator of couple distress.

Second, a pervasive sense of unhappiness with the relationship may be an indicator of severe partner relational problems in Arab *married* couples. Arab wives may disregard marital difficulties for the sake of maintaining financial support, family cohesion, and social approval (Abu-Baker, 2005). However, when marital problems become severe, the distress caused by the marriage may no longer be balanced by the gratification derived from maintaining the approval of the family and society, leading to a pervasive sense of marital dissatisfaction.

With regard to the second presentation of relationship dissatisfaction under Criterion A in the *DSM-5* criteria, "Thoughts of divorce that are more than transitory" may also be considered

TABLE 6.2 Proposed Guidelines for Partner Relationship Problems in ICD-11 (Z61.0)

Substantial and sustained dissatisfaction with the intimate relationship (e.g., pervasive unhappiness with the relationship, significant thoughts of divorce/separation)
Dissatisfaction is associated with disturbance in at least one major area of functioning, such as:
☐ Behavior (e.g., persistent and intense conflicts, pervasive withdrawal or neglect, lack of positive behaviors)
☐ Cognition (e.g., pervasive negative attributions of partner's intent)
☐ Emotion (e.g., persistent and intense anger, sadness, or apathy)
☐ Physical health (e.g., medically unexplained pain and other physical symptoms)
☐ Interpersonal interaction (e.g., social isolation, decreased involvement in social activities)
☐ Major life role activities (e.g., work, school, caregiving)

Note: This category (Z61.0) does not include any form of partner maltreatment codes (Z61.1, Z61.2, Z61.3, Z61.4, Z61.5).

an indicator of severe marital difficulties in an Arab context. Divorce is not approved of by Arab society unless the marriage is unbearably stressful (Abu-Baker, 2003, 2005). Moreover, divorce threatens the reputation and social status of Arab women (Dwairy, 2006). Given that maintaining family cohesion and meeting society's expectations are major concerns among Arabs, divorce is sought as the last resort when the couple becomes severely dysfunctional (Cohen & Savaya, 1997; Kulik & Klein, 2010; Savaya & Cohen, 1998). Therefore, because it is a step of last resort, thoughts of divorce may not be a sensitive indicator of marital problems among Arab couples and may be best considered a marker of severity rather than a diagnostic requirement for partner relational problems in the context of Arab culture.

The third presentation of relationship dissatisfaction described in the proposed *DSM-5* criteria as "perceived need of professional help for the relationship" needs to be more specific to the Arab culture. Arab couples do not often seek professional assistance and mainly rely on traditional methods to resolve their issues. They primarily seek the help of the extended family and important people or religious figures in the community (Abu-Baker, 2003). It may be more useful to specifically consider culturally specific forms of help-seeking as one of the presentations of "substantial and sustained disatisfaction with the intimate relationship" in Arab culture.

Therefore, with respect to the subjective criterion in the proposed *DSM-5* criteria (Criterion A, "relationship dissatisfaction"), defining relationship dissatisfaction in three specific ways restricts the cross-cultural applicability of the criterion. Hence, the use of a more general subjective criterion in the proposed ICD-11 guidelines ("substantial and sustained dissatisfaction with the intimate relationship") is more likely to be appropriate in Arab culture and possibly other non-Western cultural settings.

With respect to conflict resolution difficulties (under Criterion B in the *DSM-5* criteria, "interactional symptoms"), it is worth mentioning that communication in Arab couples is not characterized by authentic self-expression (Dwairy, 2006). Direct communication is not welcomed in the Arab world, especially for women. Nonegalitarian traditional gender roles put the wives in an inferior and helpless position compared to their husbands. Arab women, in traditional settings, tend to adopt a submissive and self-effacing attitude, are less likely to communicate with their husbands in a critical, confrontational, or threatening way, and are more likely to withdraw. Moreover, given that Arab society glorifies women who endure marital difficulties in silence, Arab wives may remain silent about their suffering to earn the respect of others in their community (Abu-Baker, 2005). Given these cultural considerations, conflict resolution difficulties that involve a "marked escalation of negative behavior or affect (e.g., "little" disputes quickly and frequently evolve into heated arguments)" may not be typical of Arab couples, especially in traditional settings and, when present, may indicate severe relational problems. On the other hand, withdrawal may be the norm among Arab wives, and when present, may not necessarily be indicative of relationship difficulties. Again, the more general behavioral criterion proposed in the ICD-11 is more likely to be compatible with likely presentations of interactional dysfunction among Arab couples.

With respect to cognitive symptoms (Criterion C), "perceived negative intentions" and "low relationship efficacy" may not be sensitive indicators of cognitive disturbance among Arab couples. Arabs tend to believe in predetermined fate and attribute behavior to external rather than internal factors (Dwairy, 2006). Moreover, they tend to expect problems to get resolved by external forces (Dwairy, 2006). Therefore, reports of "perceived negative intentions" and "low relationship efficacy" may not be common among distressed Arab couples and the absence of such symptoms may not necessarily rule out the presence of cognitive dysfunction. Thus, the broader cognitive criterion in the ICD-11 guidelines seems to be more appropriate for the assessment cognitive dysfunction in an Arab context.

Regarding affective symptoms (Criterion D), a few cultural aspects related to the expression of emotions are worth mentioning. First, the mind/body and the individual/others distinctions do not hold in Arab culture. Arab individuals when asked about their emotions, may not differentiate between their feelings and those of significant others. They may also not distinguish between feelings and other internal constructs (such as physical sensations, thoughts, values, etc.) fusing them altogether (Dwairy, 2006). Second, Arabs tend to express emotional distress using somatic metaphors (Al-Krenawi & Graham, 2000; Okasha, 1999). Hence, clinicians should differentiate between physical complaints that are purely somatic and those that serve as metaphoric expressions of emotional distress. Third, due to gender-dependent norms regarding emotional expression, Arab women may tend to express emotions that elicit support, such as sadness, whereas Arab men may express emotions that lead to action, such as anger or contempt (Abu-Baker, 2005). Finally, the expression of certain emotions, especially those that are usually unwelcomed by Arab society, may not occur unless in a treatment setting when there is enough rapport between the patient and the clinician.

Moreover, a few additional assessments are needed to enhance the cultural relevance of the proposed *DSM-5* criteria in an Arab context. First, given that the mind/body as well as the individual/family distinctions do not hold in Arab culture, the manifestation of a partner relational problem may also involve somatic and interpersonal in addition to behavioral, cognitive, and affective symptoms (Dwairy, 2006). Therefore, it is valuable for cross-cultural applicability that a criterion for somatic symptoms ("physical health") and a criterion for interpersonal functioning ("interpersonal interaction") were added to the diagnostic guidelines for ICD-11. In fact, somatic complaints are very common among Arab women and constitute a socially acceptable way of expressing psychological distress (Abu-Baker, 2005). Hence, these symptoms would be relatively more common and easier to detect than intrapsychic symptoms. Second, due to the major role of the family and society in determining behavior, a full assessment of contextual factors (the level of individual-family interdependence/independence, traditional/liberal gender roles, household roles, cultural beliefs and values, intrafamilial conflicts or sources of external pressures, intrafamilial coalitions or sources of support, status of the client in the family, efficiency of social coping mechanisms, etc.) is necessary to guide the treatment.

CONCLUSION

As can be seen in the direct comparison of the adequacy of criterion sets from *DSM-5* and ICD-11, the criteria proposed in the context of the ICD-11 broaden the scope of the assessment to allow a more culturally sensitive assessment of relationship functioning in the Arab world. It seems likely that this will prove true more generally. The consequence is that more specific interview questions and specific screening questionnaires may need to be developed in each specific cultural setting, but the broad guidelines proposed for ICD-11 seem well able to guide assessment of marital problems in the Arab world as well as in many other non-Western settings. Moreover, with the addition of criteria to assess somatic and interpersonal symptoms, ICD-11 guidelines for the diagnosis of a partner relational problem is more inclusive of the various possible manifestations of couple distress in Arab culture and, hence, are more culturally sensitive. Finally, more research is needed to examine the manifestation of partner relational problems in different samples from the Arab world given the cultural diversity that exists within the region.

REFERENCES

Abu-Baker, K. (2003). Marital problems among Arab families: Between cultural and family therapy interventions. *Arab Studies Quarterly, 25*(4), 53–74.

Abu-Baker, K. (2005). The impact of social values on the psychology of gender among Arab couples: A view from psychotherapy. *Israel Journal of Psychiatry & Related Sciences, 42*(2), 106–115.

Al-Krenawi, A. (1999). Women of polygamous marriages in primary health care centers. *Contemporary Family Therapy: An International Journal, 21*(3), 417–430.

Al-Krenawi, A. (2001). Women from polygamous and monogamous marriages in an out-patient psychiatric clinic. *Transcultural Psychiatry, 38*(2), 187–199.

Al-Krenawi, A., & Graham, J. R. (2000). Culturally sensitive social work practice with Arab clients in mental health settings. *Health & Social Work, 25*(1), 9–22.

Al-Krenawi, A., & Graham, J. R. (2006a). A comparison of family functioning, life and marital satisfaction, and mental health of women in polygamous and monogamous marriages. *International Journal of Social Psychiatry, 52*(1), 5–17.

Al-Krenawi, A., & Graham, J. R. (2006b). Inshallah, family, gender roles, and other issues affecting mental health and therapy for Palestinian Arab Israelis. In J. Kuriansky (Ed.), *Terror in the Holy Land* (1st ed., pp. 217–227). Westport: Praeger Publishers.

Al-Krenawi, A., Slonim-Nevo, V., & Graham, J. R. (2006). Polygyny and its impact on the psychosocial well-being of husbands. *Journal of Comparative Family Studies, 37*(2), 173–189.

Al-Krenawi, A., & Vered, S. N. (2008). The psychosocial profile of Bedouin Arab women living in polygamous and monogamous marriages. *Families in Society, 89*(1), 139–149.

American Psychiatric Association. (2000). *Diagnostic and statistical manual of mental disorders* (revised 4th ed.). Washington, DC: Author.

Barakat, H. I. (1993). *The Arab world: Society, culture, and state.* Los Angeles, CA: University California Press.

Beach, S. R. H., Wamboldt, M. Z., Kaslow, N. J., Heyman, R. E., & Reiss, D. (2006). Relational processes and mental health: A bench to bedside dialogue to guide *DSM-V*. In S. R. H. Beach, M. Z. Wamboldt, N. J. Kaslow, R. E. Heyman, M. B. First, L. G. Underwood, & D. Reiss (Eds.), *Relational processes and DSM-V: Neuroscience, assessment, prevention and treatment* (1st ed., pp. 1–20). Washington, DC: American Psychiatric Publishing, Inc.

Bebbington, P., Ghubash, R., & Hamdi, E. (1993). The Dubai community psychiatric survey: II. Development of the Socio-Cultural Change Questionnaire. *Social Psychiatry and Psychiatric Epidemiology,* 28, 60–65.

Beitin, B. K., Allen, K. R., & Bekheet, M. (2010). A critical analysis of Western perspectives on families of Arab descent. *Journal of Family Issues, 31,* 211–233.

Chaleby, K. (1988). Traditional Arabian marriages and mental health in a group of outpatients Saudis. *Acta Psychiatrica Scandinavica, 77*(2), 139–142.

Cohen, O., & Savaya, R. (1997). "Broken Glass": The divorced woman in Moslem Arab society in Israel. *Family processes, 36,* 225–245.

Douki, S., Nacef, F., Belhadj, A., Bouasker, A., & Ghachem, R. (2003). Violence against women in Arab and Islamic countries. *Archives of Women's Mental Health, 6*(3), 165–171.

Douki, S., Zineb, S. B., Nacef, F., & Halbreich, U. (2007). Women's mental health in the Muslim world: Cultural, religious, and social issues. *Journal of Affective Disorders, 102,* 177–189.

Dwairy, M. (2006). *Counseling and psychotherapy with Arabs and Muslims.* New York, NY: Teachers College.

Haj-Yehia, M. M., & Edleson, J. (1994). Predicting the use of conflict resolution tactics among engaged Arab Palestinian men in Israel. *Journal of Family Violence, 9*(1), 47–62.

Harb, C., & Smith, P. B. (2008). Self-construals across cultures: Beyond independence–interdependence. *Journal of Cross-Cultural Psychology, 39,* 178–197.

Heyman, R. E., Smith Slep, A. M., Beach, S. R. H., Wamboldt, M. Z., Kaslow, N. J., & Reiss, D. (2009). Relationship problems and the *DSM*: Needed improvements and suggested solutions. *World Psychiatry, 8,* 7–14.

Khawaja, M., & Habib, R. R. (2007). Husbands' involvement in housework and women's psychological health: Findings from a population-based study in Lebanon. *American Journal of Public Health, 97*(5), 860–866.

Khoury, B. (2003). *Sexuality in Lebanon: Between Omar Sharif and sex and the city.* Conference on Sexuality in the Middle East organized by Oxford University and the American University of Beirut, Beirut, Lebanon, December 3–5. Lecture.

Khoury, B. (2011). *Reproductive health and sexuality in Arab youth.* Conference on Youth, Sexuality, and Self-Expression in the Arab World organized by Issam Fares Institute and Goethe Institute-Lebanon, American University of Beirut, Beirut, Lebanon, April 6–7.
Kulik, L., & Klein, D. (2010). Swimming against the tide: Characteristics of Muslim-Arab women in Israel who initiated divorce. *Journal of Community Psychology, 38*(7), 918–931.
Kulik, L., & Rayyan, F. (2003). Spousal relations and well-being: A comparative analysis of Jewish and Arab dual-earner families in Israel. *Journal of Community Psychology, 31*(1), 57–73.
Markus, H. R., & Kitayama, S. (1991). Culture and the self: Implications for cognition, emotion, and motivation. *Psychological Review, 98*(2), 224–253.
Okasha, A. (1999). Mental health in the Middle East: An Egyptian perspective. *Clinical Psychology Review, 19*(8), 917–933.
Savaya, R. (1995). Attitudes towards family and marital counseling among Israeli Arab women. *Journal of Social Service Research, 21*(1), 35–51.
Savaya, R., & Cohen, O. (1998). A qualitative cum quantitative approach to construct definition in a minority population: Reasons for divorce among Israeli Arab women. *Journal of Sociology and Social Welfare, 25*(4), 157–179.
Savaya, R., & Cohen, O. (2003). Divorce among Moslem Arabs living in Israel: Comparison of reasons before and after the actualization of the marriage. *Journal of Family Issues, 24*, 338–351.
Snyder, D. K., Heyman, R. E., & Haynes, S. N. (2009). Assessing couples. In J. N. Butcher (Ed.), *Oxford handbook of personality assessment* (pp. 457–484). New York, NY: Oxford University Press.
World Health Organization. (1992). *The ICD-10 classification of mental and behavioral disorders: Clinical descriptions and diagnostic guidelines.* Geneva: Author.
World Health Organization. (1997). *Multiaxial presentation of the ICD-10 for use in adult psychiatry.* New York, NY: Cambridge University Press.
World Health Organization. (2007). *International Classification of Diseases Chapter XXI: Factors influencing health status and contact with health services (Z00–Z99).* Retrieved from http://apps.who.int/classifications/apps/icd/icd10online/index.htm?gz55.htm+z63

7

Relationship Distress: Impact on Mental Illness, Physical Health, Children, and Family Economics

Steven R. H. Beach and Mark A. Whisman

A fundamental question confronting diagnostic systems is whether it is necessary to include a description of problems in intimate relationships (i.e., relationship distress) to adequately describe factors commonly affecting mental health and mental health surveillance. Suggesting that it may be necessary, across many cultures, a satisfying marriage is one of the most important goals in life (Levinger & Huston, 1990). Marital happiness is more strongly associated with overall life satisfaction than is satisfaction in other domains, such as health, work, or children (Fleeson, 2004). When intimate relationships become distressed, the negative effects on the emotional and physical well-being of both partners can be far-reaching, with impact extending to etiology and maintenance of mental health disorders, as well as to their prevention and optimal treatment. For these reasons, and given the potential effects of relationship distress on the development, prevention, and remediation of mental health problems, enhanced assessment of intimate partner relationships seems essential to inform progress in coping with the increasing burden of mental illness worldwide. Accordingly, it is necessary to describe relationship distress more systematically and to provide guidance to those interested in enhancing public health.

Supporting the view that intimate relationships are central in the presentation of many seeking mental health services, a U.S. national survey found the most frequently cited causes of acute emotional distress were problems in intimate relationships, including divorce, separation, and other marital strains (Swindle, Heller, Pescosolido, & Kikuzawa, 2000). Other studies indicate that problems in intimate relationships are common among individuals seeking mental health services, regardless of whether they report relationship distress as their primary complaint (Lin, Goering, Offord, Campbell, & Boyle, 1996). The salience and impact of intimate relationships, like that of parenting relationships, may arise because humans are "hard-wired" to respond to problems occurring in primary family relationships (Insel & Young, 2001; Young, Francis, & Insel, 2003). This suggests that problems in intimate relationships may need to be one of the focused subcategories within the broader category of relationship problems proposed in the revised International Classification of Diseases (ICD). As we note below, studies in a number of countries have found strong associations between problems in intimate relationships and mental health outcomes (e.g., Greenstein & Davis, 2006; Lin et al., 1996; Overbeek et al., 2006), and as is suggested by Khoury and Fayad (Chapter 6, this volume), the impact of relational problems in non-Western cultural settings may be substantial as well.

Treatment of relationship distress is provided in many inpatient and outpatient mental health settings. Accordingly, clear, but flexible, guidelines for the identification of relationship distress may be useful in guiding prevention and intervention efforts, as well as identifying needs confronting those seeking services for a range of clinical and health-related disorders. Identification of the presence of intimate partner relational problems in addition to a disorder diagnosis (e.g., depression, anxiety, and other behavioral disorders) may suggest avenues for adjunctive treatment and remediation. Particularly, routine, standardized assessment of relationship distress may suggest ways to improve treatments for individual disorders, improve treatment success, and decrease the likelihood of relapse, thereby reducing the burden of mental illness and facilitate full recovery.

HOW IS RELATIONSHIP DISTRESS ASSOCIATED WITH MENTAL ILLNESS?

A first step in appreciating the potential impact of relationship distress on mental illness is understanding the mechanisms linking relationship distress with stress, decreased resilience, and the exacerbation of mental health problems. The stress generation model (Hammen, 1991) provides an overarching heuristic model that illustrates the ways in which relationship distress can become connected to various mental health problems. The model describes a circular pattern of causation between depression and the accumulation of stressful experiences. In particular, the model highlights the potential for relationship distress and symptoms of mental illness to become connected in mutually reinforcing feedback loops. In addition to providing a useful framework for integrating the broad literature on stress, social support, and depression, the stress generation framework also illustrates that individual mental health problems and relationship distress form a dynamic system with the potential to produce vicious circles. For example, persons with more symptoms of depression are less supportive toward their spouse and have lower expectations regarding support from the spouse. These negative behaviors and expectations lead to greater marital stress. Finally, completing the vicious circle, level of marital stress predicts subsequent depressive symptoms controlling for earlier symptoms (Davila, Bradbury, Cohan, & Tochluk, 1997). This demonstrates one pathway by which mental health symptoms can contribute to relationship distress that, in turn, may lead to an accumulation of additional stress and ultimately to the maintenance and/or exacerbation of symptoms. Illustrating a pathway through self-propagating processes, Joiner (2000; see also Joiner, Brown, & Kistner, 2006) highlighted excessive reassurance seeking, conflict avoidance, and withdrawal as additional factors in intimate relationships that may result from symptoms, elicit negative changes in the partner, and ultimately lead to an accumulation of stress and maintenance of symptoms. Recent research has also highlighted the role of support in producing relationship satisfaction (Pasch & Bradbury, 1998; see also Bradbury, Fincham, & Beach, 2000), suggesting that erosion of support may be another important pathway connecting relationship distress and a range of negative outcomes. For each of these pathways, a direct focus on the intimate partner relationship may be the best approach to address the self-perpetuating set of problems that maintain the disorder.

Although Hammen's (1991) stress generation model was advanced to account for associations between depression and stress, it can be expanded to account for associations between relationship functioning and other mental health problems as well. In particular, the model highlights both the role of individual problems in exacerbating partner relationship problems, as well as the role of continuing, unresolved relationship problems in prolonging or exacerbating individual problems, setting the stage for increased likelihood of recurrence and relapse of mental health problems. This perspective suggests it is possible to establish a feedback loop involving relationship distress and a particular mental or physical health problem, with the symptoms of the disorder exacerbating relationship distress even as these problems, in turn, contribute to an accumulation of stress and decrease in resilience, thereby maintaining the individual symptoms and decreasing the potential effectiveness of individual or pharmacological interventions. Interpersonal stressors are particularly important in extending and amplifying the stress generation process because they have the potential to produce greater subjective distress than do noninterpersonal stressors (Frans, Rimmo, Aberg, & Fredrikson, 2005). Given the effect of stress on mental health (e.g., Monroe, 2008), it is not surprising that stress generation effects from relationship distress may play an important role in a range of mental health problems. Additionally, this model highlights the potential for unresolved continuing relationship distress to set the stage for future recurrence and relapse. In the following sections, we elaborate aspects of this circular process by providing a selective review of research studies on the association between relationship distress and several common forms of psychopathology.

Association of Relationship Distress With Depression

Combining results across a number of studies, Whisman (2001) reported a moderate association between relationship distress and depressive symptoms for both women and men, and a significant, albeit small, gender difference in the magnitude of the association of relationship distress with symptoms of depression, with relationship distress more strongly associated with depressive symptoms for women than men. Relationship distress covaries not only with depressive symptoms but also with depressive disorders (Whisman, 2001). Likewise, in subsequent examinations of community samples there has been a robust association between concurrent relationship distress and depression (e.g., Horwtiz, Briggs-Gowan, Storfer-Isser, & Carter, 2007; Whisman, 2007).

Turning to longitudinal effects, results suggest that relationship distress may contribute to depressive symptoms over time and vice versa. For example, Beach, Katz, Kim, and Brody (2003) demonstrated longitudinal effects of relationship distress on later depressive symptoms for husbands and wives. Likewise, Davila, Karney, Hall, and Bradbury (2003) used growth curve analyses to demonstrate covariation over time between relationship distress and depressive symptoms, with a similar degree of influence going from relationship distress to depressive symptoms and from depressive symptoms to relationship distress. Similar results were obtained from a multistage stratified sample of couples from Detroit, Michigan, among whom relationship distress was associated with increased risk of depression (McLeod & Eckberg, 1993), a population-based sample in the Netherlands among whom relationship distress was associated with increased incidence of dysthymia and major depressive episodes (Overbeek et al., 2006), and in a population-based sample of over 900 married adults who did not meet criteria for 12-month major depressive episode (MDE) at baseline, among whom relationship distress was associated with a 2.7-fold increased risk for MDE during the following 12 months (Whisman & Bruce, 1999). Similarly, intimate partner physical abuse has been found to predict increased depressive symptoms over time, even after controlling for earlier symptoms and level of relationship distress (Beach et al., 2004).

Association of Relationship Distress With Anxiety Disorders

Relationship distress is also associated with anxiety disorders. In large, population-based samples of married individuals in the United States, people with anxiety disorders reported greater relationship distress than do people without anxiety disorders (Whisman, 1999, 2007). Relationship distress has also been shown to prospectively predict the onset of anxiety disorders. In a population-based sample of 3,383 people in the Netherlands, relationship distress at baseline was associated with increased risk for first (i.e., new-case onset) and total incidence of anxiety disorders (generalized anxiety disorder, panic disorder, social phobia, agoraphobia) occurring between 1 and 3 years later (Overbeek et al., 2006). Likewise, results from a multistage stratified sample of couples from Detroit, Michigan, found that relationship distress was associated with increased risk of the onset of anxiety disorders, including panic disorder, phobias, and generalized anxiety disorder (McLeod, 1994). Likewise, Chambless et al. (2002) examined the association between intimate partner interaction and anxiety disorders in a study that used both self-report and observational methods to evaluate the intimate partner communication of women with agoraphobia. Results indicated that couples in which the wife was agoraphobic were less likely than control couples to engage in positive problem solution. Furthermore, compared to husbands of control couples, husbands of women with agoraphobia were more critical of their wives; husbands of agoraphobic women did not, however, differ from husbands of control couples in terms of supportiveness.

Association of Relationship Distress With Other Psychiatric Conditions

There is also a sizable body of literature linking relationship distress with a broad category of psychiatric disorders in large and representative community samples. For example, in a large population-based community sample from Ontario, Canada, 24.5% of people with an active (i.e., 12-month) psychiatric disorder reported troubled relationships with their spouse compared to 8.9% of people without a psychiatric disorder (Goering, Lin, Campbell, Boyle, & Offord, 1996). In a reanalysis of the same data, it was found that in comparison to troubled relationships with relatives or friends, not getting along with one's spouse was more strongly associated with psychiatric disorders (Whisman, Sheldon, & Goering 2000). Furthermore, results from a population-based sample of married individuals from New Haven, Connecticut, found that people without a psychiatric disorder reported significantly more active and satisfying interactions in intimate partner relationships than did people with any disorder (Fredman, Weissman, Leaf, & Bruce, 1988). In a stratified random community sample of individuals, intimate partner relationship problems were associated with sexual dysfunctions in women, but not in men (Dunn, Croft, & Hackett, 1999). In a large population-based sample of over 2,500 married individuals from the United States, a categorical measure of relationship distress was associated with a 3.1-fold increased risk for mood disorders, a 2.5-fold increased risk for anxiety disorders, and a 2.0-fold increased risk for substance use disorders (Whisman, 1999; Whisman & Uebelacker, 2003). Intimate partner relational problems were also associated with 10 of 11 specific psychiatric disorders, with odds ratios ranging from 1.8 for alcohol use disorders to 5.7 for dysthymia.

In a population-based sample of over 900 married adults who did not have an active alcohol use disorder at baseline, baseline relationship distress was associated with a 3.7-fold increased risk for developing an alcohol use disorder during the following 12 months (Whisman, Uebelacker, & Bruce, 2006). Furthermore, the association between baseline intimate partner relational problems and alcohol use disorders remained significant when controlling for demographic variables and history of the disorder. Likewise, relationship discord, and not relationship dissolution (e.g., divorce), was found to predict the incidence of mood, anxiety, and substance use disorders (Overbeek et al., 2006), and a study of African American women showed that relationship discord was a risk factor for suicide attempts (Kaslow, Thompson, Brooks, & Twomey, 2000). Among individuals with bipolar disorder, patients who were more distressed by relatives' criticisms had greater depression and fewer well days (Miklowitz, Wisniewski, Miyahara, Otto, & Sachs, 2005), and this pattern is associated with cycles of negative interaction that increase stress for all members of the family (Miklowitz, 2004).

Relationship distress is increasingly recognized as an important predictor of maintenance following treatment gains for psychiatric conditions (e.g., Fals-Stewart, O'Farrell, & Hooley, 2001), and couple-based therapy is increasingly recognized as an important, empirically supported, treatment when relationship distress is an element of the presenting picture for psychiatric conditions, including depression (Barbato & D'Avanzo, 2008) and alcohol use disorders (Powers, Vedel, & Emmelkamp, 2008).

Association of Relationship Distress With General Distress and Impairment

In addition to mental disorders, investigators have evaluated whether relationship distress is associated with more global measures of distress and impairment. Specifying the impact of relationship distress on global measures of distress and impairment provides another window on the importance of problems in intimate relationships for the revision of the ICD.

As with the research on mental health problems, investigators have recently begun to evaluate the association between relationship distress and distress and impairment using nationally representative samples. For example, in a population-based sample of over 2,500 married and cohabiting individuals, relationship distress was associated with greater psychological distress, greater likelihood of suicide ideation, poorer perceived physical health, greater social impairment in relationships with relatives and friends, and greater work impairment (Whisman & Uebelacker, 2006). Moreover, with the exception of suicide ideation, these associations remained significant when controlling for current (i.e., 12-month) mood, anxiety, and substance use disorder, suggesting that the associations were not secondary to psychiatric disorders.

Association of Relationship Distress With Physical Health

Given the strong association of relationship distress with mental health, stress accumulation, and decreased family resilience, it is not surprising that relationship distress is also associated with physical health. For example, longitudinal data from a national sample in the United States showed that relationship distress led directly to increased physical, functional impairment and increased depressive symptoms both directly and indirectly through its impact on functional impairment (Choi & Marks, 2008). There is also a body of research showing that relationship distress is associated with a variety of negative physical health outcomes and health-related physiological processes (for a review, see Kiecolt-Glaser & Newton, 2001). For example, research has linked relationship distress with key physical outcomes, including immunological downregulation and proinflammatory response (e.g., Kiecolt-Glaser et al., 2005). This has opened the way for examination of intimate partner relational processes in the etiology and maintenance of several disease states, including heart disease, diabetes, and cancer. Of continuing interest in this literature is an apparent gender difference in the relative effect of marital status versus marital distress, with a stronger effect of marital *status* on morbidity and mortality for men than for women, but a stronger effect of marital *distress* for women than for men (Kiecolt-Glaser & Newton, 2001; Saxbe, Repetti & Nishina, 2008).

Encouraging greater attention to intimate partner relationship processes among patients with congestive heart failure, marital distress predicted 4-year survival as well as illness severity (Coyne et al., 2001). However, as with mental health problems, the relationship between physiological processes, physical health, and relationship distress may be bi-directional, with measures of physiological stress such as level of stress hormones measured in the first year of marriage predicting likelihood of subsequent divorce (Kiecolt-Glaser, Bane, Glaser, & Malarkey, 2003), and higher stress hormone reactivity in the context of problem solving predicting lower marital satisfaction 10 years later (Kiecolt-Glaser et al., 2003).

Association of Relationship Distress With Parenting Problems

Relationship distress influences both parental adjustment and parenting behavior toward children (Cummings & Davies, 2002; Erel & Burman, 1995; Krishnakumar & Buehler, 2000). Bronfenbrenner's (1986) ecological systems model emphasized the importance of understanding individuals within the multiple contexts in which they live and interact. Consistent with this model, relationship distress has received considerable attention in the research literature on parenting and child outcomes. Whereas healthy families, or families characterized by low levels of stress and conflict, have been linked to resilience and mental health and adjustment in both children and adults; unhealthy families, or families characterized by high levels of stress and conflict, have been linked to a wide range of parenting problems, such as poor discipline (Gerard, Krishnakumar, & Beuhler, 2006), increased negativity (Belsky, Youngblade, Rovine, & Vollig, 1991), and decreased warmth (Davies, Sturge-Apple, & Cummings, 2004), as well as adjustment difficulties in children, including mental illness (e.g., Cummings, Davies, & Campbell, 2000). Children from homes in which parents are experiencing high levels of conflict also demonstrate more adjustment problems (Booth & Amato, 2001). Likewise, longitudinal declines in parental marital conflict are associated with better adjustment among young adults (Amato, Loomis, & Booth, 1995). Moreover, the consequences of family conflict may persist beyond childhood and adolescence into adulthood and affect not only individual adjustment (Jones, Forehand, & Beach, 2000), but also later adult romantic relationships (Delsing, Oud, DeBruyn, & van Aken, 2003; Sabatelli & Bartle-Haring, 2003), setting the stage for transmission of the burden of mental health, physical health, and economic burden into the next generation.

An understudied aspect of the impact of relationship distress on broader family processes is the role played by paternal behavior. This is unfortunate, because intimate partner relationship conflict may often prompt paternal withdrawal (Osborne & Fincham, 1996), producing negative consequences for children's adjustment (Cummings, Goeke-Morey, & Raymond, 2004), and exacerbating conflict in the intimate partner relationship (Cowan, Cowan, Pruett, & Pruett, 2006). Recent longitudinal results suggest that paternal reports of relationship conflict are associated with decreases in positive paternal behavior toward children, and decreased child emotional security, which in turn predicts later internalizing and externalizing behavior by the child (Schacht, Cummings, & Davies, 2009).

As noted above, relationship distress may contribute to depression and other forms of psychopathology in parents, providing an additional indirect pathway from relationship distress to child outcomes. Parental depression and other mental health problems can also contribute to a range of parenting difficulties, including greater withdrawal and negative parenting (Lovejoy, Gracyk, O'Hare, & Neuman, 2000). Completing the potential for a vicious circle in this context, difficulties in the parent–child relationship can subsequently feed back to increase the parent's symptoms of poor mental health (Beach, Lei, Brody, Simons, Cutrona, & Philibert, 2012).

Association of Relationship Distress With Divorce and Marital Dissolution

Marital distress predicts divorce, which in turn is strongly associated with increases in symptoms of depression for both men and women (Wade & Pevalin, 2004), as well as child mental health outcomes. Parental divorce places offspring at risk for a wide range of negative outcomes in childhood, adolescence, and adulthood. In childhood, parental divorce is associated with internalizing and externalizing behavior problems, academic and social problems, and poor physical health (Amato, 2001; Amato & Keith, 1991; Troxel & Matthews, 2004). Experiencing parental divorce during adolescence predicts continued academic, mental health, and physical health problems, as well as risk for substance use, and teen childbearing (Hetherington et al., 1992; Hoffmann & Johnson, 1998; McLanahan, 1999). Adults who experienced parental divorce during childhood also have an increased risk for multiple mental disorders, including major depression and dysthymia, anxiety disorders, personality disorders, and alcohol and drug dependence (Kessler, Davis, & Kendler, 1997). Parental divorce also predicts lower educational attainment, occupational problems, physical health problems (including shortened lifespan), and poorer relationships with spouses, parents, and peers in adulthood.

Association of Relationship Distress With Economic Outcomes

Relationship distress is associated with problems with occupational functioning, including work loss (e.g., Forthofer, Markman, Cox, Stanley, & Kessler, 1996) and low job satisfaction (e.g., Rogers & May, 2003). This suggests the possibility that relationship distress may be related to workforce issues and economic development in a variety of ways that go beyond its effects on physical health and mental health.

Marital dissolution is associated with decreased resources for custodial parents. In the United States, divorce is associated with a nearly 40% decline in household income over the 5 years following the divorce (Sobolweski & Amato, 2005), increasing by 46% the likelihood that children in those families will grow up poor (McLanahan & Sandefur, 1994). These findings have led some to argue that promotion of marital relationships and prevention of divorce through community programs could be a cost-effective component of a broader strategy to reduce poverty—and certainly would reduce the number of children growing up in poverty in the United States (Amato & Maynard, 2007). Although these statistics represent the economic effects of marital dissolution on those in the United States, the impact will vary in countries around the world depending on social services available to custodial parents in divorcing families. At the same time, however, urbanization is increasing in many parts of the world, disrupting traditional extended family structures, and this may set the stage for rising marital dissolution rates worldwide (David, 1997). Likewise, female participation in the labor force is increasing, and this is also associated with increased likelihood of divorce (Greenstein & Davis, 2006). Accordingly, it may be that the United States provides a warning regarding the potential for the structural imbalances and social problems that can occur if public policy is not directed at supporting marital relationships as societies experience social change, particularly in those areas of the world that are experiencing rapid social change and concomitant increases in divorce (e.g., China; Wang & Zhou, 2010).

IS RELATIONSHIP ENHANCMENT/DIVORCE PREVENTION POSSIBLE?

One important function of a well-validated "relationship distress" category would be to facilitate referral for appropriate treatment and to guide public policy in support of marital success using a prevention framework. However, this function can only be effective to the extent that there are efficacious treatments and prevention programs for intimate partner relational problems. Fortunately, there are several approaches to couple therapy that have been found to be efficacious, including behavioral couple therapy, cognitive-behavioral couple therapy, emotion-focused therapy, and insight-oriented couple therapy (Snyder, Castellani, & Whisman, 2006), and at least some of these appear to be useful in the context of concurrent mental health problems (Beach & Whisman, 2011). This demonstrates considerable potential for benefit to recipients of mental health services if a category of "relationship distress" facilitated referrals of couples experiencing these problems. Similarly, community marriage education programs aimed at decreasing propensity for divorce appear to be efficacious (Stanley, Amato, Johnson, & Markman, 2006), suggesting that there is sufficient evidence to move forward with expanding dissemination efforts (Halford, Markman, & Stanley, 2008) for prevention efforts as well.

CONCLUSIONS

There are consistent links between relationship distress and the mental and physical health of adult partners and their children. These links indicate that relationship distress is implicated in the etiology and maintenance of a number of mental and physical health problems, and that treatment is likely to be less effective, and treatment gains more difficult to maintain, to the extent that relationship context is ignored (Beach & Whisman, 2011). Incorporating a well-validated category of "relationship distress" within the ICD framework will facilitate appropriate referral and better research on the consequences of referral, and will help shape relevant policy regarding prevention programs that support healthy marriage, reduce divorce, and reduce negative impacts on adults and their offspring. In particular, increased attention to relationship distress and the inclusion of a category identifying relationship distress will help efforts to better monitor and support healthy relationships while enhancing mental, physical, and economic health outcomes for adults, children, and youth.

ACKNOWLEDGMENT

We are grateful for support received from the Fetzer Institute that made the project possible.

REFERENCES

Amato, P. R. (2001). Children of divorce in the 1990s: An update of the Amato and Keith (1991) meta-analysis. *Journal of Family Psychology*, 15, 355–370.

Amato, P. R., & Keith, B. (1991). Parental divorce and adult well-being: A meta-analysis. *Journal of Marriage and Family*, *53*(1), 43–58.

Amato, P. R., Loomis, L. S., & Booth, A. (1995). Parental divorce, marital conflict, and off-spring well-being during early adulthood. *Social Forces, 73*, 895–916.

Amato, P. R., & Maynard, R. A. (2007). Decreasing nonmarital births and strengthening marriage to reduce poverty. *The Future of Children, 17*, 117–141.

Barbato, A., & D'Avanzo, B. (2008). Efficacy of couple therapy as a treatment for depression: A meta-analysis. *Psychiatric Quarterly, 79*, 121–132.

Beach, S. R. H., Katz, J., Kim, S., & Brody, G. H. (2003). Prospective effects of marital satisfaction on depressive symptoms in established marriages: A dyadic model. *Journal of Social and Personal Relationships, 20*, 355–371.

Beach, S. R. H., Kim, S., Cercone-Keeney, J., Gupta, M., Arias, I., and Brody, G. (2004). Physical aggression and depressive symptoms: Gender asymmetry in effects? *Journal of Social and Personal Relationships, 21*, 341–360.

Beach, S. R. H., Lei, M. K., Brody, G. H., Simmons, R. L., Cutrona, C., & Philibert, R. A. (2012). *DRD4* and stress generation: Transforming chronic stress into parenting stress in African American parents. *Journal of Family Psychology, 26*(1), 46–55.

Beach, S. R. H., & Whisman, M. A. (2011). Affective disorders. *Journal of Marital and Family Therapy*. doi:10.1111/j.1752-0606.2011.00243.x

Belsky, J., Youngblade, L., Rovine, M., & Vollig, B. (1991). Patterns of marital change and parent–child interaction. *Journal of Marriage and the Family, 53*, 487–498.

Booth, A., & Amato, P. R. (2001). Parental predivorce relations and offspring postdivorce well-being. *Journal of Marriage and Family, 63*, 197–212.

Bradbury, T. N., Fincham, F. D., & Beach, S. R. H. (2000). Research on the nature and determinants of marital satisfaction: A decade in review. *Journal of Marriage and the Family, 62*, 964–980.

Bronfenbrenner, U. (1986). Ecology of the family as a context for human development: Research perspectives. *Developmental Psychology, 22*, 723–742.

Chambless, D. L., Fauerbach, J. A., Floyd, F. J., Wilson, K. A., Remen, A. L., & Renneberg, B. (2002). Marital interaction of agoraphobic women: A controlled, behavioral observation study. *Journal of Abnormal Psychology, 111*, 502–512.

Choi, H., & Marks, N. F. (2008). Marital conflict, depressive symptoms, and functional impairment. *Journal of Marriage and Family, 70*, 377–390.

Cowan, C. P., Cowan, P. A., Pruett, M. K., & Pruett, K. (2006). An approach to preventing coparenting conflict and divorce in low income families: Strengthening couple relationships and fostering father involvement. *Family Process, 46*(1), 109–121.

Coyne, J. C., Rohrbaugh, M. J., Shoham, V., Sonnega, J. S., Nicklas, J. M., & Cranford, J. A. (2001). Prognostic importance of marital quality for survival of congestive heart failure. *The American Journal of Cardiology, 88*(5), 526–529.

Cummings, E. M., & Davies, P. T. (2002). Effects of marital conflict on children: Recent advances and emerging themes in process-oriented research. *Journal of Child Psychology and Psychiatry and Allied Disciplines, 43*, 31–63.

Cummings, E. M., Davies, P. T., & Campbell, S. B. (2000). *Developmental psychopathology and family process: Theory, research, and clinical implications*. New York, NY: Guilford Press.

Cummings, E. M., Goeke-Morey, M. C., & Raymond, J. (2004). Fathers in family context: Effects of marital quality and marital conflict. In M. E. Lamb (Ed.), *The role of father in child development* (pp. 196–221). Hoboken, NJ: John Wiley & Sons.

David, L. (1997). Correlates of worldwide divorce rates. *Journal of Divorce and Remarriage, 26*, 215–219.

Davies, P., Sturge-Apple, M., & Cummings, E. (2004). Interdependencies among interparental discord and parenting practices: The role of adult vulnerability and relationship perturbations. *Development and Psychopathology, 16*, 773–797.

Davila, J., Bradbury, T. N., Cohan, C. L., & Tochluk, S. (1997). Marital functioning and depressive symptoms: Evidence for a stress generation model. *Journal of Personality and Social Psychology, 73*, 849–861.

Davila, J., Karney, B. R., Hall, T. W., & Bradbury, T. N. (2003). Depressive symptoms and marital satisfaction: Within-subject associations and the moderating effects of gender and neuroticism. *Journal of Family Psychology, 17*, 557–570.

Delsing, M. J. M. H., Oud, J. H. L., DeBruyn, E. E. J., & van Aken, M. A. G. (2003). Current and recollected perceptions of family relationships: The social relations model approach to members of three generations. *Journal of Family Psychology, 17*, 445–459.

Dunn, K. M., Croft, P. R., & Hackett, G. I. (1999). Association of sexual problems with social, psychological, and physical problems in men and women: A cross sectional population survey. *Journal of Epidemiology and Community Health, 53*, 144–148.

Erel, O., & Burman, B. (1995). Interrelatedness of marital relations and parent–child relations: A meta-analytic review. *Psychological Bulletin, 118*, 108–132.

Fals-Stewart, W., O'Farrell, T. J., & Hooley, J. M. (2001). Relapse among married or cohabiting substance-abusing patients: The role of perceived criticism. *Behavior Therapy, 32*, 787–801.

Fleeson, W. (2004). The quality of American life at the end of the century. In O. G. Brim, C. D. Ryff, & R. C. Kessler (Eds.), *How healthy are we: A national study of well-being at midlife*. Chicago, IL: University of Chicago Press.

Forthofer, M. S., Markman, H. J., Cox, M., Stanley, S., & Kessler, R. C. (1996). Associations between marital distress and work loss in a national sample. *Journal of Marriage and Family, 58*, 597–605.

Frans, O., Rimmo, P. A., Aberg, L., & Fredrikson, M. (2005). Trauma exposure and posttraumatic stress disorder in the general population. *Acta Psychiatrica Scandinavica, 111*, 280–291.

Fredman, L., Weissman, M. M., Leaf, P. J., & Bruce, M. L. (1988). Social functioning in community residents with depression and other psychiatric disorders: Results of the New Haven Epidemiologic Catchment Area study. *Journal of Affective Disorders, 15*, 103–112.

Gerard, J., Krishnakumar, A., & Beuhler, C. (2006). Marital conflict, parent–child relations, and youth maladjustment: A longitudinal investigation of spillover effects. *Journal of Family Issues, 27*, 951–975.

Goering, P., Lin, E., Campbell, D., Boyle, M. H., & Offord, D. R. (1996). Psychiatric disability in Ontario. *Canadian Journal of Psychiatry, 41*, 564–571.

Greenstein, T. N., & Davis, S. N. (2006). Cross-national variations in divorce: Effects of women's power, prestige and dependence. *Journal of Comparative Family Studies, 37*, 253–273.

Halford, W. K., Markman, H. J., & Stanley, S. (2008). Strengthening couples' relationships with education: Social policy and public health perspectives. *Journal of Family Psychology, 22*(4), 497–505. doi:10.1037/a0012789

Hammen, C. (1991). *Depression runs in families: The social context of risk and resilience in children of depressed mothers*. New York, NY: Springer-Verlag.

Hetherington, E. M., Clingempeel, W. G., Anderson, E. R., Deal, J. E., Stanley-Hagan, M., Hollier, E. A., & Lindner, M. S. (1992). Coping with marital transitions: A family systems perspective. *Monographs of the Society for Research in Child Development, 57*(2–3), 1–14. doi:10.1111/j.1540–5834.1992.tb00300.x

Hoffmann, J. P., & Johnson, R. A. (1998). A national portrait of family structure and adolescent drug use. *Journal of Marriage and Family, 60*(3), 633–645.

Horwitz, S. M., Briggs-Gowan, M. J., Storfer-Isser, A., & Carter, A. S. (2007). Prevalence, correlates, and persistence of maternal depression. *Journal of Women's Health, 16*, 678–691.

Insel, T. R., & Young, L. J. (2001). The neurobiology of attachment. *Nature Reviews Neuroscience*, 2(2), 129–136.

Joiner, T. E. (2000). Depression's vicious scree: Self-propagating and erosive processes in depression chronicity. *Clinical Psychology: Science and Practice, 7*, 203–218.

Joiner, T., Brown, J., & Kistner, J. (Eds.). (2006). *The interpersonal, cognitive, and social nature of depression*. Mahwah, NJ: Erlbaum

Jones, D. J., Forehand, R., & Beach, S. R. H. (2000). Maternal and paternal parenting during adolescence: Forecasting early adult psychosocial adjustment. *Adolescence, 35*, 513–530.

Kaslow, N. J., Thompson, M. P., Brooks, A. E., & Twomey, H. B. (2000). Ratings of family functioning of suicidal and nonsuicidal African American women. *Journal of Family Psychology, 14*, 585–599.

Kessler, R. C., Davis, C. G., & Kendler, K. S. (1997). Childhood adversity and adult psychiatric disorder in the US National Comorbidity Survey. *Psychological Medicine, 27*, 1101–1119.

Kiecolt-Glaser, J. K., Bane, C., Glaser, R., & Malarkey, W. B. (2003). Love, marriage, and divorce: Newlyweds' stress hormones foreshadow relationship changes. *Journal of Consulting and Clinical Psychology, 71*, 176–188.

Kiecolt-Glaser, J. K., Loving, T. J., Stowell, J. R., Malarkey, W. B., Lemeshow, S., Dickinson, S. L., & Glaser, R. (2005). Hostile marital interactions, proinflammatory cytokine production, and wound healing. *Archives of General Psychiatry, 62*, 1377–1384.

Kiecolt-Glaser, J. K., & Newton, T. (2001). Marriage and health: His and hers. *Psychological Bulletin, 127*, 472–503.

Krishnakumar, A., & Buehler, C. (2000). Interparental conflict and parenting behaviors: A meta-analytic review. *Family Relations, 49*, 25–44.

Levinger, G., & Huston, T. L. (1990). The social psychology of marriage. In F. D. Fincham & T. N. Bradbury (Eds.), *The psychology of marriage* (pp. 19–58). New York: Guilford Press.

Lin, E., Goering, P., Offord, D. R., Campbell, D., & Boyle, M. H. (1996). The use of mental health services in Ontario: Epidemiologic findings. *Canadian Journal of Psychiatry, 41*, 572–577.

Lovejoy, M. C., Gracyk, P. A., O'Hare, E., & Neuman, G. (2000). Maternal depression and parenting behavior: A meta-analytic review. *Clinical Psychology Review, 20*, 561–592.

McLanahan, S. S. (1999). Father absence and children's welfare. In E. M. Hetherington (Ed.), *Coping with divorce, single parenting, and remarriage: A risk and resiliency perspective*. Mahwah, NJ: Erlbaum.

McLanahan, S., & Sandefur, G. (1994). *Growing up with a single parent: What hurts, what helps*. Cambridge, MA: Harvard University Press.

McLeod, J. D. (1994). Anxiety disorders and marital quality. *Journal of Abnormal Psychology, 103*(4), 767–776. doi:10.1037/0021–843X.103.4.767

McLeod, J. D., & Eckberg, D. A. (1993). Concordance for depressive disorders and marital quality. *Journal of Marriage & Family, 55*, 733–746.

Miklowitz, D. J. (2004). The role of family systems in severe and recurrent psychiatric disorders: A developmental psychopathology view. *Development and Psychopathology, 16*, 667–688.

Miklowitz, D. J., Wisniewski, S. R., Miyahara, S., Otto, M. W., & Sachs, G. S. (2005). Perceived criticism from family members as a predictor of the 1-year course of bipolar disorder. *Psychiatry Research, 136*(2–3), 101–111.

Monroe, S. M. (2008). Modern approaches to conceptualizing and measuring human life stress. *Annual Review of Clinical Psychology, 4*, 33–52.

Osborne, L. N., & Fincham, F. D. (1996). Marital conflict, parent–child relationships, and child adjustment: Does gender matter? *Merrill-Palmer Quarterly, 42*(1), 48–75.
Overbeek, G., Vollebergh, W., de Graaf, R., Scholte, R., de Kemp, R., & Engels, R. (2006). Longitudinal associations of marital quality and marital dissolution with the incidence of *DSM-III-R* disorders. *Journal of Family Psychology, 20*, 284–291.
Pasch, L. A., & Bradbury, T. N. (1998). Social support, conflict, and the development of marital dysfunction. *Journal of Consulting and Clinical Psychology, 66*, 219–230.
Powers, M. B., Vedel, E., & Emmelkamp, P. M. (2008). Behavioral couples therapy (BCT) for alcohol and drug use disorders: A meta-analysis. *Clinical Psychology Review, 28*(6), 952–962.
Rogers, S. J., & May, D. C. (2003). Spillover between marital quality and job satisfaction: Long-term patterns and gender differences. *Journal of Marriage and Family, 65*(2), 482–495.
Sabatelli, R. M., & Bartle-Haring, S. (2003). Family-of-origin experiences and adjustment in married couples. *Journal of Marriage and Family, 65*, 159–169.
Saxbe, D. E., Repetti, R. L., & Nishina, A. (2008). Marital satisfaction, recovery from work, and diurnal cortisol among men and women. *Health Psychology, 27*, 15–25.
Schacht, P. M., Cummings, E. M., & Davies, P. (2009). Fathering in family context and child adjustment: A longitudinal analysis. *Journal of Family Psychology, 23*, 790–797.
Snyder, D. K., Castellani, A. M., & Whisman, M. A. (2006). Current status and future directions in couple therapy. *Annual Review of Psychology, 57*, 317–344.
Sobolweski, J. N., & Amato, P. R. (2005). Economic hardship in the family of origin and children's psychological well-being in adulthood. *Journal of Marriage and Family, 67*, 141–157.
Stanley, S. M., Amato, P. R., Johnson, C. A., & Markman, H. J. (2006). Premarital education, marital quality, and marital stability: Findings from a large, random, household survey. *Journal of Family Psychology, 20*, 117–126.
Swindle, R., Heller, K., Pescosolido, B., & Kikuzawa, S. (2000). Responses to nervous breakdowns in America over a 40-year period: Mental health policy implications. *American Psychologist, 55*, 740–749.
Troxel, W. M., & Matthews, K. A. (2004). What are the costs of marital conflict and dissolution to children's physical health? *Clinical Child and Family Psychology Review, 7*, 29–57.
Wade, T. J., & Pevalin, D. J. (2004). Marital transitions and mental health. *Journal of Health and Social Behavior, 45*, 155–170.
Wang, Q., & Zhou, Q. (2010). China's divorce and remarriage rates: Trends and regional disparities. *Journal of Divorce and Remarriage, 51*, 257–267.
Whisman, M. A. (1999). Marital dissatisfaction and psychiatric disorders: Results from the National Comorbidity Survey. *Journal of Abnormal Psychology, 108*, 701–706.
Whisman, M. A. (2001). The association between depression and marital dissatisfaction. In S. R. H. Beach (Ed.), *Marital and family processes in depression*. Washington, DC: American Psychological Association.
Whisman, M. A. (2007). Marital distress and *DSM-IV* psychiatric disorders in a population-based national survey. *Journal of Abnormal Psychology, 116*, 638–643.
Whisman, M. A., & Bruce, M. L. (1999). Marital distress and incidence of major depressive episode in a community sample. *Journal of Abnormal Psychology, 108*, 674–678.
Whisman, M. A., Sheldon, C. T., & Goering, P. (2000). Psychiatric disorders and dissatisfaction with social relationships: Does type of relationship matter? *Journal of Abnormal Psychology, 109*, 803–808.
Whisman, M. A., & Uebelacker, L. A. (2003). Comorbidity of relationship distress and mental and physical health problems. In D. K. Snyder & M. A. Whisman (Eds.), *Treating difficult couples: Helping clients with coexisting mental and relationship disorders* (pp. 3–26). New York, NY: Guilford Press.
Whisman, M. A., & Uebelacker, L. A. (2006). Impairment and distress associated with relationship discord in a national sample of married or cohabiting adults. *Journal of Family Psychology, 20*, 369–377.
Whisman, M. A., Uebelacker, L. A., & Bruce, M. L. (2006). Longitudinal association between marital discord and alcohol use disorders. *Journal of Family Psychology, 20*, 164–167.
Young, L. J., Francis, D. D., & Insel, T. R. (2003). *The biochemistry of family commitment and youth competence: Lessons from furry mammals* (Working Paper No. 76–18). New York, NY: Institute for American Values.

8

Practical Tools for Assessing Marital or Intimate Partner Relational Problems in Clinical Practice and Public Health Settings

Steven R. H. Beach, Mark A. Whisman, Douglas K. Snyder, and Richard E. Heyman

Enhanced surveillance of relationship problems ("relationship distress with spouse or intimate partner," ICD code Z61.0) is timely both for public health applications and for optimizing mental health referrals. Depending on circumstances and the goal of the assessment, enhanced surveillance may involve the use of brief screening tools or relatively brief, semistructured interviews. There are good reasons to enhance surveillance of marital and other similar relationship problems at the community level. Marital problems are prevalent in community studies, and the most frequently cited causes of acute emotional distress are relationship problems, including divorce, separation, and other marital strains (Swindle, Heller, Pescosolido, & Kikuzawa, 2000). Likewise, maritally distressed individuals are overrepresented among those seeking mental health services (Schonbrun & Whisman, 2010) and other types of health care (Shumway, Wampler, Dersch, & Arredondo, 2004), suggesting the potential for better planning and greater efficiency in health care utilization when individuals receive appropriate marital intervention referrals (Law & Crane, 2000). For those working in public health settings, use of repeated, brief screening tools often may be optimal to provide an overview of changes within a community, region, or nation over time, or to track the impact of public policy or special initiatives in a given area, or simply to note associations with increases or decreases in other problems or resources. At the community level, therefore, there is considerable potential for increased surveillance to benefit community health and inform policy focused on increasing community resilience.

For those working in clinic settings, brief screening tools may often provide a practical approach for informing appropriate referrals for relationship problems and thus help optimize intervention in a manner that is sensitive to the potential need for attention to concomitant relationship problems. In particular, brief reliable screening tools for assessment of marital problems can be useful in providing information that is unlikely to be forthcoming from individually focused assessments and may be of importance in understanding the course and consequences of proposed interventions. Because the presence of relationship distress predicts longitudinal changes in psychiatric symptoms (e.g., Beach, Katz, Kim, & Brody, 2003; Beach & O'Leary, 1993; Davila, Karney, Hall, & Bradbury, 2003), as well as incidence of mood, anxiety, and substance use disorders (Overbeek et al., 2006; Whisman & Bruce, 1999; Whisman, Uebelacker, & Bruce, 2006), and is associated with poorer treatment outcome for mood (e.g., Kung & Elkin, 2000; Whisman, 2001), anxiety (e.g., Durham, Allan, & Hackett, 1997), and substance use disorders (e.g., Maisto, McKay, & O'Farrell, 1998), as well as relapse and recurrence following treatment (e.g., Hooley & Teasdale, 1989; O'Farrell, Hooley, Fals-Stewart, & Cutter, 1998; Whisman, 2001), the potential importance of valid screening and referral for relationship problems in clinical settings is considerable. Underscoring the potential value of appropriate referrals, couple therapies have been shown to reduce marital problems (Snyder, Castellani, & Whisman, 2006) and continue to have a beneficial impact on relationship distress when other psychiatric problems are present (Beach & Whisman, 2012). In sum, empirical findings indicate that marital and relationship distress plays an important role in the etiology, course, and treatment of a variety of psychological disorders, and underscores the potential utility of providing those engaged in surveillance of mental and physical health outcomes with simple screening tools that will allow them to reliably assess for broad changes in prevalence or to assess the need for referral to couple-based interventions in the case of many common forms of psychopathology.

One difficulty confronting both public health epidemiology and clinical decision making regarding appropriate referrals is the dichotomous nature of the outcome to be tracked and the decision to be made. Although numerous measures exist for assessing intimate relationship distress, most of these measures assess for distress on a continuum (Snyder, Heyman, & Haynes, 2005) and provide only a limited empirical basis for dichotomous decisions regarding the presence or absence of "clinically significant" relationship impairment. Accordingly, categorizing a particular couple as "distressed" or "in need of referral" requires adoption of a specific cut-point for commonly used measures. Because only a minority of couples report being "very happy" with their marriages and the presence of a psychological disorder might be expected to increase relationship stress, it is to be expected that most couples in clinical settings will report at least some transient or focused areas of relationship problems. Although these transient or limited areas of difficulty do not preclude involving the spouse in efforts to enhance support and coping within the couple as a component of clinical interventions (e.g., Cohen et al., 2010), they do not necessarily indicate a need for referral for remediation of relationship problems. Nonetheless, once a couple develops serious, pervasive, and persistent problems in their relationship, their patterns of interaction may become self-perpetuating (Epstein & Baucom, 2002). Thus, even if relationship distress is precipitated initially in response to external stress, once established, relationship problems may persist even if the external stress is removed, suggesting that there is a point of discontinuity in relationship problems that is important to recognize for practical and conceptual purposes.

To identify the point at which relationship distress becomes qualitatively different than transient or limited relationship complaints, it is possible to utilize statistical methods designed to examine patterns of covariation among indicators to determine if they are diagnostic of either latent categories (i.e., taxa) or dimensions (Ruscio, Haslam, & Ruscio, 2006; Schmidt, Kotov, & Joiner, 2004; Waller & Meehl, 1998). Such methods are collectively referred to as taxometrics. Results from taxometric analyses of self-report inventories of marital problems suggest that dimensional variation on these measures derives, in part, from an underlying discrete entity or taxon. When such methods have been used to examine marital problems, results have suggested the presence of a marital distress taxon with a base rate of approximately 0.20 for recently married couples in the United States (Beach, Fincham, Amir, & Leonard, 2005; Whisman, Beach, & Snyder, 2008), and a higher overall base rate of approximately 0.32 in a representative sample of the U.S. population (Whisman et al., 2008). Evidence for short-term stability of the taxon and construct validity has also been obtained (Whisman et al., 2008). Further, a dichotomized measure of marital distress that used a cut-score to reflect Beach et al.'s estimated 0.20 base rate was associated with increased risk of psychiatric disorders and with elevated levels of general distress and functional impairment (Whisman & Uebelacker, 2006). These findings support earlier theorizing by Gottman (e.g., Gottman, 1994; Gottman, Swanson, & Swanson, 2002) that iterative marital processes (i.e., vicious circles) may result in discontinuities between distressed versus nondistressed couples along multiple dimensions.

These results suggest that couples can be categorized as "distressed" in a nonarbitrary manner, and that the base rate of marital distress differs depending on the sample composition in terms of years married. The results support the feasibility and the value of developing simple screening tools and clear cut-points using existing screening measures to better identify couples who are "distressed" and using such tools to guide clinical decision making.

BRIEF SCREENING INSTRUMENT FOR MARITAL OR INTIMATE PARTNER RELATIONAL PROBLEMS: INSTRUMENT PSYCHOMETRICS AND RECOMMENDATIONS FOR USE

Based on these results, and to satisfy the need for an easy-to-use, but reliable guide for referrals, two screening tools—available from Western Psychological Services—are described in a recent paper (Whisman, Snyder, & Beach, 2009). Both tools are based on the Marital Satisfaction Inventory–Revised (MSI-R; Snyder, 1997) and are meant to optimize utility in diverse clinical settings. The self-report version of the screening measure (called the MSI-B) is available from Western Psychological Services and the interview version of the measure is presented in Table 8.1.

Administration and scoring of the screen is straightforward, rendering it easy to determine whether someone is a member of the relationship distress taxon and so may be in need of referral for more detailed relationship assessment. In short, the screening device is a 10-item set of yes–no questions. If the person has a score ≥4 (out of a possible 10) he or she are classified as "probably in need of further assessment and possible intervention." It is estimated that the entire classification process should require less than 5 minutes.

When the screening instrument leads to referral for further evaluation or clinical intervention, we recommend a more extensive multimodal assessment by the treating clinician (Snyder et al., 2005) incorporating multidimensional self-report measures differentiating among sources of relationship distress; behavioral samples of partners' interactions involving problem-solving and support-providing communication; and clinical interviews delineating the functional relations among specific indicators of relationship distress, individual and relationship functioning, and sources of support or stress in the couple's broader environment.

TABLE 8.1 Marital Taxon Measure

I would like to ask you some questions about you and your relationship.	(D)	(ND)
1. Do you get pretty discouraged about your relationship sometimes?	Yes	No
2. Does your partner often fail to understand your point of view on things?	Yes	No
3. Whenever you are feeling sad, does your partner make you feel loved and happy again?	No	Yes
4. Do you and your partner spend a good deal of time together in different kinds of play and recreation?	No	Yes
5. Does your partner have too little regard sometimes for your sexual satisfaction?	Yes	No
6. Are there are some serious difficulties in your relationship?	Yes	No
7. Do minor disagreements with your partner often end up in big arguments?	Yes	No
8. Just when you need it the most, does your partner make you feel important?	No	Yes
9. Is your daily life full of interesting things to do together?	No	Yes
10. Is your sexual relationship entirely satisfactory?	No	Yes

Notes: Number of D (DISTRESSED) Responses
If <4, then NONDISTRESSED (ND)
If ≥4, then DISTRESSED

Source: Material from the MSI-B © 2008 by Western Psychological Services. Reprinted by D. Snyder with permission of the publisher, WPS, 12031 Wilshire Boulevard, Los Angeles, California 90025, USA (rights@wpspublish.com).

Cultural and Developmental Consideration in Screening

It is important to note that cultural variation is likely to be present both in key indicators of marital problems and in the subjective experience of marital problems. At a minimum, there is important variation in cultural expectations, religious guidelines, and economic outlook that can affect the impact of marital problems on other domains of life, and as well as typical expression of marital complaints, sources or focus of conflict, and the impact of relationship conflict on overall well-being (e.g., Diener, Gohm, Suh, & Oishi, 2000). These considerations suggest that optimal screeners may be somewhat different for older couples relative to younger couples, and that a focus on extended family may be more important in some cultures (Bhugra & De Silva, 2000). Accordingly, there is a continuing need to develop and validate screening tools for relationship problems that can be shown to be sensitive and valid in specific cultural and developmental contexts (Chapter 6, this volume). A number of currently available, brief marital inventories may prove useful as starting points for future development of cut-points for brief screening tools. The Kansas Marital Satisfaction Inventory (KMS; Schumm et al., 1986); the Quality of Marriage Inventory (QMI; Norton, 1983); and the Couples Satisfaction Index (CSI; Funk & Rogge, 2007) all have demonstrated good validity and ability to capture substantial variance in relationship satisfaction using brief formats. However, none has yet been examined for utility with regard to identification of taxonic membership. Nonetheless, because they are well validated, they are likely to provide a useful foundation for efforts to identify brief screening tools that can be applied readily in various cultural contexts and for couples in various developmental stages of their relationships.

Who Should Be Screened?

Converging evidence suggests that the degree of connection between relationship problems and a wide range of psychological and physical difficulties is greater than would be expected based on the degree of association found between psychological and physical well-being and distress in other close relationships (Whisman, Sheldon, & Goering, 2000). Likewise, the effects on cardiovascular, endocrine, and immunological systems suggest mechanisms for influence of marital problems with regard to a range of physical health problems (Kiecolt-Glaser & Newton, 2001) as well as associations with problem behaviors in children (Grych & Fincham, 2001). Accordingly, we recommend screening for relationship problems and recording its presence when individuals are evaluated for emotional, behavioral, or physical health problems, as well as when child behavior problems are the primary focus of clinical attention.

STRUCTURED CLINICAL DIAGNOSTIC INTERVIEW FOR MARITAL OR INTIMATE PARTNER RELATIONAL PROBLEMS

In cases where the initial screening is not clear, or the measure has not been validated for the population of interest, or greater specificity is desired, it may be appropriate to use a clinical interview to assess the couple's problems and strengths in a somewhat more extended format. The interview format can be very flexible, which is useful when adapting screening for various cultural or regional contexts, but where it is feasible, it is likely that a structured format will yield increased reliability of decision making.

Criterion Set for Relationship Distress

In conducting clinical interviews, it is useful to keep in mind the broad outlines of the criterion set for "Relationship distress with spouse or intimate partner" (Z61.0 code). In particular, it is useful to keep in mind that applying the Z61.0 code requires the presence of

Z61.0—Substantial and Sustained Dissatisfaction With the Intimate Relationship (e.g., Pervasive Unhappiness With the Relationship, Significant Thoughts of Divorce/Separation)

Dissatisfaction is associated with disturbance in at least one major area of functioning such as:

- Behavior (e.g., persistent and intense conflicts, pervasive withdrawal or neglect, lack of positive behaviors)
- Cognition (e.g., pervasive negative attributions of partner's intent)
- Emotion (e.g., persistent and intense anger, sadness, or apathy)
- Physical health (e.g., medically unexplained pain and other physical symptoms)
- Interpersonal interaction (e.g., social isolation, decreased involvement in social activities)
- Major life role activities (e.g., work, school, caregiving)

substantial and sustained dissatisfaction with a spouse or intimate partner, as well as significant disturbance in functioning.

It should be noted that this category (Z61.0) does not include any form of partner maltreatment codes (Z62.1, Z62.2, Z62.3, Z62.4, Z62.5) and should not be used to indicate partner maltreatment in the relationship. However, the Relationship Distress category may be assigned jointly with a partner maltreatment category if both apply. In addition, presentations of Z61.0 may differ based on the age of the couple. For example, younger couples may be more likely to report overt or physical forms of conflict. Sexual difficulties or lack of interest may be reported more frequently for older couples, but may be less indicative of relationship distress.

It should also be noted that relationship distress has a quite variable course with some cases becoming chronic, whereas others may show substantial improvement over time. External stressors are often associated with symptomatic relapse of relationship distress. In some cultures women will be more attentive to relationship problems and so report greater relationship distress. In addition, women's health may be more influenced by relationship distress, whereas men's health may be more influenced by relationship status. However, both men and women are affected by relationship distress.

Assessment of Relationship Distress

It is the presence of multiple indicators across multiple domains that distinguishes the syndrome of relationship distress from the common experience of transient or limited marital complaints. Accordingly, the category of Relationship Distress (Z61.0) should be used only when the focus is on a *pattern* of interaction between spouses or partners, and does not reflect an isolated event. The pattern should be characterized by the presence of negative couple characteristics (including, but not limited to communication, noncommunication, or withdrawal) or the absence of positive couple characteristics, and should be associated with significant impairment in individual and/or family functioning.

Seven key indicators of relationship distress should be examined in the assessment interview: relationship dissatisfaction; relationship conflict; other negative relationship behaviors; lack of positive relationship behaviors; perceived negative intentions; perceived low relationship efficacy; and sad, angry, or apathetic affect regarding partner. These areas will typically be the primary focus for brief interview assessment. For example, it would be appropriate in the interview to examine each partner's subjective sense of overall happiness in the relationship during the past year, and especially over the past month, as well as the frequency of their thoughts of divorce/separation (where this is an option), and their perception that they would probably need external help in order for the relationship to improve. The interview allows opportunities to exclude situations where complaints are focused outside the relationship or are not producing dissatisfaction (e.g., sexual problems without accompanying relationship distress, or difficulty adjusting to infertility in an otherwise happy couple). Likewise, the interview allows exploration of conflict resolution difficulties, such as marked escalation of negative behavior or affect (e.g., "little" disputes evolve into shouting matches), or withdrawal from interactions so that problem resolution is impeded. Withdrawal can either be through leaving a discussion before it is resolved, or through more pervasive disconnectedness that impedes bringing up or resolving problems. (However, neither constructive use of time-out procedures that include later discussion of the issue nor culturally appropriate alternative approaches that result in resolution of disagreements within the dyad would not be considered as meeting this criterion.) It would be appropriate to explore other negative exchanges in the dyad, including withholding critical relationship behaviors (e.g., not contributing to childcare or household responsibilities) when this is used as a coercive strategy, or engaging in nonverbal negative behaviors at a high rate (e.g., cold shoulder, angry looks, etc.) used as a coercive strategy. Likewise, it is appropriate to explore whether there is a lack of positive exchanges in the dyad, including lack of sharing thoughts and feelings, lack of sexual and nonsexual physical intimacy, lack of other positive shared activities, and lack of emotional and tangible social support. However, assessment of lack of positive exchanges may be particularly subject to cross-cultural variation and regional differences due to local norms and expectations (e.g., Chapter 6 in this volume). In the cognitive domain, it is appropriate to explore the presence of perceived negative intentions by the partner that may indicate a distressed attributional pattern in which negative behaviors of the partner are attributed to negative personality traits, or are perceived to be done voluntarily, intentionally, and with negative intent, whereas positive behaviors of the partner are attributed primarily to transient states, performed unintentionally, or with a hidden negative intention. In the context of relationship distress, one also anticipates finding evidence of low relationship efficacy with little expectation that the relationship can improve without some form of outside involvement or help. Likewise, one anticipates that interactions with the partner and thoughts about the partner are frequently marked by intense and persistent levels of negative affect, including anger, sadness, apathy, or contempt.

Keeping these broad indicators in mind, we provide a general set of questions, in Table 8.2, which can be used to assess each indicator in the context of relationship distress. As a general rule, it is appropriate to begin a semistructured interview with broad, open-ended questions allowing the partner or couple to describe their relationship in their own words before the interviewer asks any specific, potentially leading, questions. Although the specific questions suggested are designed to elicit relevant information, it should be understood that they are merely vehicles for clarifying the presence or absence of significant, persistent problems in multiple domains of the relationship. In many cases, questions will need to be adapted to fit the needs of the couple and the cultural context, or the interviewer may need to seek out corroborating information before making a determination that particular criteria have been met.

Ideally, interview-based assessment of relationship problems would combine conjoint and individual interviews, with an initial conjoint meeting followed by separate sessions with each partner individually. This format provides maximum flexibility, independence of information, and comprehensiveness of the assessment. However, practical considerations may often preclude the combination of joint and individual interviews (e.g., if only one partner is present). Whenever separate interviews are utilized and both partners are present, it will be important for the interviewer to explain any limits to confidentiality and the circumstances under which information disclosed by one partner might be shared with the other. As is noted in the assessment chapters for partner maltreatment, there are conditions under which disclosure to partners is not advisable.

Semistructured Interview Outline

The interviewer would ordinarily begin by eliciting a short overall evaluation of the relationship in the following manner: "Now, I'm going to ask you some questions about your

TABLE 8.2 Semistructured Interview for Marital or Intimate Partner Relational Problems

	No or Below Threshold	Yes or Above Threshold
In the past month…		
(1)…have you been feeling unhappy about your relationship? (Has it been more than half of the days in the past month?)	0	1
(2)…have you had thoughts of separation or divorce, or that you'd be better off without your partner? IF YES: How long do these thoughts last?	0	1
(3) Do you think your relationship is in need of professional help?	0	1
During the past month, when you disagreed about something with your partner…		
(4)…does it escalate quickly into a major argument? (Do little problems escalate into heated arguments?)	0	1
(5)…do you or your partner leave the room, withdraw or stop talking so that it's impossible to resolve the problem?	0	1
(6) During the past month, when your partner has done something you didn't like, did you think that s/he did it on purpose or that s/he had negative intentions? Do you think it reflects a negative part of his/her personality?	0	1
(7) Do you and your partner have trouble resolving problems in your relationship to your mutual satisfaction?	0	1
(8) During the past month, how often have you felt angry or sad about your partner? (If apathy seems present) Do you feel as strongly about your partner as you did once?	0	1

relationship. Could you tell me about your relationship and any difficulties you have been having over the past month? The past year? When did these problems begin? What do you see as the source of the problems in your relationship? What do you see as the positive factors in your relationship? When do you think your relationship will get better?"

Scoring

1. Does subjective sense of overall happiness in the relationship during the past month indicate generalized unhappiness with the relationship on more days than not? (yes = 1; no = 0)
2. Are thoughts of divorce/separation present on multiple occasions and more than transitory? (yes = 1; no = 0)
3. Is there a perceived need for outside help for the relationship? (Excluded are situations in which the relationship itself is not troubled; for example, sexual problems without accompanying relationship problems, adjusting to infertility in a happy couple.) (yes = 1; no = 0)
4. Is there marked escalation of negative behavior or affect in the context of discussions (e.g., "little" disputes evolve into heated arguments)? Is this a pattern rather than a single occurrence? (yes = 1; no = 0)
5. Is there withdrawal from interaction so that resolution is impeded? Withdrawal can either be through leaving a discussion before it is resolved, or through more pervasive disconnectedness that impedes bringing up or resolving problems. Are there multiple instances? (Constructive use of time-out procedures that include later discussion of the issue would not meet this criterion.) (yes = 1; no = 0)
6. Is there evidence of a distressed attributional pattern? Negative behaviors of the partner are attributed to negative personality traits, or are perceived to be done voluntarily, intentionally, or with

negative intent. Positive behaviors of the partner are attributed to temporary states, or are perceived to be done accidentally, unintentionally, or with hidden negative intentions. Is the attributional pattern pervasive and not merely a transient response to an incident? (yes = 1; no = 0)

7. Is there evidence of very low levels of efficacy regarding conflict resolution or being able to improve the relationship? (yes = 1; no = 0)
8. Are interactions with, or thoughts about, the partner frequently marked by intense and persistent levels of anger, sadness, or apathy? (yes = 1; no = 0)

Overall Scoring

If ≥3 consider coding as Z61.0 (Relational Distress). Couple may require referral for direct focus on relationship problems. Also consider assessing for Relational Aggression. If subjective sense of overall unhappiness is not present, consider whether another code better captures the family problems (e.g., a maltreatment code, Z62; or problems related to primary support group, Z63).

The interview format outlined above is derived from Heyman, Feldbau-Kohn, Ehrensaft, Langhinrichsen-Rohling, and O'Leary (2001), who developed a semistructured interview to measure and diagnose relationship distress, aggression, and abuse. Findings from the interview significantly differentiated between distressed and nondistressed groups formed on the basis of the Marital Adjustment Test (Locke & Wallace, 1959). Distressed and nondistressed couples also differed significantly in their discussions of problem topics.

CONCLUSIONS

Screening for relationship distress is indicated when individuals are evaluated for emotional, behavioral, or physical health problems as well as when child behavior problems are the primary focus of clinical attention. In this chapter, we reviewed several brief, self-report measures and semistructured interviews that can be used in screening for relationship distress not only in clinical settings to optimize mental health referrals, but also for surveillance of relationship distress at the community level for public health applications.

REFERENCES

Beach, S. R., & O'Leary, K. D. (1993). Marital discord and dysphoria: For whom does the marital relationship predict depressive symptomatology? *Journal of Social and Personal Relationships, 10*, 405–420.

Beach, S. R. H., Fincham, F. D., Amir, N., & Leonard, K. E. (2005). The taxometrics of marriage: Is marital discord categorical? *Journal of Family Psychology, 19*, 276–285.

Beach, S. R. H., Katz, J., Kim, S., & Brody, G. H. (2003). Prospective effects of marital satisfaction on depressive symptoms in established marriages: A dyadic model. *Journal of Social and Personal Relationships, 20*, 355–371.

Beach, S. R. H. & Whisman, M. A. (2012). Affective disorders. *Journal of Marital and Family Therapy, 38*, 201–219. doi: 10.1111/j.1752-0606.2011.00243.x

Bhugra, D., & De Silva, P. (2000). Couple therapy across cultures. *Sexual & Relationship Therapy, 15*, 183–192.

Cohen, S., O'Leary, K. D., & Foran, H. (2010). A randomized clinical trial of a brief, problem-focused couple therapy for depression. *Behavior Therapy, 41*, 433–446.

Davila, J., Karney, B. R., Hall, T. W., & Bradbury, T. N. (2003). Depressive symptoms and marital satisfaction: Within-subject associations and the moderating effects of gender and neuroticism. *Journal of Family Psychology, 17*, 557–570.

Diener, E., Gohm, C. L., Suh, E., & Oishi, S. (2000). Similarity of the relations between marital status and subjective well-being across cultures. *Journal of Cross-Cultural Psychology, 31*, 419–436.

Durham, R. C., Allan, T., & Hackett, C. A. (1997). On predicting improvement and relapse in generalized anxiety disorder following psychotherapy. *British Journal of Clinical Psychology, 36*, 101–119.

Epstein, N., & Baucom, D. H. (2002). *Enhanced cognitive-behavioral therapy for couples: A contextual approach.* Washington, DC: American Psychological Association.

Funk, J. L., & Rogge, R. D. (2007). Testing the ruler with item response theory: Increasing precision of measurement for relationship satisfaction with the Couples Satisfaction Index. *Journal of Family Psychology, 21*, 572–583.

Gottman, J. M. (1994). *What predicts divorce?* Hillsdale, NJ: Erlbaum.

Gottman, J., Swanson, C., & Swanson, K. (2002). A general systems theory of marriage: Nonlinear difference equation modeling of marital interaction. *Personality and Social Psychology Review, 6*, 326–340.

Grych, J. H., & Fincham, F. D. (2001). Interparental conflict and child adjustment: An overview. In J. H. Grych & F. D. Fincham (Eds.), *Interparental conflict and child development: Theory, research, and applications* (pp. 1–6). New York, NY: Cambridge University Press.

Heyman, R. E., Feldbau-Kohn, S. R., Ehrensaft, M. K., Langhinrichsen-Rohling, K., & O'Leary, K. D. (2001). Can questionnaire reports correctly classify relationship distress and partner physical abuse? *Journal of Family Psychology, 15*, 334–346.

Hooley, J. M., & Teasdale, J. D. (1989). Predictors of relapse in unipolar depressives: Expressed emotion, marital distress, and perceived criticism. *Journal of Abnormal Psychology, 98*, 229–235.

Kiecolt-Glaser, J. K., & Newton, T. L. (2001). Marriage and health: His and hers. *Psychological Bulletin, 12*, 472–503.

Kung, W. W., & Elkin, I. (2000). Marital adjustment as a predictor of outcome in individual treatment of depression. *Psychotherapy Research, 10*, 267–278.

Law, D. D. & Crane, D. S. (2000). The influence of marital and family therapy on health care utilization in a health-maintenance organization. *Journal of Marital and Family Therapy, 26*, 281–291. doi: 10.1111/j.1752-0606.2000.tb00298.x

Locke, H. J., & Wallace, K. M. (1959). Short marital adjustment and prediction tests: Their reliability and validity. *Marriage and Family Living, 21*, 251–255.

Maisto, S. A., McKay, J. R., & O'Farrell, T. J. (1998). Twelve-month abstinence from alcohol and long-term drinking and marital outcomes in men with severe alcohol problems. *Journal of Studies on Alcohol, 59*, 591–598.

Norton, R. (1983). Measuring marital quality: A critical look at the dependent variable. *Journal of Marriage and the Family, 45*, 141–150.

O'Farrell, T. J., Hooley, J., Fals-Stewart, W., & Cutter, H. S. G. (1998). Expressed emotion and relapse in alcoholic patients. *Journal of Consulting and Clinical Psychology, 66*, 744–752.

Overbeek, G., Vollebergh, W., de Graaf, R., Scholte, R., de Kemp, R., & Engels, R. (2006). Longitudinal associations of marital quality and marital dissolution with the incidence of *DSM-III-R* disorders. *Journal of Family Psychology, 20*, 284–291.

Ruscio, J., Haslam, N., & Ruscio, A. M. (2006). *Introduction to the taxometric method: A practical guide.* Mahwah, NJ: Lawrence Erlbaum.

Schmidt, N. B., Kotov, R., & Joiner, T. E. (2004). *Taxometrics: Toward a new diagnostic scheme for psychopathology.* Washington, DC: American Psychological Association.

Schonbrun, Y. C., & Whisman, M. A. (2010). Marital distress and mental health care service utilization. *Journal of Consulting and Clinical Psychology, 78*, 732–736.

Schumm, W. R., Paff-Bergen, L. A., Hatch, R. C., Obiorah, F. C., Copeland, J. M., Meens, J. D., & Bugaighis, M. A. (1986). Concurrent and discriminant validity of the Kansas Marital Satisfaction Scale. *Journal of Marriage and Family, 48*(2), 381–387.

Shumway, S. T., Wampler, R. S., Dersch, C., & Arredondo, R. (2004). A place for marriage and family services in employee assistance programs (EAPs): A survey of EAP client problems and needs. *Journal of Marital and Family Therapy, 30*, 71–79.

Snyder, D. K. (1997). *Manual for the Marital Satisfaction Inventory–Revised.* Los Angeles, CA: Western Psychological Services.

Snyder, D. K., Castellani, A. M., & Whisman, M. A. (2006). Current status and future directions in couple therapy. *Annual Review of Psychology, 57*, 317–344.

Snyder, D. K., Heyman, R. E., & Haynes, S. N. (2005). Evidence-based approaches to assessing couple distress. *Psychological Assessment, 17*, 288–307.

Swindle, R., Heller, K., Pescosolido, B., & Saeko, K. (2000). Responses to nervous breakdowns in America over a 40-year period: Mental health policy implications. *American Psychologist, 55(7)*, 740–749.

Waller, N. G., & Meehl, P. E. (1998). *Multivariate taxometric procedures: Distinguishing types from continua.* Thousand Oaks, CA: Sage.

Whisman, M. A. (2001). Marital adjustment and outcome following treatments for depression. *Journal of Consulting and Clinical Psychology, 69*, 125–129.

Whisman, M. A., Beach, S. R. H., & Snyder, D. K. (2008). Is marital discord taxonic and can taxonic status be assessed reliably? Results from a national, representative sample of married couples. *Journal of Consulting and Clinical Psychology, 76*, 745–755.

Whisman, M. A., & Bruce, M. L. (1999). Marital distress and incidence of major depressive episode in a community sample. *Journal of Abnormal Psychology, 108*, 674–678.

Whisman, M. A., Sheldon, C. T., & Goering, P. (2000). Psychiatric disorders and dissatisfaction with social relationships: Does type of relationship matter? *Journal of Abnormal Psychology, 109*, 803–808.

Whisman, M. A., Snyder, D. K., & Beach, S. R. H. (2009). Screening for marital and relationship discord. *Journal of Family Psychology, 23*, 247–254.

Whisman, M. A., & Uebelacker, L. A. (2006). Impairment and distress associated with relationship discord in a national sample of married or cohabiting adults. *Journal of Family Psychology, 20*, 369–377.

Whisman, M. A., Uebelacker, L. A., & Bruce, M. L. (2006). Longitudinal association between marital discord and alcohol use disorders. *Journal of Family Psychology, 20*, 164–167.

PART III: CHILD MALTREATMENT

9

Child Maltreatment: Definitions, Prevalence, and Implications for Diagnosis

Amy M. Smith Slep, Richard E. Heyman, and Jill Malik

Child maltreatment includes the physical, emotional or psychological, or sexual abuse or neglect of a child by that child's caregiver(s) or other responsible party (for ease of exposition, this chapter will use "parent"). Since child maltreatment was first brought to society's consciousness (Kempe & Helfer, 1968), it was clear that maltreatment not only could result in myriad negative consequences for its victims, notably devastating injuries, chronic conditions, and death, but also could result in children emerging with few or no apparent ill effects (see Chapter 11 in this volume). Initial definitional struggles focused on whether child maltreatment was best operationalized as occurring within the child (i.e., battered child syndrome), within the parent (i.e., based only on the parental act or omission), or as relational (i.e., both the parent's act/omission and impact on the child are considered). Despite the complete lack of consensus on specific definitional criteria that remains in the child maltreatment field (e.g., Trickett, Feerick, Flanzer, & Knutson, 2006), evidenced by no agreement across state and national laws and no commonly accepted research definitions, there does seem to be some implicit consensus that a relational approach is optimal. Such an approach requires some sort of qualifying parental act and some sort of harm or endangerment of the child. This sets child maltreatment apart from most traditional diagnostic entities, which typically sit squarely within one individual. Despite lack of consensus regarding definitions of child maltreatment, it has long been clear that child maltreatment was and continues to be a tremendous problem with serious consequences born by society at large as well as victims.

In the tenth edition of the International Statistical Classification of Diseases and Related Health Problems (ICD-10; World Health Organization [WHO], 1992), child maltreatment is addressed in three sections. The first is in the Y codes "external causes of morbidity and mortality." These are codes for labeling the cause of child injuries or health conditions, and assault, including at the hands of a parent or other caregiver, is codeable as a cause. The second is in the T codes (i.e., T74), which is a category including "injury, poisoning, and certain other consequences of external causes." The T codes include notable factors that can cause injuries and other disorders. In this section, physical, sexual, and psychological abuse syndromes are listed, as are some more general categories (e.g., maltreatment syndrome unspecified). The T codes are intended to be used when maltreatment is the primary presenting problem, but perhaps without an immediate injury that was caused by the abuse, which was the case in the Y codes. The third is in the Z codes (Z61.4–61.6), which include, "factors influencing health status and contact with health services." The Z codes are recorded when the individual seeking services has a notable issue for which services may be necessary, but this issue is not a disease or injury or notable external cause. Within the Z codes, sexual abuse is defined, but physical abuse is not. Aspects of neglect are included under Z62, which includes "Other problems related to upbringing." Emotional neglect is included and defined as, "Parent talking to the child in a dismissive or insensitive way. Lack of interest in the child, of sympathy for the child's difficulties and of praise and encouragement. Irritated reaction to anxious behavior and absence of sufficient physical comforting and emotional warmth." Another aspect of neglect is covered by Z62.0, "Inadequate parental supervision and control," defined as, "Lack of parental knowledge of what the child is doing or where the child is; poor control; lack of concern or lack of attempted intervention when the child is in risky situations." Despite the inclusion of maltreatment in three places in the ICD, the lack of consistent, operationalized definitions likely hinders its routine consideration and application of these codes when warranted.

As research on child maltreatment has burgeoned, along with policies and systems to address the problem and assist families, this lack of definitional consensus remains one of the most pressing sticking points in being better able to clearly identify when maltreatment occurs and how it relates to mental and physical health. In response to this need, the United States Centers for Disease Control (CDC) developed and published uniform definitions (Leeb, Paulozzi, Melanson, Simon, & Arias, 2007). These definitions are more operationalized and detailed than typical legal definitions, and are more usable by health care providers and others in the field, but they remain rather broad and how reliably they could be applied remains unexamined in field trials. Others are beginning to struggle with how to distinguish suboptimal, nonabusive parenting from maltreatment (e.g., Wolfe & McIsaac, 2010), which can be very complex. In the next section, we will detail our program of research that extends this work by creating and testing reliable diagnostic criteria.

PROPOSED CHILD MALTREATMENT CRITERIA

Our goal in developing criteria for child physical, emotional, and sexual abuse, and neglect was to produce clear criteria that could provide clinically useful guidance and support high levels of inter-rater agreement in clinical settings. In addition, each criteria set was based on the best available scientific understanding of the development and maintenance of child maltreatment. The Appendix in this chapter displays the criteria for the child maltreatment categories. Please note that the criteria proposed for inclusion in the ICD-11 are very similar to, but not identical to those used in our research described below. In this section, we detail the research criteria. Later in this chapter, the nature of and rationale for the revisions for ICD criteria are detailed.

Both Criteria A and B were required. Criterion A involved a qualifying act or omission that was consistent with the type of maltreatment in question. Criterion B comprises the relevant physical and psychological impacts that have appeared repeatedly in the empirical literature; at least one was required for all types of child maltreatment, with the exception of sexual abuse, for which only an act was required and significant impact was assumed. Finally, Criterion C (included for physical abuse and neglect) included mitigating information that would result in an incident that otherwise met criteria for maltreatment being excluded.

Criteria for child physical abuse are found in the Appendix. Both Criterion A (act; i.e., nonaccidental use of physical force) and Criterion B (impact; i.e., more than inconsequential physical injury, reasonable potential for more than inconsequential physical injury, more than inconsequential fear reaction, significant somatic symptoms) are required, as is Criterion C (lack of mitigating circumstances; i.e., the acts were not committed to protect self from imminent harm, were not part of developmentally appropriate play, and were not committed to protect child from imminent harm).

The criteria have some subcriteria sets that have proven essential for reliable application of the criteria. As seen in the Appendix, "more than inconsequential physical injury" and "more than inconsequential fear reaction" have clarifying criteria. As we discovered during the field trials discussed below, such operationalizations are necessary to achieve high field assessor-master reviewer agreement. Finally, note that Criteria B1 (more than inconsequential injury) and B3 (more than inconsequential fear reaction) involve actual impacts, whereas B2 involves potential for more than inconsequential injury. Assessors judge whether the inherent dangerousness of the act, the degree of force used, and the physical environment in which the acts occurred constituted a significant potential for serious harm (e.g., pushing a child hard near the top of a flight of stairs, choking an adolescent hard but leaving no bruises).

Similarly, emotional abuse required Criteria A (act) and B (impact). In the case of emotional abuse, the potential impacts were emotional rather than physical. They included psychological harm in B1 (more than inconsequential fear reaction or significant psychological distress), reasonable potential for harm in B2 (either a psychiatric disorder or significant disruption of development), and somatic symptoms in B3. The potential for disorders and developmental disruption, although arguably difficult to assess, were intended to allow for the determination that particular acts or patterns of acts of emotional abuse can be determined by the assessor as significant, and likely to result in harm. However, sufficient time might not have passed to demonstrate that impact at the time of the assessment either due to the acute and severe nature of the act or the developmental stage of the child, which would make the probable impact less likely to appear until the child is older.

Sexual abuse was defined only in terms of act. Although there is evidence in the literature that sexual abuse is not necessarily dramatically impactful (e.g., Rind, Tromovitch, & Bauserman, 1998), most definitions of sexual abuse used in clinical, research, and legal settings do not include a need for demonstrable harm to the child. Rather, these acts are seen as in such violation of society's standards that they are considered abusive regardless of apparent impact. The proposed definitions included three types of acts, detailed in the Appendix: use of physical force, emotional manipulation, or a child's youth or naïveté to engage in (a) rape, (b) other sexual contact, and (c) exploitation of the child for anyone's sexual gratification in a manner than involves no direct contact with the child (e.g., photographs).

The definition of child neglect was the longest and most complex of the criteria sets, due to the variety of significant omissions that can occur. Criterion A consisted of one of the following acts or omissions, each of which are more completely defined in the Appendix: (a) lack of supervision, (b) exposure to physical hazards, (c) educational neglect, (d) health care neglect, (e) deprivation of necessities, and (f) abandonment. It is important to note that the principle underlying these categories was that the act or omission must have been egregious and deprived the child of needed, age-appropriate care. This principle allowed flexibility in applying these standards in different cultures where standards for age appropriate education, supervision, and health care might differ tremendously. For criteria for neglect to be met, there must also have been significant impact. Because of the diversity of the types of neglectful acts/omissions, all the categories of impact included in both physical and emotional abuse were included under neglect.

Below we detail the creation and testing of these criteria in a series of studies focused on partner and child maltreatment. The maltreatment criteria were developed in a multistage process described in depth elsewhere (Heyman & Slep, 2006, 2009; Slep & Heyman, 2006). The steps comprised: (a) examining the content validity and field usability of a set of maltreatment criteria already in use; (b) creating a unifying conceptualization for what constituted an above-threshold problem; (c) reviewing and adapting (where appropriate) existing operationalizations; (d) field testing and refining criteria, assessments, and decision-making process; (e) testing criteria's use in wide-scale dissemination; (f) creating criteria-informed screeners and structured clinical interviews; and (g) examining the content validity of the final criteria.

DEVELOPMENT AND TESTING OF THE CRITERIA

Before describing the results of the multistage development/testing process, some context is necessary. First, the criteria were originally developed for use in a system in which all assessments and diagnostic judgments were conducted with families with maltreatment allegations lodged against them, not with a more general clinical population. All clinical assessments were conducted by credentialed providers and decisions about whether an incident met criteria for maltreatment was made by a committee.

Because we were bootstrapping our definitions using existing definitions as a starting point, we conducted two content validity studies using the family maltreatment criteria then in use by the U.S. Department of Defense (Undersecretary of Defense, 1997). To maximize the content and clinical validity of the potential criteria, we followed Haynes, Richard, and Kubany's (1995) suggestion to conduct content validity studies using both civilian and military family maltreatment experts (Study 1) and those intended to use the definitions (i.e., field clinicians; Study 2). Study 1 (Heyman & Slep, 2006) suggested that the criteria then in force were adequate but could be improved by: (a) operationalizing terms, (b) eliminating the definitional overlap of emotional abuse and other forms of maltreatment, and (c) eliminating the requirement that clinicians predict risk of recurrence to find that incidents met criteria for child emotional abuse or child neglect. In Study 2 (Heyman & Slep, 2006), field clinicians shared the views of the experts that, despite being generally understandable and containing many key elements of maltreatment, the existing definitions were in need of increased operationalization. Further, regarding the process of decision making, clinicians reported that extradefinitional issues either influenced the decision-making process or caused the decision-making committee to blatantly overrule the definitions.

The next step was to adopt a conceptual framework. In developing the maltreatment criteria, Heyman and Slep (2006) and Slep and Heyman (2006) adopted the framework that child physical and emotional abuse and child neglect would require both a specific type of act (e.g., use of physical force for physical abuse) and a significant impact (or high potential for significant impact, such as throwing a knife at a child but not hitting him or her). Because of a presumed risk for significant impact sexual abuse, the sexual abuse conceptual framework required only a qualifying act.

Next, specific criteria were created. These were based in part on the prior U.S. Department of Defense criteria and on operationalizations in existing legal, research, or clinical definitions that were specific enough to promote reliability. Dozens of definitions were comprehensively reviewed, including the following: Child Abuse Prevention and Treatment Act (U.S. Department of Health and Human Services, 2003); CDC partner abuse definitions (Saltzman, Fanslow, McMahon, & Shelley, 1999); the Modified Maltreatment Classification System (Barnett, Manly, & Cicchetti, 1991, 1993); international and domestic agencies' definitions of child sexual abuse and related terms, including, among many others, those of the NGO Group for the Convention on the Rights of the Child, *Focal point on the sexual exploitation of children* (2000); the National Incidence Survey on Child Abuse and Neglect definitions (Sedlak & Broadhurst, 1996); state child abuse statutes (National Clearinghouse on Child Abuse and Neglect, 2003); and the U.S. Department of Defense definitions then in force with their proposed modifications (Undersecretary of Defense, 1997, 1999, 2000, 2002).

The next step (Study 3), a pilot field test at five sites (Heyman & Slep, 2006), aimed to train clinical staff and other case determination committee members at the five sites in the use of these definitions, improve iteratively the operationalizations during the field trial, and compare maltreatment decisions with those of master reviewers (from the project team). Agreement between committees and the master reviewers was moderate. Based on monitoring meetings prior to the field trial, Heyman and Slep (2006) estimated that committee decisions followed the old definitions approximately 50% of the time. Using the new definitions, however, 76% ($\kappa = 0.48$) of allegations were decided by the committees the same way as they were by master reviewers. Although this represented an improvement, neither 76% agreement nor a Cohen's kappa of 0.48 could be considered adequate.

For the second field trial, Study 4 (Heyman & Slep, 2006), several changes were made. First, to make the assessment process consistent across sites and assure that the pertinent information was being assessed, we developed a structured clinical interview that paralleled the diagnostic criteria for each form of maltreatment (a version of this interview appears in

Chapter 12 in this volume). The assessing clinicians were provided with and instructed to use these questions. Second, the composition of who served on the determination committee was altered in a manner that reduced the number of clinicians present. Third, the presentation of information was drastically altered. The former process (used in the pilot field trial) involved a summary by the assessing clinician, which often did not straightforwardly present criteria-relevant information. In Study 4, all committee members who had pertinent information presented it (e.g., assessing clinician, police, work supervisor). Fourth (and we believe critically), votes were cast for each criterion separately, aided by a computer-guided decision matrix that presented the diagnostic decisions to be made. In 92% of cases ($\kappa = 0.84$), decisions in the field about whether or not maltreatment met or exceeded diagnostic thresholds matched those of master reviewers. This exceptional level of reliability suggested that the refinement of the criteria had been successful.

Although the second trial involved field-generated decisions under real-world conditions, it was clearly an effectiveness trial and did not speak to the performance of the diagnostic system when disseminated broadly. A dissemination trial of the diagnostic system's use under typical conditions at many sites was necessary. Because the diagnostic system was being disseminated worldwide throughout the organization, we were able to randomly select 41 communities to participate in a trial. As shown in Table 9.1 (Heyman & Slep, 2006) agreement between the field-generated decisions and those of master reviewers remained high. The maintenance of adequate agreement is especially noteworthy, given the relative lack of expertise and training among the majority of those using the diagnostic criteria and the standard-operating-procedure nature of the participating sites (i.e., they were not "special volunteer test sites," as in the effectiveness trial). These results are quite encouraging and suggest that diagnostic systems for relational problems can indeed be reliably applied in real-world settings, despite the discouraging results in the general mental health diagnosis literature to date (Basco et al., 2000; Fennig, Craig, Tanenberg-Karant, & Bromet, 1994; Kashner et al., 2003; Shear et al., 2000).

GLOBAL PREVALENCE RATES

Due to the current lack of consensus on definitions, different thresholds to define child maltreatment across various cultures, and weak surveillance systems in many countries, it is difficult to report global rates of child maltreatment. However, best estimates suggest that worldwide, approximately 40 million children under the age of 15 are subjected to child abuse each year (WHO, 2001). With regard to fatal abuse, the WHO (2000) estimated 57,000 deaths attributed to homicide among children under 15 years old, with infants and toddlers

TABLE 9.1 Agreement Between Field Decisions and Master Reviewers

	Pilot Field Trial			Field Trial 2			Dissemination Trial		
Type of Maltreatment	κ	% Agreement	*n*	κ	% Agreement	*n*	κ	% Agreement	*n*
Child maltreatment (all types)	0.49	78	184	0.87	94	236	0.75	88	342
Physical	0.55	80	46	0.92	96	76	0.82	91	115
Emotional	0.24	59	27	0.89	96	47	0.73	90	60
Sexual	0.67	83	12	1.00	100	12	0.89	95	19
Neglect	0.55	81	99	0.80	91	101	0.66	84	148

(aged 0–4) at the greatest risk. The risk of fatal abuse for children varies with a country's income/region of the world, in that the rate of fatal abuse for children younger than 5 years living in low-income countries is 2 to 3 times higher (5.1–6.1 out of 100,000) than children living in high-income countries (1.8–2.2 out of 100,000). Highest rates were reported in the African region (12.7–17.9 out of 100,000) and the lowest rates were reported in the European, Eastern Mediterranean, and Western Pacific regions. Because misclassification of child fatal abuse is a widespread problem, the general consensus is that actual rates are much higher than these estimates, based on reported cases. Rates of nonfatal child abuse and neglect are based on such weak data that they should not be interpreted, as many countries do not have requirements to report or track such maltreatment.

The rate of child abuse or neglect in the United States is estimated as 1 out of 58 children (NIS-4; Sedlak et al., 2010) when demonstrable harm is used as the threshold. In the same study, when the rate of child maltreatment is 1 out of 25 children endangerment is the threshold applied to incidents. Given the patterns of rates of fatalities reviewed above, it is likely that the U.S. rates of nonfatal child maltreatment are greater than some high-income countries, but are likely much lower than in many poorer regions.

Physical Abuse

Population-based studies on rates of physical abuse considerably vary among countries. Data that are somewhat comparable across nations come from the World Studies of Abuse in the Family Environment (Ramiro, Madrid, & Amarillo, 2000). This project is a cross-national collaborative study (Chile, Egypt, India, Philippines) that focuses on establishing comparable incidence rates for harsh and moderate forms of child discipline using the Parent–Child Conflict Tactics Scale (Straus, 1995) with mothers reporting. The results from this study were compared to a study in the United States that used the same measure. Moderate physical punishment (e.g., spank child with hand/hit with object on buttocks) occurred at rates of 18% to 75% in the 6 months prior to the survey, with the highest rates reported in the Philippines and India and the lowest reported in Egypt and Chile. Severe physical punishment (e.g., hit child with an object not on buttocks) occurred at rates of 4% (Chile and the United States) to 36% (India). Other forms of severe physical abuse (e.g., kicked, burned, choked) occurred at much lower rates internationally, with the norm being 0% to 2% in the past 6 months.

Sexual Abuse

Rates of sexual abuse are also hard to estimate because the various methods used to gather and report such statistics produce very different results. For example, 0.1% of parents admit to sexually abusing their children; however, retrospective studies of adults reporting on child sexual abuse indicate much higher (although mostly by nonparental perpetrators), and much more variable rates (1%–19% for men and 0.9%–45% for women), depending on the criteria for sexual abuse used (e.g., questions from these retrospective studies often refer to history of parental sexual abuse, abuse by other family members, and nonfamily members). International studies from the 1980s report a mean lifetime prevalence of 20% for women and 5% to 10% for men (Finkelhor, 1994). The WHO (2005) reported, in both developed and developing countries that between 1% and 21% of women reported to have been sexually abused before the age of 15. In most cases, the perpetrator was a male family member *other* than the father or stepfather. Regarding sex differences, the NIS-4 reports that girls were abused five times more often than boys.

Emotional Abuse

Emotional abuse might be the most variably defined across cultures. Verbal or psychological punishment such as yelling at one's child appears to occur at fairly common rates internationally, ranging from 70% to 85% (WHO, 2002). Other forms of verbal punishment, such as cursing at or calling the child a name, occurs more variably internationally, at rates of 3% to 51%, with the lowest incidences reported in Chile and the highest in Egypt (of the countries studied).

Neglect

The combination of differing definitions and differing laws relating to the report of abuse and neglect among nations makes it nearly impossible to estimate the global prevalence of child neglect. Further, it is hard to meaningfully compare rates of neglect cross-nationally. Additionally, when national studies have been conducted, the types of neglect included have not been consistent across studies. For example, national studies from Canada and the United States looked at physical neglect, emotional neglect, abandonment, educational neglect, and inadequate supervision. According to the NIS-4, 16.2 children out of 1,000 were physically neglected, 15.9 out of 1,000 children were emotionally neglected, and 4.9 out of 1,000 were educationally neglected. All neglect combined was reported to be 30.6 out of 1,000 children.

CURRENT LIMITATIONS IN GLOBAL SURVEILLANCE SYSTEMS

Consensus regarding what defines child maltreatment, as well as how to uniformly measure maltreatment, is necessary to enable surveillance systems to produce comparable child maltreatment information across countries. Without consensus on what constitutes abuse and neglect, researchers cannot move toward a singular system to define and more accurately assess child maltreatment. Further, more population-based studies are needed that use agreed-upon operationalizations and methods for global rates to truly be surveyed and reported. However, although progress has been made to standardize definitions and report population-based prevalence rates (e.g., NIS-4), less progress has been made to standardize definitions and methodology internationally. There are several evident barriers to this progress that make it daunting and nearly impossible to achieve with current systems in place. In addition to definitional issues, many countries are reluctant to intrude on private home life and ask intrusive questions about possibly abusive parenting behaviors. However, we must move beyond concerns about intrusiveness and seek to better ensure children's safety in their homes.

In part to address these gaps, we have streamlined the research diagnostic criteria for child maltreatment detailed above for possible inclusion in the ICD-11. Their inclusion would be a first step in having globally acceptable, research-based definitions of child maltreatment that could be consistently applied by public health systems through their use of ICD codes tracking health care service utilization, morbidity, and mortality. In recognition of the time and system constraints in all countries to support coding of health conditions, it was necessary to slightly simplify the criteria, while maintaining the general approach that lead to the successful field trials. To achieve this, we recommend the ICD include both act and impact criteria, but that the injury criterion for physical abuse and neglect include any injury rather than a more than inconsequential injury, and the exclusions be omitted for ICD coding purposes. Otherwise, the criteria recommended for inclusion in the ICD-11 are consistent with the nuanced research criteria detailed earlier.

Threshold Considerations

In this section, we discuss considerations relevant to identifying thresholds distinguishing maltreatment from nonabusive, but potentially problematic parenting in general, and then we will address issues considered the thresholds as they pertain to the specific operationalizations of each type of child maltreatment. Parenting acts and omissions clearly exist along continua (Kendziora & O'Leary, 1993). In many societies, it is acceptable and even expected to use physical aggression in the discipline of children's behavior. It can also be normative to yell at and criticize children. In a smaller number of cultures, sexual activity with children is accepted under certain circumstances. Certainly, the level of independence granted to children of different ages varies tremendously from one culture to another. These continua of parental behavior and different thresholds for socially sanctioned parenting in different contexts across the globe underscore the need for a relational approach to the diagnosis of child maltreatment. There is generally global agreement in the rights of children to live in safe environments, free from risk of preventable physical and psychological injury. Thus, the proposed criteria use the impact on the child as threshold. In this way, physical discipline is considered nonabusive if the child is not significantly impacted. The three types of impact included in the criteria map on to clinical presentations of abuse—the child is significantly injured or harmed, the child is not demonstrably harmed, but is fearful with enduring symptoms that suggest the dangerousness/riskiness of what the parent did, or that neither of these things is true, but objective outsiders are afraid for the child due to the inherent dangerousness of the act/omission. These criteria are consistent with the harm and endangerment standards that are typically used but not operationalized in other definitions of child maltreatment. Furthermore, they are consistent with the categorical and agreed-upon principle that children should be safe.

It is noteworthy that the definition of caregiver–child relationship problem (discussed in Chapter 13 in this volume) differs from the child maltreatment definitions primarily in terms of the parenting acts that are considered. The acts considered under Criterion A in child maltreatment define the type of maltreatment (and the types of impacts that will be considered) and similarly define whether the parenting might constitute a type of maltreatment or be better considered under Caregiver–Child Relationship Problem. The Caregiver–Child Relationship Problem criteria are intended to be used only when the parental behavior would not be consistent with those described under the various maltreatment criteria.

There are some threshold considerations relevant to specific maltreatment types. With respect to the child physical abuse criteria, it should be noted that the threshold for injury under B(1) differs slightly from the threshold in the parallel criterion in the partner physical abuse definition used in the field trials. The criterion in child physical abuse is a "more than inconsequential injury," which excludes very minor bruises and similar mild injuries. These minor injuries constitute impact in partner physical abuse, but not in child abuse. Parenting requires routine physical handling of children. Some uses of nonaccidental physical force (stopping a child running from a parent or toward a hazard, picking up or moving a child who is aggressing or destroying something) are not only acceptable parenting behaviors also but might constitute optimal parenting in some circumstances. Furthermore, most countries and cultures find some use of physical discipline to be acceptable. Thus, societally appropriate or sanctioned acts of force could result in very minor injuries under some circumstances. We would argue that if injuries above the "more than inconsequential" threshold occur, that is an indication of an excessive amount or type of force being used and that any use of force carries some risk and the parent is responsible, even if the injury was not intended. Thus, even if the act could be considered acceptable physical discipline, if the injury resulting is more then inconsequential, then it would constitute physical child abuse. On the other hand, a parent carrying a child to bed while the child is resisting, resulting in a fingertip sized red mark that lasts for a couple of hours, is not over the threshold for abuse. This has been discussed as a "two steps beyond acceptable behavior" approach to the physical abuse thresholds. Use of physical force against one's partner is not acceptable, so use of force that results in even a very minor injury is two steps beyond acceptable behavior and therefore is over the abuse threshold. Use of physical force with one's child can be acceptable, so use of force that results in a very minor injury is only one step beyond acceptable behavior. A more significant injury indicates that the act was two steps beyond acceptable behavior and is therefore over the abuse threshold. Note that (a) the risk of injury (or danger) and fear criteria do not differ between partner and child physical abuse, and (b) for ease of use, the injury criterion thresholds for partner and child abuse were made consistent in the recommendations for the ICD-11.

The operationalizations of child and partner emotional abuse are intended to be reasonably comparable in terms of threshold, however, specific impact criteria differ to an extent to address the developmental and contextual differences between adult partners and children. Specifically with respect to child emotional abuse, there are potential criteria that are not present in the partner emotional abuse diagnosis. This is not intended to result in a lower threshold, but rather to ensure that a comparable threshold is achieved rather than what could be an unintended rising of the threshold if these criteria were omitted. The rationale is that determination of impact on young children, in particular, could be beyond the sensitivity of the current state-of-the-art assessment, as most assessment of young children is heavily reliant on parent report, which could be particularly biased in abusive families. Furthermore, some disorders do not onset until children reach certain developmental milestones (e.g., major depression). Other problems (e.g., learning disabilities, attentional problems) might require development to "bloom" and become apparent.

Finally, as discussed earlier in this chapter, child sexual abuse is defined only by the act. Demonstrated impact is not required. This is for two reasons. First, with very few exceptions, sexual acts with children are considered far out of bounds of acceptable caregiving, which makes these acts a qualitatively more extreme departure from the lower bounds of normal, but problematic, parenting than qualifying physical or emotionally abusive acts or qualifying neglectful omissions. Second, although there is heterogeneity in outcomes among sexual abuse survivors (e.g., Rind et al., 1998), it seems reasonable to assume some significant impact or risk for the development of significant impact.

IMPLICATIONS OF IMPROVED CRITERIA FOR DIAGNOSIS

More than 40 years after the introduction of child maltreatment as an area of research and clinical practice, the importance of this construct appears well accepted. The threat of child maltreatment and its importance seem well accepted in medical, research, and policy circles. At this point, the inherent utility of knowing that a child is being or has been abused or neglected in determining appropriate mental or physical health care would likely be close to universally acknowledged. However, our tools for identifying maltreatment (which are of course, contingent on definitions of maltreatment) lag far behind. Surveillance systems in developed countries are likely to miss more maltreatment than they detect and less developed countries often have no sense of its prevalence (see Leeb et al., 2007). Clinical assessment of maltreatment by providers, although they are mandated to report maltreatment in some countries, is scant. Most health care providers seem to take a "I'll know it when I see it," approach and do not routinely or systematically assess for maltreatment. However, the best prevalence information available suggests that maltreatment is, in fact, occurring in a tremendous number of children's lives. It seems probable that maltreatment plays a role in a significant number of presentations for both mental and physical disorders or injuries.

Given (a) the far-reaching effects of child maltreatment (see Chapter 11 in this volume), and (b) that treatment of children is often via the actions of the parent (e.g., parenting interventions for behavioral problems, parental administration of medications for health conditions), it seems likely that proper identification and treatment of child maltreatment issues would improve children's outcomes. Without (a) more operationalized maltreatment criteria that can be used reliably by health workers in field as well as research settings and (b) consensus on criteria that can then be implemented consistently across countries and settings, it will be difficult to advance efforts to minimize the impact of maltreatment on children's outcomes.

ACKNOWLEDGMENT

Preparation of this chapter was supported by a grant U49CE00124602 from the Centers for Disease Control and Prevention.

REFERENCES

Barnett, D., Manly, J. T., & Cicchetti, D. (1991). Continuing toward an operational definition of psychological maltreatment. *Developmental Psychopathology, 3*, 19–29.

Barnett, D., Manly, J. T., & Cicchetti, D. (1993). *Defining child maltreatment: The interface between policy and research.* In D. Cicchetti & S. L. Toth (Eds.), *Advances in applied developmental psychology: Child abuse, child development and social policy* (pp. 7–73). Norwood, NJ: Ablex Publishing.

Basco, M. R., Bostic, J. Q., Davies, D., Rush, A. J., Witte, B., Hendrickse, W., & Barnett, V. (2000). Methods to improve diagnostic accuracy in a community mental health setting. *American Journal of Psychiatry, 157*, 1599–1605.

Fennig, S., Craig, T., Tanenberg-Karant, M., & Bromet, E. J. (1994). Comparison of facility and research diagnoses in first-admission psychotic patients. *American Journal of Psychiatry, 151*, 1423–1429.

Finkelhor, D. (1994). Current information on the scope and nature of child sexual abuse. *The Future of Children, 4*, 31–53.

Haynes, S. N., Richard, D. C. S., & Kubany, E. S. (1995). Content validity in psychological assessment: A functional approach to concepts and methods. *Psychological Assessment, 7*, 238–247.

Heyman, R. E., & Slep, A. M. S. (2006). Creating and field-testing diagnostic criteria for partner and child maltreatment. *Journal of Family Psychology, 20*, 397–408.

Heyman, R. E., & Slep, A. M. S. (2009). Reliability of family maltreatment diagnostic criteria: 41 site dissemination field trial. *Journal of Family Psychology, 23*(6), 905–910.

Kashner, T., Rush, A., Suris, A., Biggs, M. M., Gajewski, V. L., Hooker, D. J., Shoat, T., & Altshuler, K. Z. (2003). Impact of structured clinical interviews on physicians' practices in community mental health settings. *Psychiatric Services, 54*, 712–718.

Kempe, C. H., & Helfer, R. E. (Eds.). (1968). *The battered child* (1st ed.). Chicago, IL: Chicago University Press.

Kendziora, K. T., & O'Leary, S. G. (1993). Dysfunctional parenting as a focus for prevention and treatment of child behavior problems. *Advances in Clinical Child Psychology, 15*, 175–206.

Leeb, R. T., Paulozzi, L., Melanson, C., Simon, T., & Arias, I. (2007). *Child maltreatment surveillance: Uniform definitions for public health and recommended data elements,* Version 1.0. Atlanta, GA: Centers for Disease Control and Prevention, National Center for Injury Prevention and Control.

National Clearinghouse on Child Abuse and Neglect. (2003). *Compendium of laws, reporting laws: Definitions of child abuse and neglect.* Ottawa, Canada: Author.

NGO Group for the Convention on the Rights of the Child. (2000). *Focal point on the sexual exploitation of children. Definitions of child sexual exploitation and related terms.* Geneva, Switzerland: Author.

Office of the Under Secretary of Defense. (1997). *DoD directive 6400.2.* Washington, DC: Office of the Under Secretary of Defense for Personnel and Readiness.

Office of the Under Secretary of Defense. (1999, May 25). *Proposed DoD directive 6400.2 (draft).* Unpublished manuscript.

Office of the Under Secretary of Defense. (2000, December 25). *Proposed DoD directive 6400.2 (draft).* Unpublished manuscript.

Office of the Under Secretary of Defense. (2002, February 22). *Proposed DoD directive 6400.2 (draft).* Unpublished manuscript.

Ramiro, L., Madrid, B., & Amarillo, M. (2000). *The Philippines WorldSAFE Study* (Final report). Manila, Philippines: International Clinical Epidemiology Network.

Rind, B., Tromovitch, P., & Bauserman, R. (1998). A meta-analytic examination of assumed properties of child sexual abuse using college samples. *Psychological Bulletin, 124*(1), 22–53.

Saltzman, L. E., Fanslow, J. L., McMahon, P. M., & Shelley, G. A. (1999). *Intimate partner violence surveillance: Uniform definitions and recommended data elements,* Ver. 1.0. Atlanta, GA: National Center for Injury Prevention and Control, Centers for Disease Control and Prevention.

Sedlak, A. J., & Broadhurst, D. D. (1996). *Third national incidence study of child abuse and neglect.* Washington: National Center on Child Abuse and Neglect.

Sedlak, A. J., Mettenburg, J., Basena, M., Petta, I., McPherson, K., Greene, A., & Li, S. (2010). *Fourth National Incidence Study of Child Abuse and Neglect (NIS-4): Report to Congress.* Washington, DC: U.S. Department of Health and Human Services, Administration for Children and Families.

Shear, M., Greeno, C., Kang, J., Ludewig, D., Frank, E., Swartz, H., & Hanekamp, M. (2000). Diagnosis of nonpsychotic patients in community clinics. *American Journal of Psychiatry, 157*, 581–587.

Slep, A. M. S., & Heyman, R. E. (2006). Creating and field-testing child maltreatment definitions: Improving the reliability of substantiation determinations. *Child Maltreatment, 11*, 217–236.

Straus, M. A. (1995). Corporal punishment of children and adult depression and suicidal ideation. In J. McCord (Ed.), *Coercion and punishment in long-term perspectives* (pp. 59–77). New York, NY: Cambridge University Press.

Trickett, P. K., Feerick, M., Flanzer, S., & Knutson, J. (2006). *Child abuse and neglect: Definitions, classification, and a framework for research*. Baltimore, MD: Brookes Publishing Co.

U.S. Department of Health and Human Services, Administration for Children and Families, Administration on Children, Youth and Families, Children's Bureau, Office on Child Abuse and Neglect. (2003). *The child abuse prevention and treatment act*. Washington, DC: U.S. Department of Health and Human Services.

Wolfe, D. A., & McIsaac, C. (2010). *Distinguishing between poor/dysfunctional parenting and child emotional maltreatment*. Prepared for the Family Violence Prevention Unit of the Public Health Agency of Canada. Unpublished report.

World Health Organization. (1992). *The ICD-10 Classification of Mental and Behavioral Disorders*. Geneva, Switzerland: Author.

World Health Organization. (2000). *World health report health systems: Improving performance*. Geneva, Switzerland: Author.

World Health Organization. (2001). *World health report mental health: New understanding, new hope*. Geneva, Switzerland: Author.

World Health Organization. (2002). Child abuse and neglect by parents and other caregivers. In E. G. Krug, L. L. Dahlberg, J. A. Mercy, A. B. Zwift, & R. Lozano (Eds.), *World report on violence and health* (pp. 57–86). Geneva, Switzerland: Author.

World Health Organization. (2005). *World health report: Make every mother and child count*. Geneva, Switzerland: Author.

APPENDIX: COMPARISON OF PROPOSED CHILD MALTREATMENT DEFINITIONS AND OTHER COMMONLY USED DEFINITIONS

TABLE 9A.1 Comparison of Child Physical Abuse Definitions: Proposed Criteria, CDC Uniform Definitions, and U.S. National Incidence Study on Child Abuse and Neglect Operationalizations

	Proposed Definitions	Maltreatment Classification System	CDC Definitions	NIS-4
Act	The nonaccidental use of physical force on the part of a child's caregiver. • Physical force includes, but is not limited to, spanking with hand, dropping, pushing, shoving, slapping, grabbing, poking, hair-pulling, scratching, pinching, restraining, shaking, throwing, biting, kicking, hitting with fist, hitting with a stick, strap, or other object, scalding, burning, poisoning, stabbing, applying force to throat, cutting off air supply, holding under water, using a weapon.	A caregiver or responsible adult [commits] other than accidental [act].	The intentional use of physical force against a child that results in, or has the potential to result in, physical injury. • Physical acts include: hitting, kicking, punching, beating, stabbing, biting, pushing, shoving, throwing, pulling, dragging, dropping, shaking, strangling/choking, smothering, burning, scalding, and poisoning.	The nonaccidental use of physical force against a child. • Physical acts include: shake, throw, or purposefully drop, hit with hand, hit with object, push, grab, drag, or pull, punch or kick.
Impact	Significant impact on the child involving any of the following: 1. More than inconsequential physical injury; 2. Reasonable potential for more than inconsequential physical injury, given the degree of force used and the physical environment in which the acts occurred; 3. More than inconsequential fear. Means for determining fear may vary with the developmental level of the child.	Act "inflicts physical injury upon a child"		Harm standard: Child must have experienced observable harm from their maltreatment. Endangerment standard: Physical acts placed the child at serious risk or harm.

Table 9A.2. Comparison of Child Sexual Abuse Definitions: Proposed Criteria, CDC Uniform Definitions, and U.S. National Incidence Study on Child Abuse and Neglect Operationalizations

	Proposed Definitions	Maltreatment Classification System	CDC Definitions	NIS-4
Act	1. Noncontact exploitation—Forcing, tricking, enticing, threatening or pressuring a child to participate in acts for anyone's sexual gratification without direct physical contact between child and offender. • Acts include, but are not limited to, exposing child's or offender's genitals, anus, or breasts; having child masturbate or watch masturbation; having child participate in sexual activity with a third person (including child prostitution); having child pose, undress or perform in a sexual fashion (including child pornography); exposing child to pornography or live sexual performance; "peeping" or other prurient watching (i.e., voyeurism) 2. Rape—Use of physical force, emotional manipulation, or a child's youth or naïveté to engage in penis-vulva or penis-anus penetration (of child, perpetrator, or both), however slight 3. Other sexual assault—Physical contact of a sexual nature between child and perpetrator not involving penis-vulva or penis-anus penetration, including, but not limited to: • Oral-genital or oral-anal contact • Non-penile penetration of vulva or rectum (for example, with hands, fingers, or objects) • Attempted penetration of the vulva or rectum • Groping, rubbing, fondling, stroking, or similar behavior—directly or through clothing	Any sexual contact or attempt at sexual contact occurs between a caregiver or other responsible adult and a child, for purposes of the caregiver's sexual gratification or financial benefit. In cases of sexual abuse, caregiver or responsible adult refers to any family member or friend who has a relationship with the child, or is in a position of authority over the child (e.g. baby-sitter).	1. Noncontact sexual abuse. Does not include physical contact of a sexual nature between the caregiver and the child. It can include: Acts which expose a child to sexual activity (e.g., pornography, voyeurism), filming of a child in a sexual manner, sexual harassment of a child, prostitution of a child. 2. Sexual act: Any completed or attempted sexual act, sexual contact with, or exploitation (i.e., noncontact sexual interaction) of a child by a caregiver. • Acts include contact involving penetration, however slight, between the mouth, penis, vulva, or anus of the child and another individual. Sexual acts also include penetration, however slight, of the anal or genital opening by hand, finger, or other object. 3. Abusive sexual content. Includes intentional touching, either directly or through the clothing of the following: genitalia, anus, groin, breast, inner thigh, buttocks.	The following comprise sexual abuse: Intrusion sex with or without force, child's prostitution or involvement in pornography with or without intrusion, molestation with genital contact, exposure/voyeurism, providing sexually explicit materials, failure to supervise child's voluntary sexual activity, and attempted/threatened sexual abuse with physical contact.

(*continued*)

Table 9A.2 Comparison of Child Sexual Abuse Definitions: Proposed Criteria, CDC Uniform Definitions, and U.S. National Incidence Study on Child Abuse and Neglect Operationalizations (*continued*)

	Proposed Definitions	Maltreatment Classification System	CDC Definitions	NIS-4
Impact	None required	None required		Harm standard: Child must have experienced observable harm from their maltreatment. Endangerment standard: Sexual acts placed the child at serious risk or harm.

Table 9A.3 Comparison of Child Emotional Abuse Definitions: Proposed Criteria, CDC Uniform Definitions, and U.S. National Incidence Study on Child Abuse and Neglect Operationalizations

	Proposed Definitions	Maltreatment Classification System	CDC Definitions	NIS-4
Act	Nonaccidental act or acts (excluding physical and sexual abusive acts) such as those listed below. Acts not listed, but of similar severity, are also eligible. • Berating, disparaging, humiliating child (or other similar behavior) • Threatening to harm child directly (including, but not limited to, threatening physical harm, abandonment, sexual assault) • Threatening to harm child indirectly (including, but not limited to, threatening suicide; threatening to, hurt, destroy, or abandon loved one, pet, or property) • Harming child's loved one, pet, or property (including exposing child to criteria-meeting or sub-threshold spouse abuse) • Confining child (a means of punishment involving restriction of movement, as by tying a child's arms or legs together or binding a child to a chair, bed, or other object, or confining a child to an enclosed area [such as a closet]) • Scapegoating child • Coercing the child to inflict pain on him/herself (including, but not limited to, ordering child to kneel on split peas for long periods) • Disciplining child (through physical or nonphysical means) excessively (i.e., extremely high frequency or duration, though not meeting physical abuse criteria)	Persistent or extreme thwarting of children's basic emotional needs. This category also includes parental acts that are harmful because they are insensitive to the child's developmental level. These needs include, but are not limited to, the following: 1. Psychological safety & security: the need for a family environment free of excessive hostility and violence, and the need for an available and stable attachment figure. 2. Acceptance and self-esteem: the need for positive regard and the absence of excessively negative or unrealistic evaluation, given the child's particular developmental level. 3. Age-appropriate autonomy: the need to explore the environment and extra-familial relationships, to individuate within the bounds of parental acceptance, structure, and limit setting, without developmentally inappropriate responsibility or constraints placed on the child. These are acts of maltreatment that may be scored solely as Emotional maltreatment or that may be scored in conjunction with other subtypes of maltreatment	Intentional caregiver behavior that conveys to a child that s/he is worthless, flawed, unloved, unwanted, endangered, or valued only in meeting another's needs. Can be continual or episodic. Behaviors may include: blaming, belittling, degrading, intimidating, terrorizing, isolating, restraining, confining, corrupting, exploiting, spurning, or otherwise behaving in a manner that is harmful, potentially harmful, or insensitive to the child's developmental needs, or can potentially damage the child psychologically or emotionally. 1. Terrorizing includes caregiver behavior that is life-threatening, makes a child feel unsafe, sets unrealistic expectations of the child with threat of loss, harm, or danger if expectation is not met, threatens or perpetrates violence against a child. 2. Isolating occurs when a caregiver forbids, prevents, or minimizes a child's contact with others.	Acts include the following: close confinement (e.g., tying/binding), verbal assaults and emotional abuse, threats of sexual abuse (without contact), threats of other maltreatment, terrorizing the child, and administering unprescribed substances.

(continued)

Table 9A.3 Comparison of Child Emotional Abuse Definitions: Proposed Criteria, CDC Uniform Definitions, and U.S. National Incidence Study on Child Abuse and Neglect Operationalizations (*continued*)

	Proposed Definitions	Maltreatment Classification System	CDC Definitions	NIS-4
Impact	Adverse effect upon the child's psychological well-being	Significant impact on the child involving any of the following: 1. Psychological harm, including either a. More than inconsequential fear reaction b. Significant psychological distress (Major Depressive Disorder, Posttraumatic Stress Disorder, Acute Stress Disorder, or a constellation of symptoms similar to other psychiatric disorders) related to the act(s) 2. Reasonable potential for psychological harm a. The act (or pattern of acts) creates reasonable potential for the development of a psychiatric disorder (at or near diagnostic thresholds) related to, or exacerbated by, the act(s). The child's level of functioning and the risk and resilience factors present should be taken into consideration; b. The act (or pattern of acts) carries a reasonable potential for significant disruption of the child's physical, psychological, cognitive, or social development 3. Stress-related somatic symptoms (related to or exacerbated by the acts) that significantly interfere with normal functioning		Harm standard: Child must have experienced observable harm from their maltreatment. Endangerment standard: Emotional acts (or omissions) placed the child at serious risk or harm.

Table 9A.4 Comparison of Child Neglect Definitions: Proposed Criteria, Maltreatment Classification System, CDC Uniform Definitions, and U.S. National Incidence Study on Child Abuse and Neglect Operationalizations

	Proposed Definitions	Maltreatment Classification System	CDC Definitions	NIS-4
Act	Egregious act(s) or omission(s) on the part of the child's caregiver that deprives the child of needed age-appropriate care. 1. *Lack of supervision*: Egregious absence or inattention. Child's age and level of functioning should be considered in making determination about level of supervision required. A child's accident is not evidence of caregiver neglect, unless the lack of supervision was clearly below the level of supervision expected from caregiver. 2. *Exposure to physical hazards*: Inattention to child's safety by exposing child to physical dangers (including, but not limited to, exposed wiring; broken glass; non-secured, loaded guns in the house; illegal drugs in home; dangerous or unhygienic pets; asking child to perform dangerous activities; driving while intoxicated with child in vehicle). 3. *Educational neglect*: Knowingly allowing the child to have extended or frequent absences form school, neglecting to enroll the child in some type of home schooling or public or private education, or preventing the child from attending school for other than justifiable reasons (when education is compulsory by law) 4. *Medical neglect:* Refusal or failure to provide appropriate, medically indicated health care (including, but not limited to, failure to obtain appropriate medical, mental health, dental care) although the parent is financially able to do so or was offered other means to do so. It includes withholding of medically indicated treatment for a child with life threatening conditions.	1. Physical neglect—When a caregiver or responsible adult fails to exercise a minimum degree of care in meeting the child's physical needs. Failure to provide includes not meeting children's physical needs in any of the following domains: • Supplying the child with adequate food. • Ensuring that the child has clothing that is sanitary, appropriate for the weather and permits the child freedom of movement. • Providing adequate shelter • Ensuring adequate medical, dental, and mental health care • Ensuring the child's adequate hygiene 2. Lack of supervision—A caregiver or responsible adult does not take adequate precautions to ensure a child's safety in and out of the home, given the child's particular emotional and developmental needs. • Supervision—failing to take steps to ensure that the child is engaging in safe activities	Failure by a caregiver to meet a child's basic physical, emotional, medical/dental, or educational needs. 1. Inadequate supervision: Failure by the caregiver to ensure that the child engages in safe activities and uses appropriate safety devices, to ensure that the child is not exposed to unnecessary hazards, or to ensure appropriate supervision by an adequate substitute caregiver. 2. Exposure to violent environments: Caregiver intentionally fails to take available measures to protect the child from pervasive violence within the home, neighborhood, or community. 3. Educational neglect: Caregiver fails to provide access to adequate education (frequent absences from school, does not enroll the child in school, or to drop out of school if under 16 years old).	1. Physical neglect: Refusal to allow or provide needed care for diagnosed condition or impairment, unwarranted delay or failure to seek needed care, refusal of custody/abandonment, illegal transfers of custody or unstable custody arrangements, inadequate supervision, nutrition, personal hygiene, clothing, or shelter. 2. Educational neglect: Permitted chronic truancy or failure to register or 3. Emotional neglect: Inadequate nuturance/affection, domestic violence, knowingly permitting drug/alcohol abuse or other maladaptive behaviors, refusal to allow or provide needed care for diagnosed emotional or behavioral impairment/problem, overprotectiveness, inadequate structure, inappropriately advanced expectations, exposure to maladaptive behaviors and environments.

(*continued*)

Table 9A.4. Comparison of Child Neglect Definitions: Proposed Criteria, Maltreatment Classification System, CDC Uniform Definitions, and U.S. National Incidence Study on Child Abuse and Neglect Operationalizations *(continued)*

Proposed Definitions	Maltreatment Classification System	CDC Definitions	NIS-4
5. *Deprivation of necessities*: The failure to provide age-appropriate nourishment, shelter and clothing. Includes non-organic failure to thrive, a type of child neglect evidenced by an infant's or young child's failure to adequately grow and develop to or above the third percentile in height and weight when no organic basis for this deviation is found. Must be determined by a competent medical authority. 6. *Abandonment*: The caregiver is absent and does not intend to return or is away from the home for more than 24 hours without having arranged for an appropriate surrogate caregiver. NO IMPACT ("B") CRITERION IS NECESSARY FOR ABANDONMENT TO BE DEEMED NEGLECT.	• Environment—Failing to ensure that the child is playing in a safe area. Refers to immediate physical dangers inside or outside the home such as broken glass, unguarded electrical fixtures, toxic chemicals, and firearms. • Substitute care—Failing to provide for adequate substitute care in the caregiver's absence, or mental or physical incapacity.	4. Medical/dental neglect: Caregiver fails to provide adequate access to medical, vision, or dental care for the child (does not administer prescribed medications, refuses to take the child for needed medical attention or seek timely medical attention). 5. Physical neglect: Caregiver fails to provide adequate nutrition, hygiene, or shelter; fails to provide clothing that is adequately clean, appropriate size, or adequate for the weather. 6. Emotional neglect: Caregiver ignores the child or denies emotional responsiveness or adequate access to mental health care.	

Table 9A.4. Comparison of Child Neglect Definitions: Proposed Criteria, Maltreatment Classification System, CDC Uniform Definitions, and U.S. National Incidence Study on Child Abuse and Neglect Operationalizations (*continued*)

	Proposed Definitions	Maltreatment Classification System	CDC Definitions	NIS-4
Impact	Significant impact on the child involving any of the following: 1. More than inconsequential physical injury; 2. Psychological harm, including either a. Child's more than inconsequential fear reaction; or b. Significant psychological distress (Major Depressive Disorder, Posttraumatic Stress Disorder, Acute Stress Disorder, or a constellation of symptoms similar to other psychiatric disorders) related to the act(s) or omission(s) 3. Stress-related somatic symptoms (related to or exacerbated by the acts) that that significantly interfere with normal functioning. 4. Given the act or omission in this incident, there was significant reasonable potential for more than inconsequential physical injury; 5. Reasonable potential for psychological harm a. Given the child's level of functioning and the risk and resilience factors present, the act (or pattern of acts) poses reasonable potential for the development of a psychiatric disorder (including sub-threshold symptomology); b. The act (or pattern of acts) creates a reasonable potential for significant disruption of the child's physical, psychological, cognitive, or social development	None required		Harm standard: Child must have experienced observable harm from their maltreatment. Endangerment standard: Neglectful acts (or omissions) placed the child at serious risk or harm.

10

Child Maltreatment Relational Diagnosis Using ICD Codes: Considerations for Low- and Middle-Income Settings

Mokhantšo G. Makoae

How society defines a problem determines the manner by which we confront it.
—Jonathan M. Mann, 1999

Child maltreatment (CM) is a global problem affecting the survival, health, and development of children negatively. CM has fatal and nonfatal consequences as well as long-term negative health outcomes for individuals affected during childhood (see Chapter 11 in this volume). Particularly integral to development of prevention planning for CM is early identification of the problem (Leeb, Paulozzi, Melanson, Simon, & Arias, 2008). Currently the incidence of CM, the use of health services due to CM-related illness and injury, as well as CM consequences for child health outcomes in low- and middle-income countries (LMIC) are not well understood. This is because, as in many high-income countries, CM is predominantly conceptualized as a child protection problem, and there are a lack of tools and systems in most LMIC to support identification and reporting of the problem. LMIC are at different stages of standardizing their national health statistics including child health statistics to reflect all factors that affect the health and well-being of children, including CM. The use of the International Classification of Diseases and Related Health Problems (ICD) can enhance health sources of CM information to provide evidence for its prioritization in policy agendas. It is important that as the ICD evolves, attempts are made to improve CM identification and reporting in resource-poor settings.

This chapter will examine the extent of use of ICD-10 codes in health systems in general, and its use for diagnosing CM in LMICs in particular. Institutional arrangements, policy requirements, and practices of health professionals in relation to recognizing, documenting, and reporting CM as a public health issue, as well as some of the impeding factors to effective ICD use will be discussed.

CHILD MALTREATMENT INFORMATION SOURCES AND SYSTEMS

Child morbidity and mortality due to parents' and caregivers' actions and inactions toward children irrespective of intent are common yet severely underestimated. International literature (Jenny & Isaac, 2006; Schnitzer, Covington, Wirtz, Verhoek-Oftedahl, & Palusci, 2008) provides evidence that CM-related deaths tend to be undercounted due to surveillance systems that rely on single instead of multiple sources of CM data. They indicate that the most relied upon sources, child welfare agencies records and death certificates, seriously undercount deaths due to child abuse and neglect by parents and caregivers. Weak health information systems with limited information on the incidence, injury, and causes of death are a common problem in developing countries (Smith & Barss, 1991). This situation can be attributed to several factors.

First, institutional arrangements in most countries contribute to the invisibility of this phenomenon in child health profiles. The silence about CM in health data is also due to unlinked information systems. For example, health, law enforcement, and child protection agencies use different definitions that satisfy their mandates, and there is little communication between agencies. Consequently, responses that could have an effect on CM tend to be sectoral and less integrated, but more importantly, child health problems that could be attributed to CM remain invisible in clinical settings. Child abuse and neglect-related morbidity as a reason for seeking emergency and trauma services, as well as maltreatment-related injuries, are more likely to be diagnosed in pediatric departments and specialized children's hospitals than general hospitals. However, reviews of children's death certificates and hospital discharge records reveal consistent underreporting of fatal and nonfatal CM (Crume, DiGuiseppi, Byers, Sirotnak, & Garrett, 2002; Schnitzer, Slusher, Kruse, & Tarleton, 2011; Trokel et al., 2006).

Second, despite the health consequences of CM it is globally conceptualized almost exclusively as a child welfare problem and its occurrence may be overlooked in clinical settings. The burden of CM is seen in relation to child protection indicators (Gilbert et al., 2009) without reference to the health dimension of the burden. Consequently, CM receives little attention in child health services because physicians underdiagnose and underreport it (Flaherty & Sege, 2005; Schnitzer et al., 2011). For example, CM may not be recognized due to lack of training about CM among health professionals and data coders (Bannon & Carter, 2003; Flaherty & Sege, 2005; Scott, Tonmyr, Fraser, Walker, & McKenzie, 2009). This results in poor capturing of CM-related injuries, health conditions, and death; and translates into inaccurate estimates of CM based on child health information systems at the country level. The potential of health information systems in complementing social welfare agencies in recording and reporting CM while also highlighting the health costs of the problem is less recognized in LMICs.

Third, lack of policy or poor implementation of standard procedures and guidelines for documenting CM in clinical settings contribute to a poor understanding of CM incidence in developing countries. Health authorities are less likely to prioritize child abuse and neglect in sectoral child well-being strategies and surveillance systems. McKenzie and Scott (2011) state that child protection agencies produce most of the statistics on child abuse and neglect while other sectors also mandated to prevent and respond to CM do not customarily produce the data, or if they collect the information it tends to be in a manner that truncates maltreatment. The situation is improving in high-income contexts, since increasingly, health care services are considered critical in providing information on CM (McKenzie & Scott, 2011).

Furthermore, even in LMICs that produce relatively good quality health statistics, the focus tends to be on unintentional injuries, such as road traffic accidents, and mainly on fatal injuries. Nonfatal injuries and the circumstances under which they occur are less monitored in health care services. For example, although the burden of disease analysis combines fatal and nonfatal health outcomes, published statistics on the outcomes of childhood injuries in developing countries are on mortality (Lopez, Begg, & Bos, 2006), and data on childhood injury-related morbidity are not routinely published.

The level of recognition may also vary by type of CM, with child neglect receiving less attention than child physical and child sexual abuse. This is mainly because physical abuse cases seeking medical attention can have injuries, and the need for medicolegal evidence and the explicit health consequences of sexual abuse, such as sexually transmitted infections and adolescence pregnancy, are better understood. Child protection practitioners experience ethical dilemma in situations where caregivers live in chronic poverty and their capacity to care for children is diminished by inequitable circumstances beyond their control—"circumstantial neglect" (Loffell, 2007). Expectedly, clinicians may treat injuries such as burns or malnutrition without clarifying their link to child abuse and neglect. Health professionals may not spend enough time with patients and caregivers to obtain a comprehensive patient history or interview parents and caregivers in detail to determine the link between observed diagnosis and parental behavior. Underreporting by parents of younger children and underdetection of maltreatment by child protection agencies for older children (Gilbert et al., 2009) are recognized as threats to complete national statistics for children affected by physical, sexual, and psychological abuse. Health services are not immune to such threats to obtaining complete data, but overall consciousness about the problem can improve information on how CM affects public health in LMICs.

In medical settings practitioners may prioritize treatment and overlook the equally important mandated responsibility to determine child abuse and neglect or report such cases as stipulated in various countries' child protection laws. For example, pediatric malnutrition and burns are common problems in LMICs. However, research on burns may focus on the management of wounds (Kingu & Mazwai, 2010; Shonubi et al., 2005), even though some the injuries could be due to child abuse. All these factors affect the accuracy of the statistics reported, thus understating the extent of CM and its consequences for child health care resources and long-term health needs for society.

HEALTH CARE PROFESSIONALS' ROLE IN PRODUCING CHILD MALTREATMENT DATA AND CHALLENGES

It is necessary for health care professionals to report both nonfatal and fatal consequences of CM but currently statistics severely underrepresent the former. Stone et al. (1999) refer to a similar situation reported by the Centers for Disease Control and Prevention (CDC) of data gaps in nonfatal assaults and an emphasis on homicide information. Child health indicators in most countries do not reflect the contribution of child abuse and neglect to child morbidity and health costs in the public health sector. This can be attributed to several factors, including poor recording of the information in clinical settings. Determining the level of awareness of health professionals about CM as a public health concern is one of the prerequisites for ensuring that they identify and record related diagnosis in medical records with sufficient detail. However, both systemic and individual factors contribute to the problem of underestimating CM in health settings.

Health professionals play an important role in the production of adequate statistics pertaining to the impact of CM on children's health but in LMICs there are insufficient frameworks, infrastructure, and policy enforcement to support this responsibility. Countries lack effective surveillance systems for CM in their health systems, but most importantly child protection and child health information systems remain unlinked. The problem is further complicated by child protection and child health being viewed as mandates of different professions such that even where state institutional arrangements could facilitate integration of these two subareas of child well-being, successes in one do not filter into the other.

LMIC's child protection registers tend to be underdeveloped compared with child health monitoring systems, yet the potential of the latter in augmenting traditional sources of child development indicators, especially for children under 5 years of age, is neglected in policy. In many instances evidence on health services' contribution to this goal is not visible in national reports. Often, child protection data are reported without specifying the sources, especially the health information systems at national, subnational, or regional levels. Clinicians have a role in supporting efforts to prevent and respond to CM by providing surveillance data for evidence-based interventions for individual children and at the population level.

Studies stress the child protection role of health professionals in relation to surveillance. O'Donnell et al. (2010) investigated the extent to which children with hospital admission due to assault, maltreatment, or sexually transmitted infection before 14 years of age also had contact with child protection services. They also identified injuries commonly linked to CM and reported to child protection. They concluded that the health system was effective in recognizing and reporting "real cases" of CM, a high proportion of which were also found in the child protection system, thus highlighting the reliability of routine child health data for tracking CM. In fact, health professionals are more likely than child protection agencies to "know" children affected by fatal child abuse and child neglect (Newton et al., 2010). McKenzie, Scott, Fraser, and Dunne (2011) found that about 29% of CM cases linked with hospital and child protection records were presented to health services before becoming known to child protection agencies. The need for health workers of different categories, including antenatal care providers to recognize child protection issues in routine clinical encounters has been examined (Lazenbatt & Greer, 2009). The benefit of integrated surveillance systems and increasing enforcement of reporting was illustrated in a recent study in Saudia Arabia (Al-Eissa & Almuneef, 2010). They concluded that identification and reporting of CM increased due to the introduction of child protection centers in health facilities accompanied by enforcement of mandatory reporting of child abuse and neglect cases by health professionals. Poor integration of services perpetuates the common misconception that locates CM exclusively in the child welfare domain, thus making CM peripheral to health professionals' responsibilities even though it affects health outcomes significantly.

The consequences of overlooking child abuse and neglect in clinical settings by simply documenting diagnosed health conditions without providing information about the clinician's assessment of the context of health problem and referring the family to child protection services for proper investigation and possible support are far-reaching. Figure 10.1 illustrates possible trajectories of interventions for child injuries under different clinical assumptions: CM and no CM, and child outcomes. Health practitioners can optimize the benefits of both systems of intervention by integrating child protection values and practice in routine child health care; this is in the best interest of a child. Sometimes clinicians' decisions regarding whether to report a CM case will be influenced by their anticipation of cumbersome child protection procedures that ensue following such notifications, their self-perception of their CM competencies, and consequences for their professional reputation. Nevertheless, the opportunity of health services to enhance child protection is buttressed by evidence that in many instances, children who die from maltreatment would have been seen by health care professionals for abuse-related symptoms before formally reported to child protection services.

THE ICD CODES

The ICD is a diagnostic framework that has been used and adapted in many countries since 1948, when the system ceased to be a mere list of causes of death—then known as the International List of Causes of Death—ILCD (Jette et al., 2010). The system was developed by the World Health Organization (WHO, 1992) and adopted by many countries to code documented information on clinical records and death certificates pertaining to causes of morbidity and mortality, respectively, as well as monitor the kind of diagnoses that result in the need for health resources in the form of treatment and clinical investigation. The WHO (1992/1996/2006) is currently reviewing the 10th revision of the ICD—ICD-10 published in 1992. This process will produce the 11th revision of this diagnostic framework, a process this volume was, in part, based on.

According to the Colorado Department of Public Health and Environment (2001, p. 1) through the ICD, the goal of the WHO is to "promote international comparability in the collection, classification, processing and presentation of mortality statistics." This coding system is contained in 21 chapters of the ICD-10, and clinical professionals use the codes as a guide when describing diagnosis and treatment choices while trained data coders use them to convert written medical records into alphanumeric codes that constitute the ICD system.

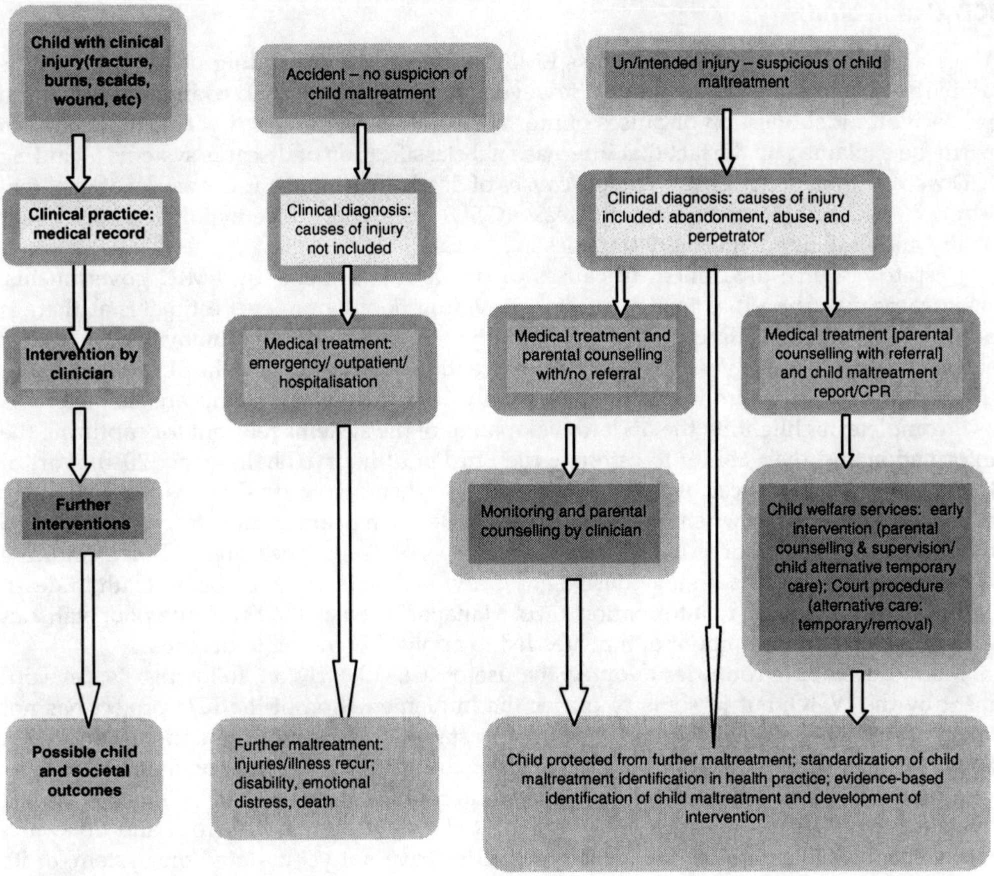

FIGURE 10.1 Possible trajectories and child outcomes of intervention for child injuries under different clinical assumptions.

Note: Low- and middle-income country frameworks for identifying, recording, tracking, and responding to maltreatment in health care services need improvement, including the consistent use of globally recognized medical recording practices, such as the International Classification of Diseases and Related Health Problems (ICD) as required, in some instances, by law.

The codes indicate clinical diagnosis and external causes of morbidity, and mortality, which examining physicians are expected to record for purposes of disease and health management. The information is also used for surveillance of diseases, reasons for consulting health services, and causes of injury and death globally. The environmental events and circumstances that cause injuries and death indicate the risk factors that contribute to the burden of disease in specific localities, countries, and globally, thus helping planners to identify strategies for curbing health problems affecting populations and policy makers to make informed decisions about priority actions. Within the public health system, information about disease and injury causing children to use health care services would be available from hospital trauma and emergency departments, pediatric wards, and outpatient departments, as well as community health clinics. A health professional provides authenticated information pertaining to the outcome of clinical consultation in a medical record that becomes a valuable source of local, national, and international data. The information feeds into the health information system of a country and can be part of vital statistics.

ICD Use in LMICs

There are variations within and across LMICs in terms of ICD coding utilization and the usability of the produced data varies. However, most importantly, ICD coding has been used primarily for identification of causes of mortality and less for morbidity. This tendency can partly be explained by the fact that international classification of diseases systems including ICD were originally designed to report causes of deaths. Within the frameworks of vital registration (VR) and global burden of disease (GBD) researchers have mainly assessed availability and usability of mortality statistics in LMICs.

Despite resource investment in causes of death data systems by LMIC governments, researchers describe VR as inadequate for providing population-level estimates as there is an urban-hospital bias (Rao, Bradshaw, & Mathers, 2004). Additional innovative measures such as verbal autopsies (VA) used to monitor trends in death causes in the developing countries (Byass, 2007) are also inadequate. Generally, countries' data systems are characterized as incomplete, highlighting the underdevelopment of the systems relevant for capturing the information and their ability to estimate the burden of injury (Bhalla et al., 2010). Part of the reason is the practices of health professionals when recording diagnoses in everyday clinical encounters and when recording causes of death in death certificates, which can also influence lay interpretation of death causes. Reviews of death certificates in LMICs indicate that health professionals do not consistently provide details of the cause of death in death certificates thus leading to information gaps. Mahapatra et al. (2007) attribute poor statistics to lack of skill and the amount of time needed to apply ICD coding to diagnoses.

Many developing countries adopted the use of ICD-10 early on, following its development by the WHO, but in some countries the implementation of the ICD project has not taken off, placing various countries at different stages of ICD implementation (Bah, 2009). Some countries that have a widespread use of the ICD-10 codes for organizing medical records in hospitals include Brazil since 1998 (Laurenti & Buchalla, 2005), China since 2002 (Deloitte LLP, 2011), India since 2000 (Kumar et al., 2007), and South Africa and Botswana more recently. Other sub-Saharan Africa countries have not yet adopted the system, or its use is limited to institutional deaths (e.g., Kenya and Mozambique; Rao et al., 2004). Several countries in Africa, Asia, and Latin America have ICD-coded cause-of-death data of acceptable quality available from in-hospital death records and VR of population subsets (Bhalla et al., 2010; Murray, Lopez, Barofsky, Bryson-Cahn, & Lozano, 2007).

Where ICD-10 is used for documentation of morbidity, rationale tends to emphasize its efficiency in supporting the billing system. It is plausible that there are even fewer LMICs that apply ICD for identification of causes of child morbidity due to CM or as a reason for contacting health care services. Describing the state of hospital records in LMIC, Marszalek and De Villiers (2006, p. 15) stated, "the quality of records varies among institutions. Some hospitals have computerized data, while others may keep no records whatsoever. ... Thorough documentation is essential in providing an invaluable database for researchers, but morbidity statistics are unfortunately scarce." In many sub-Saharan Africa countries physicians do not ascribe the strict application of cause-of-death ICD guidelines. It is suggested that conducting physicians' medical records reviews and physician training on ICD-sensitive recording of causes of death would be a necessary investment (Murray et al., 2007). The use of abbreviations and producing incomplete medical records especially for unfamiliar conditions such as CM affect data quality. To promote documenting of CM, WHO and United Nations International Children's Emergency Fund (UNICEF) need to increase awareness about the ICD codes for CM and encourage their use.

Health care professionals are the bedrock of reliable national health data but it is equally important that institutional frameworks and resource capacity support the compilation, processing, analysis, and reporting of all kinds of data needed to profile public health status. There has been progress in collecting reliable statistics on child health and development indicators in LMICs. For example, the Integrated Management of Childhood Illnesses (IMCI) strategy for promotion, prevention, cure, and rehabilitation of children under 5 years of age in primary health care facilities has been successfully implemented with the support of United Nation (UN) agencies. The inclusion of CM as an additional indicator of child health and well-being in national health information systems is crucial but requires a more active role of health professionals in child protection matters and supporting institutional resources. It also requires awareness among health professionals about the various uses of the data obtained from medical records at local, national, and international levels. For example, most countries have ratified the UN Convention on the Rights of the Child (CRC) and submit health status reports to UN agencies such as UNICEF and the WHO. Efficient health information systems that feed into the global statistics are needed for monitoring progress toward meeting national obligations to protect children. ICD-supported health information requires support through international cooperation by way of countries situation assessments, training, institutional strengthening, and information systems framework development across sectors.

Various factors affect the extent of data usability. First, there is a problem of negligence by health professionals who use the diagnostic categories of the ICD-10 for ill-defined causes of death leading to unusable information for health policy and planning (Mathers, Lopez, & Murray, 2006). Second, there are many deaths that occur in the community making in-hospital deaths only a crude measure of the overall deaths that occur in any poor resource context. Deaths recorded by nonmedical authorities are less likely to be ICD-compliant and provide details about circumstances leading to death. This situation is even more applicable to young children's data, especially if their deaths are not due to trauma or accidents; hence there is a high proportion of "undetermined causes" category or "natural causes" in public data sources.

Factors that influence countries to provide high quality data on CM in child health profiles vary. They may be political, systemic, and individualistic in nature, sometimes relating to ICD use in general or specifically to CM codes. However, challenges faced by health personnel and data coders in the production of health statistics on nonfatal and fatal CM in developing countries need to be researched. In particular, there is little understanding of how the use and nonuse of ICD codes in pediatric settings affects national child health statistics.

Policy enforcement is weak even in some of the countries that have laws obliging health professionals to use ICD for documenting diagnoses. A survey of the WHO member states' ICD coding capacity for morbidity and mortality data (Walker & McKenzie, 2004) found that apart from low response rate by LMICs—27% of Southeast Asia region and 30% of Africa region—several indicators suggested low capacity to implement ICD-10, including low involvement by hospitals, medical officers, and clinical coders in the coding of mortality data and the perceived need for ICD training in 71 of the 99 analyzed countries. Marszalek and De Villiers (2006) attribute poor documentation of medical records in LMICs including, South Africa, to a chronic shortage of staff in public hospitals. Health systems in LMICs are weak because of shortage of professional personnel as indicated by doctor–patient population ratios that far exceed WHO recommendations. Consequently, health care providers in public health settings—emergency departments, pediatric hospital units, and outpatient departments—face serious time constraints that affect the quality of their interaction and communication with patients.

Child Maltreatment Identification in Clinical Settings

CM is underestimated in child health databases and is generally invisible as a cause of child morbidity and death (Flaherty & Sege, 2005; McKenzie & Scott, 2011; Scott et al., 2009). CM could be invisible because health professionals record diagnoses in a manner that does not allow the use of ICD codes for child abuse and neglect leading to misrepresentation of data. This could be because they lack awareness about the link between CM and some of the health conditions they attend to, or they lack awareness about CM codes in the ICD system. All these factors lead to nonuse of the relevant codes and limit the potential benefit of health information systems to identify the incidence and types of CM, their effect on child well-being, and survival and ability to monitor treatment costs and outcomes. For example, the need to address the public health consequences of CM is not yet part of health strategies in place in many countries. As McKenzie and Scott (2011) indicate, the problem will remain intractable unless disease diagnosis, hospitalization, and child protection data are integrated to produce an evidence base for developing interventions for child well-being.

There are two broad categories of ICD-10 codes used for classifying current CM as cause of morbidity. First, Chapter XIX codes (S00–T98) are "Injury, poisoning and certain other consequences of external causes" of injury or diseases. They include T74 codes for classifying "maltreatment syndromes" for children (and adults). The codes are used to specify clinically identified diseases or injuries that typify *effects* of neglect or abandonment and abuse. The T74 maltreatment syndromes are used to identify the nature of current injury, disease, or psychological condition that is a consequence of different forms of maltreatment. As McKenzie and Scott (2011) indicate, T74 codes are used for conclusive diagnosis. They should be used with age specification expansion characters to indicate when a patient is a child. In addition, clarity on the nature of the condition can be enhanced by including the external cause code in Chapter XX.

Chapter XX (V01–Y98) codes are for classifying "External causes of morbidity and mortality." They include broad categories of environmental events and circumstances as the cause of injury, poisoning, and other negative effects (WHO, 1992, 2006). They also include codes used for coding homicide and injuries inflicted by another person with intent to injure or kill, by any means, including attempted acts. The X85–Y09 codes are used to classify homicide and injury caused by assault using various substances, objects, and elements.Y04 and Y05 codes are specifically used to identify injuries and death caused by another person using bodily force—Y04 "assault by bodily force;" Y05 for "sexual assault by bodily force" (including sodomy and rape). Y06 code is for "neglect and abandonment;" and Y07 is for "other maltreatment syndromes," which entail a combination of mental cruelty, physical abuse, sexual abuse, and torture. Y06 and Y07 are used for conclusive diagnoses of maltreatment. Including information about the age of a patient and the perpetrator category improves specificity (e.g., Y06.1 would show an injury or death caused by parental neglect or abandonment). Y04 and Y05 codes are useful for injury surveillance but lack specificity needed to identify child physical and sexual abuse. As such medical records produced without CM-specific codes will lead to underestimation of CM incidence. The cause for undercounting will be different from concerns raised by McKenzie and Scott (2011) who refer to strict criteria of inclusion while using codes that are internationally applied. This limitation will be discussed in relation to South Africa's ICD use for child abuse by a children's hospital and ongoing mortality surveillance systems.

Despite availability of ICD codes for CM, research shows that even in high-income countries, there are variations in practices among pediatricians and other primary health care professionals in relation to documenting injuries in clinical setting. Potential sources of data, including medical records are often not documented in a manner that injuries and morbidity could be linked to CM. Similarly, reports of CM to child protection services for investigation are rare or not reflected as such in national child well-being data. Research has identified several contributing factors. Scott et al. (2009, p. 792) argue that "[i]dentification of inflicted injury in children in a clinical setting can be complex and confronting for medical and nursing staff." Newton et al. (2010) conducted a systematic review of six studies that evaluated changes in emergency department practitioners' behavior in relation to documenting child abuse. Some of the factors that influence professionals' decisions include their consideration of the likely consequences of their involvement. For most practitioners, consequences considered include benefits for children and affected families (preventing further abuse, facilitating provision of services including alternative placement), concern with time demands and damaging relationships with clients; avoiding court processes involved in the investigation of child abuse reports, and working relationship with child protection services (CPS) especially CPS inability to provide feedback on their decisions following investigations, as well as lack of confidence due to limited knowledge in identifying child abuse (David, 2005, Flaherty & Sege, 2005; Newton et al., 2010). Some professionals may advocate for routine screening of parenting problems by child health professionals as part of regular health visits. If health professionals are conscious about the relevance of relational problems in clinical practice and understand their own role in child protection, they can be critical about young children's health conditions that are due to external causes and these will reflect in their medical records.

Researchers have also noted the inherent limitations of ICD codes used specifically for CM. Schnitzer et al. (2011) indicate that ICD codes are inadequate when it comes to capturing physical abuse, and medical, physical, and supervisory neglect as causes of diagnosed clinical conditions in children under 10 years old. Their analysis highlighted undercounting of CM as a common problem even when practitioners adhered to guidelines. This occurs because surveillance usually includes cases coded with explicit CM codes (e.g., T74 codes) and excludes medical records where injuries and illnesses are suggestive of probable or possible maltreatment based on the literature and contextual indicators. For example, parents' or caregivers' failure to follow a child's free medical treatment and take a child for vaccine despite availability of free health care services and immunization programs for young children should alert health practitioners to care practices. However, it is common to focus on issues relating to access and lack of information. Health professionals' practices when they document CM findings in medical records will determine whether or not children's injuries and other morbidities (e.g., malnutrition) receive the necessary attention that could lead to improved identification and implementation of enhanced protocols and support for children, families. and health practitioners.

Applications and Benefits of Using the ICD for Child Maltreatment Data

Although the ICD coding system is increasingly being used worldwide due to its promotion by the WHO and noticeable benefits in categorizing health problems for planning, the use of ICD codes for CM surveillance in clinical settings is limited with many countries not prioritizing CM in their health information systems. Developing countries have different practices with regard to the utilization of the ICD for health data derived using ICD codes—ranging from nonuse to a relatively elaborate use of the coding system. Whether the system is used or not, and the extent of its use to inform child health in any country, reflect the challenges of using this classification system.

The effective application of ICD at various levels of health delivery primarily depends on examining health practitioner's awareness about CM diagnostic codes and subjective decisions during each clinical encounter. For example, they influence the amount of detail they include when they write medical records. Scott et al. (2009) state that it is important that medical records and death certificates support the use of ICD codes and minimize misdiagnosis of CM-related morbidity and mortality. Hazlewood (2003) identifies the advantages of using ICD-10 as going beyond just identifying and classifying diseases and injuries "to include risk factors that are frequently encountered in a primary care setting" thus providing the necessary level of precision in clinical information that can allow evidence-based interventions.

The benefits of using ICD for CM surveillance, research, and developing policies and plans for child protection are well documented. A recent systematic literature review of ICD use for documenting CM (Scott et al., 2009) identified the following four purposes:

approximating child abuse incidence, estimating risk of injury and death by describing the patterns and characteristics of child abuse, evaluation of ICD codes used for child abuse across data sources to validate coding used and, finally, research articles on the use of ICD to estimate CM health costs.

Maintaining strong health information systems is critical to effective planning and meeting the needs of populations in developing countries but the challenges are numerous (Oak, 2007). González-Izquierdo et al. (2010) and Scott et al. (2009) state that when ICD-10 codes are used for diagnosis and recording clinical findings on CM as well as the circumstances under which injuries and other medical conditions occur in detail, the codes help with identification and classification of fatal and nonfatal child abuse and neglect. ICD-coded information improves the reliability of CM information and can be used to assess this dimension of children's well-being and support provision of evidence-based child protection services ranging from prevention, to early identification, to intervention. According to the CDC, state surveillance of CM is foremost in the public health approach process (Leeb et al., 2008). In particular, hospital discharge records and emergency department visits have been identified as relevant to capturing routine child health information suggestive of CM; "they document disease and injury morbidity that is severe enough to require medical attention" (Schnitzer et al., 2011, p. 4), and the frequency of emergency visits positively correlates with substantiated child protection reports (Spivey, Schnitzer, Kruse, Slusher, & Jaffe, 2009).

In low- and middle-income settings, the ICD system could enhance the IMCI strategy and be used to determine the circumstances of injuries. But such an approach assumes a broad conceptualization of child protection that recognizes CM as a public health problem. The approach becomes less effective when health policy does not support an integrated strategy or prioritize CM such that health professionals internalize the objective of child protection. The tendencies discussed above will be illustrated through a South Africa example, one of the developing countries where ICD-10 adoption is considered to have generated useful lessons (Bah, 2009).

The South Africa Case Study

South Africa has high levels of interpersonal violence that contribute significantly to child injuries and nonnatural fatalities (Donson, 2009; Seedat, Van Niekerk, Jewkes, Suffla, & Ratele, 2009; Statistics South Africa, 2007). Violence consequences include child sexual and physical injuries that lead to medical treatment in hospitals (Lammers, Martin, Andrews, & Seedat, 2010).The annual injury mortality surveillance report for 2008 indicated that violence was the leading cause of nonnatural deaths with 31% (9,151) of all deaths (31,177) in participating cities recording it. Additionally, 397 deaths (1.3%) were infants and children aged between infancy and 14 years of age; and 686 (2.2%) were adolescents aged 15 to 19 years (Donson, 2009). Finally, the Child PIP (problem identification program) has been implemented in some of the hospitals, beginning in 2000, to analyze hospital mortality information for children younger than 5 years of age. The Child PIP system has encountered a difficulty of identifying injury-related childhood deaths in nationwide annual audits of the causes of mortality for children under 5 years of age cared for in hospitals. Only 38 "other accidents/poisoning deaths," 8 "abuse-related deaths," and 7 "burns" were recorded in pediatric medical wards (Stephen et al., 2006). The root cause could be a lack of consciousness among some of the health professionals about ICD requirements and their role in producing information that is informed by the system's coding standards.

The latest report (Stephen, Bamford, Patrick, & Wittenberg, 2011) shows that between 2005 and 2009, nonaccidental injury, abuse-related, and neglect, and homicide accounted for 68 (0.3%) of hospital child deaths.

Although the country's death registration system has improved since 1998, a significant proportion of violence-related deaths are still documented inadequately, thus creating gaps in surveillance data (Rao et al., 2004). In 2005 a high number of deaths—65.3% of 52,478 deaths due to nonnatural causes—could not be classified accordingly and were accorded "events of undetermined intent" category (Statistics South Africa, 2007). The 2008 injury mortality surveillance report shows that out of 2,729 (9.5%) nonnatural deaths with undetermined cause, 516 (18.9%) were children aged between less than 1 year and 4 years, 39 (1.4%) were aged 5 to 9 years, 38 (1.4%) were aged 10 to 14 years, and 93 (3.4%) were adolescents aged 15 to 19 years (Donson, 2009). Violence researchers and the national statistics office using ICD codes identified data gaps but the contribution of both confirmed and suspected CM to child health outcomes using ICD codes have not received research and policy attention in the country.

In practice, there is bias toward collecting mortality data according to international standards while efforts to collect comparable morbidity data remain less focused. A useful explanation for this disparity is provided by Bah (2009) who rightly states that the two parts of ICD-10-derived information for mortality and morbidity belong to two different information subsystems (national statistics offices and health care systems, respectively). These institutions are driven by different players (state institutions and private sector institutions, respectively) whose actions do not have the same consequences. For example, the "no-ICD-10 code, no pay" policy (Bah, 2009; National ICD-10 Task Team, 2010) in South Africa has motivated health care providers who make submissions for billing and reimbursement to privately run medical schemes to adopt ICD-10 coding for diagnostic purposes; failure to do so would impact severely on their revenue flow. Their counterparts in the public health sector may not feel equally obliged despite the fact that ICD use is a legal requirement in the country (see Tzitzivacos, 2007). Nonuse of ICD is a challenge and some of the factors that can enhance its use have been identified.

On the one hand, the importance of enforcing legislation and making ICD mandatory in public health facilities has been identified as necessary (Jette et al., 2010) but in South Africa this has not yet led to significant changes. ICD-10 was adopted by the Department of Health in 1996 and the maintenance of the system became the responsibility of the National Health Information System of South Africa (NHISSA; Department of Health & Council of Medical Schemes, 2004). Since 2005, all health care practitioners were required by law to use the ICD-10 system. However, these institutional and legal provisions have not yet translated into consistent and standardized professional practice when documenting CM in clinical settings. The situation may give the impression that the legislative requirements of the Medical Schemes Act 131 of 1998 are only compulsory to private health providers. The necessary detail that would allow categorization of diagnosis is not included in medical records. The use of ICD codes is fragmented and lacks the necessary level of specificity that allows comparison of data across the national health information district subsystems and globally.

On the other hand, Bah (2009, p. 49) predicts that "[t]he more health care financing tends towards insurance-based system, the more important billing and clinical coding becomes." This change could be expected as South Africa moves toward the National Health Insurance (NHI) system. Presently, private health funders seem to be optimizing the benefits of the coding system in relation to guaranteed payment of bills, and this goal seems to supersede ICD primary function as a tool for collecting standardized country statistics.

Information Systems for Child Maltreatment and ICD Use

The health information system is district based, and similar to injury mortality data, there are several information sources for nonfatal injuries and illnesses affecting children. Sources of information are primary health care facilities (private and public), hospital outpatient departments, hospital wards, emergency departments, trauma units, and specialized academic children's hospitals. Dawes, Willenberg, & Long (2006) argue that research on the health consequences of interpersonal violence for children is constrained by the inadequacy of data systems that do not include data elements that enable such analysis. The inconsistent use of the ICD codes in clinical settings could be seen as one of the factors impeding effective reporting and interventions for CM.

Currently, clinicians do not necessarily adhere to international guidelines and write descriptions of diagnoses including CM in detail. But factors that influence their decisions as well as awareness of the implications of their actions for policy implementation have not been systematically investigated. More importantly, despite the well-documented concern about the high magnitude of CM in the country, policy guidelines on clinical surveillance are unavailable, hence varied practices across health and research institutions.

At the basic level, coding guidelines would entail the use of codes for external causes of morbidity and mortality, and codes for identifying the nature of injury or disease due to CM. In addition, the fourth character for identification of the perpetrator of identified external cause or morbidity and mortality would be included as this is also important for surveillance purposes (e.g., Y06.1 for injury, illness, or death caused by neglect and abandonment by a parent).

The current status is that Y05, Y06, and Y07 codes are used for mortality surveillance in the data coordinated by Statistics South Africa. Table 10.1 shows coding of external causes of death for the 1997 to 2007 period from the national database. It shows a high number of deaths of children and adolescents (18 years or under) due to external causes (sexual assault, neglect, abandonment, and other maltreatment syndromes). A major limitation of this national source of data, however, is that Statistics South Africa does not use the fourth character in its coding system for causes of unnatural causes of death. The perpetrator is not specified in some of the death certificates or may not be included during data capturing. The utility of ICD-coded injury mortality data compiled by Statistics South Africa is further limited by poor reporting of intent leading to a high proportion of cases under the "undetermined intent" category. The situation leads to data with limited usability since it may not be comparable to other countries' statistics, but most importantly, its usefulness for planning prevention programs is diminished.

The use of three-character codes is inadequate for classifying the causes of death due to injury since they fail to identify the perpetrator (hospital child death audits use Y04–Y06 for abuse or neglect-related injuries and X85–Y05 and Y07–Y09 codes for homicides). Both as clinicians' and clinical coders' practice, the consequences of three-character codes and inadequate documentation of circumstances under which children become injured negatively affect the identification of CM and its reporting.

In addition, T74 codes show the consequences (injury, disease, or psychological condition) that are due to CM, yet these codes are not part of the country's morbidity system. Furthermore, institutions seem to follow different practices when it comes to documenting

TABLE 10.1 External Causes of Death Affecting Children and Adolescents, South Africa—1997 to 2007

ICD-10 Code: Cause of Death	Number of Reported Deaths	Children and Adolescents (No.)	Children and Adolescents (%)
Y05: "Sexual assault by bodily force": Includes rape and sodomy	67	25	37
Y06: Neglect and abandonment	683	141	20.6
Y07: "Other maltreatment syndrome": Includes mental cruelty, physical abuse sexual abuse, and torture	41	13	31.7
Total child and adolescent deaths	791	179	22.6

Source: Statistics South Africa mortality dataset (Professor D. Bradshaw, Medical Research Council of South Africa—personal communication—October 6, 2010).

clinical information on child injury. The Red Cross War Memorial Children's Hospital is the largest referral academic hospital for children in South Africa based in the Western Cape Province. Since 2008 the hospital policy obliges health professionals to use ICD-10 codes. Y04.9 is used for physical abuse and Y05.9 code is used for sexual assault abuse-related morbidity and mortality (Professor Sebastian Van As, personal communication). Although further details are provided in the form of the fourth character, this is the expansion character used for assault "by unspecified person." Marszalek and De Villiers (2006) report morbidity data obtained from a hospital in the province in which ICD categories used to characterize morbidity profiles of admissions to the hospital were "S or T"—injury, poisoning, effects of foreign bodies, burns and others, as well as "V or X or Y" for transport accident, other accidental injury, assault or self-harm, and other external causes of injury.

The data have limited use because of their lack of precision, and they may not be comparable globally. The major weaknesses include lack of a consistent practice regarding the use of ICD codes, nonuse of CM-specific codes, and inconsistent recording of perpetrators of abuse in children's medical records. The data are useful in as far as they show the extent of violence against children, which in the case of South Africa, is a relatively advanced priority.

Furthermore, there has been a concern about definitional dissonance and its implications for generating reliable CM statistics. The new Children's Act (No. 38 of 2005, as amended) defines a child as an individual under 18 years of age. The definition of "a child" varies across some of the key institutions that constitute the important sources of child health information. Health data on child sexual abuse is captured (though not routinely reported) through the District Health Information System (DHIS), a component of the National Health Information System of South Africa (NHIS/SA) that collects routine health data monthly for monitoring and evaluation of priority health programs. While child health indicators such as nutritional status, mortality, and morbidity data are part of the system, CM is not one of the areas of focus in the health sector. Dawes et al. (2006) identified some of the weaknesses in the DHIS as its definition of a child as individuals under the age of 14, which is inconsistent with the law. Consequently, data on older children cannot be captured and they disappear into the adult statistics in the DHIS. For example, Marszalek and DeVilliers (2006) analyzed morbidity data from hospital admissions for "adult patients," which was defined as anyone over 13 years of age. Similarly, the Red Cross War Memorial Children's Hospital located in the Western Cape Province is the only specialized hospital in the country but sees children under 13 years of age only. Although the facility uses ICD-10 codes it only has data on a subset of children in the province.

There is a consensus that in South Africa morbidity statistics are not complete; the available morbidity data may not necessarily be in accordance with ICD coding while that which is ICD coded may show variability in code application. There is variability between public health institutions and health providers who provide services to clients under medical schemes. Mainly medical records submitted by health professionals for billing would in most cases conform to ICD coding system whereas most of the medical records from public health facilities may neither be coded nor compiled to support ICD coding by coders and record review for research purpose. Researchers have mainly applied codes to hospital admissions records retrospectively (Marszalek & De Villiers, 2006; Naidoo, 2009). But the accuracy of the records may be limited since they are not revised when patients are discharged and reliance on personnel who are not ICD trained further reduces data reliability (Naidoo, 2009).

Bah (2009) discussed factors that can facilitate the adoption of ICD coding in the developing countries based on what is considered the South Africa success story. However, challenges for documenting CM data in routine health records in LMICs are not documented. Generally, health practitioners perceive the application of ICD as onerous. Most health systems are faced with problems of shortages of health professionals. They are expected to focus on what may be considered as priority health problems and the sector's direct responsibilities for which there are clear performance goals. These include diseases that are part of a government's reporting obligations within various international frameworks. A lack of policies that prioritize CM as a public health problem exacerbates the problem of underestimating the phenomenon.

Patterns of childhood injuries and age could indicate CM but they are not reliable clinical markers on the basis of which pediatricians should make referrals to child protection services (Woodman et al., 2009). Although the consequences of failing to screen a child for CM risk may be dire, the view that in poor resource settings health professionals would not have the "luxury" of conducting lengthy interviews to get to the bottom of circumstances that lead to child injury or illness is common, but needs to be considered critically. For example, screening tools for CM to be used in conjunction with the existing systems for monitoring young children's morbidity and mortality would fill an important gap. This strategy would require integrating CM in the assessment of risk factors for childhood illnesses. In South Africa, the role of health services in child protection is illustrated by the evolution of infrastructure and provision of curative and rehabilitative services in specialized children's hospitals, clinics, and specialized centers that work closely with child protection and law enforcement agencies as referral entities.[1]

The key question is how health professionals can contribute evidence to effective planning based on their findings as providers of health services to children and their families. Being ICD aware is desirable but in many ways introduces complexities to routine examination and medical record production in clinical settings. Decisions made by health practitioners and challenges they encounter when confronted with suspected or confirmed cases of CM in clinical settings have been documented in the developed countries. Medical records written in such cases will depend on several factors including the knowledge of health professionals about the link of CM with other symptoms, their confidence to diagnose CM, the resources needed to diagnose, and the implications of including legal services as well as own professional considerations. Some health practitioners may have the perception that ICD-10 is complicated and time-consuming making it less attractive to use unless compliance is enforced. But this view overlooks the importance of producing accurate health data that can be used with efficiency to support public health decisions and families at risk. Without clear policies of states' support for health professionals who may become embattled in legal processes, clinicians are likely to avoid reputational and livelihood risks and treat the injury or medical condition clinically and ignore maltreatment. A recent study in Saudi Arabia has reported that change of attitude regarding the relevance of CM in the health domain has led to increased recognition and recording of CM cases in health facilities (Al-Eissa & Al-Muneef, 2010). Studies are needed in LMICs to assess the competencies of health professionals to recognize and respond to child abuse and neglect as well as their attitudes toward their legal obligation to report child abuse to authorities.

Although studies have focused primarily on physical injury, there is an equal need to analyze medical records of children in health facilities such as community health care centres, day hospitals, emergency or casualty departments, and pediatric wards to determine how child neglect, especially inadequate supervision, could be the underlying cause of clinical conditions such as burns, ingestion of poisonous agents and dangerous objects, malnutrition, dehydration, and other childhood illnesses preventable by immunization. It is important to document such incidents accordingly by contextualizing them within the child protection framework by including details on the adequacy of parental supervision and care in addition to structural and systemic problems. Schnitzer et al. (2008) found that in two of the three U.S. jurisdictions they studied, fatality rates due to child neglect were two to six times higher than fatalities attributed to physical abuse. A small-scale study based on the reviews of children's court inquiries (Makoae, Dawes, Loffell, & Ward, 2008) found that poisoning and medical neglect were reasons statutory interventions were implemented, however, such reports emanated from child protection agencies.

CONCLUSIONS

Growing research and surveillance on CM using administrative information sources in the health sector attests to the widespread understanding that child protection information systems do not provide all data pertaining to CM incidence, a situation believed to be more serious in LMICs than in high-income settings. LMICs have not yet made progress toward integrating CM into clinical practice and child health data. Although there are improvements in the development of child health systems generally following the implementation of IMCI, focus has mainly been on the monitoring of health indicators for children under 5 years of age for both morbidity and mortality related to disease. For older children's health and nonfatal injuries in general the same shortcomings that characterize documentation of adult morbidity and nonfatal injuries apply—data gaps on the causes of morbidity and reasons for seeking health care services are common problems. Recognition and some degree of documentation of CM take place in academic and specialized children's hospitals as well as in those hospitals that participate in surveillance initiatives for "under-five" mortality. However, there is uncertainty regarding reporting of CM identified in clinical settings to child protection services and maintaining linked cases between the two systems.

One of the important steps toward obtaining CM statistics from a country's health care system is applying the ICD codes to health conditions diagnosed by clinicians and to their causes. Countries vary in their use of ICD. Some LMICs have adopted ICD for nonbilling purposes and apply it widely in public health facilities, others have a narrow use of ICD codes in that they apply them primarily for billing and mortality surveillance with unclear practices when it comes to tracking morbidity; yet there are many countries that do not document mortality and morbidity records according to ICD at all. Conducting assessments of where various LMICs are with both clinical CM surveillance and ICD use in the health system would be necessary for determining the capacity of countries to implement ICD use for reporting injuries and health conditions that are caused by maltreatment.

The factors that determine the use of ICD vary across countries. Although it is necessary for countries to enact legislation and enforce policy on ICD use, it is not predictable that ICD codes for CM will be applied. Nevertheless, the Saudi Arabian case shows improvements in clinical recognition of CM following policy enforcement. To change the common view that CM is solely a concern for social welfare, health sector role players including policy makers and practitioners need to prioritize CM and integrate it into existing child health monitoring systems. That would increase recognition and improve documentation of CM in health settings. Both are necessary for complementing child protection statistics but most importantly, the approach will improve the visibility of CM in the public health domain; this is necessary in planning effective intersectoral interventions. Investments by the global community under the leadership of national ministries of health and welfare in partnership with WHO and UNICEF are needed to increase the use of ICD for CM morbidity and mortality by promoting both the codes for definite and suspected CM diagnoses, forms of injury, and conditions treated and procedures. These are needed for recognition of this problem and its consequences in policy agenda.

Certainly the current global focus on injury mortality and the burden of disease surveillance influences clinical practice. This focus can hamper a comprehensive assessment of interpersonal violence against children and delineation of the risk factors if the level of awareness about CM among clinical personnel and coders is low. Although child physical abuse and child sexual abuse tend to be identified, amid the problems mentioned, child psychological abuse and neglect seem to fall through the cracks. In particular, evidence of identification of CM by other health care practitioners, including therapists is unavailable. Health care information systems do not reflect routine care information on confirmed and suggestive CM and health professionals' practices in relation to documenting child injuries and child abuse in medical records are a concern. Nonuse of T74 codes in South Africa as one of the success stories in ICD adoption points that tracking CM within the health sector requires enforcement and monitoring of mandatory reporting of child physical injuries, sexual abuse, emotional abuse, and neglect.

There is a lack of scientific evidence in LMICs on how health professionals respond to identified CM in clinical settings and how they contribute to ensuring that children receive comprehensive care and child protection services. In order to improve understanding on the patterns and health consequences of CM health care professionals need to strive for producing detailed medical records that reflect the medical and child protection dimensions of the diagnoses they make in children including relational problems with parents and caregivers. Otherwise CM injury and illness are likely to be addressed as purely medical problems while overlooking the element of abuse.

The current policy and research focus on violence and injury deaths limit have led to CM forms associated with violence—physical abuse and sexual abuse—receiving some attention in national statistics. There is gross underidentification and underreporting of nonfatal CM even for sexual acts involving children and use of physical force yet they equally have far-reaching consequences for health and development. The common view that it is difficult to conduct child neglect assessment in the context of widespread disadvantage and poverty without wrongfully blaming parents inadvertently encourages uncritical findings. Health practitioners who succeed to assess and document undernourishment, stunting, burns, or poisoning using the CM lens will improve child outcomes significantly. Nonuse of T74 codes is a concern in these settings because it means that CM-specific health conditions are not reported. A revised ICD coding system that encourages documentation according to the different forms of CM while reflecting the specific acts and empirical consequences other than death will improve the visibility of CM in public health agenda.

NOTE

1. In South Africa, the Thuthuzela Care Centre model is a prototype of such interdepartmental and public-donor collaborations for the provision of care, therapy, and rehabilitation to children affected by sexual violence. The centers are located within major hospitals—currently there are 10 centers in 6 provinces.

REFERENCES

Al-Eissa, M., & Al-Muneef, M. (2010). Child abuse and neglect in Saudi Arabia: Journey of recognition to implementation of national prevention strategies. *Child Abuse & Neglect, 34*, 28–33.

Bah, S. (2009). Strategies for managing the change from ICD-9 to ICD-10 in developing countries: The case of South Africa. *Journal of Health Informatics in Developing Countries*, 3(2), 44–49.

Bannon, M. J., & Carter, Y. H. (2003). Paediatricians and child protection: The need for effective education and training. *Archives of Disease in Childhood, 88*, 560–562. doi:10.1136/adc.88.7.560

Byass, P. (2007). Who needs cause-of-death-data? *PLoS Medicine*, 4(11), e333. doi:10.1371/journal.pmed.0040333

Colorado Department of Public Health and Environment. (2001). *New International Classification of Diseases (ICD-10): The history and impact*. Retrieved November 14, 2010, from www.cdphe.state.co.us/hs/

Crume, T. L., DiGuiseppi, C., Byers, T., Sirotnak, A. P., & Garrett, C. J. (2002). Underascertaining of CM fatalities by death certificates, 1990–1998. *Pediatrics, 110*(2 pt 1), e18.

David, T. J. (2005). Child abuse and paediatricians. *Journal of the Royal Society of Medicine, 98*, 229–231.

Dawes, A., Willenberg, I., & Long, W. (2006). *Indicators for child protection. Report for the Research Directorate, Department of Social Services & Poverty Alleviation*. Provincial Government of the Western Cape. Cape Town: Human Sciences Research Council.

Deloitte LLP, (2009) *ICD-10: Turning regulatory compliance into strategic advantage*. Washington, DC: Deloitte Centre for Health Solutions.

Department of Health & Council of Medical Schemes (2006) *ICD-10 Implementation Review: January 2004-October 2006*. http://www.medicalschemes.com/files/ICD10%20Codings/ICD10_Implementation_Review_October2006.pdf

Donson, H. (2009). *A profile of fatal injuries in South Africa, 2008: Annual report for South Africa based on the National Injury Mortality Surveillance System (NIMSS)*. MRC-UNISA Crime, Violence and Injury Lead Programme. South Africa: Medical Research Council.

Flaherty, E. G., & Sege, R. (2005). Barriers to physicians identification and reporting of child abuse. *Pediatric Annuals, 34*(5), 349–356.

Gilbert, R., Widom, C. S., Browne, K., Fergusson, D., Webb, E., & Janson, S. (2009). Burden and consequences of CM in high-income countries. *Lancet, 373*, 68–81.

González-Izquierdo, A., Woodman, J., Copley, L., van derMeulen, J., Brandon, M., Hodes, D.,..., Gilbert, R. (2010). Variation in recording of CM in administrative records of hospital admissions for injury in England, 1997–2009. *Archives of Diseases in Childhood, 95*, 918–925. doi:10.1136/adc.2009.180216

Hazlewood, A. (2003). *ICD-9-CM to ICD-10-CM: Implementation issues and challenges.* AHIMA's 75th Anniversary National Convention and Exhibit Proceedings, October 2003. Retrieved September 27, 2010, from www.ahima.org/downloads/pdfs/about/ICD-10-Resources.pdf

Jenny, C., & Isaac, R. (2006). The relation between child death and CM. *Archives of Diseases in Childhood, 91*, 265–269. doi:10.1136/adc.2004.066696

Jette, N., Quan, H., Hemmelgarn, B., Drosler, S., Maass, C., Moskal, L.,..., Ghali, W. A. (2010). The development, evolution and modifications of ICD-10: Challenges to the international comparability of morbidity data. *Medical Care, 48*, 1105–1110.

Kingu, H. J., & Mazwai, E. L. (2010). A review of burn care at an emerging centralised burns unit. *South African Journal of Surgery, 48*, 53–58.

Lammers, K., Martin, L., Andrews, D., & Seedat, S. (2010). Reported rapes at a hospital rape centre: Demographic and clinical profiles. *South African Medical Journal, 100*, 362–363.

Lazenbatt, A., & Greer, J. (2009). Safeguarding and protecting children in maternity services: Implications for practice. *Child Care in Practice, 15*, 313–326.

Leeb, R. T., Paulozzi, L., Melanson, C., Simon, T., & Arias, I. (2008). *CM surveillance: Uniform definitions for public health and recommended data elements, Version 1.0.* Atlanta, GA: Centers for Disease Control and Prevention, National Center for Injury Prevention and Control.

Loffell, J. (2007). Monitoring the situation of children in statutory care. In A. Dawes, R. Bray, & A. Van der Merwe (Eds.), *Monitoring child well-being: A South African rights-based approach* (pp. 293–327). Cape Town: Human Sciences Research Council Press.

Lopez, A. D., Begg, S., & Bos, E. (2006). Demographic and epidemiological characteristics of major regions, 1990–2001. In A. D. Lopez, C. D. Mathers, M. Ezzati, D. T. Jamison, & C. J. L. Murray (Eds.), *Global burden of disease and risk factors.* Washington: Oxford University Press and the World Bank.

Mahapatra, P., Shibuya, K., Lopez, A. D., Coullare, F., Notzon, F. C., & Szreter, S. (2007). Civil registration systems and vital statistics: Successes and missed opportunities. *The Lancet, 370*, 1653–1663. doi:10.1016/S0140–6736(07)61308–7

Makoae, M., Dawes, A., Loffell, J., & Ward, C. L. (2008). *Children's court inquiries in the Western Cape.* Final report to the Research Directorate, Department of Social Development, Provincial Government of the Western Cape. Cape Town: Human Sciences Research Council. Retrieved from www.hsrc.ac.za

Mann, J. M. (1999). Human rights and AIDS: The future of the pandemic. In J. M. Mann, S. Gruskin, M. A. Grodin, & G. A. Annas (Eds.), *Health and human rights* (pp. 216–226). New York: Routledge.

Marszalek, J., & De Villiers, P. J. T. (2006). Morbidity profile of admissions to GF Jooste Hospital, Manenberg, Cape Town. *South African Family Practice, 48*(6), 15–15e. Retrieved from www.safpj.co.za

Mathers, C. D., Lopez, A. D., & Murray, C. J. L. (2006). The burden of disease and mortality by condition: Data, methods, and results for 2001. In A. D. Lopez, C. D. Mathers, M. Ezzati, D. T. Jamison, & C. J. L. Murray (Eds.), *Global burden of disease and risk factors.* Washington: Oxford University Press and the World Bank.

McKenzie, K., & Scott, D. A. (2011). Using routinely collected hospital data for CM surveillance: Issues, methods and patterns. *BMC Public Health, 11*(7), 1–10.

McKenzie, K., Scott, D., Fraser, J. A., & Dunne, M. P. (2011). Assessing the concordance of health and child protection data for "maltreated" and "unintentionally injured" children [electronic version]. *Injury Prevention.* doi:10.1136/ip.2011.031849

Murray, C. J. L., Lopez, A. D., Barofsky, J. T., Bryson-Cahn, C., & Lozano, R. (2007). Estimating population cause-specific mortality fractions from in-hospital mortality: Validation of a new method. *PLoS Medicine, 4*(11), e326. doi:10.1371/journal.pubmed.0040326

Naidoo, A. (2009). *Trends in adult admissions at Tambo Memorial Hospital, Gauteng, between 2005 and 2007.* Unpublished research report submitted to the Faculty of Health Sciences, University of Witwatersrand, Johannesburg, in partial fulfillment of the requirements for the Degree of Masters of Public Health, November. Retrieved June 15, 2011, from http://wiredspace.wits.ac.za/handle/10539/8795

National ICD-10 Task Team (2010). *ICD-10 Implementation Review: January 2004–March 2010.* South Africa: Ministry of Health and Council of Medical Schemes. Retrieved June 9, 2011, from www.dhsolutions.co.za

Newton, A. S., Zou, B., Hamm, M., Curran, J., Gupta, S., Dumonceaux, C., & Lewis, M. (2010). Improving child protection in the emergency department: A systematic review of professional interventions for health care providers. *Academic Emergency Medicine, 17*(2), 117–125.

Oak, M. R. (2007). A review on barriers to implementing health informatics in developing countries. *Journal of Health Informatics in Developing Countries, 1*, 19–22. Retrieved December 10, 2010, from www.jhidc.org/index.php/jhidc/article/view/3

O'Donnell, M., Nassar, N., Leonard, H. M., Matthews, R. P., Patterson, Y. G., & Sanley, F. J. (2010). The use of cross-jurisdictional population data to investigate health indicators of CM. *The Medical Journal of Australia, 193*(3), 142–145.

Rao, C., Bradshaw, D., & Mathers, C. D. (2004). Improving death registration and statistics in developing countries: Lessons from sub-Saharan Africa. *Southern African Journal of Demography, 9*, 79–97.

Schnitzer, P. G., Slusher, P.L., Kruse, R. L., & Tarleton, M. M. (2011). Identification of ICD codes suggestive of CM. *Child Abuse & Neglect, 35*, 3–17.

Schnitzer, P. G., Covington, T. M., Wirtz, S. J., Verhoek-Oftedahl, W., & Palusci, V. J. (2008). Public health surveillance of fatal CM: Analysis of 3 state programmes. *American Journal of Public Health, 98*, 296–303.

Scott, D., Tonmyr, L., Fraser, J., Walker, S., & McKenzie, K. (2009). The utility and challenges of using ICD codes in CM research. A review of existing literature. *Child Abuse & Neglect, 33*, 791–808.

Seedat, M., Van Niekerk, A., Jewkes, R., Suffla, S., & Ratele, K. (2009). Violence and injury in South Africa: Prioritising agenda for prevention. Health in South Africa. *The Lanet, 374*, 1011–1022. Retrieved September 19, 2009, from www.thelancetglobalhealthnetwork.com/wp-content/uploads/Health-in-South-Africa-5.pdf

Shonubi, A. M. O., Akiode, O., Musa, A. A., Salami, B. A., Kingu, H. A., & Mohaleroe, P. (2005). Thermal injuries in under-4-year-old children: The Lesotho experience. *African Journal of Medicine and Medical Sciences, 34*, 77–80.

Smith, G. S., & Barss, P. (1991). Unintentional injuries in developing countries: The epidemiology of a neglected problem. *Epidemiologic Reviews, 13*, 228–266.

Spivey, M. I., Schnitzer, P. G., Kruse, R. L., Slusher, P., & Jaffe, D. M. (2009). Association of injury visits in children and CM reports. *The Journal of Emergency Medicine, 36*(2), 207–214.

Stephen, C.R., Bamford, L.J., Patrick, M.E., & Wittenberg, D.F. (2011). *Saving children 2009: Five years of data: Sixth survey of child health care in South Africa*. Pretoria, South Africa: Tshepesa Press, MRC, CDC.

Stone, D. A., Kharasch, S. J., Perron, C., Wilson, K., Jacklin, B., & Sege, R. D. (1999). Comparing pediatric intentional injury surveillance data with data from publicly available sources: Consequences for a public health response to violence. *Injury Prevention, 5*, 136–141.

Trokel, M., Wadimbba, A., Griffith, J., & Sege, R. (2006) Variation in the diagnosis of child abuse in severely injured infants. *Pediatrics*, 117, 722–728.

Tzitzivacos, D. (2007). The International Classification of Diseases, 10th edition (ICD-10). *CME, 25*(1), 8–10.

Van As, S. (October 6, 2010). *The use of ICD-10 codes at Red Cross War Memorial Children's hospital*. Personal communication.

Walker, S., & McKenzie, K. (2004). *Report on findings of the ICD-10 coder needs assessment surveys*. WHO Family of International Classifications Network. Meeting held at Reykjavik, Iceland, October 24–30. WHOFIC/04.027. Retrieved May 12, 2011, from http://eprints.qut.edu.au/19665/1/19665.pdf

Woodman, J., Lecky, F., Hodes, D., Pitt, M., Taylor, B., & Gilbert, R. (2009). Screening injured children for physical abuse or neglect in emergency departments: A systematic review. *Child: Care, Health and Development, 36*, 153–164.

World Health Organization. (1992). *International statistical classification of diseases and related health problems, tenth revision*. Geneva, Switzerland: Author.

World Health Organization (2006). *The world health report—2006*. Geneva, Switzerland: World Health Organization.

11

Psychological, Physical, and Economic Consequences of Child Maltreatment

Tamara Del Vecchio, Amy M. Smith Slep, and Richard E. Heyman

Child maltreatment is a public health concern of substantial magnitude. It can cause death, serious injury, and mental health difficulties for children and impact children, their families, and the larger society. Child maltreatment is a broad term and includes "physical, emotional or psychological, or sexual abuse or neglect of a child by that child's caregiver(s) or other responsible party" (Chapter 9 in this volume), resulting in a significant impact on the child. Although additional forms of child maltreatment, including child slavery and prostitution, result in significant psychological and physical harm to children, the following review will be limited to caregiver–child relationships.

PREVALENCE

There is no internationally agreed upon definition of child maltreatment; therefore, global estimates for the prevalence of child maltreatment are difficult to obtain. Nonetheless, a review of child physical abuse (CPA) estimates in high-income countries, including the United States, the United Kingdom, Canada, and Australia, found 1-year prevalence rates of 4% to 16% (Gilbert et al., 2009). Childhood prevalence of neglect is estimated at 6% to 12% in U.S. and UK samples (Gilbert et al., 2009). A review of 21 primarily from English-speaking and Northern European countries, including the United States, found a range of prevalence rates of 7% to 36% for female and 3% to 29% for male victims of child sexual abuse (CSA; Finkelhor, 1994). Across all studies, female-to-male ratios were approximately 1.5–3:1. A telephone survey of 2,000 U.S. children aged 10 to 16 years found a lifetime prevalence rate for attempted and completed CSA at 10.5%; 1-year incidence rate of incidence rate of 3.2% for girls and 0.6% for boys (Finkelhor & Dziuba-Leatherman, 1994). In contrast, Madu and Peltzer (2000) found a prevalence rate of 54.2% in a sample of 414 South African high school students.

The proportion of incidence rates across abuse type also varies by country. For instance, in Canada, 40% of reports were neglect, 31% physical abuse, 19% emotional abuse, and 11% sexual abuse (Trocmé, Tourigny, MacLaurin, & Fallon, 2003). This is in contrast to Australia where 31%, 28%, 24%, and 16% of reports were of emotional abuse, physical abuse, neglect, and sexual abuse, respectively (Hatty & Hatty, 2001). There is a high rate of co-occurrence among the abuse types (Gilbert et al., 2009; Higgins & McCabe, 2001). It is estimated that about 35% to 64% of victims of child maltreatment experience more than one type of maltreatment (Donga et al., 2004; Edwards, Holden, Felitti, & Anda, 2003; Manly, Kim, Rogosch, & Cicchetti, 2001). Cultural differences in child rearing beliefs and practices, in addition to differing definitions of abuse cross-culturally, likely influences prevalence rates.

Witnessing intimate partner violence can be considered a form of child maltreatment, depending on the impact to the child. The 1985 National Family Violence Survey data (Gelles & Straus, 1994) indicates that 17.9% of respondents with children at home reported physical partner aggression in the past year. Over three-fourths of children in homes with partner physical maltreatment are exposed to it directly (i.e., witnessing or hearing it; Mahoney, Donnelly, Boxer, & Lewis, 2003; O'Brien, John, Margolin, & Erel, 1994); nearly all children in such homes are exposed when indirect effects (e.g., seeing sequelae; exposure to maternal depression) are considered (Kitzmann, Gaylord, Holt, & Kenny, 2003). Child victimization co-occurs with child exposure to partner violence at high levels (i.e., median co-occurrence of partner physical maltreatment and CPA appears to be over 40%; Appel & Holden, 1998).

CHILD MALTREATMENT AND MENTAL HEALTH

Child maltreatment predicts the development of behavioral and emotional difficulties. In childhood, victimization consistently predicts a variety of externalizing behavior problems, including aggression, inattention-hyperactivity, conduct problems, and adolescent delinquency, as well as internalizing problems such as depression (Johnson, Cohen, Kasen, & Brook, 2002a; Maschi, Morgen, Hatcher, Rosotto, & Violette, 2009; Teisl & Cicchetti, 2008). In addition to increased risk for behavior problems, child maltreatment victimization is also associated with increased suicidal ideation and behavior in early adulthood (Evans, Hawton, & Rodham, 2005; Fergusson, Boden, & Horwood, 2008). Specifically, female victims, compared to nonabused counterparts, were more likely to have made at least one suicide attempt by age 21 (Silverman, Reinherz, & Giaconia, 1996).

Research into the long-term consequences of child maltreatment has found that victimization in childhood is a significant risk factor for the development of later mental health difficulties (Kaplan, Pelcovitz, & Labruna, 1999; Kendall-Tackett, Williams, & Finkelhor, 1993; Malinosky-Rummell & Hansen, 1993; Putnam, 2003). In an analysis of a birth cohort of New Zealand–born children, Fergusson et al. (2008) examined the linkage between exposure to CSA and CPA and mental health problems in adulthood. Greater exposure to CSA and CPA was associated with increased rates of major depression, anxiety disorders, antisocial personality disorder, and substance dependence. The associations between exposure and mental health outcomes were similar for males and females. A longitudinal community study of 375 young adults conducted by Silverman et al. (1996) found the adolescents who were physically abused were at higher risk of depression, posttraumatic stress disorder (PTSD), antisocial behavior, and substance abuse at age 21. However, the increased risk in maltreated children may partly reflect the family context in which the maltreatment occurred (Fergusson et al., 2008; Fergusson & Lynskey, 1997). For victims of child maltreatment, early intervention targeting children and their families may be warranted before symptoms develop into more problematic conditions.

Neglect often co-occurs with physical or sexual maltreatment and few studies have examined the unique effect of neglect on child mental health. Some of the most influential work on the effects of neglect and later cognitive difficulties comes from studies on children who experience extreme neglect in institutionalized settings. The English and Romanian Adoptees (ERA) study examined the effect of severe neglect during the first 3½ years for children who were eventually adopted (Beckett et al., 2006). The ERA study found that even after at least 7½ years in adoptive homes, the neglected children still exhibited cognitive deficits, IQ scores on average 15 points below non-neglected adoptees. Moreover, work by Pollak et al. (2010) found that early neglect was associated with visual memory, attention, and inhibitory control deficits. The severity of neglect in toddlerhood also predicts externalizing problems and aggression in middle childhood (Manly et al., 2001). Taken together, the impact of early neglect on long-term mental health functioning emphasizes the need for early intervention. Expectedly, victims of neglect and/or abuse are 1.75 times more likely to experience PTSD as adults compared to individuals who did not experience neglect and/or abuse (Widom, 1999).

Regarding CSA, a meta-analysis of 37 empirical studies found a significant effect of CSA on depression, suicide, and PTSD (Paolucci, Genius, & Violato, 2001). Furthermore, a 10-year review conducted by Putnam (2003) found CSA to be associated with a number of mental health conditions, including depression, borderline personality disorder, substance abuse, dissociative identity disorder, bulimia nervosa, and posttraumatic stress disorder (PTSD). However, history of CSA specifically, as compared to other categories of abuse, is also associated with sexualized behavior and participation in risky sexual behavior including prostitution (Noll, Trickett, & Putnam, 2003; Widom & Ames, 1994). Moreover, Fergusson et al. (2008) found that CSA accounted for 13% of the variance in later mental disorders as compared to 5% for CPA. In a longitudinal study, Banyard, Williams, and Siegel (2001) found that female victims of CSA reported higher levels of several mental health outcomes in adulthood, including anxiety, depression, and dissociation, than nonvictims. In addition to greater risk for sexual re-victimization, victims of CSA also reported greater exposure to nonsexual trauma in childhood and adulthood. The additional trauma mediated the relation between sexual abuse victimization status and mental health outcomes suggesting that perhaps early maltreatment places a child at risk for re-victimization, and in turn, additional negative psychological outcomes. Dishearteningly, only about one-third to half of sexual abuse victims ever discloses the experience to others (Finkelhor, 1994; May-Chahal & Cawson, 2005).

A meta-analysis of 118 studies of children exposed to partner violence, which can be considered one possible presentation of emotional abuse (Kitzmann et al., 2003) found that, on a host of outcomes (internalizing problems, externalizing problems, social problems, academic problems, negative affect/distress, negative cognitions), exposed children fared significantly worse than nonexposed children. Overall, the effect size ($d = -0.34$) indicated that about two thirds of exposed children are functioning worse than nonexposed controls. Specifically, exposed children, when compared to those exposed only to verbal aggression, evidence significantly more externalizing and "other psychological" problems (e.g., thought problems), more negative affect/distress, and more intervention in parental disputes. However, exposed children did not differ from physically abused children. Finally, children dually exposed to partner violence and physical victimization faired worse than nonvictimized partner violence-exposed children on externalizing and total psychological problems.

THEORETICAL MODELS APPLICABLE TO THE CHILD MALTREATMENT–NEGATIVE CHILD OUTCOME ASSOCIATION

Social Learning Theory

Social learning theory (e.g., Bandura, 1977, 1986) postulates that behavior is the product of reciprocal influences among varying environments and one's behavioral and cognitive/affect systems. Future behavior is shaped by the consequences experienced for prior behavior. Patterson's coercion theory (1982; Reid, Patterson, & Snyder, 2002) is an example of an operant approach to the effects of family aggression on child aggression. Patterson postulated that family members often respond to aversive behaviors with aversive behaviors, escalating in aversiveness until one person capitulates. The person who "wins" is positively reinforced for escalating; the person who "loses" is negatively reinforced via the other's cessation of aversive behavior. Because each one "wins" sometimes and "loses" other times, the overall negative spiral becomes more likely, as each person tries to coerce the other into submission. Thus, coercion theory helps explain how negative escalation sequences are reinforcing for both parties, despite their unpleasant and destructive qualities. Once learned, these behaviors can be applied in nonfamilial interpersonal situations, placing a child on a trajectory toward increasingly serious conduct problems (as summarized in Reid et al., 2002). These processes, while most studied in parent–child dyads, likely also occur among couples (e.g., Slep & Heyman, 2002), creating a family culture in which aggression is reinforced.

Learning can also be accomplished vicariously (i.e., by watching stimulus-response chains enacted by others). The importance of modeling in the acquisition of aggressive and anxious behavior is well-established (see Huesmann, 1997; Mineka & Hamida, 1998, for recent reviews), as are a number of elements of the model that increase learning (e.g., similarity of the model to the observer, whether the model struggles to perform the behavior or does so effortlessly; see Chance, 1993). Modeling is often posited as a likely mechanism contributing to child externalizing problem links (e.g., Onyskiw & Hayduk, 2001).

Further, people develop predictions of outcomes of behavioral enactment that moderate their performance of target behavior(s). Efficacy expectancies (i.e., predictions about whether one has the ability/means to carry out a target behavior) and outcome expectancies (i.e., predictions about what the likely consequences would be from carrying out the target behavior) are two leading examples. This is the basis of social information processing models, which have gained increasing support not only in accounting for aggression and behavior problems in children (e.g., Dodge & Schwartz, 1997) but also in the maltreatment area (e.g., Grych, Wachsmuth-Schlaefer, & Klockow, 2002; Rossman, 1998).

Social Information Processing

Research consistently suggests that aggressive acts are predicted by distortions in cognitive perceptions of social cues. Among the most widely accepted explanations of this phenomenon is social information processing theory proposed by Dodge (1986). Social information processing theory illustrates the relation between cognitions regarding social interactions and the expression of aggressive responses (Crick & Dodge, 1994). Processing of social information occurs in six stages where distorted cognitions in any stages are linked to maladaptive behavioral responses. The theory states that the way a child interprets the intent of a person's actions determines the child's response to that action. Thus, when children attribute hostile intentions to others, they react in aggressive and defensive ways. Hostile attributions are correlated with a child's age and gender (Orobio de Castro, Veerman, Koos, Bosch, & Monshouwer, 2002). Specifically, boys and younger children have been found to exhibit higher levels of hostile attributions than do girls and adolescent populations.

In a study investigating multiple forms of maltreatment, Price and Glad (2003) also found that maladaptive representations of social situations mediate the relation between maltreatment and aggressive behaviors. In addition, Pollak and Tolley-Schell (2003) found that physically abused children overattend to angry faces, however, victimized children did not differ from nonvictimized children when presented with happy faces. These findings suggest that abuse children do not demonstrate overall attentional problems, but may be hypersensitive to anger. This hypersensivity is likely adaptive in the context of the abuse experience, however, hypervigilance to anger cues represents a cognitive distortion that may result in an increase in aggressive responding in other contexts.

Attachment Theory

Attachment theory (e.g., Ainsworth, Blehar, Waters, & Wall, 1978; Bowlby, 1969) focuses on the primacy of the caregiver–caretaker relationship in establishing people's representations of the interpersonal world. These representations are first formed via interactions with the primary caregiver (typically the mother) but are updated in later development via relationships with important others (e.g., romantic partners). Waters and Cummings (2000, p. 165) summed up the theory's view of developing infants as one of a "competence-motivated infant using its primary caregiver as a secure base from which to explore and, when necessary, as a haven of safety and a source of comfort. Within this framework, the child's tie to its mother reflects the operating characteristics of an underlying control system that collates information about the infant's state, the state of the environment, and past and current access to the caregiver."

Because of its emphasis on the security of the child–caregiver bond, attachment theory has been central to developing specific theories of the effects of maltreatment on child functioning. Cummings and Davies's Emotional Security Hypothesis (e.g., Davies & Cummings, 1994) is perhaps the most extensively studied and best-validated example of an attachment-informed approach. The Emotional Security Hypothesis suggests that emotional security is a goal that motivates and directs children's reactions to events, such as child maltreatment, in their environment. Under this model, child maltreatment does not have a direct impact on child outcomes. Rather, it is the extent to which elements of the maltreatment threaten or disrupt the child's sense of security that drives his or her responses, which, over time, can evolve into patterns that are generally maladaptive but serve in the moment to help the child regain security (Cummings & Davies, 1996).

There may be a critical period for the development of social attachments. To examine the effects of early experience in social development, Wismer Fries, Ziegler, Kurian, Jacoris, and Pollak (2005) studied severely neglected institutionalized children after they transitioned into appropriate home environments. Neglected children failed to show hormonal responsivity after physical contact with their caregivers as evidenced by a lack of increase in levels of oxytocin, a neuropeptide associated with social bonding. Thus, early neglect might impact the ability to develop attachments to caregivers.

CHILD MALTREATMENT AND PHYSICAL HEALTH AND BRAIN DYSFUNCTION

The World Health Organization estimates the homicide rate of children at 2 per 100,000 for children younger than 15 years; children younger than 4 years are at greatest risk with an estimated 5.8 and 4.8 deaths per 100,000 for males and females, respectively (World Health Organization, 2002). Some child deaths fail to be recognized as homicide; therefore these reports are likely underestimating the rates of intentional deaths to children via maltreatment. A 10-year retrospective study evaluated children aged 0 to 4 years with injuries requiring hospitalization (DiScala, Sege, Li, & Reece, 2000). Child abuse was indicated in 10.6% of injuries. Maltreated children were primarily injured by battery (53%); however, causes also included suffocation, strangulation, shaking, pulling, and throwing. In addition, the victimized children were more likely to sustain intracranial, thorax, abdominal, and significantly more severe injuries, and be admitted into intensive care.

In addition to the serious physical harm that can directly result from child maltreatment, trauma experience can also result in poor physical health and neurological dysfunctions through indirect and less well-understood mechanisms. Child neglect and sexual abuse are associated with obesity and risk for type 2 diabetes during childhood an early adulthood (Johnson et al., 2002a; Lissau & Sorensen, 1994; Noll, Zeller, Trickett, & Putnam, 2007; Thomas, Hypponen, & Power, 2008). Furthermore, although research on the long-term effect of maltreatment is limited, the health impact of early childhood maltreatment appears to last well in later adulthood. In a sample of 21,000 adults over 60, the Depression and Early Prevention of Suicide in General Practice Study Group found an increased rate of poor health behaviors, including smoking and elevated drinking levels, in those who were victims of physical or sexual abuse (Draper et al., 2008). Furthermore, victimization was associated with a greater risk of medical disease for both sexes, and increased reports of myocardial infarction and stroke for women. The association between abuse status and medical outcomes were significant, even after controlling for mental health levels.

Evolutionarily functional, innate, organized behavioral patterns exist to respond to danger (e.g., fight/flight response) and can be shaped through environmental interaction. Although humans, like all animals, are born with perceptual and behavioral systems to scan for and respond to danger, these systems are plastic and responsive to environmental influences. LeDeux (2002) posited two information pathways, a danger-related pathway from the thalamus to the amygdala and a slower, nonthreat-based pathway from the cortex to the amygdala. The former, although adaptive in the face of real environmental dangers, can become primed to such an extent via traumatic experience that hyperarousal and hypervigilance result. The latter, although more accurate, is not evolutionarily advantageous in danger-rich environments. Thus, through exposure to a dangerous, traumatic environment, neural connections can be formed and strengthened that favor attention to danger cues in social information processing.

Hyperaroused physiological responses to minor stressors can result from learned responses to trauma (Perry, Pollard, Blakley, Baker, & Vigilante, 1995). This use-dependent model assumes that the development of the brain is affected by response patterns to experience, and trauma experiences in childhood can result in irreparable damage to the developing brain. These responses, which begin as adaptive responses, can become maladaptive psychological symptoms. For example, an increased release of norepinephrine, which modulates the body's fight or flight response to threat, accompanies a hyperarousal response to trauma. Initially, hyperarousal occurs in response to trauma cues, however, stimulus generalization causes reactivation of this stress-response system in response to more minor stressors.

Moreover, child maltreatment has negative effects on the hypothalamic–pituitary–adrenocortical system (HPA) and is associated with long-term cortisol elevations and short-term variations, that is, elevated afternoon levels of cortisol (Hart, Gunnar, & Cicchetti, 1996; Perry et al., 1995/). Modification to the stress-response system affects associated systems and may cause tachycardia, hypertension, and neuroendocrine abnormalities (DeBellis et al., 1994a; DeBellis, Lefter, Trickett, & Putnam, 1994b; Ito et al., 1993). As summarized by Crittenden (1998, p. 19):

> Experience with fear-eliciting stimuli lead[s] to potentiated response states in which the individual is hypervigilant with regard to stimuli indicative of danger, responds more rapidly to such stimuli, and responds with great amplitude. The more intense and frequent the danger that is experienced early in life and throughout life, the more rapid, protective, affect laden and preconscious will be the response.... This has implications for children of unpredictable, chaotic, overwhelmed, or affectively labile parents.

Clearly, neurobiological theories of trauma are tremendously important to understanding the effects of maltreatment on a host of child outcomes, as trauma has the potential to fundamentally change the way in which children process information and respond to the environment at the neurological and physiological levels (Repetti, Taylor, & Seeman, 2002). Not surprisingly, evidence of trauma and posttraumatic stress symptoms has been found among maltreated children (Widom, 1999), suggesting that the effects of abuse might be, in part, a function of neurobiological changes caused by trauma.

CHILD MALTREATMENT AND ECONOMIC OUTCOMES

There is an economic impact of child maltreatment both directly (e.g., medical care) and indirectly (e.g., decreased educational attainment, secondary mental and physical health outcomes). It is difficult to quantify the indirect costs of medical and mental health treatment, for example, nonemergency medical treatment as a result of maltreatment, long-term health problems, and treatment for the victim, family members, and perpetrator. Furthermore, child maltreatment occurs at a significant cost to society as a whole; victims of child maltreatment are more likely to engage in high-risk behaviors such as sexual promiscuity that impacts society in terms of sexually transmitted diseases and unwanted pregnancies, which both come with significant economic impacts. There are also increased risks for substance use and obesity, costly public health concerns. Moreover, child maltreatment is associated with low skilled employment, lower IQ and academic achievement, and lower high school graduation rates (Gilbert et al., 2009; Veltman & Browne, 2001). Prevent Child Abuse America estimates the total direct cost of child maltreatment, including hospitalization, child welfare services, mental health services, and law enforcement activities in the United States at $33 billion annually (Wang & Holton, 2007). An additional $70 billion is estimated to cover indirect costs, including special education, juvenile delinquency, adult criminal justice system, and loss of productivity to society. The societal impact of child maltreatment may be greater in countries with limited economic resources to address the mental and physical health needs.

Developing countries are less able to ameliorate the outcomes of child maltreatment resulting in greater vulnerability to its economic costs.

CONCLUSIONS

As compared to children who had not experienced any victimization, those who had been abused exhibited more severe adverse behavioral and emotional outcomes that can persist well into adulthood. In addition to physical harm experienced by abused children, childhood trauma may result in irreversible changes to brain function and physical health. Although primary prevention is the goal, secondary prevention may lessen the impact of child maltreatment. Failure to assess and intervene early in cases of child maltreatment may be detrimental to child mental health and disallow the opportunity to reduce the probability of these negative outcomes. Such early assessment and intervention would be tremendously enhanced by the existence of consistent criteria for defining child maltreatment that could be used globally.

REFERENCES

Ainsworth, M., Blehar, M., Waters, E., & Wall, S. (1978). *Patterns of attachment*. Hillsdale, NJ: Erlbaum.

Appel, A. E., & Holden, G. W. (1998). The co-occurrence of spouse and physical child abuse: A review and appraisal. *Journal of Family Psychology, 12*(4), 578–599.

Bandura, A. (1973). *Aggression: A social learning analysis*. Englewood Cliffs, NJ: Prentice Hall.

Bandura, A. (1986). *Social foundations of thought and action: A social and cognitive theory*. Englewood Cliffs, NJ: Prentice Hall.

Banyard, V. L., Williams, L. M., & Siegel, J. A. (2001). The long-term mental health consequences of child sexual abuse: An exploratory study of the impact of multiple traumas in a sample of women. *Journal of Traumatic Stress, 14*, 697–715.

Beckett, C., Maughan, B., Rutter, M., Castle, J., Colvert, E., Groothues, C., Kreppner, J.,…, Sonuga-Barke, E. J. S. (2006). Do the effects of early severe deprivation on cognition persist into early adolescence? Findings from the English and Romanian adoptees study. *Child Development, 77*, 696–711.

Bowlby, J. (1969). *Attachment and loss* (Vol. 1). New York, NY: Basic Books.

Chance, P. (1993). *Learning and behavior* (3rd ed.). Pacific Grove, CA: Brooks/Cole.

Crick, N. R., & Dodge, K. A. (1994). A review and reformation of social information-processing mechanisms in children's social adjustment. *Psychological Bulletin, 115*, 74–101.

Crittenden, P. M. (1998). Dangerous behavior and dangerous contexts: A 35-year perspective on research on the developmental effects of child physical abuse. In P. K. Trickett & C. J. Schellenbach (Eds.), *Violence against children in the family and the community* (pp. 11–38). Washington, DC: American Psychological Association.

Cummings, E., & Davies, P. (1996). Emotional security as a regulatory process in normal development and the development of psychopathology. *Development & Psychopathology, 8*, 123–139.

Davies, P. T., & Cummings, E. M. (1994). Marital conflict and child adjustment: An emotional security hypothesis. *Psychological Bulletin, 116*, 387–411.

DeBellis, M. D., Chrousos, G. P., Dorn, L. D., Burke, L. Helmers, K., Kling, M. A.,…, Putnam, F. W. (1994a). Hypothalamic–pituitary–adrenal axis dysregulation in sexually abused girls. *Journal of Clinical Endocrinology and Metabolism, 78*, 249–255.

DeBellis, M. D., Lefter, L., Trickett, P. K., & Putnam, F. W. (1994b). Urinary catecholamine excretion in sexually-abused girls. *Journal of the American Academy of Child and Adolescent Psychiatry, 33*, 320–327.

DiScala, C., Sege, R., Li, G., & Reece, R. M. (2000). Child abuse and unintentional injuries: A 10-year retrospective. *Archives of Pediatrics & Adolescent Medicine, 154*, 16–22.

Dodge, K. A. (1986). A social information processing model of social competence in children. In M. Perlmutter (Ed.), *Minnesota symposia on child psychology* (Vol. 18, pp. 77–125). Hillsdale, NJ: Erlbaum.

Dodge, K. A., & Schwartz, D. (1997). Social information processing mechanisms in aggressive behavior. In D. M. Stoff & J. Brelling (Eds.), *Handbook of antisocial behavior* (pp. 171–180). New York, NY: John Wiley & Sons.

Donga, M., Andaa, R. F., Felitti, V. J., Dubea, S. R., Williamson, D. F., Thompsona, T. J.,…, Giles, W. H. (2004). The interrelatedness of multiple forms of childhood abuse, neglect, and household dysfunction. *Child Abuse & Neglect, 28*, 771–784.

Draper, B., Pfaff, J. J., Pirkis, J., Snowdon, J. J., Lautenschlager, N. T. Wilson, I., & Almeida, O. P. (2008). Long-term effects of childhood abuse on the quality of life and health of older people: Results from the depression and early prevention of suicide in general practice project. *Journal of American Geriatrics Society, 56*, 262–271.

Edwards, V. J., Holden, G. W., Felitti, V. J., & Anda, R. F. (2003). Relationship between multiple forms of childhood maltreatment and adult mental health in community respondents: Results from the adverse childhood experiences study. *American Journal of Psychiatry, 160*, 1453–1460.

Evans, E., Hawton, K., & Rodham, K. (2005). In what ways are adolescents who engage in self-harm or experience thoughts of self-harm different in terms of help-seeking, communication and coping strategies? *Journal of Adolescence, 28*, 573–587.

Fergusson, D. M., Boden, J. M., & Horwood, L. J. (2008). Exposure to childhood sexual and physical abuse and adjustment in early adulthood. *Child Abuse & Neglect, 32*, 607–619.

Fergusson, D. M., & Lynskey, M. T. (1997). Physical punishment/maltreatment during childhood and adjustment in young adulthood. *Child Abuse & Neglect, 21*, 617–630.

Finkelhor, D. (1994). The international epidemiology of child sexual abuse. *Child Abuse & Neglect, 18*, 409–417.

Finkelhor, D., & Dziuba-Leatherman, J. (1994). Children as victims of violence: A national survey. *Pediatrics, 94*, 413–420.

Gelles, R. J., & Straus, M. A. (1994). *Physical violence in American families, 1985* (3rd release) [computer file]. Durham, NH: University of New Hampshire Family Research Laboratory [producer], 1988. Ann Arbor, MI: Inter-University Consortium for Political and Social Research [distributor], 1994.

Gilbert, R., Widom, C. S., Browne, K., Fergusson, D., Webb, E., & Janson, S. (2009). Burden and consequences of child maltreatment in high-income countries. *Lancet, 373*, 68–81.

Grych, J. H., Wachsmuth-Schlaefer, T., & Klockow, L. L. (2002). Interparental aggression and young children's representations of family relationships. *Journal of Family Psychology, 16*, 259–272.

Hart, J., Gunnar, M., & Cicchetti, D. (1996). Altered neuroendocrine activity in maltreated children related to depression. *Development and Psychopathology, 8*, 201–214.

Hatty, S. E., & Hatty, J. (2001). Australia. In B. Schwartz-Kenney, M. Epstein, & M. McCauley (Eds.), *Child abuse: A global view* (pp. 1–16). Westport, CT: Greenwood Publishing Group.

Higgins, D. J., & McCabe, M. P. (2001). Multiple forms of child abuse and neglect: Adult retrospective reports. *Aggression and Violent Behavior, 6*, 547–578.

Huesmann, L. R. (1997). Observational learning of violent behavior: Social and biosocial processes. In A. Raine, P. A. Brennen, D. P. Farrington, & S. A. Mednick (Eds.), *Biosocial bases of violence* (pp. 69–88). London, UK: Plenum.

Ito, Y., Teicher, M. H., Glod, C. A., Harper, D., Magnus, E., & Gelbard, H. A. (1993). Increased prevalence of electrophysiological abnormalities in children with psychological, physical, and sexual abuse. *Journal of Neuropsychiatry and Clinical Neurosciences, 5*, 401–408.

Johnson, J. G., Cohen, P., Kasen, S., & Brook, J. S. (2002a). Childhood adversities associated with risk for eating disorders or weight problems during adolescence or early adulthood. *American Journal of Psychiatry, 159*, 394–400.

Kaplan, S. J., Pelcovitz, D., & Labruna, V. (1999). Child and adolescent abuse and neglect research: A review of the past 10 years. Part I: Physical and emotional abuse and neglect. *Journal of the American Academy of Child and Adolescent Psychiatry, 38*, 1214–1222.

Kendall-Tackett, K. A., Williams, L. M., & Finkelhor, D. (1993). Impact of sexual abuse on children: A review and synthesis of recent empirical studies. *Psychological Bulletin, 113*, 164–180.

Kitzmann, K. M., Gaylord, N. K., Holt, A. R., & Kenny, E. D. (2003). Child witnesses to domestic violence: A meta-analytic review. *Journal of Consulting and Clinical Psychology, 71*, 339–352.

LeDeux, J. (2002). *Synaptic self: How our brains become who we are.* New York, NY: Viking Press.

Lissau, I., & Sorensen, T. I. (1994). Parental neglect during childhood and increased risk of obesity in young adulthood. *Lancet, 343*, 324–327.

Madu, S. N., & Peltzer, K. (2000). Risk factors and child sexual abuse among secondary school students in the Northern Province (South Africa). *Child Abuse & Neglect, 24*, 259–268.

Mahoney, A., Donnelly, W. O., Boxer, P., & Lewis, T. (2003). Marital and severe parent-to-adolescent physical aggression in clinic-referred families: Mother and adolescent reports on co-occurrence and links to child behavior problems. *Journal of Family Psychology, 17*, 3–19.

Malinosky-Rummell, R., & Hansen, D. J. (1993). Long-term consequences of childhood physical abuse. *Psychological Bulletin, 114*, 68–79.

Manly, J. T., Kim, J. E., Rogosch, F. A., & Cicchetti, D. (2001). Dimensions of child maltreatment and children's adjustment: Contributions of developmental timing and subtype. *Development and Psychopathology, 13*, 759–782.

Maschi, T., Morgen, K., Hatcher, S. S., Rosato, N. S., & Violette, N. M. (2009). Maltreated children's thoughts and emotions as behavioral predictors: Evidence for social work action. *Social Work, 54*, 135–143.

May-Chahal, C., & Cawson, P. (2005). Measuring child maltreatment in the United Kingdom: A study of the prevalence of child abuse and neglect. *Child Abuse & Neglect, 29*, 969–984.

Mineka, S., & Hamida, S. (1998). Observational and nonconscious learning. In W. O'Donohue (Ed.), *Learning and behavior therapy* (pp. 421–439). Needham Heights, MA: Allyn and Bacon.

Noll, J. G., Trickett, P. K., & Putnam, F. W. (2003). A prospective investigation of the impact of childhood sexual abuse on the development of sexuality. *Journal of Consulting and Clinical Psychology, 71*, 575–586.

Noll, J. G., Zeller, M. H., Trickett, P. K., & Putnam, F. W. (2007). Obesity risk for female victims of childhood sexual abuse: A prospective study. *Pediatrics, 120*, 361–367.

O'Brien, M., John, R. S., Margolin, G., & Erel, O. (1994). Reliability and diagnostic efficacy of parents' reports regarding children's exposure to marital aggression. *Violence and Victims, 9*, 45–62.

Onyskiw, J. E., & Hayduk, L. A. (2001). Process underlying children's adjustment in families characterized by physical aggression. *Family Relations: Interdisciplinary Journal of Applied Family Studies, 50,* 376–385.

Orobio de Castro, B., Veerman, J. W., Koops, W., Bosch, J. D., & Monshouwer, H. J. (2002). Hostile attribution of intent and aggressive behavior: A meta-analysis. *Child Development, 73,* 916–934.

Paolucci, E., Genuis, M., & Violato, C. (2001). A meta-analysis of the published research on the effects of child sexual abuse. *The Journal of Psychology, 135,* 17–36.

Patterson, G. R. (1982). *Coercive family process.* Eugene, OR: Castalia Publishing Company.

Perry, B., Pollard, R., Blakley, T., Baker, W., & Vigilante, D. (1995). Childhood trauma, the neurobiology of adaptation, and "use-dependent" development of the brain: How "states" become "traits." *Infant Mental Health Journal, 16,* 271–291.

Pollak, S. D., Nelson, C. A., Schlaak, M. F., Roeber, B. J., Wewerka, S. S., Wiik, K. L.,…, Gunnar, M. R. (2010). Neurodevelopmental effects of early deprivation in postinstitutionalized children. *Child Development, 81,* 224–236.

Pollak, S. D., & Tolley-Schell, S. A. (2003). Selective attention to facial emotion in physically abused children. *Journal of Abnormal Psychology, 112,* 323–338.

Price, J.M., & Glad, K. (2003). Hostile attributional tendencies in maltreated children. *Journal of Abnormal Child Psychology, 31,* 329–343.

Putnam, F. W. (2003). Ten-year research update review: Child sexual abuse. *Journal of the American Academy of Child and Adolescent Psychiatry, 42,* 269–278.

Reid, J. B., Patterson, G. R., & Snyder, J. (Eds.). (2002). *Antisocial behavior in children and adolescents: A developmental analysis and model for intervention.* Washington, DC: American Psychological Association.

Repetti, R. L., Taylor, S. E., & Seeman, T. E. (2002). Risky families: Family social environments and the mental and physical health of offspring. *Psychological Bulletin, 128,* 330–366.

Rossman, B. B. R. (1998). Descartes's error and posttraumatic stress disorder: Cognition and emotion in children who are exposed to parental violence. In G. W. Holden, R. Geffner, & E. N. Jouriles (Eds.), *Children exposed to marital violence* (pp. 223–256). Washington, DC: American Psychological Association.

Silverman, A. B., Reinherz, H. Z., & Giaconia, R. M. (1996). The long-term sequelae of child and adolescent abuse: A longitudinal community study. *Child Abuse & Neglect, 20,* 709–723.

Slep, A. M. S., & Heyman, R. E. (2002). *Emotional regulation and intimate violence.* National Institute of Mental Health/(1 R01 MH067043–01). Stony Brook, NY: State University of New York at Stony Brook.

Teisl, M., & Cicchetti, D. (2008). Physical abuse, cognitive and emotional processes, and aggressive/disruptive behavior problems. *Social Development, 17,* 1–23.

Thomas, C., Hyponnen, E., & Power, C. (2008). Obesity and type 2 diabetes risk in mid-adult life: The role of childhood adversity. *Pediatrics, 121,* 1240–1249.

Trocmé, N. M., Tourigny, M., MacLaurin, B., & Fallon, B. (2003). Major findings from the Canadian incidence study of reported child abuse and neglect. *Child Abuse & Neglect, 27,* 1427–1439.

Veltman, M. W. M., & Browne, K. D. (2001). Three decades of child maltreatment research: Implications for the school years. *Trauma, Violence, & Abuse, 2,* 215–239

Wang, C., & Holton, J. (2007). *Total estimated cost of child abuse and neglect in the United States: Statistical evidence.* Chicago, IL: Prevent Child Abuse America. Retrieved October 1, 2010, from www.preventchildabuse.org/about_us/media_releases/pcaa_pew_economic_impact_study_final.pdf

Waters, E., & Cummings, E. M. (2000). A secure base from which to explore close relationships. *Child Development, 71,* 164–172.

Widom, C. S. (1999). Posttraumatic stress disorder in abused and neglected children grown up. *American Journal of Psychiatry, 156,* 1223–1230.

Widom, C., & Ames, M. (1994), Criminal consequences of childhood sexual victimization. *Child Abuse & Neglect, 18,* 303–318.

Wismer Fries, A. B., Ziegler, T. E., Kurian, J. R., Jacoris, S., & Pollak, S. D. (2005). Early experience in humans is associated with changes in neuropeptides critical for regulating social behavior. *Proceedings of the National Academy of Sciences, 102,* 17237–17240.

World Health Organization. (2002). World report on violence and health: Summary. Geneva: Author. Retrieved October 1, 2010, from www.who.int/violence_injury_prevention/violence/world_report/en/summary_en.pdf

12

Practical Tools for Assessing Child Maltreatment in Clinical Practice and Public Health Settings

Amy M. Smith Slep, Richard E. Heyman, Jeffery D. Snarr, and Heather M. Foran

Child maltreatment can be challenging to assess. In many settings, parents may be less than forthcoming. Children, depending on age and context, can be unreliable reporters. Many professionals who are comfortable asking about a range of topics are squeamish about assessing possible maltreatment, afraid they will misunderstand, make a difficult situation worse, intrude on a private family matter, or drive a family in need of care away. These challenges are exacerbated by the fact that there has not been consensus on what constitutes maltreatment, making it difficult to know how an assessment should best proceed. In this chapter, we will briefly discuss some of the issues relevant to assessing child maltreatment clinically, and present two assessment tools developed in concert with the child maltreatment definitions presented in Chapter 9 in this volume.

Enhanced surveillance of child maltreatment is necessary for both child welfare and public health applications, as well as for appropriately managing clinical services for parents and children. Depending on circumstances and the goal of the assessment, enhanced surveillance may involve the use of brief screening tools that indicate risk and that would trigger additional assessment to determine if specific incidents of maltreatment had occurred. There are good reasons to enhance surveillance of child maltreatment. As thoroughly reviewed by Del Vecchio, Slep, and Heyman (Chapter 11, this volume), child maltreatment is strikingly prevalent and has major public health impacts. As discussed by Makoae (Chapter 10, this volume), child welfare and public health systems are typically not integrated, and health care providers are in a particularly good position to identify cases of maltreatment prior to extremely severe incidents and fatalities, which provides these families with the potential to obtain the support they need. Given the psychological and physical consequences of maltreatment, and the prevalence of maltreatment in the general population, one can imagine that more routine screening of maltreatment among families seeking mental health and medical services for children would have the potential of promoting empirically supported parenting interventions (e.g., Triple P; Sanders, 1999, 2008; Parent–Child Interaction Therapy; Eyberg & Robinson, 1982) as a way of further addressing the children's presenting conditions. Routine administration of screening measures in public health settings would also enable community-level tracking of risk, which might be useful when broader initiatives are put in place to reduce violence or mitigate the impact of stressors such as poverty.

ASSESSMENT CONSIDERATIONS

There are several issues that warrant consideration in the assessment of child maltreatment. First, it is essential to carefully match the context and the assessment tool. In child welfare systems, it is essential to assess whether an alleged incident occurred, and if so, whether it was above or below the threshold for labeling an incident maltreatment. This requires a very different type of assessment than what might best suit mental health providers who screen parents of children coming to their clinics to determine whether they are at elevated risk for maltreatment to incorporate that into the treatment plan. In this case, it may be undesirable to directly assess maltreatment, which necessitates determining whether the provider has a reasonable suspicion of abuse and might require reporting the parent to the child welfare system. Finally, surveillance data is likely to be most accurate if those data can be collected anonymously, which is not a viable option for health care providers seeking information about the patient sitting in the exam room. Anonymous assessments help lessen reporting biases that contribute to parents trying to "fake good" on questionnaires; identifiable assessments likely lead to significant underreporting on direct assessments of maltreatment.

One must also consider the age and developmental level of the child in question. Some behaviors, such as shaking, are not particularly harmful to older children, but are potentially fatal to infants. Once children are verbal, they can participate in interviews, and once they can read, they can complete questionnaires. One must be sensitive to the cognitive level of the child, and match the level of detail sought to what the child is capable of. A preschooler being inconsistent in reports of how long ago something occurred is to be expected and does not negate an otherwise credible report. Children are subject to reporting biases as well. Children might be concerned for their own or their siblings' safety. They might fear getting their parents in trouble. Context can dramatically affect the quality of an assessment with a child.

ASSESSMENT TOOLS

Existing Measures

Perhaps the best-known assessment tool assessing risk for physical child abuse is the Child Abuse Potential Inventory (CAP; Milner, 1986). It is a 160-item self-report measure consisting of statement respondents agree/disagree with, 77 of which comprise the total Abuse Risk subscale. Although all items assess risk factors of child physical abuse, none directly assess violence toward children. The reliability of CAP scores is very good (test–retest reliabilities from 1 day to 3 months: 0.75 –0.91; Milner, 1986). The validity is also well established. Scores on the CAP Abuse Risk subscale discriminate between abusive and nonabusive parents well (Milner, 1986, 1994; Milner, Gold, & Wimberley, 1986), especially under ideal conditions.

This widely used measure clearly has strong psychometrics, but also a number of other attractive qualities. First, it does not directly assess parenting behavior, which makes it useful when clinicians may want to understand risk for maltreatment without confronting maltreatment directly. This also makes the CAP a useful measure for parents referred for an incident of abuse, who might be sensitized to reporting on the parenting, and understanding risk for additional incidents might be critical. Second, it has validity scales that can indicate when a parent is trying to "fake good," which can happen when parents are being evaluated for their fitness, as in the case of custody evaluations, for example.

On the other hand, because it does not directly assess maltreatment, it is not helpful in determining whether an incident was below or above a maltreatment threshold. Also, it was developed specifically in reference to child physical abuse perpetrators and may not be as sensitive and specific in identifying psychological or sexual abuse, or neglect, perpetrators. Because it is designed to be administered to the perpetrating parent, it cannot help in identifying children at risk for maltreatment. Finally, the full scale is rather long, which makes it difficult to use as a screening tool.

To address the concern about the length of the measure, Ondersma, Chaffin, Mullins, and LeBreton (2005) developed a shortened form of the CAP, the Brief Child Abuse Potential Inventory (BCAP). The BCAP, comprising 24 abuse and 9 validity items, was developed to fit on one page and to be a viable screening tool. It was empirically developed using data on the complete CAP and has strong psychometrics. Using receiver operator characteristic (ROC) curves, the area under the curve for the BCAP was 98% when predicting CAP cutoff scores, with sensitivity and specificity over 0.90 when using both less and more conservative CAP cutoff scores as the criteria. BCAP scores were also able to predict future abuse, with CAP scores not adding significantly to the prediction afforded by the BCAP. Thus, in screening situations where the objective is to identify risk for child abuse and the potential perpetrator is available to complete the screen, the BCAP is a strong option.

There have been other screening tools proposed in the literature, though none are as developed as the CAP and BCAP. These have primarily been developed for use in pediatric or other medical care settings to screen for families that are at elevated risk for parents' use of physical aggression or physical abuse (Feigelman et al., 2009; Woodman et al., 2009). Woodman and colleagues (2009) conducted a systematic review to determine whether risk markers might be sensitive and specific enough to be used as screeners for child abuse in emergency department settings. They included items such as repeated emergency visits, child age, and type of injury. They concluded that none of the factors they investigated were accurate enough predictors of child abuse to be used as screeners. Feigelman et al. (2009) evaluated the ability of two items from the Parent Screening Questionnaire, a 20-item scale designed to assess risk factors for child abuse, to successfully identify families engaged in harsh physical punishment at pediatric visits. The questions were, "(1) Do you often feel your child is difficult to take care of?" and "(2) Do you sometimes find you need to hit/spank your child?" (p. 271). As a screener for harsh physical discipline, these two items had only modest sensitivity (the highest was when either question was endorsed, 57%), but reasonably good specificity (71%–98%, depending on the criterion [psychological aggression or physical assault] and whether one or both questions were used). Given its brevity, however, this may still be a useful conversation starter in primary care and other medical settings.

The Binghamton Childhood Abuse Screen is designed to identify people with a history of childhood abuse in a nonface valid manner (Castelda, Levis, Rourke, & Coleman, 2007). This measure was based on one initially developed to identify patients with a history of sexual abuse (Sexual Abuse Questionnaire; Lock, Levis, & Rourke, 2005). It was then extended to be a screener for a wider range of victimization and a series of studies were undertaken to improve its psychometrics. The final scale consists of 36 items and was designed to be administered to adults. Given that it was developed using undergraduate student samples, the scale could likely be successfully administered to adolescents as well. The psychometrics reported suggest possible utility as a screening device, with sensitivities and specificities at optimal cut scores ranging from 0.65 to 0.75 and 0.60 to 0.57, respectively. Thus, the scale was nearly as successful at identifying those with child physical abuse histories and child sexual abuse histories.

In the following section, we detail two types of measures. The first type is brief parent report questionnaire screeners for child physical and psychological abuse. The second type is a series of structured interviews that support the diagnostic criteria for child maltreatment detailed in Chapter 9 in this volume.

BRIEF SCREENING INSTRUMENT FOR CHILD MALTREATMENT: INSTRUMENT PSYCHOMETRICS AND RECOMMENDATIONS FOR USE

Screener Development

As described in more detail by Heyman et al. (2012b), we used two large population surveys (2006 survey, $N = 69{,}228$; 2008 survey, $N = 76{,}518$) to develop and cross-validate a short screening test for child physical abuse and child emotional abuse. For both types of maltreatment, the questions operationalized the criteria presented in Chapter 9 in this volume. That is, child physical abuse comprises nonaccidental acts of physical force that result, or have reasonable potential to result, in physical harm to a child or which evoke significant fear in the child; emotional abuse comprises nonaccidental verbal or symbolic acts of that result in significant or reasonable potential for psychological harm to a child. Thus, the questions to parents presented inquired about parental acts and the impact on children.

Both years' surveys included a measure of family maltreatment that was developed, refined, and tested over a several-year period to operationalize the criteria in this volume (see Heyman, Snarr, Slep, & U.S. Air Force Family Advocacy Program, 2012a). The child physical abuse module comprised 18 items assessing the commission of various aggressive acts in the previous year engaged in by respondents toward each of their four youngest children (e.g., "I spanked child on the bottom with a bare hand." "I hit child with a fist."). Parents indicated whether they did the behavior (a) to teach, (b) to punish, and/or (c) because they were frustrated/lost their cool. Reasons were provided because pilot work indicated that parents were more willing to report these behaviors of questionable social desirability if they could provide the reasons for their behavior. Follow-up questions asked about (a) where on the child's body the acts were directed and (b) whether injuries resulting from acts endorsed.

The child emotional abuse module inquired about the frequency of 10 behaviors toward the child (e.g., "I called child names that could really hurt," e.g., "worthless," "stupid," "slut," etc.). Follow-up questions asked, "What happened as a result?" and included several psychological impacts (e.g., "child seemed down or depressed for more than 2 weeks afterward").

To derive the screener, we used the 2006 sample and dichotomized all acts as either endorsed or not (1 or 0). We then computed a dichotomous summary variable for every possible combination of up to 10 items; the summary variable indicated whether any one of the items in the combination had been endorsed. For each summary variable, we then calculated its sensitivity (i.e., abuse identified by those screener items/all cases of that type of abuse) and specificity (i.e., abuse not indicated by those screener items/all noncases). The optimally predictive combination of as few items as possible was then selected for both types of abuse. All analyses were conducted separately for men and women reporters. Finally, after deriving the screeners, we cross-validated them by calculating their sensitivity and specificity in the 2008 sample.

Sensitivity and Specificity

Child Physical Abuse

For child physical abuse, three items were needed for a screener with high sensitivity (but only modest specificity): spank on the bottom with a bare hand, slapped child's hand, and grabbed (see Appendix—Screener Form A). Sensitivity was 97% to 98% and specificity was 51% to 52% (same in the cross-validation). Thus, the screener captured 98% of parents who met criteria for child physical abuse, but had a high false positive rate resulting in modest specificity. These three items would work well in a two-stage screening design (e.g., Rothman & Greenland, 1998), as they can quickly eliminate parents who would *not* meet criteria for child physical abuse. The second stage (an interview) could then distinguish parents who are truly abusive from those who were false positives. Further, if time allowed an additional question (and some additional false positives), sensitivity goes up to 98.8% to 99.7% (with specificity reduced to 43%–46%) by adding, "Using a belt, electrical cord, switch, or some similar object, I hit or spanked my child." We should note that because the parents' reports of their children's injury and/or fear were the defining elements to distinguish parental aggression from abuse (for all reports other than high-inherent-risk-for-injury acts), it is highly likely that some of the "false positives" are actually true positives who minimized the reporting of the impact of their acts on their children.

Because of the high sensitivity but modest specificity, we have included an alternative screener (see Appendix—Screener Form B). The alternative form adds the fourth act described above and several impacts. (Note that several distractor impacts are included to reduce response biases: #5 "Child stopped misbehaving" and #8 "Child behaved better in the future.") Parents who indicate an act in items 1 to 4 and an impact on items 6, 7, or 9 would be considered to have reported child physical abuse.

Child Emotional Abuse

For child emotional abuse, four items were needed for a screener with high sensitivity and specificity: calling child names that could really hurt, using harsh verbal discipline, threatening to harm something important to child, threatening to hurt or abandon child, and mocking/putting child down in front of others (see Appendix—Screener Form C). Sensitivity was 93% and specificity was 97% (92% and 97%, respectively, in the cross-validation). Sensitivity was 95% to 98% and specificity was 91% to 92% (97%–98% and 92%–93%, respectively, in the cross-validation).

Administration

Procedure

Like all measures of sensitive health information, participants should complete the abuse screener privately (i.e., away from the other parent and, ideally, away from the children). It is important that parents understand the implications of their answers prior to administration. If the administration is for surveillance purposes and the data will be anonymous, that should be made clear. If the screener is being administered for clinical purposes, the clinicians need to be clear about whether their purpose is to identify abuse, which will require a follow-up interview, or whether their purpose is to identify risk, which can be done with the screener alone.

Time to Complete

All forms of the screener take very little time to complete. For example, the version that captures both child physical and emotional abuse (Appendix—Screener Form D) is only eight items, and thus could be completed in a couple of minutes. The more complete version that has child physical abuse acts and impacts and child emotional abuse (Screener Form E) is 14 items that would take between 5 and 10 minutes to complete.

Settings

Given the brevity of the screener, it could be used wherever there is an interest in screening for possible child maltreatment (e.g., doctors' offices, clinics, epidemiological studies). However, due to the required two-stage screening for child physical abuse, such settings would have to be prepared to discuss physical acts toward children and their impacts with parents who screen positive.

Scoring

Scoring is straightforward. For physical and emotional abuse items (Appendix—Screener Forms A, C, and D), a single act in the past 12 months is a sensitive (and, in the case of child emotional abuse, specific) indicator of abuse. In Screener Forms B and E, acts and impacts are assessed, and thus they indicate both components of the physical abuse criteria directly. Two-stage screening is still advisable, to ensure that the acts and impacts described were not answered in error or would not meet exclusionary criteria (e.g., acts were done to protect the child from physical harm in the environment, such as yank a child's arm to prevent him/her from getting hit by a car).

Follow-Up to a Positive Screen

As noted above, the physical abuse screener requires two-stage screening to sort out true from false positives. Although the child emotional abuse screener has high sensitivity and specificity, like all screeners, it is not a perfect predictor of actual abuse. Interviewing parents who screen positive is still an important practice.

STRUCTURED CLINICAL DIAGNOSTIC INTERVIEW FOR CHILD

Maltreatment

A series of structured clinical interviews have been developed and field tested as part of our work to develop the child maltreatment definitions used in the field trials described elsewhere (Chapter 9, this volume) and that form the basis of the definitions proposed for inclusion in the International Statistical Classification of Diseases and Related Health Problems (ICD-11). There are separate interviews for each form of maltreatment, and for different likely reporters, including the alleged perpetrator, the alleged victim, and a nonoffending parent or other witness (e.g., older sibling). Each interview assesses both the current incident that is being considered and the most severe recent incident. This allows the assessing clinician to understand the severity of maltreatment that may have occurred in the past, which is critical in treatment planning. Although a variant of this interview was used in the field trials (Heyman & Slep, 2006, 2009; Slep & Heyman, 2006) evaluating the definitions, the psychometrics of these interviews have not been evaluated. The interviews are included in the Appendix.

As can be seen from the interviews, they were created using the same approach taken in the Structured Clinical Interview for the *Diagnostic and Statistical Manual* (*DSM*; e.g., First, Spitzer, Gibbon, & Williams, 2002). The interviews can be used together, or separately, depending on the needs of the case. Interviewers should be familiar with the research diagnostic criteria for child maltreatment (see Chapter 9, this volume) prior to administering the structured interview, as this is critically important in helping the interviewer recognize when to probe for additional detail from the respondent.

Administration

Procedure

Like all measures of sensitive health information, participants should complete this interview privately. It is important that parents understand the limitations of confidentiality that might apply to their answers prior to administration. These interviews are best suited to situations where clearly determining whether incidents of parental behavior meet criteria for child maltreatment. For this reason, they are a good fit to research purposes with parents or children who are already involved in the child welfare system, or where the interview can be conducted anonymously. Anonymous interview data, while logistically challenging, can be arranged. Interviews can be conducted over the phone with no record of the phone number or other identifying information, for example. These interviews are also a good fit to child welfare applications, where an investigation of maltreatment leading to a determination is part of the purpose of the assessment.

Time to Complete

The interviews vary in length of time to complete by (a) how many of the interviews are to be administered and (b) how complex the incidents to be assessed are. One module of the interview typically requires approximately 10 to 15 minutes to complete.

Scoring

Scoring instructions parallel those used in the Structured Clinical Interview for the *DSM* and are included in the interview form. Each criterion is scored for present or absent. If an act criterion and impact criterion are met, then maltreatment is scored.

Follow-Up to a Positive Interview

If an interview is scored as maltreatment, or is not but raised concerns, it is critical to address safety concerns. If in a clinical setting, this could involve planning with the child or parent for the child's safety, as well as making appropriate referrals to child welfare. In a research setting, it is important that safety protocols are in place that would connect the research participant with an appropriate provider to develop safety plans and provide resources. In clinical settings, it is important to also consider what diagnoses might be comorbid. For instance, if this was an interview with an older child, are there comorbid depression or anxiety disorders? Ideally, the information gleaned from the interview will promote more precise treatment planning, which will improve the health and well-being of children and their families. In addition, more precise child maltreatment research will ultimately result in improved prevention efforts.

ACKNOWLEDGMENT

Preparation of this chapter was supported by a grant U49CE00124602 from the Centers for Disease Control and Prevention.

REFERENCES

Castelda, B. A., Levis, D. J., Rourke, P. A., & Coleman, S. L. (2007). Extension of the Sexual Abuse Questionnaire to other abuse categories: The initial psychometric validation of the Binghamton Childhood Abuse Screen. *Journal of Child Sexual Abuse, 16*, 107–125.

Eyberg, S. M., & Robinson, E. (1982). Parent–child interaction training: Effects on family functioning. *Journal of Clinical Child Psychology, 11*, 130–137.

Feigelman, S., Dubowitz, H., Lane, W., Prescott, L., Meyer, W., Tracy, J. K., & Kim, J. (2009). Screening for harsh punishment in a pediatric primary care clinic. *Child Abuse & Neglect, 33*, 269–277.

First, M. B., Spitzer, R. L., Gibbon, M. & Williams, J. B. W. (2002). *Structured clinical interview for DSM-IV-TR axis I disorders—patient edition*. New York: Biometrics Research Department.

Heyman, R. E., & Slep, A. M. S. (2006). Creating and field-testing diagnostic criteria for partner and child maltreatment. *Journal of Family Psychology, 20*, 397–408.

Heyman, R. E., & Slep, A. M. S. (2009). Reliability of family maltreatment diagnostic criteria: 41 site dissemination field trial. *Journal of Family Psychology, 23*, 905–910.

Heyman, R. E., Snarr, J. D., Foran, H. M., Makin-Byrd, K., Slep, A. M. S., & U.S. Air Force Family Advocacy Program. (2012a). *High sensitivity screening for child physical and emotional abuse*. Manuscript submitted for publication.

Heyman, R. E., Snarr, J. D., Slep, A. M. S., & U.S. Air Force Family Advocacy Program. (2012b). *Validity of a measure of clinical significant intimate partner violence and child abuse*. Manuscript submitted for publication.

Lock, T. G., Levis, D. J., & Rourke, P. A. (2005). The Sexual Abuse Questionnaire: A preliminary examination of a time and cost efficient method in evaluating the presence of childhood sexual abuse in adult patients. *Journal of Child Sexual Abuse, 14*, 1–26.

Milner, J. S. (1986). *The Child Abuse Potential Inventory manual—Second edition*. DeKalb, IL: Psytec.

Milner, J. S. (1994). Assessing physical child abuse risk: The child abuse potential inventory. *Clinical Psychology Review, 14*, 547–583.

Milner, J. S., Gold, R. G., & Wimberley, R. (1986). Prediction and explanation of child abuse: Cross-validation of the Child Abuse Potential Inventory. *Journal of Consulting and Clinical Psychology, 54*, 865–866.

Ondersma, S. J., Chaffin, M. J., Mullins, S. M., & LeBreton, J. M (2005). A brief form of the Child Abuse Potential Inventory: Development and validation. *Journal of Clinical Child & Adolescent Psychology, 34*, 301–311.

Rothman, K. J., & Greenland, S. (1998). *Modern epidemiology* (2nd ed). Hagerstown, MD: Lippincott-Raven.

Sanders, M. R. (1999). The Triple P–Positive Parenting Program: Towards an empirically validated multilevel parenting and family support strategy for the prevention of behavior and emotional problems in children. *Clinical Child and Family Psychology Review, 2*, 71–90.

Sanders, M. R. (2008). The Triple P—Positive Parenting Program as a public health approach to strengthening parenting. *Journal of Family Psychology, 22*, 506–517.

Slep, A. M. S., & Heyman, R. E. (2006). Creating and field-testing child maltreatment definitions: Improving the reliability of substantation determinations. *Child Maltreatment, 11*, 217–236.

Woodman, J., Lecky, F., Hodes, D., Pitt, M., Taylor, B., & Gilbert, R. (2009). Screening injured children for physical abuse or neglect in emergency departments: A systematic review. *Child: Care, Health and Development, 36*, 153–164.

APPENDIX: SCREENERS

SCREENER FORM A: CHILD PHYSICAL ABUSE

Below is a list of behaviors that parents often use to deal with their children's misbehavior (e.g., when children disobey, are aggressive, don't follow instructions, break rules, provoke their parents, etc.).

- The following questions ask how you have responded to misbehavior in the past 12 months.
- For each child, check all boxes that apply.

	I did this...			
During the past 12 months... (For each child, check all that apply)	**...to teach**	**...to punish**	**...because I was frustrated/lost my cool**	**I never did this**
1. I spanked child on the bottom with a bare hand				
Youngest child	☐	☐	☐	☐
2nd youngest child	☐	☐	☐	☐
3rd youngest child	☐	☐	☐	☐
4th youngest child	☐	☐	☐	☐
2. I slapped child's hand				
Youngest child	☐	☐	☐	☐
2nd youngest child	☐	☐	☐	☐
3rd youngest child	☐	☐	☐	☐
4th youngest child	☐	☐	☐	☐
3. I grabbed child				
Youngest child	☐	☐	☐	☐
2nd youngest child	☐	☐	☐	☐
3rd youngest child	☐	☐	☐	☐
4th youngest child	☐	☐	☐	☐

SCREENER FORM B: CHILD PHYSICAL ABUSE (INCLUDING IMPACT)

Below is a list of behaviors that parents often use to deal with their children's misbehavior (e.g., when children disobey, are aggressive, don't follow instructions, break rules, provoke their parents, etc.).

- The following questions ask how you have responded to misbehavior in the past 12 months.
- For each child, check all boxes that apply.

During the past 12 months... (For each child, check all that apply)	I did this... ...to teach	...to punish	...because I was frustrated/lost my cool	I never did this
1. I spanked child on the bottom with a bare hand				
Youngest child	☐	☐	☐	☐
2nd youngest child	☐	☐	☐	☐
3rd youngest child	☐	☐	☐	☐
4th youngest child	☐	☐	☐	☐
2. I slapped child's hand				
Youngest child	☐	☐	☐	☐
2nd youngest child	☐	☐	☐	☐
3rd youngest child	☐	☐	☐	☐
4th youngest child	☐	☐	☐	☐
3. I grabbed child				
Youngest child	☐	☐	☐	☐
2nd youngest child	☐	☐	☐	☐
3rd youngest child	☐	☐	☐	☐
4th youngest child	☐	☐	☐	☐
4. Using a stick, hairbrush, or some other hard object, I hit or spanked child				
Youngest child	☐	☐	☐	☐
2nd youngest child	☐	☐	☐	☐
3rd youngest child	☐	☐	☐	☐
4th youngest child	☐	☐	☐	☐

How often did the following happen as a result?	*1 time*	*2 times*	*3-5 times*	*6-10 times*	*11-20 times*	*More than 20 times*	*Never*	*Not this year, but has happened in the past*
5. Child stopped misbehaving	1	2	3	4	5	6	0	☐
6. Child had pain the next day	1	2	3	4	5	6	0	☐
7. Child had a bruise or welt	1	2	3	4	5	6	0	☐
8. Child behaved better in the future	1	2	3	4	5	6	0	☐
9. Child had a sprain, broken bone, or cut that required stitches	1	2	3	4	5	6	0	☐

SCREENER FORM C: CHILD EMOTIONAL ABUSE

Children can be very frustrating. All parents at one time or another say or do things that they don't really mean or that they wouldn't usually do if they weren't feeling so frustrated.

- The following questions ask how you have responded to your child in the past 12 months.
- For each child, check all boxes that apply.

	I did this...					
During the past 12 months... (For each child, check all that apply)	**Less than once a week**	**Once a week**	**Once or twice a day**	**Three to five times a day**	**Five to ten times a day**	**More than ten times a day**
1. I verbally disciplined my child harshly						
Youngest child	☐	☐	☐	☐	☐	☐
2nd youngest child	☐	☐	☐	☐	☐	☐
3rd youngest child	☐	☐	☐	☐	☐	☐
4th youngest child	☐	☐	☐	☐	☐	☐

	I did this...					
	Once or twice	**Less than once a month**	**Once a month to once a week**	**Once a week to once a day**	**More than once a day**	**I never did this**
2. To send a message to my child, I harmed something important to him/her, (e.g., child's favorite object or pet)						
Youngest child	☐	☐	☐	☐	☐	☐
2nd youngest child	☐	☐	☐	☐	☐	☐
3rd youngest child	☐	☐	☐	☐	☐	☐
4th youngest child	☐	☐	☐	☐	☐	☐
3. I threatened to seriously hurt my child, threatened to abandon him/her, or made similar kinds of threats						
Youngest child	☐	☐	☐	☐	☐	☐
2nd youngest child	☐	☐	☐	☐	☐	☐
3rd youngest child	☐	☐	☐	☐	☐	☐
4th youngest child	☐	☐	☐	☐	☐	☐
4. To send a message to my child, I harmed something important to him/her (e.g., child's favorite object or pet)						
Youngest child	☐	☐	☐	☐	☐	☐
2nd youngest child	☐	☐	☐	☐	☐	☐
3rd youngest child	☐	☐	☐	☐	☐	☐
4th youngest child	☐	☐	☐	☐	☐	☐
5. I did things such as mock child, put child down in front of others, spit at child, etc.						
Youngest child	☐	☐	☐	☐	☐	☐
2nd youngest child	☐	☐	☐	☐	☐	☐
3rd youngest child	☐	☐	☐	☐	☐	☐
4th youngest child	☐	☐	☐	☐	☐	☐

SCREENER FORM D: COMBINED CHILD PHYSICAL AND EMOTIONAL ABUSE

Below is a list of behaviors that parents often use to deal with their children's misbehavior (e.g., when children disobey, are aggressive, don't follow instructions, break rules, provoke their parents, etc.).

- The following questions ask how you have responded to misbehavior in the past 12 months.
- For each child, check all boxes that apply.

	I did this...			
During the past 12 months... (For each child, check all that apply)	**...to teach**	**...to punish**	**...because I was frustrated/lost my cool**	**I never did this**
1. I spanked child on the bottom with a bare hand				
Youngest child	☐	☐	☐	☐
2nd youngest child	☐	☐	☐	☐
3rd youngest child	☐	☐	☐	☐
4th youngest child	☐	☐	☐	☐
2. I slapped child's hand				
Youngest child	☐	☐	☐	☐
2nd youngest child	☐	☐	☐	☐
3rd youngest child	☐	☐	☐	☐
4th youngest child	☐	☐	☐	☐
3. I grabbed child				
Youngest child	☐	☐	☐	☐
2nd youngest child	☐	☐	☐	☐
3rd youngest child	☐	☐	☐	☐
4th youngest child	☐	☐	☐	☐

Children can be very frustrating. All parents at one time or another say or do things that they don't really mean or that they wouldn't usually do if they weren't feeling so frustrated.

- The following questions ask how you have responded to your child in the past 12 months.
- For each child, check all boxes that apply.

(continued)

SCREENER FORM D: COMBINED CHILD PHYSICAL AND EMOTIONAL ABUSE *(continued)*

During the past 12 months... (For each child, check all that apply)	I did this... Less than once a week	Once a week	Once or twice a day	Three to five times a day	Five to ten times a day	More than ten times a day
4. I verbally disciplined my child harshly						
Youngest child	☐	☐	☐	☐	☐	☐
2nd youngest child	☐	☐	☐	☐	☐	☐
3rd youngest child	☐	☐	☐	☐	☐	☐
4th youngest child	☐	☐	☐	☐	☐	☐
5. To send a message to my child, I harmed something important to him/her, (e.g., child's favorite object or pet)						
Youngest child	☐	☐	☐	☐	☐	☐
2nd youngest child	☐	☐	☐	☐	☐	☐
3rd youngest child	☐	☐	☐	☐	☐	☐
4th youngest child	☐	☐	☐	☐	☐	☐
6. I threatened to seriously hurt my child, threatened to abandon him/her, or made similar kinds of threats						
Youngest child	☐	☐	☐	☐	☐	☐
2nd youngest child	☐	☐	☐	☐	☐	☐
3rd youngest child	☐	☐	☐	☐	☐	☐
4th youngest child	☐	☐	☐	☐	☐	☐
7. To send a message to my child, I harmed something important to him/her (e.g., child's favorite object or pet)						
Youngest child	☐	☐	☐	☐	☐	☐
2nd youngest child	☐	☐	☐	☐	☐	☐
3rd youngest child	☐	☐	☐	☐	☐	☐
4th youngest child	☐	☐	☐	☐	☐	☐
8. I did things such as mock child, put child down in front of others, spit at child, etc.						
Youngest child	☐	☐	☐	☐	☐	☐
2nd youngest child	☐	☐	☐	☐	☐	☐
3rd youngest child	☐	☐	☐	☐	☐	☐
4th youngest child	☐	☐	☐	☐	☐	☐

SCREENER FORM E: COMBINED CHILD PHYSICAL (INCLUDING IMPACT) AND EMOTIONAL ABUSE

Below is a list of behaviors that parents often use to deal with their children's misbehavior (e.g., when children disobey, are aggressive, don't follow instructions, break rules, provoke their parents, etc.).

- The following questions ask how you have responded to misbehavior in the past 12 months.
- For each child, check all boxes that apply.

(continued)

SCREENER FORM E: COMBINED CHILD PHYSICAL (INCLUDING IMPACT) AND EMOTIONAL ABUSE *(continued)*

During the past 12 months... (For each child, check all that apply)	I did this... ...to teach	...to punish	...because I was frustrated/lost my cool	I never did this
1. I spanked child on the bottom with a bare hand				
Youngest child	☐	☐	☐	☐
2nd youngest child	☐	☐	☐	☐
3rd youngest child	☐	☐	☐	☐
4th youngest child	☐	☐	☐	☐
2. I slapped child's hand				
Youngest child	☐	☐	☐	☐
2nd youngest child	☐	☐	☐	☐
3rd youngest child	☐	☐	☐	☐
4th youngest child	☐	☐	☐	☐
3. I grabbed child				
Youngest child	☐	☐	☐	☐
2nd youngest child	☐	☐	☐	☐
3rd youngest child	☐	☐	☐	☐
4th youngest child	☐	☐	☐	☐
4. Using a stick, hairbrush, or some other hard object, I hit or spanked child				
Youngest child	☐	☐	☐	☐
2nd youngest child	☐	☐	☐	☐
3rd youngest child	☐	☐	☐	☐
4th youngest child	☐	☐	☐	☐

How often did the following happen as a result?	*1 time*	*2 times*	*3-5 times*	*6-10 times*	*11-20 times*	*More than 20 times*	*Never*	*Not this year, but has happened in the past*
5. Child stopped misbehaving	1	2	3	4	5	6	0	☐
6. Child had pain the next day	1	2	3	4	5	6	0	☐
7. Child had a bruise or welt	1	2	3	4	5	6	0	☐
8. Child behaved better in the future	1	2	3	4	5	6	0	☐
9. Child had a sprain, broken bone, or cut that required stitches	1	2	3	4	5	6	0	☐

Children can be very frustrating. All parents at one time or another say or do things that they don't really mean or that they wouldn't usually do if they weren't feeling so frustrated.

- The following questions ask how you have responded to your child in the past 12 months.
- For each child, check all boxes that apply.

(continued)

SCREENER FORM E: COMBINED CHILD PHYSICAL (INCLUDING IMPACT) AND EMOTIONAL ABUSE *(continued)*

During the past 12 months... (For each child, check all that apply)	I did this... Less than once a week	Once a week	Once or twice a day	Three to five times a day	Five to ten times a day	More than ten times a day
10. I verbally disciplined my child harshly						
Youngest child	☐	☐	☐	☐	☐	☐
2nd youngest child	☐	☐	☐	☐	☐	☐
3rd youngest child	☐	☐	☐	☐	☐	☐
4th youngest child	☐	☐	☐	☐	☐	☐

	I did this... Once or twice	Less than once a month	Once a month to once a week	Once a week to once a day	More than once a day	I never did this
11. To send a message to my child, I harmed something important to him/her (e.g., child's favorite object or pet)						
Youngest child	☐	☐	☐	☐	☐	☐
2nd youngest child	☐	☐	☐	☐	☐	☐
3rd youngest child	☐	☐	☐	☐	☐	☐
4th youngest child	☐	☐	☐	☐	☐	☐
12. I threatened to seriously hurt my child, threatened to abandon them, or made similar kinds of threats						
Youngest child	☐	☐	☐	☐	☐	☐
2nd youngest child	☐	☐	☐	☐	☐	☐
3rd youngest child	☐	☐	☐	☐	☐	☐
4th youngest child	☐	☐	☐	☐	☐	☐
13. To send a message to my child, I harmed something important to him/her (for example, child's favorite object or pet)						
Youngest child	☐	☐	☐	☐	☐	☐
2nd youngest child	☐	☐	☐	☐	☐	☐
3rd youngest child	☐	☐	☐	☐	☐	☐
4th youngest child	☐	☐	☐	☐	☐	☐
14. I did things such as mock child, put child down in front of others, spit at child, etc.						
Youngest child	☐	☐	☐	☐	☐	☐
2nd youngest child	☐	☐	☐	☐	☐	☐
3rd youngest child	☐	☐	☐	☐	☐	☐
4th youngest child	☐	☐	☐	☐	☐	☐

Structured Interview for Relational Problems

Child Physical Abuse

Child Physical Abuse	Child Physical Abuse Criteria	
Now I'm going to ask you some questions about things that sometimes go on between a parent and a child at some time or another.		
In the past year... ...have you done any of these things to your child? (Show category 1 CHILD physical force list to interviewee)	A. Nonaccidental use of physical force by a child's parent/caregiver: spanking with hand; dropping; pushing; shoving; slapping; grabbing or yanking limbs or body; throwing; poking; hair-pulling; scratching; pinching; restraining or squeezing; shaking; biting	? 1 2 3
Ok, how about any of these? (show category 2 CHILD physical force list to interviewee)	throwing objects at; kicking; hitting with fist; hitting with a stick, strap, belt, or other object; scalding; burning; poisoning; stabbing; applying force to throat; strangling or cutting off air supply; holding under water; using a weapon.	? 1 2 3
What about anything similar but not listed here?	any other nonaccidental use of physical force IF NONE ARE CODED "3," SKIP TO THE NEXT MODULE	? 1 2 3
Think about what you would consider to be the most serious incident. I'm going to ask you some questions about your child. You may not know some of these details, but just answer to the best of your ability.	B. Significant impact on the child as evidenced by any of the following:	? 1 2 3
Sometimes when things get physical, people notice marks, bruises, or cuts. Did your child have any? If NO: What about pain? (How long did that last?) If NO: What about any other injury?	(1) More than inconsequential physical injury.	? 1 2 3
"Again, I'd like you to think about the most serious physical incident in the past year. I'd like you to tell me exactly what happened in the incident. Please be as detailed as if you were watching it on a video screen and describe for me everything that you see, from the beginning to the end." ("Where were you when this happened") ("How hard was [act] on a scale of 1-10, with 1 being feather-light and 10 being as hard as possible?")	(2) Reasonable potential for more than inconsequential physical injury given the inherent dangerousness of the act, the degree of force used and the physical environment in which the acts occurred An injury involving any of the following: a. Any injury to the face or head b. More than superficial bruise(s) c. More than superficial cut(s) / scratch(es) (i.e., requires pressure to stop bleeding) d. Bleeding e. Welts f. Loss of consciousness	? 1 2 3

(continued)

Child Physical Abuse *(continued)*

Child Physical Abuse	Child Physical Abuse Criteria				
	g. Loss of functioning (including, but not limited to, sprains, broken bones, detached retina, loose or chipped teeth) h. Heat exhaustion or heat stroke i. Damage to internal organs j. Disfigurement (including, but not limited to, scarring) k. Swelling lasting at least 24 hours l. Pain felt (a) in the course of normal activities and (b) at least 24 hours after the physical injury was suffered.				
"Was your child afraid, either during or after the incident? (What was s/he afraid of?) (How long did it last?)"	(3) More than inconsequential fear reaction a. Child's fear (verbalized or displayed) of bodily injury to self or others AND	?	1	2	3
If YES to fear: "I'm going to ask you some questions about specific ways that the(se) incident(s) may have affected your child.	b. At least one of the following signs of fear or anxiety lasting at least 48 hours				
"Did your child think about the incident(s) when s/he didn't want to or did thoughts about it come to him/her suddenly when s/he didn't want them to? (Tell me about that…)"	(1) Persistent intrusive recollections of the incident	?	1	2	3
"Did s/he go out of his/her way to avoid people, places, or things related to the incident? (Tell me about that…)"	(2) Marked negative reactions to cues related to incident, as evidenced by any of the following: a. Avoidance of cues	?	1	2	3
"What about getting very upset when something reminded him/her of the incident(s)?"	b. subjective or overt distress to cues	?	1	2	3
"What about physical symptoms — like breaking out in a sweat, breathing heavily or irregularly, or his/her heart pounding or racing?"	c. physiological hyperarousal to cues	?	1	2	3
"What about finding him/herself acting or feeling as if s/he were back in the incident?"	(3) Acting or feeling as if incident is recurring	?	1	2	3
Since the incident(s)…	(4) Persistent symptoms of increased arousal, as evidenced by any of the following				
… has your child had trouble sleeping?	a. Difficulty falling or staying asleep	?	1	2	3
… has your child been unusually irritable? What about outbursts of anger?	b. Irritability or outbursts of anger	?	1	2	3
…has your child had trouble concentrating?	c. Difficulty concentrating	?	1	2	3
…has your child been watchful or on guard even when there was no reason to be?	d. Hypervigilance	?	1	2	3

(continued)

Child Physical Abuse *(continued)*

Child Physical Abuse	Child Physical Abuse Criteria	
...has your child been jumpy or easily startled, like by sudden noises?	e. Exaggerated startle response	? 1 2 3
	B1 IS CODED 3 OR B2 IS CODED 3 OR (B3a IS CODED "3" AND AT LEAST ONE OF B3b (1–4) IS CODED "3")	1 3
	C. The acts of physical force were NOT committed for any of the following reasons:	IF NOT CODED "3," SKIP TO THE NEXT MODULE
You said that you have [ACTS] and that, as a result, your child had [IMPACTS]. In any of these incidents, did your [ACTS] come after s/he had already used physical force? (IF YES, "In what percentage of the incidents had s/he used force first?") (IF 100% - "In what percentage of the incidents was s/he still in the act of using force when you [ACT]?)	C1. Act(s) DID NOT OCCUR ONLY to protect self from imminent physical harm because child was in the act of physical force a. There exists an incident when the child DID NOT use force first or WAS NOT still in the act of using force when self's act(s) occurred. b. Self's act(s) was/were NOT SOLELY to stop child's use of physical force.	a. 1 3 b. 1 3
(IF 100%, "Was there ever a time that your [ACTS] occurred for some other reason than to stop your child's use of force?") (IF NO, "Did you ever do more than was necessary to stop your child from using force?")	c. Self's act(s) used MORE THAN minimally sufficient force to stop child's use of physical force.	1 3 PHYSICAL AGGRESSION DUE TO SELF-DEFENSE OF PHYSICAL ACT
	C1. Act(s) by self DID NOT OCCUR ONLY to protect self from imminent physical harm because partner was in the act of physical force	1 3 PHYSICAL AGGRESSION IN PLAY
(If not clear from prior questions) In any of the times you have [ACTS] and that, as a result, your child had [IMPACTS], were your [ACTS] happening in play? (If YES, "In what percentage of the incidents did your [ACTS] happen in play?)	C2. Act(s) by self DID NOT ALWAYS occur in developmentally appropriate play.	1 3 IF C1a, b, and c ALL ARE CODED "1," CODE C1 "1" AND SKIP TO THE NEXT MODULE
(If not clear from prior questions) In any of the times you have [ACTS] and that, as a result, your child had [IMPACTS], did you [ACTS] to protect your child or someone else from physical harm? (If YES, "Tell me about such a time.) ("In what percentage of the incidents did your [ACTS] happen to protect your child or someone else?")	C3. Act(s) by self WERE NOT ALWAYS to directly protect child or another person from imminent physical harm (including, but not limited to, pushing child out of the way of a car, taking weapon away from suicidal child, stopping child from inflicting injury on another person). Note: Subsequent actions that were not directly protective (e.g., whipping child for running into the street) would not meet this criterion.	1 3 PHYSICAL AGGRESSION TO PROTECT

Note: ? = inadequate information, 1 = absent or false, 2 = subthreshold, 3 = threshold or true.

Child Emotional Abuse

Child Emotional Abuse	Child Emotional Abuse Criteria	
Now I'm going to ask you about other kinds of things that happen between parents and children at some time or another. In the past year...	A. Verbal or symbolic acts (excluding physically aggressive acts and sexual abuse) by a parent/caregiver with the potential to cause psychological harm to the child. Such acts include, but are not limited to:	
Have you scolded, criticized, or humiliated your child?	(1) Berating, disparaging, degrading, humiliating child	? 1 2 3
Have you threatened your child (like saying you were going to hurt or leave him/her)?	(2) Threatening child (including, but not limited to, indicating/implying future physical harm, abandonment, sexual assault)	? 1 2 3
Have you harmed or abandoned, or threatened to harm or abandon, someone or thing your child cares about?	(3) Harming/abandoning—or indicating that the parent/caregiver will harm/abandon—people/things that child cares about, such as pets, property, loved ones (including exposing child to criteria-meeting or subthreshold child maltreatment)	? 1 2 3
Have you confined your child?	(4) Confining child (a means of punishment involving restriction of movement, as by tying a child's arms or legs together or binding a child to a chair, bed, or other object, or confining a child to an enclosed area [such as a closet])	? 1 2 3
Have you blamed your child a lot for things that go wrong?	(5) Scapegoating child	? 1 2 3
Have you ordered your child to do something painful, like kneeling on rice for a while?	(6) Coercing the child to inflict pain on him/herself (including, but not limited to, ordering child to kneel on hard objects such as split peas or rice for long periods; ordering the child to ingest a highly spiced food, spice, or herb)	? 1 2 3
Have you been very harsh with disciplining your child?	(7) Disciplining child (through physical or nonphysical means) excessively (i.e., extremely high frequency or duration, though not meeting physical abuse criteria)	? 1 2 3
What about anything similar?	(8) Any other psychologically harmful acts	? 1 2 3
	B. At least one of the following features:	IF NO ITEMS 1–8 ARE CODED "3", SKIP TO THE NEXT MODULE
	(1) Psychological harm, including either a. More than inconsequential fear reaction	
Because of [ACT], was your child ever afraid? (What was s/he afraid of?) (How long did it last?)"	i. Fear (verbalized or displayed) of bodily injury to self or others AND	? 1 2 3

(continued)

Child Emotional Abuse *(continued)*

Child Emotional Abuse	Child Emotional Abuse Criteria				
If YES to fear: "I'm going to ask you some questions about specific ways that the(se) [ACTS] may have affected your child	ii. At least one of the following signs of fear or anxiety lasting at least 48 hours				
"Does your child think about the [ACTS] when s/he didn't want to or did thoughts about it come to him/her suddenly when s/he didn't want them to? (Tell me about that…)"	(a) Persistent intrusive recollections of the incident	?	1	2	3
"Does your child go out of his/her way to avoid people, places, or things related to the [ACTS]? (Tell me about that…)"	(b) Marked negative reactions to cues related to incident, as evidenced by any of the following i. Avoidance of cues	?	1	2	3
"What about getting very upset when something reminded your child of the [ACTS]?"	ii. Subjective or overt distress to cues	?	1	2	3
"What about physical symptoms — like breaking out in a sweat, breathing heavily or irregularly, or heart pounding or racing?"	iii. Physiological hyperarousal to cues	?	1	2	3
"What about your child finding him/herself acting or feeling as if you were back in the [ACTS]?"	(c) Acting or feeling as if incident is recurring	?	1	2	3
Since the [ACTS]…	(d) Persistent symptoms of increased arousal, as evidenced by any of the following				
… has your child had trouble sleeping?	i. Difficulty falling or staying asleep	?	1	2	3
… has your child been unusually irritable? What about outbursts of anger?	ii. Irritability or outbursts of anger	?	1	2	3
…has your child had trouble concentrating?	iii. Difficulty concentrating	?	1	2	3
…has your child been watchful or on guard even when there was no reason to be?	iv. Hypervigilance	?	1	2	3
…has your child been jumpy or easily startled, like by sudden noises?	v. Exaggerated startle response	?	1	2	3
	B.(1)a.: B.(1).a.i. IS CODED 3 AND AT LEAST ONE OF B.(1).a.ii. (a–d) IS CODED "3")	?	1	2	3
How did [ACTS] affect your child? (If needed: "As a result of [ACTS], did your child feel depressed? Sad? Lonely? Did your child have crying spells?"	b. Significant psychological distress (i.e., psychiatric disorders at or near diagnostic thresholds)	?	1	2	3
	(2) Reasonable potential for psychological harm. Note: The child's level of functioning and the risk and resilience factors present should be taken into consideration.	?	1	2	3

(continued)

Child Emotional Abuse *(continued)*

Child Emotional Abuse	Child Emotional Abuse Criteria				
	a. The act (or pattern of acts) creates reasonable potential for the development of a psychiatric disorder (at or near diagnostic thresholds) related to, or exacerbated by, the act(s). Note: The child's level of functioning and the risk and resilience factors present should be taken into consideration. b. The act (or pattern of acts) carries a reasonable potential for significant disruption of the child's physical, psychological, cognitive, or social development. A significant disruption would involve development that is substantially worse than would have been expected, given the child's developmental level and trajectory before alleged maltreatment.	?	1	2	3
After the [ACTS], how was your child's physical health? Did your child feel sick a lot? What kinds of problems was your child experiencing? (If YES, "How did [feeling sick] affect your child's everyday life?")	(3) Stress-related somatic symptoms (related to or exacerbated by the acts) that significantly interfere with normal functioning.	?	1	2	3
	AT LEAST ONE OF B.(1)a., B.(1)b., B.(2)a., B.(2)b., or B.(3) IS CODED 3.	?	1	2	3

Note: ?=inadequate information , 1 = absent or false, 2=subthreshold , 3= threshold or true.

Child Sexual Abuse

Child Sexual Abuse	Child Sexual Abuse Criteria				
Now I'm going to ask you about other kinds of things that can happen between a parent and a child. In the past year... Have you touched your child in a sexual way?	A. Any of the following acts involving a child and intended to provide sexual gratification to an adult offender. Sexual gratification involves sexual arousal or pleasure or appealing to prurient interest of the offender; it does not require overt evidence of arousal (e.g., erection, vaginal lubrication, ejaculation, orgasm) (1) Use of physical force, emotional manipulation, or a child's youth or naïveté to engage in penis-vulva or penis-anus penetration (of child, perpetrator, or both), however slight.	?	1	2	3
	(2) Physical contact of a sexual nature between child and perpetrator not involving penis-vulva or penis-anus penetration, including, but not limited to: a. Oral-genital or oral-anal contact	?	1	2	3

(continued)

Child Sexual Abuse *(continued)*

Child Sexual Abuse	Child Sexual Abuse Criteria				
	b. Non-penile penetration of vulva or rectum (e.g., with hands, fingers, or objects)	?	1	2	3
	c. Attempted penetration of the vulva or rectum	?	1	2	3
	d. Groping, rubbing, fondling, stroking, or similar behavior—directly or through clothing	?	1	2	3
What about having your child do things like posing or viewing sexual material or body parts?	(3) Non-contact exploitation—Forcing, tricking, enticing, threatening, or pressuring a child to participate in acts for anyone's sexual gratification without direct physical contact between child and offender. Acts include, but are not limited to, exposing child's or offender's genitals, anus, or breasts; having child masturbate or watch masturbation; having child participate in sexual activity with a third person (including child prostitution); having child pose, undress or perform in a sexual fashion (including child pornography); exposing child to pornography or live sexual performance; "peeping" or other prurient watching (i.e., voyeurism).	?	1	2	3
	AT LEAST ONE OF A(1), A(2)a–d, OR A(3) IS CODED 3.	?	1	2	3

Note: ? = inadequate information, 1 = absent or false, 2 = subthreshold, 3 = threshold or true.

Child Neglect

Child Neglect	Child Neglect Criteria
Now I'm going to ask you about other kinds of things that parents sometimes do. In the past year… Have there been times when your child was left unattended, either at home, in the car, or somewhere else? (Tell me about that.) (Think of the time when s/he was left unattended the longest. Tell me about that.) (What was s/he doing?) (What were you doing at the time?) (Where was s/he in relation to you or another caregiver?)	A. Egregious act(s) or omission(s) on the part of the child's caregiver that deprive the child of needed age-appropriate care. Note: Egregious acts or omissions show striking disregard for child's well-being. As such, they are not merely examples of inadvisable or deficient parenting, but must clearly fall below the lower bounds of normal parenting. (1) Lack of supervision: Egregious absence or inattention. Child's age and level of functioning should be considered in making determination about level of supervision required. Note: Leaving children ten or older unattended in a vehicle for brief periods of time in a safe area does not meet this criterion.

(continued)

Child Neglect *(continued)*

Child Neglect	Child Neglect Criteria
Children sometimes encounter situations in which there are dangers, where they could get sick or hurt. In the past year, has your child been exposed to any of these situations? (Hand "Dangerous Situations" card). (Tell me about that.)	(2) Exposure to physical hazards: Inattention to child's safety by exposing child to physical dangers (including, but not limited to, exposed wiring; broken glass; hazardous chemicals, non-secured, loaded guns in home; illegal drugs in home; dangerously unhygienic living conditions; dangerous or unhygienic pets; asking child to perform dangerous activities; driving while intoxicated with child in vehicle).
In the past year, has your child attended school regularly? Have there been any times when s/he did not go to school, other than when s/he was too sick to go?	(3) Educational neglect: Knowingly allowing the child to have extended or frequent absences from school, neglecting to enroll the child in appropriate home schooling or public or private education, or preventing the child from attending school for other than justifiable reasons (when education is compulsory by law).
Think of all the times in the past year when your child may have needed medical care, medicine, dental care, or mental health care. In what percentage of those situations did you get him/her medical care? (IF LESS THAN 100%, "Think about the time when your child most needed medical care but didn't get it. Tell me about that.") (What did you do to try to get him/her health care?)	(4) Health care neglect: Refusal or failure to provide appropriate health care (including, but not limited to, failure to obtain appropriate medical, mental health, dental care, medications, medically indicated services or procedures) although the parent was financially able to do so or was offered other means to do so.
In the past year, has there been a time when your child has not had enough food, shelter, or clothing?	(5) Deprivation of necessities: The failure to provide age-appropriate nourishment, shelter and clothing. Includes non-organic failure to thrive (which must be determined by a competent medical authority), a type of child neglect evidenced by an infant's or young child's failure to adequately grow and develop in height and weight when no organic basis for this deviation is found.
In the past year, have you ever been away from your child for more than 24 hours? (IF YES, "In what percentage of those times did you arrange for someone else to care for your child?") (IF LESS THAN 100%, "Think about the time(s) when you were away from your child but didn't have someone else care for him/her. Tell me about that.)	(6) Abandonment: The caregiver is absent and does not intend to return or is away from the home for more than 24 hours without having arranged for an appropriate surrogate caregiver. NO IMPACT ("B") CRITERION IS NECESSARY FOR ABANDONMENT TO BE DEEMED NEGLECT.

(continued)

Child Neglect *(continued)*

Child Neglect	Child Neglect Criteria				
Sometimes when parents [NEGLECT ACT], children get marks, bruises, or cuts. Did your child have any? If NO: What about pain? (How long did that last?) If NO: What about any other injury?	B. Significant impact on the child as evidenced by any of the following: (1) More than inconsequential physical injury. An injury involving any of the following: a. Any injury to the face or head b. More than superficial bruise(s) c. More than superficial cut(s) / scratch(es) (i.e., requires pressure to stop bleeding) d. Bleeding e. Welts f. Loss of consciousness g. Loss of functioning (including, but not limited to, sprains, broken bones, detached retina, loose or chipped teeth) h. Heat exhaustion or heat stroke i. Damage to internal organs j. Disfigurement (including, but not limited to, scarring) k. Swelling lasting at least 24 hours l. Pain felt (a) in the course of normal activities and (b) at least 24 hours after the physical injury was suffered. (2) Psychological harm, including any of the following a. More than inconsequential fear reaction				
Because of [NEGLECT ACT], was your child ever afraid? (What was s/he afraid of?) (How long did it last?)"	i. Fear (verbalized or displayed) of bodily injury to self or others AND	?	1	2	3
If YES to fear: "I'm going to ask you some questions about specific ways that the(se) [NEGLECT ACT/IES] may have affected your child	ii. At least one of the following signs of fear or anxiety lasting at least 48 hours				
"Does your child think about the [NEGLECT ACT] when s/he didn't want to or did thoughts about it come to him/her suddenly when s/he didn't want them to? (Tell me about that…)"	a. Persistent intrusive recollections of the incident	?	1	2	3
"Does your child go out of his/her way to avoid people, places, or things related to the [NEGLECT ACT]? (Tell me about that…)"	b. Marked negative reactions to cues related to incident, as evidenced by any of the following i. Avoidance of cues	?	1	2	3
"What about getting very upset when something reminded your child of the [NEGLECT ACT]?"	ii. Subjective or overt distress to cues	?	1	2	3
"What about physical symptoms — like breaking out in a sweat, breathing heavily or irregularly, or heart pounding or racing?"	iii. Physiological hyperarousal to cues	?	1	2	3
"What about your child finding him/herself acting or feeling as if you were back in the [NEGLECT ACT]?"	c. Acting or feeling as if incident is recurring	?	1	2	3

(continued)

Child Neglect *(continued)*

Child Neglect	Child Neglect Criteria				
Since the [NEGLECT ACT]...	d. Persistent symptoms of increased arousal, as evidenced by any of the following				
... has your child had trouble sleeping?	i. Difficulty falling or staying asleep	?	1	2	3
... has your child been unusually irritable? What about outbursts of anger?	ii. Irritability or outbursts of anger	?	1	2	3
...has your child had trouble concentrating?	iii. Difficulty concentrating	?	1	2	3
...has your child been watchful or on guard even when there was no reason to be?	iv. Hypervigilance	?	1	2	3
...has your child been jumpy or easily startled, like by sudden noises?	v. Exaggerated startle response	?	1	2	3
	B.(2): B.(2).a.i. IS CODED 3 AND AT LEAST ONE OF B.(2).a.ii. (a–d) IS CODED "3")	?	1	2	3
How did [ACTS] affect your child? (If needed: "As a result of [ACTS], did your child feel depressed? Sad? Lonely? Did your child have crying spells?"	iii. Significant psychological distress (i.e., psychiatric disorders, at or near diagnostic thresholds) related to, or exacerbated by, the act(s)	?	1	2	3
After the [NEGLECT ACTS], how was your child's physical health? Did your child feel sick a lot? What kinds of problems was your child experiencing? (If YES, "How did [feeling sick] affect your child's everyday life?")	(3) Stress-related somatic symptoms (related to or exacerbated by the acts) that that significantly interfere with normal functioning	?	1	2	3
(For (5) and (6), if unclear) I'd like you to think about the most serious [NEGLECT ACT] in the last year. I'd like you to tell me exactly what happened in the incident. Please be as detailed as if you were watching it on a video screen and describe for me everything that you see, from the beginning to the end." ("Where were you when this happened")	(4) Reasonable potential for more than inconsequential physical injury given the act(s)/omission(s) and child's physical environment "More than inconsequential physical injury": An injury involving any of the following: a. Any injury to the face or head b. More than superficial bruise(s) c. More than superficial cut(s) / scratch(es) (i.e., requires pressure to stop bleeding) d. Bleeding e. Welts f. Loss of consciousness g. Loss of functioning (including, but not limited to, sprains, broken bones, detached retina, loose, or chipped teeth) h. Heat exhaustion or heat stroke i. Damage to internal organs j. Disfigurement (including, but not limited to, scarring) k. Swelling lasting at least 24 hours Pain felt in the course of normal activities and at least 24 hours after the physical injury was suffered.	?	1	2	3

(continued)

Child Neglect *(continued)*

Child Neglect	Child Neglect Criteria				
	(5) Reasonable potential for psychological harm, as evidenced by either or the following:	?	1	2	3
	a. The act (or pattern of acts) creates reasonable potential for the development of a psychiatric disorder (at or near diagnostic thresholds) related to, or exacerbated by, the act(s). **Note:** The child's level of functioning and the risk and resilience factors present should be taken into consideration.	?	1	2	3
	b. The act (or pattern of acts) carries a reasonable potential for significant disruption of the child's physical, psychological, cognitive, or social development. A significant disruption would involve development that is substantially worse than would have been expected, given the child's developmental level and trajectory evident before alleged maltreatment.	?	1	2	3

Note: ? = inadequate information, 1 = absent or false, 2 = subthreshold, 3 = threshold or true.

13

Caregiver–Child Relational Problems: Definitions and Implications for Diagnosis

Amy M. Smith Slep and Tuula Tamminen

Parenting, and what constitutes good and suboptimal caregiving, has been the focus of research for quite a long time. Rich areas of inquiry have developed focusing on general parenting (e.g., Maccoby & Martin, 1983), attachment (e.g., Sroufe, Carlson, Levy, & Egeland, 1999), managing misbehavior (e.g., Baumrind, 1967; Dowling, Slep, & O'Leary, 2010), and nearly every aspect of child development that parents might play a role in (see Chapter 15, this volume). Each area has a strong theoretical foundation and supports an array of empirical work highlighting the importance of parenting behavior to child development and well-being. Although dysfunctional or suboptimal parenting has been the focus of a great deal of work, parenting behavior has typically been considered along a continuum. Even qualitatively distinct parenting styles (e.g., Baumrind, 1967) are not thought of as "healthy" and "dysfunctional."

In the past several years, however, a subset of parenting researchers and clinicians are beginning to conceive of dysfunctional parent–child or caregiver–child relationships as a clinical problem distinct from child psychopathology. Research on a clinically distinct construct of caregiver–child relational problems is still relatively new. This stands in contrast to the area of couples relationship problems, where the notion of a clinically distressed relationship that was separable from either individual's functioning has been part of the field from its inception (see Chapter 5, this volume). This likely came from clinical presentation. Couples in conflicted or dysfunctional relationships sought help without a clear focus on one or the other's individual functioning. On the one hand, it seems intuitive that the same thing can happen with parents and children. However, the tradition has been to focus on the sequelae of the relational problems (e.g., parent's depression; child's conduct problem) rather than the relational problem per se. We argue that a caregiver–child relational diagnosis would facilitate appropriate recognition, definition, and labelling of these situations, rather than instead attributing the cause of the problem to the child (or parent) and his or her individual disorder.

Most of the research relevant to creating a caregiver–child relational diagnosis has focused on parenting. The vast majority of the time, the criteria described in this chapter will likely be applied to dysfunctional parent–child relationships. However, we have chosen to label the diagnosis as caregiver–child relational problem to acknowledge that although children are most often raised by parents, this is not always the case. Sometimes extended family or close friends take on the raising of a child. In these instances, it is important that the label of the disorder not be overly restrictive with respect to the biological relation between the caregiver and child. It is not our intent, however, in developing these criteria, to include the child's relationship with anyone who is ever in a more minor caregiving role, which could include a teacher, babysitter, or relatives who might be with a child for a relatively short period of time, compared with a heavily involved caregiver who is, or is functioning as, a parent.

A relationship diagnosis is, by its nature, relational and independent of whether the people in the relationship have any individual disorder(s). Although the conceptual shift away from psychopathology in either person in the relationship and toward interventions that focus on the caregiver–child relationship is one that is new, it is noteworthy that the treatments of choice for many child (and adolescent) disorders focus on parenting or the parent–child relationship (e.g., oppositional defiant disorder, attachment disorder, attention deficit disorder, substance abuse). The apportioning of family interventions to nominally address either child or parent psychopathology is apparent from Hahlweg's review of the impact of caregiver–child problems (Chapter 15, this volume). The only applied context in which parenting-focused treatments were not in service of treating a child disorder was when the parent was referred for parenting interventions as a result of allegations of child maltreatment.

Because caregiver–child relational problems are dependent on the quality of fit and interaction between the caregiver and child, the disorder is thus specific to that relationship (Dollberg, Feldmen, Keren, & Guedeney, 2006; Savonlahti et al., 2005; ZERO TO THREE, 1994, 2005). These problems might not spill over into other relationships either the caregiver or the child has. Developmental studies on early interaction and brain functions indicate the following model for possible psychopathological processes: If, for example, a mother's depression affects her interaction with her infant and if her infant starts to become withdrawn and less responsive in their mutual interaction, their relationship has become disturbed. If the situation persists long enough and/or is serious enough, they may have a relationship disorder specific to their mother–infant relationship even after the mother's depression has resolved.

Of course, what one learns in caregiver–child relationships can become more generalized, which can, ultimately, lead to individual problems. If the infant in this example starts to behave in a similar way with others, including the father and other caregivers, the infant's relational processes have been affected. If the infant shows similar behavior in all her or his relationships, the disorder has generalized and the infant is probably also suffering from a depression (Field, 1992; Gerhold, Laucht, Texdorf, Schmidt, & Esser, 2002). At that point, what began as a relational disorder contributed to the development of an individual disorder.

Because the tradition in research on parenting is to treat parenting as a continuum from functional to dysfunctional, and because clinicians have worked around the lack of a caregiver–child relational diagnosis by labeling a disorder in the child, the parent, or both, this chapter begins with a discussion of the rationale for adopting a caregiver–child relational diagnosis. As detailed below, much of the rationale for caregiver–child relational disorders draws largely on research with infants and young children, and early parenthood and parenting, although many issues presented here are also relevant for school-aged children, adolescents, and their parents. This is consistent with a developmental psychopathology perspective, where it is optimal to trace the origins of any ultimately dysfunctional process from the beginning of human life, bearing in mind that many relational issues are transgenerational. We will also present criteria for caregiver–child relational problems that are currently under consideration for inclusion in the International Classification of Diseases (ICD-11; World Health Organization). These criteria were developed in parallel with others described in this volume and have been the focus of initial clinical research field trials.

WHY SHOULD CLASSIFICATION SYSTEMS INCLUDE A CAREGIVER–CHILD RELATIONSHIP DIAGNOSIS?

Given the well-developed array of diagnoses that exist to classify and help organize treatments for problems experienced by both children and adults, including a number of child diagnoses that are often treated with parent-focused interventions (e.g., parent training,

Brestan & Eyberg, 1998), is it really necessary to include caregiver–child relational diagnosis as well in classification systems such as the ICD? In the section below, we review arguments that have been made in recent years to isolate dysfunctional relational processes from child and adult psychopathology.

Filling Clear Gaps in Individual-Focused Classification

Convincing evidence from diverse research fields and universal clinical experiences show how the parent–child relationship and parenting practices, especially in infancy and early childhood, when brain and mind development is so exceptional and essential, affect the child's mental maturation. The key elements for human mental development, according to the current scientific models are (a) genes, (b) primary relationships, and (c) self-directed and self-regulated brain and mind maturation (Drury et al., 2010; Fox, Levitt, & Nelson, 2010; Sameroff, 2004; Sameroff & Fiese, 2000; Schore, 2001a; Swain, Lorberbaum, Kose, & Strathearn, 2007).

The parent–child relationship buffers, modulates, and mediates psychopathological risks arising from the child, parent, family broader environment, or combinations thereof (Gunnar, 1998; Laucht, Esser, & Schmidt, 2001; Tronick & Weinberg, 1997; Zeanah, Boris, & Scheeringa, 1997). The mutual adaptation capacity in parent–child interaction protects the psychological well-being of both partners, but especially that of the developing child (Mäntymaa, 2006; Trevarthen & Aitken, 2001; Tronick et al., 1998). Cumulating evidence has begun to show that distorted relational processes between parent and child can also crucially exacerbate and even create psychopathology-producing risks. One or both partners may become symptomatic to the point of an individual diagnosis, but the vulnerability of the developing brain and mind may cause life-long effects (e.g., stress-hormone reactions, attachment behaviors, emotion regulation; Crittenden, 1995; Gunnar, Brodersen, Krueger, & Rigatuso, 1996a; Gunnar, Brodersen, Nachmias, Buss, & Rigatuso, 1996b; Kaufman & Charney, 2001; Liu & Diorio, 1997; Schore, 2001b; Siegel, 2001).

Thus, there is accumulating evidence of a gap in the current classification systems that focus on individual psychopathology. Although the research on parent–child or caregiver–child relational disorders is just beginning, it does not follow that inclusion of such a disorder must await the completion of that research. If a gap between a body of relevant research data and the categories in any classification system becomes clear, the usefulness of the system will rapidly decrease. If the widely and well-accepted academic understanding of developmental psychopathology enters the classification systems too slowly (e.g., because of the time required for empirical validation) the research and clinical relevance of the system will be confined mainly to administrative purposes.

Apparent Content Validity and Clinical Utility

The need to assess parenting and relationship problems and disorders has become important particularly in child psychiatry. Recently developed, multiaxial classification systems have been the most widely used and best accepted systems in the field of infant, child, and adolescent psychiatry (Egger, 2009). These seem to reflect, in a relevant way, the existing clinical reality and are more meaningful for designing treatments and evaluating outcomes than merely labeling the child's symptom profile. The possibility that a provider might assess both individual problems and relational difficulties separately but simultaneously may be more important the younger the child is. In early childhood, it has even been documented that the possibility of making relational diagnoses (rather than forcing clinicians to only label individuals) improves the accuracy and quality of the diagnostic assessment of infants (Davies et al., 2006; Skovgaard, 2010). This suggests that there may be significant clinical utility in adding caregiver–child relational problems to the ICD, in addition to the mental disorders that are already considered.

Improving Treatment

The ultimate purpose of any diagnostic classification system is to help individuals in need and to offer them appropriate treatments and services. The same is true of relationship disorders. The principal factor for human suffering, and also for satisfaction, seems to be the quality of close relationships.

Clinical experiences from different parts of the world show that parents having relationship difficulties with their children, particularly during early parenthood, first seek help in their normal support systems, and if that is not enough, they seek help increasingly from elsewhere. With a more advanced classification system for relationship disorders it would be possible to better assess who needs what. To a large extent, diagnostic systems such as the ICD drive how clinicians and researchers conceptualize the field in which they work. By providing ways for clinicians to do more than label individuals, it is likely that more accurate evaluations of relational difficulties would be conducted. A common framework for classifying caregiver–child relationship disorder would influence research and data collection systems, and help providers choose interventions. This will likely influence treatment not only for parents and children with no disorders, other than caregiver–child relational disorder, but also for children or parents whose assessments indicate they do not have relational disorders but may have individual disorders.

Facilitating Prevention

Furthermore, within developmental psychopathology, one can also argue that treating problematic parenting and general parent–child relationship problems can serve a preventive purpose and might mitigate risk for children developing a variety of mental health problems (see Fonagy, 1998; Sanders, Markie-Dadds, & Turner, 2003; Schechter et al., 2010). A shift of focus from waiting for behavior problems and other disorders to become entrenched and then intervening to, instead, identifying problematic parent–child relationships and intervening early is a cost-effective solution and leads to improved public health (see Sanders et al., 2003). An exclusive reliance on treating individual disorders increases costs for individuals and societies (Heckman, 2009; Nagle, 2009).

Reducing Stigma

Clear, objective, and psychometrically sound diagnostic criteria can help reduce stigma and blaming and increase patients' openness to intervention. In the same way that, historically, it was more stigmatizing to call a person "insane" or a "mental patient" than "chronically depressed," it is more accusatory to talk about poor parenting or being a bad parent than to describe a parent–child dyad as having a caregiver–child relational problem. The label is helpful, but it is also critical to have operationalized, clear diagnostic criteria. This helps parents and providers both understand whether the relationship is impaired significantly enough for it to be considered clinically problematic and ensure neither thinks the other is merely applying personal opinions to the problems at hand. If objective criteria can be used, identifying problems and addressing them can seem less personal and blaming.

Improving Infrastructure to Identify and Support Parenting Globally

Existing research shows that caregiver–child relational disorders can be treated in many different ways and in diverse contexts, mainly by using human resources (Sameroff, 2004; Schechter et al., 2006). Unlike some interventions, though, these human resources may not necessarily need to be very highly trained. In many poor and developing countries, paraprofessional human resources might be more easily and readily available for intervening in human suffering than other treatment resources. Clinical experience and some studies document that treating early parent–infant relationship disorders in poor and developing countries—which is where the vast majority of young children live—with simple but focused relationship interventions, seems to be possible, practical, and effective (Cooper et al., 2009; Vanderwert, Marshall, Nelson, Zeanah, & Fox, 2010).

In addition, based on some anthropological and epidemiological studies, it seems that at least some basic human relational processes, such as communality, in some developing countries could support the psychological well-being of individuals better than in modern, high-income countries (Kagitcibasi, 2005; Keller et al., 2004). Also, certain features of early parenting practices common to certain cultures in low-income countries might promote healthy development better than some relational practices in, for example, Western culture. The need for a more specific understanding and classification of relational processes, their disorders, and their healthy or unhealthy effects is increasingly apparent, but difficult to achieve. Inclusion of caregiver–child relational diagnoses in the ICD would facilitate research to identify and support these processes.

Facilitating Research and Infrastructure Development

In recent decades, the role of diagnostic classification systems in promoting or impeding advancements with respect to aspects of mental health both in research and clinical fields has become quite clear. International classification systems are powerful tools also in affecting decision making at different levels (e.g., development of treatments and services, funding of research, provision of services through the sanctioned public health infrastructure). It is imperative that these classification systems are comprehensive and reflect the existing research. In this case, the importance of a diagnosis focusing on parent–child or caregiver–child relational problems is strongly supported by the literature, as detailed above. If classification systems are consistent with the state of the science, they can facilitate further development and translation to application. If systems do not include all relevant aspects of psychopathology, their effects may be detrimental.

DEFINING CAREGIVER–CHILD RELATIONAL PROBLEMS

Earlier Definitions

In ICD-10 (World Health Organization, 1992), parent–child problems (excluding maltreatment, which is discussed elsewhere in this volume [Chapter 9]) are addressed in the Z codes. The Z codes include, "factors influencing health status and contact with health services" and are recorded when the individual seeking services has a notable issue for which services may be necessary, but this issue is not a disease, injury, or notable external cause. Within the Z codes, several codes apply to some aspect of problematic parenting or parent–child relationships. Most are covered in Z62, which includes other problems related to upbringing. This section includes some aspects of parenting that could overlap with neglect in many classification systems, and includes the following specific categories and accompanying definitions:

- Z62.0, Inadequate parental supervision and control (i.e., "lack of parental knowledge of what the child is doing or where the child is; poor control; lack of concern or lack of attempted intervention when the child is in risky situations")
- Z62.1, Parental overprotection; pattern of upbringing resulting in infantilization and prevention of independent behavior
- Z62.3, Hostility toward and scapegoating of child (i.e., "negative parental behavior specifically focused on the child as an individual, persistent over time, and pervasive over several child behaviors [e.g., automatically blaming the child for any problems in the household or attributing negative characteristics to the child])
- Z62.4, Emotional neglect of child (i.e., "parent talking to the child in a dismissive or insensitive way; lack of interest in the child, of sympathy for the child's difficulties, and of

praise and encouragement; irritated reaction to anxious behavior and absence of sufficient physical comforting and emotional warmth")

- Z62.5, Other problems related to neglect in upbringing (i.e., "lack of learning and play experience")
- Z62.6, Inappropriate parental pressure and other abnormal qualities of upbringing (i.e., parents forcing the child to be different from the local norm, either sex-inappropriate [e.g., dressing a boy in girl's clothes], age-inappropriate [e.g., forcing a child to take on responsibilities above her or his own age], or otherwise inappropriate [e.g., pressing the child to engage in unwanted or too difficult activities]).

In addition to these categories found in Problems with Upbringing, Z63.1 refers to "problems in relationship with parents and in-laws" within "other problems related to primary support group, including family circumstances." In this way, problems with parenting (specifically excluding maltreatment) are included in Z62 and other problems with the parent–child relationship (excluding maltreatment and problems with upbringing) are considered separately, but both are included. That said, many of these categories are not clearly defined, have not been the product of or subject to research, and are generally not consistently assessed or reliably applied. To help address these concerns, other approaches to conceptualizing parent–child problems been developed.

From the developmental psychopathology perspective, it can be argued that disordered caregiver–child relationships are more important and potentially dangerous to younger children. Therefore it is understandable that researchers and professionals in infant mental health have been pioneers in developing a classification of caregiver–child relational processes and problems. In 1994, the first edition of the Diagnostic Classification of Mental Health and Developmental Disorders of Infancy and Early Childhood (DC 0–3, ZERO TO THREE, 1994) was published after seven years of work by a multidisciplinary expert group. In this multiaxial system, Axis II is the very first international attempt to present a caregiver–child relationship disorder classification with six different categories, one of them having three subcategories:

- 901 Overinvolved
- 902 Underinvolved
- 903 Anxious/Tense
- 904 Angry/Hostile
- 905 Mixed
- 906 Abusive
  - 906a Verbally Abusive
  - 906b Physically Abusive
  - 906c Sexually Abusive

In the DC 0–3 manual, descriptions for all these diagnostic categories are presented according to the three levels mentioned above. First, behavioral quality includes concepts such as degree of sensitivity or insensitivity in responding, contingent or noncontingent responsivity, genuineness of involvement or concern, regulation, predictability and the quality of structuring, and mediating of the environment. These features of parent–infant interaction are specifically described in each category. Second, affective tone descriptions refer to the emotional tone that characterizes each category. Third, psychological involvement focuses on parental attitudes and perceptions of the child. This conceptualization of caregiver–child disorders mapped well onto the literature regarding the important facets of parenting and parent–child relationships. However, it could be argued that it was too complex to include in a classification system that is more general, or to be applied in all but specialized aspects of the health care system.

Ten years later, this system was revised (DC 0–3R, ZERO TO THREE, 2005). These categories were replaced by a different approach evaluating the functional level of the parent–child relationship with the Parent–Infant Relationship Global Assessment of Functioning Scale

(PIR-GAS). With this, the putative disorders were turned into the Relationship Problems Checklist (RPCL). This shift occurred to acknowledge the lack of empirical support for specific caregiver–child relationship disorders based on the earlier framework and to make the system more consistent with the upcoming revision of the *Diagnostic and Statistical Manual* (*DSM-5*; Egger & Emde, 2011). On the PIR-GAS, which has a dimensional scale from 0 to100, the quality of the infant–parent relationship ranges from well adapted to severely impaired, and scores are classified as:

- 81–100 Adapted Relationship
- 41–80 Features of a Disordered Relationship
- 0–40 Disordered Relationship

Again, in the PIR-GAS there are 10 dimensionally organized descriptions of parent–child interaction and the quality of the functioning of both partners and the dyad. So far it seems that this approach, too, is clinically useful, although it may still be overly complex for inclusion in a comprehensive diagnostic system, such as the ICD. Primary healthcare providers may not be able to complete the observational assessment and characterize parent–child relationships on 10 dimensions, in addition to addressing other physical and developmental considerations, within typical time constraints.

Within the past 10 years, Heyman and Slep (e.g., Heyman & Slep, 2006, 2009; Slep & Heyman, 2006) had success in developing operationalized definitions for maltreatment (the extreme end of disordered parenting) that were reliably implemented in field trials and a dissemination trial. More recently, the approach taken in these successful, specific, parenting-relevant, relational disorders was extended to include nonabusive caregiver–child relational disorder. In the following section, we present this definition and its rationale. For a review of the maltreatment definitions, see Chapter 9, this volume.

Proposed Definitions

The criteria set for caregiver–child relational problem were based on the approach used with the other relational criteria described elsewhere in this volume (Chapter 8 and Chapter 9). Conceptually, the goal of the criteria set was to operationalize thresholds above which to consider caregiver–child problems to be clinically significant while specifically excluding parenting issues that would not also meet criteria for child abuse or neglect. Although we considered distinguishing between problems of parenting, which might be important etiological influences on some child mental disorders, and problems with the caregiver–child relationship, which likely has complex and reciprocal relationships with the mental health of both parent or other caregiver and child, we ultimately decided that an omnibus caregiver–child relationship problem category would be most relevant and minimize the burden placed on health care providers and administrative systems, while still capturing the key constructs in a manner consistent with the existing literature. Caregiver–child relational problem parallels partner relational problem, where the impact and symptoms can be borne by either party in the relationship—the parent, the child, or both. It is noteworthy that the specific "B" symptoms that are necessary for this diagnosis parallel the dimensions included in the DC 0–3 system (ZERO TO THREE, 1994), including behavioral, affective, and cognitive (referred to as psychological involvement) facets of relationship distress.

Caregiver–child relational problem addresses strained and distressing or unhappy relationships, where the distress is the thing that causes the impacts or symptoms. It captures dysfunctional, but nonabusive parenting, as well, through parenting's impact on child behavior and caregiver affect and cognition. It may also be applicable to clear cases of parental alienation syndrome (e.g., Bernet, 2008), where a child is manipulated to reject one parent over the other. The rejected parent's distress and both the parent's and child's affect, cognitions, and behavior can be affected in such instances. All types of parent–child issues that rise to the level of impact required for diagnosis are likely to have significant implications for the child's, and possibly caregiver's, mental health. The specific criterion sets are presented in Table 16.1 in Chapter 16 of this volume.

The caregiver–child criteria sets were the newest sets developed in this effort to map out relational disorders and are the only disorders proposed in this effort that have not been extensively empirically tested. That said, steps were taken to promote reliability and validity, and initial field trials are currently under way. First, the same general strategy was used to develop these criteria as the maltreatment criteria—a) existing operationalizations were reviewed to identify useful elements and conceptualizations, b) the initial criteria were developed, and c) the initial criteria were reviewed by experts, and then modified. Second, the conceptual frame for the diagnosis and criteria set was based on that for partner relational problems, all of which have been subject to fairly extensive empirical evaluation. Third, possible elements of validated criteria sets were included verbatim in the caregiver–child diagnostic criteria (e.g., impact). Thus, although this criteria set is relatively new, there is reason to believe that they will perform comparably to the other diagnostic criteria proposed when they are subject to evaluation.

Caregiver–child relational disorder, with relationship dissatisfaction as its defining element, is applicable to relationships with both younger children (as detailed earlier in this chapter) as well as to relationships with adolescents, where power is less imbalanced, and conflict is typical. Although not considered in the literature, it seems likely that Caregiver–child relational disorder might have the same complex and reciprocal relationship with depression among postpubescent teens and adult caregivers that partner relational disorder has, where both could cause the other, and treating the relational problem might be sufficient to cause the remission of the depression (see Chapter 7, this volume, for more discussion). It is also likely that caregiver–child relational disorder could be secondary to some child disorders—perhaps especially substance use and conduct problems, which can include lying to and fighting with parents as central features of the disorders. Because empirically based treatments for these disorders (e.g., Henggeler & Schaeffer, 2010; Waldron, Turner, & Ozechowski, 2006) often include family components, it could be that the presence of comorbid parent–child relational problems would indicate or counterindicate particular treatment options that may require more or less of the parent, and be based on different assumptions about the parent's current level of investment in the child and relationship.

It is important that all the diagnoses related to caregiving–child physical abuse, child emotional abuse, child sexual abuse, child neglect, and caregiver–child relational problem are used in conjunction with one another. A child could be very unhappy in his relationship with his parent and clearly meet criteria for a parent–child relational problem, but this is because of pervasive maltreatment. In scenarios such as these, the more restrictive maltreatment diagnosis should be applied rather than labeled a parent–child relational problem. Not doing so would shift the locus of the problem from the parent and his or her actions to the relationship between the parent and child. This shift, if it resulted in interventions aimed at the relationship generally, could exacerbate negative outcomes for the child and could be interpreted as validating the parent's actions. Precision in assessing and labeling maltreatment when it exists, and caregiver–child relational problems being secondary to that maltreatment when it exists, will be critical in optimal treatment matching.

Threshold Considerations

Clearly, there are relational difficulties and relationship-specific problems at times in nearly all relationships. More mundane conflicts and unhappiness between children and caregivers are commonplace. To meet criteria for caregiver–child relational problem, symptoms must be more pervasive than typical unhappiness. When the criteria are met, the overall functioning of the child and caregiver in their interactions is significantly impaired, and the level of distress during their interaction is prominent. The mutual adaptation capacity and flexibility of the dyad has been exceeded due to relational conflicts that do not find resolutions (Mäntymaa, 2006). In a disordered parent–child relationship, the child's healthy mental development is endangered.

In the criteria set forth for caregiver–child relational problem, we have been fairly inclusive. The threshold is that one or both parties are experiencing or displaying distress about or as a result of the relationship. One could be appropriately concerned that these criteria would result in high false negative rates, capturing a large number of families in the normative range. This is why the diagnosis also requires significant impact, which is designed to ensure that only clinically significant levels of caregiver–child relational problems are captured.

Assessment

Some of the first work leading to the conceptualization of a parent or caregiver–child relationship disorder diagnosis was observational research on infant–parent interactions. It has become clear that disordered relationships are observable at young ages and are experienced by both partners of the relationship (e.g., Schechter et al., 2010; ZERO TO THREE, 1994, 2005). Observational assessment techniques and various specific assessment methods for dyadic interaction are now available and can be important in such an assessment process. These techniques can be used to assess whether or not a parent–infant/young child relationship disorder is present (Gleason, 2009; Stern-Bruschweiler & Stern, 1989; ZERO TO THREE, 1994, 2005), and even more assessment instruments are available for use with parents and older children (e.g., Arnold, O'Leary, Wolff, & Acker, 1993). These assessments focus on: (a) behavioral quality of the interaction, (b) affective tone of the interaction, and (c) psychological involvement in the interaction. Interactions can be assessed several times and/or by several persons. Even people with diverse training and cultural backgrounds are less prone to presentation biases and allow assessment of problems with young children and infants who could not complete self-report measures or interviews. Assessment of caregiver–child relational disorder is discussed in more detail elsewhere in this volume (Chapter 16).

In practice, assessment of most mother–infant dyads for possible relational difficulties might be easier to achieve than one might think. Most countries and societies have at least some services for pregnant mothers and for young children. The perinatal period is unique because of population-wide contacts with health care (or other support) systems through much of the globe. This offers exceptional opportunities for mental health prevention. It has been shown that it is possible to include assessments of, and support for, early parent–infant relationships in these mother-and-baby services in developed and developing countries (Boris et al., 2008; Chisholm et al., 2007; Cooper et al., 2009; Puura et al., 2005; Schechter et al., 2006).

Cultural Context

Relational processes and relationships, including parenting, are influenced by cultural contexts. Anthropological studies argue that early parenting practices and certain features of early parent–child interaction are the aspects of human life most strongly regulated in today's world by cultural contexts (Greenfield, Keller, Fuligni, & Maynard, 2003; Quinn, 2005). Any culture is powerfully carried on from one generation to the next during early parenting and parent–child relationships because the brain development of a new individual ensures that meanings, values, attitudes, and behavioral models preferred in a given culture will become the structural functioning of the developing brain (LeDoux, 2002; Trevarthen & Aitken, 2001).

Of course, the categories of a diagnostic classification system need to be universal and relevant in different cultural contexts, and this applies to relationship disorders, too. However, the identification and assessment of relational processes and disorders may need to be more culturally sensitive than the assessments of individuals. Fortunately, new cross-cultural studies focusing on similarities rather than differences in early parenting have pointed out universal features of early parent–child relationships (Cote & Bornstein, 2009). These findings serve as a basis for developing and using universal categories in addressing caregiver–child relationship disorders. Also, the present understanding of relationship disorders that endanger the child's healthy development can, when these disorders are properly identified and treated, promote children's mental health on the individual level and children's human rights on the cultural level.

To ensure the diagnostic criteria developed are culturally, as well as developmentally sensitive, we have included the second criterion focused on impact. Significant impact on the child and caregiver is a critical component in the definitions and ensures the diagnosis is limited to relationships that are experienced as significantly problematic by the partners in it. Thus, many aspects of parenting might be seen as problematic and out of the bounds of acceptable in one culture and accepted in another. However, regardless of the culture, if the caregiver–child relationship is distressed, and there is a significant negative impact of that distress as defined in the criteria, it is clear that the problem is important enough to that caregiver or child in that context to be labeled and addressed.

Implications of Criteria for Diagnosis

Despite the overwhelming evidence that parenting and parent–child relationships have tremendous influence on both children's and adults' well-being, the field has only recently tried to establish diagnostic criteria that would allow clinically important caregiver–child relation dysfunction to be assessed, identified, and labeled as such. Although this clearly has not slowed research on the importance of parenting, or on leveraging improvements in parenting and parent–child relationships in clinical intervention, it likely has had negative implications. Researchers research what exists. When there is no nomenclature and no clear definition, the construct does not become a focus. Thus, although we know that dysfunctional parenting is a key etiological element in the development of conduct disorder (e.g., Patterson, 1982; antisocial boys), we know little about how much dysfunctional parenting is sufficient for a detrimental impact to occur. Furthermore, the lack of a distinct threshold can keep clinicians from recognizing the problem and those with the problem from seeking treatment. Defining clinically significant caregiver–child relational problems is a key first step in advancing research, treatment, and public health agendas to foster healthy parent–child relationships.

ACKNOWLEDGMENT

Preparation of this chapter was supported by grant U49CE00124602 from the Centers for Disease Control and Prevention.

REFERENCES

Arnold, D. S., O'Leary, S. G., Wolff, L. S., & Acker, M. M. (1993). The Parenting Scale: A measure of dysfunctional parenting in discipline situations. *Psychological Assessment, 5*, 137–144.

Baumrind, D. (1967). Child care practices anteceding three patterns of preschool behavior. *Genetic Psychology Monographs, 75*(1), 43–88.

Bernet, W. (2008). Parental alienation disorder and *DSM-V. The American Journal of Family Therapy, 36*, 349–366.

Boris, N. W., Brown, L. A., Thurman, T. R., Rice, J. A., Snider, L. M., Ntaginira, J., & Nyirazinyoyne, L. (2008). Depressive symptoms among youth heads-of-household in Rwanda: Correlates and implications for intervention. *Archives of Pediatric and Adolescent Medicine, 162*, 836–843.

Brestan, E. V., & Eyberg, S. M. (1998). Effective psychosocial treatments of conduct-disordered children and adolescents: 29 years, 82 studies, and 5,272 kids. *Journal of Clinical Child Psychology, 27*, 180–189.

Chisholm, D., Flisher, A., Lund, C., Patel, V., Saxena, S., Thornicroft, G., & Tomlinson, M. (2007). Scale up services for mental disorders: A call for action. *Lancet, 370*, 1241–1252.

Cooper, P. J., Tomlinson, M., Swartz, L., Landman, M., Molteno, C., Stein, A., . . . , & Murray L. (2009). Improving quality of mother–infant relationship and infant attachment in socioeconomically deprived community in South Africa: Randomised controlled study. *British Medical Journal, 14*, 338:b974.
Cote, L., & Bornstein, M. H. (2009). Child and mother play in three U.S. cultural groups: Comparisons and associations. *Journal of Family Psychology, 23*, 355–363.
Crittenden, P. M. (1995). Attachment and risk for psychopathology: The early years. *Journal of Developmental and Behavioral Pediatrics, 16*, S12–S16.
Davies, W. H., Satter, E., Berlin, K. S., Sato, A. F., Silverman, A. H., Fischer, E. A.,. . . , & Rudolph, C. D. (2006). Reconceptualizing feeding and feeding disorders in interpersonal context: The case for a relational disorder. *Journal of Family Psychology, 20*(3), 409–417.
Dollberg, D., Feldman, R., Keren, M., & Guedeney, A. (2006). Sustained withdrawal behaviour in clinic referred and nonreferred infants. *Infant Mental Health Journal, 27*, 292–309.
Dowling, C. A., Slep, A. M. S., & O'Leary, S. G. (2010). Understanding preemptive parenting: Relations with toddlers' misbehavior, overreactive and lax discipline, and praise. *Journal of Clinical Child and Adolescent Psychology, 38*, 850–857.
Drury, S. S., Theall, K. P., Smyke, A. T., Keats, B. J., Egger, H. L., Nelson, C. A.,. . . , Zeanah, C. H. (2010). Modification of depression by COMT val158met polymorphism in children exposed to early severe psychosocial deprivation. *Child Abuse and Neglect, 34*(6), 387–395.
Egger, H. (2009). Psychiatric assessment of young children. *Child and Adolescent Psychiatry Clinic of North America, 18*(3), 559–580.
Egger, H., & Emde, R. (2011). Developmentally-sensitive diagnostic criteria for mental health disorders in early childhood: *DSM-IV*, RDC-PA and the revised DC: 0–3. *American Psychologist, 66*(2), 95–106.
Field, T. M. (1992). Infants of depressed mothers. *Development and Psychopathology, 4*, 49–66.
Fonagy, P. (1998). Prevention, the appropriate target of infant psychotherapy. *Infant Mental Health Journal, 19*, 124–150.
Fox, S. E., Levitt, P., & Nelson, C. A. (2010). How early experiences influence the development of brain architecture. *Child Development, 81*, 28–40.
Gerhold, M., Laucht, M., Texdorf, C., Schmidt, M. H., & Esser, G. (2002). Early mother–infant interaction as a precursor to childhood social withdrawal. *Child Psychiatry and Human Development, 32*, 277–293.
Gleason, M. M. (2009). Relationship assessment in clinical practice. *Child and Adolescent Psychiatric Clinics of North America, 19*, 581–591.
Greenfield, P. M., Keller, H., Fuligni, A., & Maynard, A. (2003). Cultural pathways through universal development. *Annual Review of Psychology, 54*, 461–490.
Gunnar, M. R. (1998). Quality of early care and buffering of neuroendocrine stress reactions: Potential effects on the developing human brain. *Preventive Medicine, 27*, 208–211.
Gunnar, M., Brodersen, L., Krueger, K., & Rigatuso, J. (1996a). Dampening of adrenocortical reactivity during early infancy: Normative changes and individual differences. *Child Development, 67*, 877–889.
Gunnar, M. R., Brodersen, L., Nachmias, M., Buss, K., & Rigatuso, J. (1996b). Stress reactivity and attachment security. *Developmental Psychobiology, 29*, 191–204.
Heckman, J. J. (2009). Skill formation and the economics of investing in disadvantaged children. *Science, 312*, 1900–1902.
Henggeler, S. W., & Schaeffer, C. M. (2010). Treating serious emotional and behavioural problems using multisystemic therapy. *Australian and New Zealand Journal of Family Therapy, 31*, 149–164.
Heyman, R. E., & Slep, A. M. S. (2006). Creating and field-testing diagnostic criteria for partner and child maltreatment. *Journal of Family Psychology, 20*, 397–408.
Heyman, R. E., & Slep, A. M. S. (2009). Reliablity of family maltreatment diagnostic criteria: 41 site dissemination field trial. *Journal of Family Psychology, 23*(6), 905–910.
Kagitcibasi, C. (2005). Autonomy and relatedness in cultural context: Implications for self and family. *Journal of Cross-Cultural Psychology, 36*, 403–422.
Kaufman, J., & Charney, D. (2001). Effects of early stress on brain structure and function: Implications for understanding the relationship between child maltreatment and depression. *Development and Psychopathology, 13*, 451–471.
Keller, H., Yovsi, R., Borke, J., Kärtner, J., Jensen, H., & Papaligoura, Z. (2004). Developmental consequences of early parenting experiences: Self-recognition and self-regulation in three cultural communities. *Child Development, 75*, 1745–1760.
Laucht, M., Esser, G., & Schmidt, M. H. (2001). Differential development of infants at risk for psychopathology: The moderating role of early maternal responsivity. *Developmental Medicine and Child Neurology, 43*, 292–300.
LeDoux, J. E. (2002). *Synaptic self—How our brains become who we are*. New York, NY: Viking Press.
Liu, D., & Diorio, J. (1997). Maternal care, hippocampal glucocorticoid receptors, and hypothalamic–pituitary–adrenal responses to stress. *Science, 277*, 1659–1662.
Maccoby, E. E., & Martin, J. A. (1983). socialization in the context of the family: Parent–child interaction. In E. M. Hetherington (Ed.), *Handbook of child psychology, socialization, personality, and social development* (Vol. 4, pp. 1–101). New York, NY: Wiley.

Mäntymaa, M. (2006). Early mother–infant interaction: Determinants and predictivity. Academic dissertation. Acta Universitatis Tamperensis 1144. Tampere: Tampereen yliopistopaino Oy Juvenes Print. Electronic version: Acta Electronica Universitatis Tamperensis 519. Retrieved from http://acta.uta.fi

Nagle, G. A. (2009). *The economics of infant mental health*. In C. H. Zeanah (Ed.), *Handbook of infant mental health* (3rd ed., pp. 580–590). New York, NY: Guilford Press.

Patterson, G. R. (1982). *Coercive family process*. Eugene, OR: Castalia.

Puura, K., Davis, H., Cox, A., Tsiantis, J., Tamminen, T., Ispanovic-Radojkovic, V.,…, Vizacou, S. (2005). The European early promotion project: Description of the service and evaluation study. *International Journal of Mental Health Promotion, 7*(1), 17–31.

Quinn, N. (2005). *Finding culture in talk: A collection of methods*. New York, NY: Palgrave MacMillan.

Sameroff, A. (2004). Ports of entry and mother–infant interventions. In A. Sameroff, S. C. McDonough, & K. L. Rosenblum (Eds.), *Treating parent–infant relationship problems*. New York, NY: Guilford Press.

Sameroff, A. J., & Fiese, B. H. (2000). Models of development and developmental risk. In C. H. Zeanah (Ed.), *Handbook of infant mental health* (2nd ed., pp. 3–19). New York, NY: Guilford Press.

Sanders, M. R., Markie-Dadds, C., & Turner, K. M. T. (2003). Theoretical, scientific and clinical foundations of the Triple P-Positive parenting program: A population approach to the promotion of parenting competence. *Parenting Research and Practice Monograph, 1*, 1–24.

Savonlahti, E., Pajulo, M., Ahlqvist, S., Helenius, H., Korvenranta, H., Tamminen, T., & Piha, J. (2005). Interactive skills of infants with their high-risk mothers. *Nordic Journal of Psychiatry, 59*, 139–147.

Schechter, D. S., Myers, M. M., Brunelli, S. A., Coates, S. W., Zeanah, C. H., Davies, M.,…, Liebowitz, M. R. (2006). Traumatized mothers can change their minds about their toddlers: Understanding how a novel use of videofeedback supports positive change of maternal attributions. *Infant Mental Health Journal, 27*(5), 429–447.

Schechter, D. S., Willheim, E., Hinojosa, C., Scholfield-Kleinman, K., Turner, J. B., McCaw, J.,…, Myers, M. M. (2010). Subjective and objective measures of parent–child relationship dysfunction, child separation distress, and joint attention. *Psychiatry, 73*(2), 130–144.

Schore, A. N. (2001a). Effects of a secure attachment relationship on right brain development, affect regulation, and infant mental health. *Infant Mental Health Journal, 22*, 7–66.

Schore, A. N. (2001b). The effects of early relational trauma on right brain development, affect regulation, and infant mental health. *Infant Mental Health Journal, 22*, 201–269.

Siegel, D. J. (2001). Toward an interpersonal neurobiology of the developing mind: Attachment relationships, "mindsight", and neural integration. *Infant Mental Health Journal, 22*, 67–94.

Skovgaard, A. M. (2010). *Mental health problems and psychopathology in infancy and early childhood – A epidemiological study*. Academic dissertation. Faculty of Health Sciences, Copenhagen University.

Slep, A. M. S., & Heyman, R. E. (2006). Creating and field testing child maltreatment definitions: Improving the reliability of substantiation determinations. *Child Maltreatment, 11*, 397–408.

Sroufe, I. A., Carlson, E. A., Levy, A. K., & Egeland, B (1999). Implications of attachment theory for developmental psychopathology. *Development and Psychopathology, 11*, 1–13.

Stern-Bruschweiler, N., & Stern, D. N. (1989). A model for conceptualizing the role of the mother's representational world in various mother–infant therapies. *Infant Mental Health Journal, 10*, 142–156.

Swain, J. E., Lorberbaum, J. P., Kose, S., & Strathearn, L. (2007). Brain basis of early parent–infant interactions: Psychology, physiology, and in vivo functional neuroimaging studies. *Journal of Child Psychology and Psychiatry, 48*, 262–287.

Trevarthen, C., & Aitken, K. J. (2001). Infant intersubjectivity: Research, theory and clinical application. *Journal of Child Psychology and Psychiatry, 42*, 3–48.

Tronick, E. Z., Bruschweiler-Stern, N., Harrison, A. M., Lyons-Ruth, K., Morgan, A. C., Nahum, J. P.,…, Stern, D. N. (1998). Dyadically expanded states of consciousness and the process of therapeutic change. *Infant Mental Health Journal, 19*, 290–299.

Tronick, E. Z., & Weinberg, M. K. (1997). Depressed mothers and infants: Failure to form dyadic states of consciousness. In L. Murray & P. Cooper (Eds.), *Postpartum depression and child development* (pp. 54–81). New York, NY: Guilford Press.

Vanderwert, R. E., Marshall, P. J., Nelson, C. A., Zeanah C. H., & Fox, N. A. (2010). Timing of intervention affects brain electrical activity in children exposed to severe psychosocial neglect. *PLoS One, 5*(7), 114–115.

Waldron, H. B., Turner, C. W., & Ozechowski, T. J. (2006). Profiles of change in behavioral and family interventions for adolescent substance abuse and dependence. In H. A. Liddle & C. L. Rowe (Eds.), *Adolescent substance abuse: Research and clinical advances* (pp. 357–374). New York, NY: Cambridge University Press.

World Health Organization. (1992). *ICD-10: International statistical classification of diseases and related health problems*. Geneva, Switzerland : Author.

Zeanah, C. H., Boris, N. W., & Scheeringa, M. S. (1997). Psychopathology in infancy. *Journal of Child Psychology and Psychiatry and Allied Disciplines, 38*(1), 81–99.

ZERO TO THREE. (1994). *Diagnostic classification of mental health and developmental disorders in infancy and early childhood*. Washington, DC: Author.

ZERO TO THREE. (2005). *Diagnostic classification of mental health and developmental disorders in infancy and early childhood* (rev. ed.). Washington, DC: Author.

14

Applicability, Generalizability, and Considerations in China

Wenhong Cheng

Chinese are experiencing transitions from a traditional culture to a modern, pluralistic culture due to the quick development of the economy and increases in global communications over the past 30 years. This changing process produces a number of challenges for families. Traditional parents' education style is challenged by the societal change and the child's need for development within the new society. These conflicts may promote societal and individual development, but also may lead to problematic, conflicted parent–child interaction, and the formation of pathological family structures that could disrupt children's development. A recent Chinese school survey of 6- to 16-year-olds found that 7% of children scored in the clinical range on emotional symptoms such as anxiety or depression (Zhang, Yang, Huang, Liu, & Sun, 2010). Parents' mental health or other problems may impact the children's environment and the parent–child interactions, which may contribute to children's mental health problems. This creates several challenges for child health care professionals under the current context, especially since there are huge gaps between the need for services from Chinese families and resources available in the child mental health field.

BACKGROUND OF PARENTING CHANGES IN CHINA

China has a long cultural history that consciously or unconsciously affects Chinese society, family, and parenting style. The main theme of a traditional parent–child relationship is that parents teach children to be obedient and respect the values of parents, family, and society. This differs from Western countries where more focus is placed on teaching children to be independent people whose inherent value should be respected (Xi & Zhen, 2008). Since ancient times, Chinese parents have placed a strong emphasis on the education of their children according to the society's and family's needs, but less emphasis was placed on setting goals related to children's individual needs, strengths, and difficulties. Parents were the center in the family and their views, wishes, and ideas were considered something their children should similarly acquire. They also believed that children should obey parents to be a "good child."

Psychology was considered not as science but as mentalism and was forbidden from the 1960s to 1979. During that time, individual choice of career was forbidden; to be a laborer in the country was the highest social value for an adult and any academic education was considered as nonsense or even harmful. Many young people abandoned their studies and left urban regions for rural areas following the government's call for work in the rural areas. In the 1980s, many of them returned to the cities but were unable to pass the examination for university or college and thus remained in manual labor jobs and low social and economic conditions. Consequently, that generation did not get sufficient or high-quality academic instruction in school, which led them to feel quite regretful for what they had missed later when they became parents. They thus had a higher expectation of their only child (according to governmental one-child policy) to fulfill their missed and interrupted dreams, when the society's value of school-based education shifted. The high expectations placed on children's school achievement from parents limited children's free time and left them feeling quite exhausted without time to address their own needs for psychological development.

In addition, children and parents simultaneously had to adapt to the shift from a planned economy to a rapidly growing market economy with a more open foreign policy. This brought many changes for families. The focus of social values changed from moral value to more of a focus on economic value as demonstrated by material attainments and wealth rather than being a "good person." Focus also shifted to valuing working more and at a higher intensity level than before. Living and working location became more transient; many people now immigrate from villages and small cities to big cities for work, education, and life. This increased mobility makes life more unstable compared to the past when there was less change in location. During the 1950s to 1990s, it was rare for people to move to cities or even communities for living and work, so that the family's environment remained stable. Today, changing communities and immigration to different cities, counties, or nations are becoming a more and more frequent phenomenon, which creates many different kinds of living environments and places a burden on children to adjust to new environments.

CHANGE OF PARENTING STYLES AND ENVIRONMENT

Because of the reforming and opening foreign policy, and the national one-child policy from 1980s, there have been more challenges on parent–child relationship development. After the cultural revolution, a child's educational achievement was considered paramount to guarantee good work with high social status and income in the future. The child's school achievement was becoming the center of attention and the major task for most Chinese families. Thus, families put large amounts of time and money into their child's study. Today, many parents give up their own time after work to supervise their child's homework for many hours. This comes at a cost to other types of leisure activities with their child, to their child's interests, to their own interests and life goals, and to their child's development in other ways (e.g., peer relationships).

In some quickly economically developing, but low-education-level, counties many children are sent to live in a teacher's home or boarding schools because parents believe the teachers or schools can teach the children better behavioral discipline to do well in their studies and become an independent and successful person in the future. These parents, with little formal education themselves, had low confidence in their own ability and knowledge to provide good education and parenting to children. Here the Chinese parents hope their children could be independent and be able to achieve a career successfully in the society without the parents' help, but they worry about the increasing competition in the society for their children and fear that their children will end up in situations similar to themselves.

"Children left behind in the rural areas" (Lin et al., 2010) and "rural migrant children in cities" (Zhou, Gao, Sun, & Luo, 2011) are new phenomena and prevalent in rural areas. At the same time, more citizens migrate from small cities to large urban centers for work. The increased pressure of work has led to parents having less time in the home, which makes parenting a child, without the help of grandparents, very difficult for many families. In the rural areas, many children only see their parents for less than a month per year. In the cities, many young white-collar parents, who earn a high income but have heavy work schedules, leave their children with grandparents or a babysitter during the week. They only see their children on the weekend, but are often too tired to spend time with them and satisfy their need for family activities. For these reasons, many children's main caregivers are grandparents in both urban and rural areas, especially in the early phase of childhood. Parents usually begin to take a more active role in parenting when the child starts school because parents believe it is important for their child. Research data show that about 70% children receive intergenerational care in Beijing and 50% in the whole country. This phenomenon has led some children to be at high risk for problems with care (e.g., neglect/underprotection or undercontrol due to spoiling and poor parent–child relationships), and the problems become especially prominent when the child becomes a teenager.

Marriage has also been impacted by the societal changes. Divorce rates have increased since the 1980s. The China Home Career statistics report in 2009 found that 2.468 million couples had divorced, an increase of 8.8% over the previous year. Most couples who divorce tend to be young (born after the 1970s). Some divorced couples who were born before the 1970s still live together after the divorce due to stigma against divorce, motivation to keep it a secret, and for economic reasons. Many distressed couples also choose to remain in the marriage to provide their child with a relatively more integrated home environment or due to fear of being viewed negatively and rejected by relatives, colleagues, or other people who know them. Although stigma against marital dissolution has lessened in the past 10 years in economically developed areas, traditionally divorce is condemned by Chinese society and is considered a personality deficit or symptom of an immoral and unhealthy person. When there is significant marital discord but impediments to divorce, it is associated with the following: (a) infidelity becomes a problem for a family if divorce is not "allowed"; (b) conflicts including quarrels and violence between couples increases; (c) the child is exposed to the parental conflict and violence and some of the negative emotion between the couple is directed at the child; and (d) couples live separately because of their poor relationship and the child is raised mainly by one parent.

Different generations and regions have different values placed on marriage or divorce; this makes it more difficult for the couples and child when the pressure is not only from couples, but also from grandparents, relatives, or other people in the communities. This kind of social environment leads to stress, pressure, and confusion for the child whose parents have relationship conflicts, in addition to impacting parenting.

PROBLEMS DUE TO CHANGE OF PARENTING

The change of parenting under the current social context could lead to parent–child relationship problems and child emotional and behavioral problems. Clinical data show that the most common pathological family structures in modern China (Ren, 2006) are:

1. *Enmeshment and disengagement:* For example, mother at home enmeshed with child, both of them disengaged from father who is out of the family with a poor marital relationship. This is a typical kind of parent–child relationship in Chinese families when there is marital distress. This type of pattern is associated with child academic problems, oppositional and defiant behaviors, poor peer relationships, in addition to poor relationships with both parents at home.
2. *Coalition:* For example, mother and child are opposed to and in conflict with father. In this situation, the child may have difficulty becoming independent from mother and experience social anxieties as well as difficulty forming relationships with peers or other individuals outside the family.
3. *Triangulation:* For example, given that the Asian culture emphasizes "filial piety," in some third-generation families, the grandmother replaces the mother's role, leading to division or ill-defined family roles. In these families, a grandmother may have the most authority, but also spoil the child, so that the child has no effective discipline in a conflicted family. Conflict related to this pattern may be more apparent and clinically significant in some Chinese families due to the one-child policy.

Many Chinese parents with poor marital relationships do not feel that divorce is an option because of fear that their child will lose good integrated family care and because of the stigma associated with divorce in China. Chinese distressed couples are more likely to keep marital problems a secret and choose to live together with conflict rather than seeking out help or a divorce, which highlights a cultural difference in distressed couples in many Western countries where divorce rates are higher than in China. Poor marital relationships in the same living space tend to be difficult for children in the family, leading to children sacrificing their own space and having to take on more responsibility, which has more harmful effects for the children than the adverse effects of divorce status (Jekielek, 1998; Yu & Du, 2008).

Clinical observations reveal many parenting problems: general lack of parenting knowledge and skills; poor parent–child matching problems; poor understanding of and appropriate response to children who suffer from psychological problems (Cheng et al., 2006); and parents' difficulty in dealing with their own problems leading them to "use" the child to resolve their own distress. These parenting problems are risk factors for children to develop a variety of internalizing and externalizing behavior problems (Han et al., 2010), such as overuse of the Internet (Hu, 2008), premature departure from home and/or school, becoming involved romantically too early and becoming pregnant, delinquency and risk behavior, interrupted relationships with peers and/or teachers, and poor relationships with parents. Children's mental problems also impact the parents and lead to marital problems, anxious and depressed symptoms, and interrupted social and/or work life.

SIGNIFICANCE OF ESTABLISHING CAREGIVER–CHILD RELATIONSHIP PROBLEMS

It will be very important for clinicians in China that the definition of caregiver–child relationship problem is established in the diagnostic system. It could help more clinicians understand the child as part of a family system, rather than always placing the child's mental disorder diagnosis as the center of the problem. It will be helpful to promote more active and appropriate interventions for children, as well as to increase social awareness on building healthy parent–child relationships. Having a more specified definition of caregiver–child relationship problem will allow clinicians to emphasize specific patterns of parents and child's involvement, distress and dysfunction within relationships, instead of more general words to describe the family relationships, which could be more helpful for informing specific intervention strategies.

HOW DOES ONE DEFINE THE PARENT–CHILD RELATIONSHIP AS A PROBLEM?

The identification of a parent–child relationship problem is now important in China, but the challenge is how it should be defined. The following issues are important considerations in the assessment of a parent–child relationship problem:

1. What is the boundary between the normal and abnormal parent (caregiver)–child relationship given the current and historical background of China? Compared with Western countries, the Chinese are more family oriented and family members are much more dependent on each other (Li & Liang, 2005). For example, Chinese children do not usually sleep alone until they become adolescents, which might be seen from a Western perspective as too close of a relationship between parents and children.
2. Parenting style is based on culture and we must be careful about cultural differences when defining the normal boundary in order to avoid too broad a diagnosis in some countries. For an example, it is common for Chinese parents in the first few years after immigrating to America to be careful not to beat their child, which is a quite normal parenting practice in China when parents see that their child has poor behavior and they try to teach him or her good behavior. But in America, if Chinese parents beat their child to teach him or her good behavior, they might be accused of physically abusing their child and lose parenting rights to raise the child. At times, the child will be sent to another family or children's home that is considered to be more fit for the child. This obviously might make more problems for the child and family in some cases. A Chinese study in Baotou City in the Province of Inner Mongolia surveyed the frequency and degree of parents' physical maltreatment behavior to children younger than 6 years old in the past year by using parents' self-administered questionnaire. This showed the prevalence of physical maltreatment by parents in the past year was 74.0%, of which 67.3% was minor violence (Wang, Chen, & Ma, 2007). The prevalence is higher than that of Western countries or even some other places in China. This may be related to the personality and value

of people in this minority area, but not related to the real meaning of physical maltreatment. In areas such as these, it may be important to assess the purpose/intention of the physical maltreatment, as well as the degree of control with which a caregiver administers the corporal punishment, as a way of determining whether there is a caregiver–child relationship problem, or child physical abuse, taking into account the norms of that society. If 74% of the families were determined to have problems with parenting, it will be difficult for that society to accept this concept and diagnosis.

3. How should caregiver–child relationship problems be distinguished from individual mental health problems in parents or children? For example, children with a parent who has a mental illness are at high risk for mental illness or a mental disorder themselves (Yu & Du, 2008), and vice versa. How does one define the parent (caregiver)–child relationship as purely a relationship problem? A relationship problem must be mainly relational and independent of whether the partners of the relationship have any individual disorders or not, but sometimes this is difficult to differentiate. As an example, let us take a mother with depression. Usually a mother with recently remitted depression may still be able to relate to her child in a passive and negative manner. Should we consider the parent–child relationship as a factor in multiaxis diagnosis or an independent disorder? With infants, it is more likely the latter, but with older children, more likely the former.
4. Establishing subcategories based on different reasons for parent–child relational problems, such as, disorder due to poor parenting knowledge or skills, parent–child mismatch relationship problem, disorder due to dysfunctional parenting after child suffers from disease, and disorder due to dysfunctional parenting due to parents' own problems. This kind of differentiation will be useful to guide clinicians as to how to take different perspectives on understanding and treating parent–child relational problems.

HOW DO CHINESE THERAPISTS TREAT PARENT–CHILD PROBLEMS AND CHILD BEHAVIORAL OR EMOTIONAL PROBLEMS?

Almost all Chinese child psychiatrists and child psychotherapists work in public hospitals with heavy patient loads in urban areas. The heavy caseload leaves limited time for assessment and psychological treatment of each child patient with his or her family. The way in which the Chinese psychiatrists work with children varies, depending on whether they have received any specialized training (e.g., whether or not they received psychiatry training in child development and psychotherapy). The most common practice for child psychiatrists in working with children is to interview one clinical case within 20 minutes, and provide some general psychological tests such as the Achenbach Child Behavior Rating scale (CBCL; Achenbach, 1991), family environment and function assessment scale, and other scales depending on specific problems or disorders (e.g., child depression scale) to make a psychiatric diagnosis and treatment plan.

If psychotherapy is to be offered, a 90-minute child and family functional and relational assessment is done. Therapy sessions are usually 30 to 90 minutes, depending on the kind of therapy and age of children. The most popular psychotherapy for children and their caregivers in hospitals are cognitive behavior therapy and structural family therapy, but in nonhospital-based organizations it is sandplay therapy. There has been much development in adult psychotherapy since the early 1980s in China, but child psychotherapy development has lagged behind. However, Chinese mental health workers are increasingly recognizing the important role of family in child mental problems evaluation and treatment. As an example, colleagues in the Shanghai Mental Health Center now provide eight parallel sessions of family group and adolescent group therapy for clinical adolescent cases with anxiety disorder.

CURRENT STATE OF CLINICAL PRACTICE IN CHINA

Many Chinese studies have shown that parent–child relational problems are common in both school-based and clinical populations. However, given the extremely small number of relevant professionals (i.e., only several hundred nationwide for a huge child/adolescent population of 247 million; www.stats.gov.cn, 2009), children's mental health problems or disorders are greatly under recognized and misunderstood by school teachers, family members, and communities. Children who are sent to clinics by their families may frequently be misdiagnosed and mistreated by adult psychiatrists or pediatricians who lack adequate training in child mental health diagnosis and treatment, and by some child psychiatrists who mainly work with children addressing medical diagnoses and treatment.

In the most recent decade, in large cities, children's mental health is attracting more and more attention from Chinese society, government, school, family, and mental health professionals. Mental health professionals are interested in learning more about assessment and treatment of children and their families. In Shanghai, for example, there is a project underway to establish a school-based mental health system that is integrated across several agencies, including the mental health center, pediatric hospital, school mental health organization, and the government education system. However, to move forward, more professionals trained in child mental health are necessary to ensure proper diagnosis and treatment for Chinese families.

REFERENCES

Achenbach, T. M. (1991). *Manual for the Child Behavior Checklist/4–18 and 1991 Profile.* Burlington, VT: University of Vermont.

Cheng, W., Liu, Y., Fan, J., Tang, H., Li, M., Wang, Z. (2006). Help seeking behavior of depressive adolescents and parents. *Chinese Journal of Clinical Psychology, 14*(6), 606–608.

Han, X., Zhou, H., Han, J., Hu, M., Liu, X. (2010). Psychological factors influencing children behavioral problems in family. *Journal of Huazhong University of Science and Technology, Health Sciences, 39*(5), 720–723, 730.

Hu, J. X. (2008). Influence of parental rearing pattern with juvenile internet addiction disorder. *Clinical Medicine, 28*(8), 24–26.

Jekielek, S. M. (1998). Parental conflict, marital disruption and children's emotional well-being. *Social Forces, 76*(3), 905–935.

Li, Y., & Liang, C. (2005). Different family culture viewpoints between Chinese and Western countries and the application of family psychotherapy. *Chinese Journal of Clinical Rehabilitation, 48*(9), 125–127.

Lin, X., Shen, M., Wang, L., Wang, Y. (2010). Meta-analysis on the mental health of the left-in-home children in rural China. *Acta Med Univ Sci Technol Huazhong, 39*(2), 228–231.

Ren, Z. (2006). The ill parents–children interaction and morbid family structure, the analysis about the several Chinese family of having problem. *Journal of Shandong University, 5,* 122–125.

Wang, F., Chen, J., & Ma, Y. (2007). The prevalence of physical maltreatment by parents in 810 kindergarten children. *Chinese Journal of School Health, 28*(11), 987–988, 990.

Xi, Z., & Zhen, G. (2008). Culture differences in parenting aim. *Advances in Psychological Science, 1,* 84–90.

Yu, Y., & Du, Y. (2008). Parents conflict and child mental health. *Shanghai Archives of Psychiatry, 20*(4), 240–242.

Zhang, G., Yang, Y., Huang, Y., Liu, S.-J., & Sun, X.-L. (2010). Epidemiological investigation on depression among 6–16 years old children and adolescents in Chengdu. *Chinese Mental Health Journal, 24*(3), 211–214.

Zhou, W., Gao, W., Sun, X., & Luo, J. (2011) Psychological resilience features of urban migrant children and rural left-behind children in Sichuan Province of China. *Journal of Beijing University, 43*(3), 386–390.

15

Parent–Child Relational Problems: The Psychological, Physical, and Economic Consequences

Kurt Hahlweg

At the moment, the World Health Organization (WHO) is revising the International Classification of Diseases (ICD-10). As is the case with the *Diagnostic and Statistical Manual of Mental Disorders* (*DSM-IV*), the ICD-10 is limited in its acknowledgment of relational factors, especially with regard to providing guidelines for clinical case management. Relational factors are coded under the Z codes (problems related to social environment), for example, Z61.4: problems related to sexual abuse of child; Z62.0: inadequate parental supervision and control; Z62.3: hostility toward child; Z62.4: emotional neglect; Z63.0: problems in relationship with spouse or partner; Z63.5: disruption of family by separation and divorce.

This situation provides an opportunity to suggest recommendations regarding the classification of relational processes in ICD-11, and in this chapter, the focus is on problems in parent–child relationships. Familial relational processes are integral to the diagnosis and treatment of mental, emotional, and behavioral (MEB) disorders in children and adolescents. In this chapter the risk and protective factors in the development of MEB disorders and their psychological, physical, and economical impact will be discussed.

PREVALENCE OF MEB DISORDERS AND CHILD MALTREATMENT

The mental health of children and adolescents is an epidemiological outcome of considerable public health relevance because of the high prevalence of MEB disorders in children and adolescents. Approximately 20% of children in Western, industrialized countries experience the signs and symptoms that constitute internalizing (e.g., anxiety/depression, social withdrawal) or externalizing (e.g., oppositional defiance, aggression) *DSM-IV* disorders (Belfer, 2008; O'Connell, Boat, & Warner, 2009; Patel, Flisher, Hetrick, & McGorry, 2007). More specifically, in the German BELLA-study by Ravens-Sieberer et al. (2008), 16% showed emotional symptoms, 15% conduct problems, and 14% hyperactivity/inattention disorder. Left untreated, externalizing disorders in childhood tend to persist and evolve into more antisocial behaviors in adulthood. In addition to the costs of treating such problems, social costs include school dropout, unemployment, family breakdown, drug and alcohol misuse, increased delinquency and risky behaviors, and interference with meaningful relationships among family members and friends. Furthermore, these mental health problems are highly persistent, often carrying forth into adulthood (Ihle & Esser, 2002). Thus, attending to the mental health needs of children and adolescents is a key component of child and adult public health.

Besides MEB disorders, child maltreatment (CM) is another significant public health problem. CM includes four major subtypes: physical, sexual, emotional abuse, and neglect. The prevalence figures are staggering: International studies demonstrate that, depending on the country, one quarter to half of all children report severe and frequent physical abuse; approximately 20% of females and 5% to 10% of males report sexual abuse as children. The extent of emotional abuse such as witnessing intimate partner violence (IPV) and neglect is unknown (Gonzales & MacMillan, 2008). Noll (2005) reports an increased risk of sexual abuse for children whose mothers have been a victim of sexual violence themselves. Thus, CM not only affects the current victims but also the future generation.

Unfortunately, health care services for mental health disorders and CM in children and adolescents are lacking—not only in the United States, but in Europe in general. In fact, a fifth of the countries in the European region lack mental health programs for children and adolescents. Even where services are available, 75% of the parents of affected children and adolescents do not make use of counseling or treatment options, indicating that mental health problems are being inadequately addressed (Ravens-Sieberer et al., 2008).

RISK AND PROTECTIVE FACTORS FOR HEALTHY CHILD DEVELOPMENT

Health depends on developing psychological, behavioral, and social competencies built on a foundation of safety, stability, and nurturance that is laid down early in life and that buffers against early adversity. Parental mental health and substance abuse problems; significant social deprivation or neglect; physical, sexual, and emotional abuse; and exposure to violence between parents or other adults are examples of breakdowns in the protective and nurturing environments children need to become healthy adolescents and adults. Early exposure to such adversities has been linked to many emotional, behavioral, and physical health problems. Associated emotional and behavioral problems include aggression, conduct disorder (CD), delinquency, antisocial behavior, substance abuse, IPV, teenage pregnancy, anxiety, depression, and suicide. Furthermore, a history of adverse exposures has been associated with health risks such as smoking and health problems such as obesity, diabetes, ischemic heart disease, and sexually transmitted diseases (Repetti, Taylor, & Seeman, 2002).

O'Connell et al. (2009) define a risk factor as a measurable characteristic of a subject that precedes and is associated with an outcome. Risk factors can occur at multiple levels, including biological, psychological, family, community, and cultural levels. Risk factors can be variable (there is within-subject change over time) or fixed (e.g., gender, ethnicity, genotype). Causal risk factors are those that are modifiable by an intervention and for which modification is associated with change in outcomes. A risk factor that cannot be changed by an intervention or for which change in the factor has not been demonstrated to lead to a change in an outcome is considered a variable marker. In Table 15.1 most often cited risk factors are summarized. Simple linear cause-and-effect relationships among variables and child outcomes cannot be assumed. These variables likely interact and cumulate over the development of a child (Bloomquist & Schnell, 2002).

The exposures to these factors pose a substantial risk for short- and long-term health through several mechanisms (see Table 15.1; O'Connell et al., 2009). For instance, chronic exposure to stress (e.g., chronic aggressive parental conflict) can accumulate and lead to potentially irreversible changes in the interrelated brain circuits and hormonal systems that regulate stress (e.g., sympathetic–adrenomedullary system [SAM], hypothalamic–pituitary–adrenocortical [HPA] system). These exposures also increase the risk of engaging in health-risk behaviors such as smoking, substance abuse, overeating, and unsafe sexual behaviors associated with a variety of long-term adverse health outcomes. Exposure to these adversities also might contribute to poor health by compromising the development of skills that influence income and socioeconomic status. Whether a young child is exposed to adversities is strongly associated with that child's social and economic environment. Children from households with lower income and lower parental education and who live in communities with greater concentrations of disadvantage are more likely to be exposed to CM, family and community violence, and parental mental health and substance abuse problems. Exposure to these adversities exacerbates and sustains socioeconomic, racial, and ethnic health disparities across generations. Therefore, reducing exposure to early adversity may be important to reducing health disparities.

TABLE 15.1 Summary of Risk Factors (RF) Associated With Mental, Emotional, and Behavioral (MEB) Disorders in Children and Adolescents

Child Biological RF
• Genetic predisposition
• Central nervous system abnormalities
• Difficult temperament, such as negative affect, difficult to soothe, and lower activity
Parent RF
• Psychopathology (depression, antisocial behavior, substance abuse)
• Stress
Parent–Child Interaction RF
• Parent–child attachment problems
• Inadequate supervision
• Coercive parenting (inconsistent, harsh parenting)
• Physical abuse and other forms of maltreatment
Family RF
• Couple conflict
• Family violence
• Single parenthood
• Divorce/separation
Social and Peer RF
• Negative peer–child interactions
• Social information-processing deficiencies and distortions
• Rejection
Contextual RF
• Socioeconomic status/poverty
• Neighborhood problems
• Community violence
• Stressful life events
• Violent media

Safe, stable, and nurturing relationships and environments for children counter the adverse exposures that occur during childhood and compromise their health over the lifespan. Protective factors are defined as characteristics at the individual, family, or community level that are associated with a lower likelihood of problem outcomes. The distinctions between risk factors discussed above can also be applied to protective factors. The term "protective factors" has also been used to refer to interactive factors that reduce the negative impact of a risk factor on a problem outcome, or resilience. It is often difficult to distinguish the effect of protective factors from that of risk factors, because the same variable may be labeled as either depending on the direction in which it is scored (see Table 15.2; e.g., good parenting versus poor parenting, high self-esteem versus low self esteem; O'Connell et al., 2009).

Research has identified well-established risk and protective factors for MEB disorders at the individual, family, school, and community levels. However, the pathways by which these factors influence each other to lead to the development of disorders are not well understood.

Table 15.2 Summary of Protective Factors (PF) Associated With the Prevention of Mental, Emotional, and Behavioral (MEB) Disorders in Children and Adolescents

Child PF
• Good intellectual functioning
• Appealing, sociable behavior
• Self-efficacy, self-confidence
• High self-esteem
• Talents
• Faith
Family PF
• Close relationship to caring parent figure
• Authoritative parenting: warmth, structure, high expectations
• Socioeconomic advantages
• Connections to extended supportive family networks
Extrafamilial Context PF
• Bonds to prosocial adults outside the family
• Connections to prosocial organizations
• Attending effective schools

Specific risk and protective factors have been identified for many of the major disorders, such as specific thinking and behavioral patterns for depression or cognitive deficits for schizophrenia. In addition, nonspecific factors, such as poverty and aversive experiences in families (e.g., marital conflict, poor parenting), schools (e.g., school failure, poor peer relations), and communities (e.g., violence), have been shown to increase the risk for developing most MEB disorders and problems.

BIOSOCIAL MODEL OF FAMILY INTERACTION AND CHILDREN'S HEALTH

Troxel and Matthews (2004) proposed a framework (see Figure 15.1) for understanding how early family environments contribute to the development of children, specifically linking marital conflict and dissolution to children's psychological and physical health, which can help to guide the following literature review. The model assumes several direct and indirect pathways linking marital factors with increased morbidity and mortality across the lifespan. The model posits that the effects of marital conflict and dissolution will be primarily mediated through parenting behaviors (Path A; compromised discipline, e.g., harsh and inconsistent parenting), diminished warmth and affection (cold, unresponsive, angry parenting styles), low acceptance, decreased parental supervision, negative parent–child communication). Decreased parental supervision may then directly lead to increased physical health problems in adolescents (Paths N, M; e.g., alcohol/drug use, tobacco, sexual promiscuity).

Deteriorating affective and verbal/nonverbal parent–child communication may lead (Path C) to the child's

1. inability to regulate emotion (Path G), which may lead to depression, anxiety and/or anger, may elicit health risk behaviors, and result in cardiovascular morbidity and mortality, hypertension, and—in case of depression—to suppressed immune functioning.
2. Social skills deficits, and insufficient coping behavior (Path H) may be linked with conflictual, aggressive peer relationships and rejection, and greater distress in their own relationships, thus adversely influence children's social networks and reducing stress-buffering interpersonal relationships. This may lead to poorer recovery from acute illness and increased risk of morbidity/mortality.

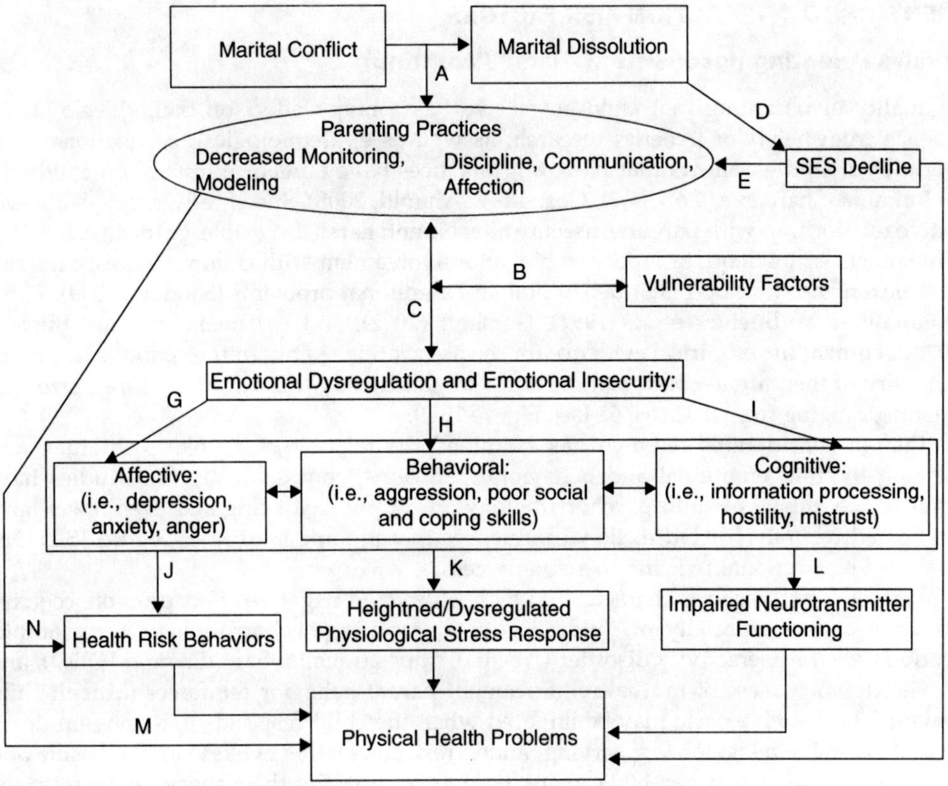

Source: Troxel and Matthews (2004).

FIGURE 15.1 Biopsychosocial model of marital conflict/dissolution and children's physical health.

3. Information processing styles (Path I) may be characterized by hostility and mistrust toward others, leading to heightened vigilance and aggressive behavior, which may lead to chronic sympathetic arousal and increased cardiovascular risk.
4. Stable parental conflict over years is a chronic stressor for children. This may lead to dysregulated physiological stress responses, for example, (a) hyperactivity of the SAM system and dysregulation of the HPA axis (Path K), and—maybe—(b) to altered serotonergic functioning (Path L). These biological stress dysregulations may increase the risk for chronic somatic illness, for example, cardiovascular disease, diabetes, and infectious illness.
5. Decline in socioeconomic status (Paths D, F), which is often the consequence of divorce, and is associated with "substantial income decline,..., high rates of job instability, and relocation to less desirable neighbourhoods, with high crime rates, poor schools, and inadequate services" (Troxel & Matthews, 2004, p. 48). Greater exposure to family and environmental stress may lead to poorer health, lower educational attainment, and increased internalizing and externalizing child disorders.

Troxel and Matthews (2004) review "yields consistent evidence documenting the consequences of marital conflict and dissolution to children's physical health status and risk trajectories. Moreover, studies linking marital conflict and dissolution to diminished parent practises and indices of emotional dysregulation provide suggestive evidence for pathways from early family environments to long-term health consequences" (p. 49).

In the following section, the literature on parent–child relational risk factors and its impact on the psychological consequences is reviewed keeping the aforementioned model as a framework in mind.

PARENT–CHILD INTERACTION RISK FACTORS

Coercive Parenting (Inconsistent, Harsh Parenting)

The quality of parenting that children receive has a major effect on their development. Evidence from behavior genetics research, as well as epidemiological, correlational, and experimental studies, shows that parenting practices have a major influence on children's development (Shanahan, Copeland, Costello, & Angold, 2008). Specifically, a lack of a warm positive relationship with parents; insecure attachment; harsh, inflexible, or inconsistent discipline practices; inadequate supervision of and involvement with children increase the risk that children will develop major behavioral and emotional problems (Sanders, 1999). Three meta-analyses by Buehler et al. (1997), Gershoff (2002), and Krishnakumar and Buehler (2000) document the empirical evidence for the associations between interparental conflicts, the quality of the parent–child relationship, and children's MEB disorders. Effect-sizes are moderate, ranging from 0.32 to 0.62 (see Figure 15.2).

Although considerable research has examined the relation of couple functioning and parenting to child emotional and behavioral problems, comparatively few studies have examined the impact of child psychopathology on couple well-being and even fewer have investigated recursive or bidirectional influences that are apparent from Figure 15.2. One example of bidirectionality is the coercion process.

Parent–child interactions characterized by hostility and negative affect promote coercive interaction cycles, especially in children with disrupting psychopathology, for example, attention-deficit hyperactivity disorder (ADHD), oppositional defiant disorder (ODD), and CD. Through a process of mutual reinforcement parent behavior reinforces difficult child behavior. The coercive cycle may be initiated when the child responds to a parental directive with aversive behavior (e.g., crying, anger, resistance); this evokes similar hostile and angry emotions from the parents, causing parents to intensify their angry response to the child, followed in turn by stronger resistance and anger by the child. The coercion process starts when the parent gives in, leading to the withdrawal of the directive by the parent and reinforces the child for resistance and negatively reinforces the parent, because the angry behavior of the child, for example, crying, stops (Patterson, 1982; Scaramella & Leve, 2004). In the case of externalizing disorders, these interactions become habitual over time. Therefore, parent training needs to incorporate those parental practices that are successful in stopping the coercion process (Burke, Pardini, & Loeber, 2008) and the life-course persistent

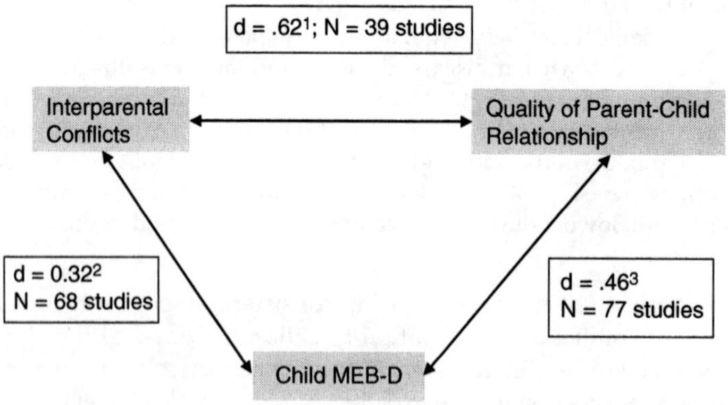

Sources: Buehler et al. (1997), Gershoff (2002), and Krishnakumar and Buehler (2000).

FIGURE 15.2 Meta-analyses: Association of parental variables and child mental, emotional, and behavioral disorders (MEB-D).

pathway from childhood to adult disorders may be best interrupted early in life, when these behavioral patterns are more easily modified.

Studies have shown that parenting is strongly affected by child psychopathology (Heinrichs, Conrath, Degen, & Snyder, under review). For example, parents of children with a clinical disorder such as ADHD, ODD, CD, or with significant child behavior problems will report more parenting distress (e.g., Duchovic, Gerkensmeyer, & Wu, 2009), a lower sense of competence and self-efficacy regarding parenting of their child (Maniadaki, Sonuga-Barke, Kakouros, & Karaba, 2005), and more individual psychological distress symptoms, especially in mothers with regard to depressive symptoms (Beck, Hastings, & Daley, 2004). In a recent study Burke et al. (2008) noted further that ODD and CD may differentially impact families because the latter involves more norm violations outside the home (less parental involvement), whereas ODD directly impacts the parent–child relationship.

FAMILY RISK FACTORS

Marital/Couple Conflict

The parents' own relationship as a couple has notable effects on their child's well-being. This impact of the couple's relationship on their child well-being results from several factors (Repetti et al., 2002): (a) after parents argue with each other, each parent is more likely to be negative in interacting with the child; (b) parents who argue with each other struggle to work together as a team to parent their child; and (c) frequent arguments between parents create a broad negative environment in which the child is raised.

The belief that marital relationships are critically related to child development and outcome has been a cornerstone of clinical and scientific literature throughout the 20th century. Marital conflict between the partners can take many forms, and may have positive and negative elements. It is healthy to discuss relationship conflicts in constructive ways. By contrast, avoidance or withdrawal from couple or family conflict may be more detrimental than engaging in openly angry and hostile heated arguments. Discussion of differences in opinion can be helpful and useful if the argument led to conflict resolution and fair problem solving. However, destructive couple conflict, for example, verbal aggression, personal insult, defensiveness, withdrawal, nonverbal hostility, and physical aggression, constitute a family risk factor and predicts child behavior problems more accurately than marital apathy and covert tension do (Grych & Fincham, 1990). Marital conflict and aggression are linked with multiple negative influences and pathways to children's development. The negative effects are not only brought about by the direct exposure to couple conflict but also through changes in parenting and other parent risk factors such as depression or alcohol problems (Cummings & Davies, 2010; Krishnakumar & Buehler, 2000).

Marital Conflict/Divorce and Child Adjustment

Couple conflict is a common occurrence even in harmonious and stable relationships and most children, even from high conflict homes, do not develop behavior problems. Zimet and Jacob (2002) summarized the state of the art taking studies of the impact of divorce into account:

1. Negative child outcomes are more strongly associated with marital conflict than divorce.
2. Conflict and discord in intact, nonclinical families (as well as treatment seeking families) is similarly related to the risk of child psychopathology.
3. Children from divorced families appear to have higher levels of well-being than children from intact, high-conflict families.
4. The negative effects of divorce on children are significantly reduced when predivorce functioning/conflict is taken into account.
5. Continued conflict between parents after divorce exacerbates negative child adjustment, whereas behavioral problems in children decrease when conflict also decreases after divorce.

The review came to the conclusion that marital conflict and discord are more significant to child maladjustment than family intactness and that process dimensions (e.g., parent hostility) explain a greater amount of negative child outcome variance than structural dimensions (Cummings & Davies, 2010; Zimet & Jacob, 2002).

In order to understand the complexities of influences associated with relations between children and marital conflict, Cummings and Davies (2010) provided a framework for a process-oriented approach (see Figure 15.3), focusing on "Emotional Security Theory EST" as a guiding conceptualization.

> Illustrating a "direct pathway" of influence [path 2 in Figure 15.3], exposure to destructive intraparental conflict increases children's vulnerability to psychological problems by undermining their emotional security in the interparental relationship—that is, children's confidence in their parents ability to manage discord, and to preserve family and marital stability. .... The erosion of children's confidence in their parents as sources of protection and support within the attachment relationship accounts for many of the deleterious effects of parenting difficulties (e.g. unresponsiveness, intrusiveness, low warmth) on children's psychological adjustment (paths 1, 4). ... In addition, the effects of marital conflict may be moderated by the operation of other family processes, such as family conflict or cohesion (path 5). (Cummings & Davies, 2010, pp. 31–32)

Child negative outcomes have included externalizing problems (e.g., CD, aggressiveness, delinquency, antisocial behavior), internalizing problems (e.g., depression, anxiety, withdrawal), as well as poor social skills characterized often by hostility and sibling and peer social problems. Couple conflict is also linked with poor school grades and problems in intellectual achievements. These school problems may be due to children's attention difficulties and sleep problems as a result of ongoing parental conflict (Cummings & Davies, 2010; Grych & Fincham, 1990). Associations between couple conflict and children's behavior problems are moderate in magnitude, for example, Erel and Burman (1995) found a mean effect size of 0.46 (meta-analyzing over 80 studies). When analyzing the association between marital conflict and child development, it seems to be important to document those elements of conflict that specifically contribute to negative outcomes (Zimet & Jacob, 2002).

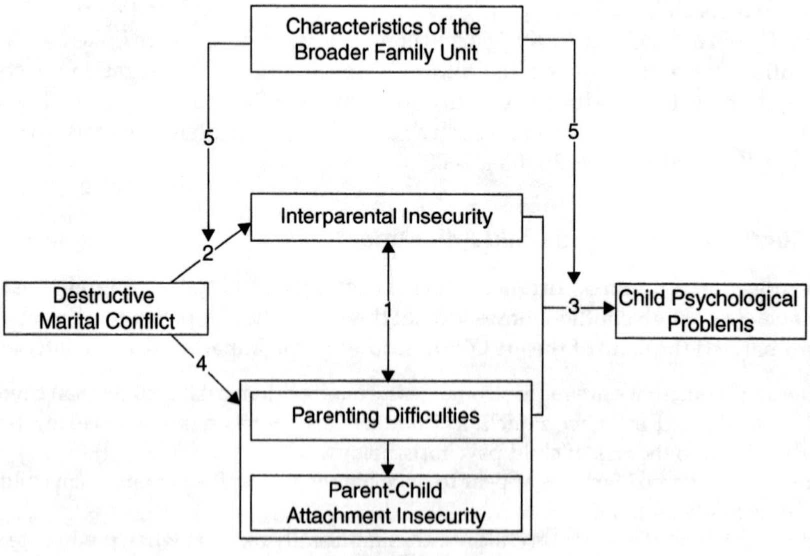

Source: Reprinted with permission from Guilford Press, Cummings and Davies (2010).

FIGURE 15.3 Multiple pathways underlying associations between destructive marital/couple conflict and child psychological problems.

Frequency

The more children are exposed to conflict the more likely they show distress, disturbed behavior, and heightened reactivity when exposed to future conflicts.

Intensity

High intensity conflict, particularly when physical violence is involved, strongly contributes to emotional problems, social skill impairments, and behavior problems.

Content

Certain conflict topics may be more threatening to children. When the topic pertains to the child, he or she is more likely to experience feelings of helplessness, fear, dysphoria, shame, and negative self-evaluation. Children may feel responsible for the parent's arguments, because they perceive themselves as the source of tension. Child-related content has been more often linked with internalizing outcomes.

Resolution

Consistently less negative reactions have been observed in children who experienced their parents as having resolved their conflicts. When anger between parents is unresolved, children experience distress and anger, and perceive the event as far more negative than when anger is resolved (Cummings & Davies, 2010).

Family Violence

In the United States, approximately 12.5% of men are physically aggressive (e.g., grab, push, slap, hit) toward their wives. Approximately 1.5 to 2 million women are severely assaulted by their husbands per year and 10 million children witness this violence. In Germany, the 1-year prevalence rate of physical aggression among partners between 20 and 45 years old is approximately 8.5% (Wetzels, Greve, Mecklenburg, Bilsky, & Pfeiffer, 1995). Up to 50% of married couples experience spousal violence at some point during the course of their marriages.

Recent U.S. research suggests that these data underestimate the number of children exposed to violence (data for Europe is not available). Smith Slep and O'Leary (2005) report prevalence rates of 49%, with 24% reporting severe physical aggression (e.g., beat up, kicked, slammed against a wall, chocked, hit with an object, burned). Physical violence often occurs with other forms of interspousal aggression (kicking furniture, throwing objects) and psychological maltreatment (e.g., insults, threats, silent treatment for days and weeks) that may also evoke negative affect and distress in children in the same way as direct interspousal aggression. Couple aggression puts children's safety at risk, because partner violence increases the likelihood of parent–child aggression. Domestic violence and CM are highly correlated. In those homes the rate of physically abused and neglected children are 15 times higher than the U.S. national average (Osofsky, 2003). In families in which the wife is battered, 60% to 75% of children are also battered.

Approximately 30% (15.5 million) of U.S. children live in homes in which some form of couple violence has occurred, and 13% of children experienced at least one incidence of witnessing severe partner violence during the past year (McDonald, Jouriles, Ramisetty-Mikler, Caetano, & Green, 2006). It is estimated that approximately 40% to 50% of children exposed to couple violence show extreme behavioral problems (Jouriles, Mahoney, Norwood, McDonald, & Vincent, 1996). Domestic violence can become part of an *intergenerational cycle of violence*. Studies showed (Osofsky, 2003) that children and adolescents who witnessed and were victims of violence were more likely to become perpetrators of violence than those who were not exposed. When witnessing violence the children learn that violence (a) is part of family relationships; (b) is an appropriate way to resolve conflicts; (c) is a way of controlling other people; and (d) the perpetrator in intimate relationships often goes unpunished.

Divorce/Separation

About 55% of American, and 40% to 45% of Australian, English, German, and Swiss first marriages end in divorce. About 50% of the divorces occur in the first 7 years of the marriage. In 2006, 200,000 couples got divorced in Germany. Many other couples, about 10% to 25% (for Germany: 1.6–4 million), live in stable but unhappy relationships for various reasons, for example, the financial implications of divorce, personal and cultural expectations about divorce, or because no alternative partner is available. As painful as the experience of divorce is for many people, about 75% of divorced men and 66% of divorced women remarry within 3 years. Unfortunately, the divorce rate in second marriages is even higher than in first marriages. Often, the public and researchers have taken a pathogenic view of divorce and have focused on the stresses and adverse outcomes associated with marital breakup. However, it should also be recognized that divorce can offer an escape from an unhappy, abusive, conflictual, or demeaning marriage and an opportunity to build new, more harmonious, fulfilling relationships, and increase personal growth and individuation (Hahlweg, Baucom, Grawe-Gerber, & Snyder, 2010).

The extent of the social problems posed by destructive couple conflict and the following separation/divorce is staggering. Approximately half of all children in the United States will experience parental divorce. However, across the United States and Europe, the separation rate of unmarried parents is higher than the divorce rate of married parents (Kiernan, 2003). In an analysis of family breakdown among 14,600 parents with 5-year-old children using data from the UK Millennium Cohort Study, Callan et al. (2006) found that 9% of *married* parents, 26% of *cohabiting* parents, and 60% of self-described *closely involved* parents had split up before their child's fifth birthday. Combining the latter two categories means 35% of *unmarried* couples split up during this period.

Single Parenthood

In the United States, approximately 50% of children will grow up in single-parent families for at least some portion of their childhood. Relatively little is known about the relation of children's well-being and parental or family conflict in single-parent families despite the high number of children affected. The few studies show that those children are at higher risk for behavioral and emotional problems, child abuse and neglect, academic problems in school, substance use problems, and physical health problems than for children in two-parent families (Amato, 2005). Conflict in single-parent families may be higher than in two-parent families due to the lack of stability in these relationships with a higher rate of cohabitating partners, the financial situation, worse living conditions, bad schooling, and other challenges that often accompany single-parent status (Cummings & Davies, 2010).

PARENT RISK FACTORS

Parent Psychopathology

Parent psychopathology has been identified as a risk factor. For example, parents who have antisocial personality disorder have been found to have more children with aggressive and conduct problems and sons of substance-abusing fathers are more likely to exhibit higher levels of aggression and ADHD than sons of nonsubstance-abusing fathers. Parents with anxiety disorders are more likely to have anxious children than their nonanxious counterparts. Some of the association may be due to shared genes. However children also learn anxious reactions via parental modeling, and reinforcement of anxious behaviors and parental overcontrol and intrusiveness seem to reinforce child inhibition (O'Donnell et al., 2009).

Depression

Depression is a common, universal, and debilitating public health problem. The Global Burden of Disease study by the WHO (Murray & Lopez, 1997) determined that depression accounts for more disability worldwide than any other condition during the middle years of adulthood. For some with depressive episodes, periods of depression may resolve in a few weeks or months. However, it has been estimated that, for 30% to 50% of adults, depression is recurrent or chronic. In the United States, 16.2% of adults reported major depression in their lifetime, while another 4.1% reported meeting a milder but chronic form of depression (dysthymia). Depression, due to its recurrent nature, leads to sustained individual, family, and societal costs, and approximately 15.6 million children under 18 years of age are living with an adult who had major depression in the past year. Depression in parents can have serious biological, psychological, behavioral, and social consequences, especially for children who rely on a parent for caregiving, material support, and nurturance. The current policy environment does not encourage a two-generation (i.e., parent, child) identification, treatment, and prevention strategy for adults with depression (National Research Council, 2009).

Parenting Practices

Less is known about parenting in depressed fathers relative to mothers, but most of the findings from the smaller number of studies are consistent with the findings about mothers. Depression in mothers is significantly associated with more hostile, negative, coercive parenting, and with more disengaged (withdrawn) parenting, and with less positive (warmth) parenting, with low to moderate effect sizes. In a meta-analysis of 46 observational studies, mother's depression was associated with negative/coercive behaviors and less positive interaction with their children, especially those children with externalizing behaviors (Lovejoy, Graczyk, O'Hare, & Neumann, 2000).

The poorer parenting qualities may not improve to levels comparable to those of never-depressed parents, despite remission or recovery from episodes of depression. These patterns of parenting have been found in depressed mothers of infants and young children, as well as in depressed mothers of school-age children and adolescents (Cummings & Davies, 2010; Lovejoy et al., 2000; National Research Council, 2009).

Child Functioning

Depression in parents has been consistently associated with a number of behavior problems and psychopathology in children, including higher rates of depression, earlier age of onset, longer duration, greater functional impairment, higher likelihood of recurrence, higher rates of anxiety, and higher rates and levels of severity of internalizing and externalizing symptoms and disorders in children and adolescents (Cummings & Davies, 2010; Lovejoy et al., 2000; National Research Council, 2009).

Prevention

Although treatment of depression is critical, many families also need professional intervention to reduce children's risk. To date, no intervention has to been proven to be acceptable, feasible, and effective in preventing psychological disorder and impairment in offspring of parents with depression. The Keeping Families Strong program (Riley et al., 2008) is the first attempt to develop such a preventive intervention and is in its pilot test phase.

STRESS

Child poverty is a critical problem in the United States and Europe and has been linked to multiple sources of risk. In 2006, almost 17% of children (approximately 13 million) in the

United States were poor, and 20% of children were under the age of 6. The main effects of poverty are difficult to isolate because economic disadvantage is associated with many of other disadvantages that threaten child development. However, studies have shown consistently that economic disadvantage is associated with less positive and more negative parenting. Parental psychosocial distress (e.g., depression) may be most harmful for low-income families because of the other risks these families face (Barnett, 2008).

COSTS

"Preventing mental, emotional, and behavioral (MEB) disorders among young people is one of the soundest investments a society could make" (O'Connell et al., 2009, p. 241). Cost-effectiveness depends on the perspective of a decision maker, for example a health care provider or the society as a whole. The provider incurs the costs for the intervention and derives some benefits (e.g., reduced future health care costs). However, major benefits of the intervention may be realized in other sectors of society, for example, education (less disruptions in classroom) or criminal justice (fewer days in jail). MEB disorders are associated with increased morbidity and reduced quality of life due to psychological suffering and increased risk of physical illnesses for the patient. These disorders may also lead to negative health consequences for family members, victims of crime, or peers.

The annual costs for MEB disorders in 2007 totaled approximately $247 billion, taking direct and indirect costs into account (O'Connell et al., 2009). CM also exacts an enormous toll on society, resulting in costs associated with utilization of administrative services and systems, child treatment services, long-term impact, and next generation victimization. Costs associated with child abuse and neglect in the United States are estimated to be over $94 billion per year in 2001 dollars (Fromm, 2001).

The annual total economic costs per person under the age of 25 are approximately $2,400 ($500 for mental health service costs and $1,900 in general health, productivity, and crime-related costs). More specifically, data from the Fast Track project showed that youth with CD incurred social cost of more than $70,000 over a 7-year period (Foster et al., 2005). A study in England showed that children with a CD diagnosis incurred public service cost more than 10 times higher than those with no MEB diagnosis by the age of 28 (Scott et al., 2001).

In summary, the economic, social, and personal costs of MEB disorders among children and adolescents are very high, and it seems worthwhile to improve our preventive and therapeutic interventions to reduce these costs.

CONCLUSION

This review emphasizes that familial relational processes, specifically of parent–child relational problems, are clearly associated with the development of MEB disorders in children and adolescents and should be integral to the diagnosis, assessment, and treatment. Therefore the inclusion of family relational processes should be of high priority in the development of ICD-11. It will help to improve the effectiveness of the treatment and the prevention of MEB disorders and it is very likely to reduce costs for society. Inclusion of a family relational process category may also improve the referral system and may allow better research of the influences of parent–child relational processes on treatment and long-term outcome.

REFERENCES

Amato, P. R. (2005). The impact of family formation change on the cognitive, social, and emotionally well-being of the next generation. *The Future of Children, 15*(2), 75–96.

Barnett, M. (2008). Economic disadvantage in complex family systems: Expansion of family stress models. *Clinical Child and Family Psychology Review, 11*,145–161.

Beck, A., Hastings, R., & Daley, D. (2004). Prosocial behavior and behavior problems independently predict maternal stress. *Journal of Intellectual and Developmental Disability, 29*, 339–349.

Belfer, M. L. (2008). Child and adolescent mental disorders: The magnitude of the problem across the globe. *Journal Child Psychology Psychiatry, 49,* 226–236.

Bloomquist, M. L., & Schnell, S. V. (2002). *Helping children with aggression and conduct problems.* New York, NY: Guilford.

Buehler, C., Anthony, C., Krishnakumar, A., Stone, G., Gerard, J. & Pemberton, S. (1997). Interparental conflict and youth problem behaviors: A meta-analysis. *Journal of Child and Family Studies, 6,* 233–247.

Burke, J. D., Pardini, D. A., & Loeber, R. (2008). Reciprocal relationship between parental behavior and disruptive psychopathology from childhood through adolescence. *Journal of Abnormal Child Psychology.* doi:10.1007/s1082–008-9219–7

Callan, S., Benson, H., Coward, S., Davis, H., Gill, M., Grant, H.,…, Rowthorn, R. (2006). *Breakdown Britain: Fractured families.* London: Social Policy Justice Group.

Cummings, E. M., & Davies, P. T. (2010). *Marital conflict and children. An emotional security perspective.* New York, NY: Guilford.

Duchovic, C. A., Gerkensmeyer, J. E., & Wu, J. (2009). Factors associated with parental distress. *Journal of Child and Adolescent Psychiatric Nursing, 22,* 40–48.

Erel, O., & Burman, B. (1995). Interrelatedness of marital relations and parent–child relations: A meta-analytic review. *Psychological Bulletin, 118,* 108–132.

Foster, E. M., Jones, D. E., & Conduct Problems Research Group. (2005). The high costs of aggression: Public expenditures resulting from conduct disorder. *American Journal of Public Health, 25*(9), 1767–1772.

Fromm, S. (2001). *Total estimated cost of child abuse and neglect in the United States: Statistical evidence.* Report submitted by Prevent Child Abuse America to the Edna McConnell Clark Foundation.

Gershoff, E. T. (2002). Punishment by parents and associated child behaviors and experiences: A meta-analytic and theoretical review. *Psychological Bulletin, 128,* 539–579.

Gonzales, A., & MacMillan, H. L. (2008). Preventing child maltreatment: An evidence-based update. *Journal of Postgraduate Medicine, 54,* 280–286.

Grych, J. H., & Fincham, F. D. (1992). Interventions for children of divorce: Toward greater integration of research and action. *Psychological Bulletin, 111,* 434–454.

Hahlweg, K., Baucom, D. H., Grawe-Gerber, M., & Snyder, D. K. (2010). Strengthening couples and families: Dissemination of interventions for the treatment and prevention of couple distress. In K. Hahlweg, M. Grawe-Gerber, & D. H. Baucom (Eds.), *Enhancing couples: The shape of couple therapy to come* (pp. 3–30). Göttingen, Germany: Hogrefe.

Heinrichs, N., Conrath, A.-L., Degen, M., & Snyder, D. K. (2010). The link between child emotional and behavioral problems and couple functioning. *Family Science, 1* (3), 152 - 172.

Ihle, W., & Esser, G. (2002). Epidemiologie psychischer Störungen im Kindes- und Jugendalter. Prävalenz, Verlauf, Komorbidität und Geschlechtsunterschiede. *Psychologische Rundschau, 53,* 159–169.

Jouriles, E. N., Mahoney, A., Norwood, W. D., McDonald, R., & Vincent, J. P. (1996). Physical violence and other forms of marital aggression: Links with children's behavior problems. *Journal of Family Psychology, 10,* 223–234.

Kiernan, K. (2003) *Cohabitation and divorce across nations and generations.* Centre for Analysis of Social Exclusion, LSE, CASE, paper 65.

Krishnakumar, A., & Buehler, C. (2000). Interparental conflict and parenting behaviors: A meta-analytic review. *Family Relations, 49*(1), 25–44.

Lovejoy, M. C., Graczyk, P. A., O'Hare, E., & Neumann, G. (2000). Maternal depression and parenting behaviour: A meta-analytic review. *Clinical Psychology Review, 20,* 561–592.

Maniadaki, K., Sonuga-Barke, E., Kakouros, E., & Karaba, R. (2005). Maternal emotions and self-efficacy beliefs in relation to boys and girls with ADHD. *Child Psychiatry and Human Development, 35,* 247–263.

McDonald, R., Jouriles, E. N., Ramisetty-Mikler, S., Caetano, R., & Green, C. E. (2006). Estimating the number of American children living in partner-violent families. *Journal of Family Psychology, 20,* 137–142.

Murray, J. L., & Lopez, A. D. (1997) *The global burden of disease.* Boston: World Health Organization.

National Research Council. (2009). *Depression in parents, parenting, and children. Opportunities to improve identification, treatment, and prevention.* Washington, DC: National Academy of Science.

Noll, J. G. (2005). Does childhood sexual abuse set in motion a cycle of violence against women? What we know and what we need to learn. *Journal of Interpersonal Violence, 20,* 455–462.

O'Connell, M. E., Boat, T., & Warner, K. E. (Eds.). (2009). *Preventing mental, emotional, and behavioral disorders among young people: Progress and possibilities.* Washington, DC: Institute of Medicine; National Research Council.

Osofsky, J. D. (2003). Prevalence of children's exposure to domestic violence and child maltreatment: Implications for prevention and intervention. *Clinical Child and Family Psychology Review, 6*(3), 161–170.

Patel, V., Flisher, A. J., Hetrick, S., & McGorry, P. (2007). Mental health of young people: A global public-health challenge. *Lancet, 369,* 1302–1313.

Patterson, G. R. (1982). *Coercive family process.* Eugene, OR: Castalia.

Ravens-Sieberer, U., Wille, N., Erhart, M., Bettge, S., Wittchen, H.-U., Rothenberger, A.,…, BELLA Study Group. (2008). Prevalence of mental health problems among children and adolescents in Germany: Results of the BELLA study within the National Health Interview and Examination Survey. *European Child Adolescent Psychiatry, 17*(Suppl. 1), 22–33.

Repetti, R. L., Taylor, S. E., & Seeman, T. E. (2002). Risky families: Family social environments and the mental and physical health of offspring. *Psychological Bulletin, 128*(2), 330–366.

Riley, A. W., Valdez, C. R., Barrueco, S., Mills, C., Beardslee, W., Sandler, I., & Rawal, P. (2008). Development of a family-based program to reduce risk and promote resilience among families affected by maternal depression: Theoretical basis and program description. *Clinical Child and Family Psychology Review, 11*, 12–29.

Sanders, M. R. (1999). Triple P-Positive Parenting Program: Towards an empirically validated multilevel parenting and family support strategy for the prevention of behavior and emotional problems in children. *Clinical Child and Family Psychology Review, 2*, 71–90.

Scaramella, L. V., & Leve, L. D. (2004). Clarifying parent–child reciprocities during early childhood: The early childhood coercion model. *Clinical Child and Family Psychology Review, 7*, 89–107.

Scott, S., Knapp, M., Henderson, J., & Maughan, B. (2001). Financial costs of social exclusion: Follow-up study of antisocial children into adulthood. *British Medical Journal, 323(7306)*, 191.

Shanahan, L., Copeland, W., Costello, E. J., & Angold, A. (2008). Specificity of putative psychosocial risk factors for psychiatric disorders in children and adolescents. *Journal of Child Psychology and Psychiatry, 49*, 34–42.

Smith Slep, A. M., & O'Leary, S. G. (2005). Parent and partner violence in families with young children: Rates, Patterns, and connections. *Journal of Consulting and Clinical Psychology, 73*, 435–444.

Troxel, W. M., & Matthews, K. A. (2004). What are the costs of marital conflict and dissolution to children's physical health? *Clinical Child and Family Psychology Review, 7*, 29–58.

Wetzels, P., Greve, W., Mecklenburg, E., Bilsky, W., & Pfeiffer, Ch. (1995). *Kriminalität im Leben alter Menschen. Eine altersvergleichende Untersuchung von Opfererfahrungen, persönlichem Sicherheitsgefühl und Kriminalitätsfurcht.* Band 105 Schriftenreihe des Bundesministeriums für Familie, Senioren, Frauen und Jugend. Stuttgart, Germany: Kohlhammer.

Zimet, D. M., & Jacob, T. (2002). Influences of marital conflict on child adjustment: Review of theory and research. *Clinical Child and Family Psychology Review, 4*, 319–335.

16

Practical Tools for Assessing Caregiver–Child Relationship Problems

Marianne Z. Wamboldt and Anthony R. Cordaro, Jr.

Pediatric professionals evaluating children or adolescents with emotional and behavioral problems often try to discern whether the child's home environment, particularly their interactions with their primary caregivers, is part or all of the cause of the child's difficult behaviors. This discernment is difficult, because children with difficult temperament or behaviors tend to elicit more negative reactions from their caregivers (Ganiban, Ulbricht, Saudino, Reiss, & Neiderhiser, 2010). Nonetheless, several prospective, genetically controlled, studies have indicated that certain components of parenting, while perhaps elicited from the child, lead to an increase in negative child behaviors over time (e.g., Narusyte et al., 2011). Similarly, many interventions that promote parenting that is a "better fit" for the child lead to a decrease in child behavior problems (Bor, Sanders, & Markie-Dadds, 2002). Thus, the usefulness of being able to accurately identify caregiver–child relationship problems seems clear if the goal is to decrease childhood behavioral and emotional problems.

In addition, there is mounting evidence that the quality of the caregiver–child relationship can play an important role in modifying the outcome of psychiatric and physical disorders in children. For example, expressed emotion has been shown to impact treatment response in a number of illnesses, including cognitive behavioral therapy for adolescents with social anxiety (García-Lopez, Muela, Espinosa-Fernandez, & Diaz-Castela, 2009), family focused therapy for adolescents with bipolar disorder (Miklowitz et al., 2009), attention-deficit hyperactivity disorder (ADHD; Sonuga-Barke et al., 2008), and pediatric asthma (F. S. Wamboldt, Wamboldt, Gavin, Roesler, & Brugman, 1995). Appropriate coding of the presence or absence of a caregiver–child relationship problem may help to explain differential outcomes for pharmaceutical or therapeutic interventions for children with a variety of mental and physical illnesses.

The World Health Organization is revising the International Classification of Diseases (ICD-11) to possibly elaborate some of the current "Z codes," which include a variety of descriptions of parent–child relationship difficulties (see Chapter 13, this volume). Current codes in the Z section are typically one-line descriptors, and do not include criteria from which to evaluate whether that code is appropriate or not. This lack of specificity often means that these codes are seldom used in health care settings, let alone public health situations or in research (Beach, Wamboldt, Kaslow, Heyman, & Reiss, 2006). Improved criteria would help lead to increased research into parent–child relational issues, including the ability for epidemiologists and public health workers to document frequency of the problem, and whether a variety of preventive interventions can improve the relationship between caregivers and children in a way that reduces overall mental health burden in children (e.g., Sanders, 2012).

In summary, there is growing evidence that relational constructs have clinical importance and thus it is increasingly important for clinicians to have a clearly defined way of classifying and identifying a relational problem between a parent (or primary caregiver) and child. This chapter will provide some suggestions for interviews, structured observations, and self-report measures that may be utilized by clinicians or researchers to help in making this assessment.

INTERVIEWS AND OBSERVATIONAL ASSESSMENTS FOR CAREGIVER–CHILD RELATIONAL PROBLEMS

When dealing with young children and infants, direct interviewing of the child is often not possible or helpful. However, over the years a number of structured observational assessments of young children have yielded reliable and predictive assessments of their attachment to a particular caregiver.

Child Focused

Strange Situation Procedure

The Strange Situation procedure, originally developed by Mary Ainsworth, has linked the degree to which caregivers exhibit sensitive and consistent parenting to the behavioral patterns of young children when faced with a standardized stressor. Typically done with children aged 12 months through 24 months, the procedure involves set times of having the child with caregiver and interviewer, then having the caregiver leave the room while child is left with the interviewer, then having the caregiver return. The coding system looks at the child's response to the departure of the caregiver, as well as their response upon the caregiver's return. Differential patterns of attachment, for example, secure, insecure, and disorganized, and so on are coded based on the child's reactions and behaviors during this procedure. This paradigm has been shown to be neither a product of infant characteristics, nor culturally bound, as attachment patterns with the same infant and different caretakers can be different, as well as attachment patterns can change over time and are sensitive to changes in parenting (Sroufe, 1985). Interestingly, and not surprisingly, some infants are more vulnerable to neglectful or intrusive parenting than others, and recent research may be identifying some of the genetic links to this vulnerability (Luijk et al., 2011).

The Ainsworth Strange Situation paradigm remains primarily a research tool, as it needs to be set up in a standardized manner. However, astute clinicians may choose to observe semistandardized separations of young children and their caregivers, for example, in a clinical interview or physical exam setting, and may glean important information as to the type of attachment the child exhibits toward the caregiver.

As discussed in Chapter 13 in this book, early research using such observations in structured situations has led to the development of elegant codes of infant–caregiver relationships, as elucidated in the DC 0–3 (e.g., Schechter et al., 2010; ZERO TO THREE, 2005).

Dyad Focused

Once children are into the school years, roughly aged 8 to 9 years and older, they can participate in semistructured interviews. Typically, these interviews involve interviewing one child or adolescent alone, interviewing the caregiver alone, and then interviewing both together for the interviewer to reach a consensus code. In a semistructured interview, there are certain prompts the interviewer must ask, but then the interviewer can ask further questions to elicit enough information that the interviewer makes a criterion-based judgment encompassing all of the information gleaned from both child and parent. While these interviews can be used in research settings, they are often quite useful in clinical settings as well, as they guide the clinician into areas of inquiry.

Parent–Child Relationship Scale (PCRS)

The PCRS is a scale based on questions about the caregiver–child relationship embedded in one of the earlier semistructured interviews developed to assess child and adolescent psychopathology. The Child and Adolescent Psychiatric Assessment (CAPA; Angold & Costello, 2000) includes 10 probes that ask about caregiver–child shared activities, time spent together, conflictual or warm interactions, and so on. These questions are asked of both child and caregiver. There are time and intensity-based criterion for whether to code the answers as problematic or not, and the scored answers can be summarized yielding a scale with good internal reliability, construct, and divergent validity (M. Z. Wamboldt, Wamboldt, Gavin, & McTaggart, 2001).

Structured Interview for Relational Problems

The relationship disorder working group has proposed new criterion for the Caregiver–Child Relationship Problem (see Table 16.1) and is in the process of testing whether mental health professionals can reliably code Caregiver–Child Relationship Problems using these criteria. As part of the field trial, a semistructured interview was developed, based on the Structured Interview for Relational Problems by Slep and Heyman (see Table 16.2).

TABLE 16.1 Proposed Diagnostic Criteria for Caregiver–Child Relational Problem

This category should be coded as positive if there is substantial and sustained dissatisfaction within a caregiver–child relationship associated with significant disturbance in functioning. This problem should be considered only within the child's primary caregiving relationships, which may include relationships with parents, grandparents, or other significant long-term caregivers. The specific dyad should be identified.

Criterion A: Caregiver–child relationship dissatisfaction or distress occurs more days than not during the past month.

Examples may include:

- Pervasive sense of unhappiness with the relationship by either caregiver or child.
- For child, thoughts of running away or fantasies of having another caregiver.
- For caregiver, wishing child were totally different or not born, or thoughts of relinquishing care of the child.

Parental alienation, that is, the child allies himself strongly with one parent (the preferred parent) and rejects a relationship with the other parent (the alienated parent) without cause. Parental alienation usually occurs in the context of high-conflict separation or divorce.

Perceived need of professional help for the relationship.

Criterion B: Considering the developmental needs of the child and the sociocultural context, dissatisfaction is associated with disturbance in at least two major areas of functioning (i.e., behavior, cognition, emotion, or health).

Examples may include:

1. Behavioral Symptoms
   a. Conflict resolution difficulties, such as
      i. persistent and intense conflicts
      ii. pervasive withdrawal or neglect so that resolution is impeded
   b. Lack of positive behaviors (e.g., sharing thoughts, feelings, activities, affection) or support
   c. Failure to socialize child through nonexistent or poorly enforced limits
   d. Poor monitoring of child's activities and child concealment of activities
   e. Caregiver overinvolvement in child's activities
   f. Child's persistent rejection, denigration, and criticism of the alienated parent without cause

2. Cognitive Symptoms
   Pervasive negative attributions of caregiver or child intent, for example
   a. Negative behaviors pervasively attributed to negative personality traits or are perceived to be done voluntarily, intentionally, or with negative intent.
   b. Positive behaviors are pervasively attributed to temporary states or are perceived to be done accidentally, unintentionally, or with hidden negative intentions.

(continued)

TABLE 16.1 Proposed Diagnostic Criteria for Caregiver–Child Relational Problem (*continued*)

3. Emotional Symptoms
   Interactions with or thoughts about the other are frequently marked by intense and persistent levels of
   a. Anger
   b. Contempt
   c. Sadness, or
   d. Apathy
4. Health Symptoms
   a. Exacerbation of medical or psychological symptoms and/or
   b. Significant interference with provision of medical or psychological care

Exclusion criteria: Do not code if caregiver behaviors meet criteria for maltreatment or neglect. Psychological abuse is characterized by one or more verbal or symbolic acts of parenting that are clearly outside of the cultural norms, and are, or have reasonable potential to be, harmful to the child. Caregiver–child relational problems include parenting that is more within the normal range, but has a negative impact on the child. Do not code if criteria for reactive attachment disorder (RAD) are met.

TABLE 16.2 Semistructured Interview for Caregiver–Child Relationship Problem

Caregiver–Child Relational Problem	**Codes 1 = no; 2 = subthreshold; 3 = present**			
Now I'm going to ask you some questions about your relationship with your child. We are going to focus on how you have been getting along over the past month.				
Tell me a bit about your relationship with your child/parent. (What is your relationship like? What kinds of things do you like to do with your child/parent? How do you show affection for your child/parent? How much time do you spend with him/her? How involved do you think parents should be with children? Do you think children should be independent? Can you tell me about that?)				
During the past month, when you disagreed about something with your child/parent…	(1) Behavioral symptoms			
…does it escalate quickly into a fight? If YES: How often does this happen?	a. Marked escalation of negative behavior or affect by both the caregiver and child (e.g. "little" disputes quickly and frequently evolve into heated arguments)	1	2	3
…do you or your child/parent leave the room, withdraw or stop talking so that it's impossible to resolve the problem? If NO: Do the two of you bring up or resolve problems?	b. Pervasive withdrawal so that resolution is impeded. Note: Withdrawal can be either through leaving a discussion before it is resolved or through more pervasive disconnectedness that impedes bringing up or resolving problems.	1	2	3
(For caregiver) How do you discipline your child? For what kinds of things does s/he get punished? How is s/he punished? How long does s/he get punished? What would your child say is the worst or most unpleasant way you have disciplined him/her?	c. (For caregiver) Excessive or inappropriate discipline (not meeting criteria for child abuse)	1	2	3

(continued)

TABLE 16.2 Semistructured Interview for Caregiver–Child Relationship Problem (*continued*)

Caregiver–Child Relational Problem	Codes 1 = no; 2 = subthreshold; 3 = present			
(For child) How does your parent discipline you? For what kinds of things do you get punished? How are you punished? How long do you get punished? What is the worst or most unpleasant way your parent has disciplined you?				
(If unclear) What kinds of limits are set in your home? What happens when those limits are broken?				
(For caregiver) Has your child ever physically threatened or hit you?	d. (For child) Excessive or inappropriate physical altercations or threats toward caregiver.	1	2	3
(For child) Have you ever physically threatened or hit your parent?				
What kinds of rules are there for your child/you? How do you and your child/parent make decisions together? (Does anyone you are close to think you/your parent are overprotective? What about overinvolved?) (IF YES, "Why do they think so?")	(2) Over-involvement: Considering the developmental needs of the child and the socio-cultural context, caregiver-child relationship is overly involved (e.g., excessive pressure to engage in a single activity or interest that is disliked; active interference in a key major life activity; relating in a manner inappropriate for developmental age of the child).	1	2	3
(For caregiver) What kinds of activities does your child participate in? How important is it for you that s/he participates in [ACTIVITY]? Has s/he ever said or acted like she didn't want to do [ACTIVITY] anymore? How did you respond?				
(For child) What kinds of activities do you participate in? How important is it for your parent that you participate in [ACTIVITY]? Do you still want to participate in [ACTIVITY]? How does your parent respond?				
How often do you or your child/parent do positive things for each other (like sharing thoughts or feelings or being affectionate)?	(3) Under-involvement: Considering the developmental needs of the child and the socio-cultural context, caregiver-child relationship exhibits under-involvement (e.g., failure to socialize child through nonexistent or poorly enforced limits, lack of positive or supportive behaviors, failure to adequately monitor a child).	1	2	3
(For caregiver) For what kinds of things does your child need your support? What kind of support does s/he need for his/her schoolwork? What about other activities? What about problems or conflicts? How do you handle this? Is there anything your child wants to do that s/he is not allowed to do? Can you tell me about that?				

(*continued*)

TABLE 16.2 Semistructured Interview for Caregiver–Child Relationship Problem (*continued*)

Caregiver–Child Relational Problem	**Codes 1 = no; 2 = subthreshold; 3 = present**			
(For child) For what kinds of things do you need your parent's support? What kind of support does s/he give for your schoolwork? What about other activities? What about problems or conflicts? Is there anything you want to do that you are not allowed to do? Can you tell me about that?				
(For caregiver) How do you monitor where your child is and what s/he is up to? How do you make sure s/he is safe? How often is s/he alone/away from adult supervision? Where? For how long? (If an older child: How often do you check in with each other? How? What are your rules about this?)				
(For child) Do you need to tell your parent where you are and when you will be back? How often?				
	Cognitive symptoms: Pervasive pattern of negative attributions regarding the other's intentions:			
During the past month, when your child / your parent has done something you didn't like, did you think that s/he did it on purpose or that s/he had negative intentions? (Do you think that it reflects a negative part of his/her personality?)	Negative behaviors pervasively attributed to negative personality traits or are perceived to be done voluntarily, intentionally, or with negative intent.	1	2	3
What about when your child/parent did something nice — what do you think his/her reasons for doing it were?	Positive behaviors are pervasively attributed to temporary states or are perceived to be done accidentally, unintentionally, or with hidden negative intentions.	1	2	3
	Affective symptoms: Interactions with or thoughts about the other are frequently marked by intense and persistent levels of			
During the past month, how often have you felt anger about your child/parent or the relationship?	Anger or contempt	1	2	3
During the past month, how often have you felt sad about your child/parent or the relationship?	Sadness	1	2	3
(If apathy seems present) How would you describe how you feel about your child/parent? (Would you say you don't care one way or the other?)	Apathy	1	2	3
Sum the number of "3" scores from above.	**Total areas scored "3" =**			
If ≥2 areas are scored "3", then Criterion B is met.				
	Criterion A. Relationship dissatisfaction during the past month:			

(*continued*)

TABLE 16.2 Semistructured Interview for Caregiver–Child Relationship Problem (*continued*)

Caregiver–Child Relational Problem	Codes 1 = no; 2 = subthreshold; 3 = present			
In the past month...				
...have you been feeling unhappy about your relationship? (Has it been more than half of the days in the past month?) ...(for child) have you thought about running away or having a different parent? (Has it been more than half of the days in the past month?) ...(for caregiver) have you thought of relinquishing care of your child or wish that they were not yours? (Has it been more than half of the days in the past month?)	(1) Pervasive sense of unhappiness with the relationship, more days than not	1	2	3
Do you think your relationship is in need of professional help?	(2) Perceived need for professional help for the relationship. Also score it if you as a clinician feel there is need for professional help regarding their relationship	1	2	3
Sum the number of "3" scores from above.				
If ≥ 1 area is scored "3," then Criterion A is met.				

Clinicians participating in the field trial range in education from master's level therapists, psychology interns, child psychiatry residents, to psychologists and psychiatrists with several decades of experience. Anecdotally, the trainees have voiced appreciation for the structure of the interview and find it easy to use and instructive to them as to areas that they need to focus on in their treatment. More experienced clinicians have likewise found the more specific criteria useful for elucidating whether there is a caregiver–child relationship problem, instead of, or in addition to, a child with a primary psychiatric diagnosis. Similarly, caregivers and children have expressed appreciation of an interview that focuses on their relationship in depth with specific criteria, and when done by more experienced interviewers, families report the interview is more akin to a regular therapy session rather than a diagnostic evaluation. This field trial should be completed in 2012, and results will be published accordingly.

Caregiver Focused

The initial studies of expressed emotion (EE) used the Camberwell Family Interview (CFI) with the primary relatives living with young adults with schizophrenia following their first hospitalization. The interview was designed to capture the affective climate directed from a relative toward the family member with the disease and is coded based on the verbal content and vocal tone for three dimensions: criticism, hostility, and emotional overinvolvement. Relatives were rated as high in expressed emotion if they had high ratings in any or all of the three categories. High EE as measured by the CFI was shown to be a powerful predictor of relapse with the original studies showing that 76% of patients who returned to households with high EE relatives relapsed, whereas only 28% of patients in low EE households relapsed (Brown, Birley, & Wing, 1972). The length of time to administer and score the CFI makes it a difficult tool to use for larger-scale research projects.

Five-Minute Speech Sample (FMSS)

Magana et al. (1986) developed the FMSS as a brief measure that captures many of the same qualities as the longer CFI. In this procedure, a relative is asked to speak about his or her thoughts and feelings about the target child and describe their relationship in a 5-minute monologue. Similar to the CFI, the FMSS is coded according to verbal content and vocal tone and includes ratings of criticism and emotional overinvolvement. A high EE rating is given for high ratings in at least one category. The majority of the EE literature concerning children and adolescents has utilized the FMSS, and studies have shown that it is a useful measure cross-culturally (McGuire & Earls, 1994; Shimodera et al., 1999; Uehara et al., 1999). However, there may be some limitations for the use of the FMSS when assessing parents of young children. In some studies, this measurement may be a proxy for parenting stress, as opposed to a relationship variable (Baker, Heller, & Henker, 2000).

CLINICIAN ASSESSMENTS AND SELF-REPORT MEASURES FOR CAREGIVER–CHILD RELATIONAL PROBLEMS

Clinician Assessments

There are a number of rating scales that are useful for clinicians to use after assessing a child within his/her family situation. Some of these are useful for assessment of the entire family climate within which the child lives, whereas others are more specific to a caregiver–child dyad.

Global Assessment of Relational Functioning (GARF; Group for the Advancement of Psychiatry Committee on the Family, 1996)

The Group for the Advancement of Psychiatry developed a scale that describes and quantifies the relational context within which patients live and problems occur. The GARF was intended to serve as a device that alerts clinicians to pay attention to the evaluation not only of individuals but also of relational functioning. The GARF is analogous to Axis V of the *Diagnostic and Statistical Manual of Mental Disorders* (*DSM*) GAF scale (Global Assessment of Functioning) that is used to assess individual functioning, and is in fact published as Appendix B of the *DSM Text Revision* (*DSM-IV-TR*). The GARF is a composite derivative of three major dimensionalized constructs: joint problem solving, organization, and emotional climate. The GARF was applied with high reliability by raters with little clinical experience to a sample of family members of patients with bipolar disorder. GARF ratings discriminated between families rated high and low in expressed emotion, with families rated as high in emotional overinvolvement showing the lowest relational functioning scores (Dausch, Miklowitz, & Richards, 1996). It has also been shown to exhibit good interrater reliability in Brazil (Mello, Blay, & Kohn, 2007), as well as good reliability and validity (Denton, Nakonezny, & Burwell, 2010; Stein, Hilsenroth, Pinsker-Aspen, & Primavera, 2009). The GARF can be seen in Table 16.3. This scale is not particularly focused on caregiver–child functioning, but rather on the entire family system. However, it may be useful in clinical settings to alert clinicians to consider the impact of the caregiver–child relationship on the difficulties presenting in the child.

The Parent Infant Relationship Global Assessment Scale (PIR-GAS)

PIR-GAS was developed more specifically to assess the relationship between young children (ages 0–3 years) and their caregiver(s). It is embedded in the Diagnostic Classification Zero to Three (2005), and rates relationships on a scale of 0 to 100, with anchor points for each assessment. This is similar to the GARF, but more pertinent to younger children. It has been translated into over eight languages, used in a number of countries (Oztop & Uslu, 2007; Skovgaard et al., 2007; Stein et al., 2009), and shown to predict problematic behaviors in young children (Skovgaard et al., 2008).

Self-Report Measures

There are several paper/pencil measures that can be administered to either the caregiver or the child. Results from these measures may be helpful for the clinician to assess whether there is a caregiver–child relationship problem, even though there are not yet clinical "cut off" scores for these measures.

Perceived Criticism Measure (PCM)

The PCM is a four-item self-report questionnaire about how critical a person feels another person is toward them and vise versa, along with how upsetting this criticism may be to the person. It uses a 10-point Likert Scale response (Hooley & Parker, 2006) and takes less than 5 minutes to complete and is simple to score. Studies have shown that patient's distress by a relative's criticism is associated positively with worse depression scores and less days well at 1 year follow-up for bipolar patients (Miklowitz, Wisniewski, Miyahara, Otto, & Sachs, 2005), and PCM scores were an important predictor of relapse at 9 months for unipolar depression (Hooley & Teasdale, 1989). The PCM scores have predicted relapse in anxiety, unipolar depression, bipolar depression, OCD, and substance abuse problems (Hooley, Miklowitz, & Beach, 2007).

Parent Bonding Index-Brief Current (PBI-BC)

The PBI-BC is an eight-item scale that is completed by the child. It was developed from the PBI for use by adolescents and measures two dimensions of the caregiver–child relationship as perceived by the child: parental care versus rejection, and control versus autonomy (Klimidis, Minas, & Ata, 1992a). The care/rejection dimensional score has shown negative correlations with psychopathology scores, whereas the control/autonomy dimensional score has positive correlations with psychopathology (Klimidis, Minas, Ata, & Stuart, 1992b). This scale can be seen in Table 16.4.

Parenting Stress Index (PSI)

The PSI is a 101-item measure that a parent fills out marking on a 1 to 5 scale how much they agree or disagree with a statement. There is an optional 19-item stressful life events scale. The PSI captures the level of stress in certain areas of the parent's life that is associated with negative parent–child relationships and behavioral problems in children. It includes two domains: a parent domain, which includes parent characteristics (e.g., level of self-competence) and social areas (e.g., marital quality) and a child domain, which includes child characteristics. The use of the PSI may help identify parents who are over-taxed and thus at risk of not being able to parent effectively and have worse parent–child relationships (whether it be from internal, social, or child factors; Abidin & Wilfong, 1989).

CONCLUSION

In summary, there are a number of methods that can be used to assess the child's relationship with their primary (or other) caregiver. Earlier research showed that assessment of the type of attachment the child has with that caregiver can be helpful in understanding the interactions between caregiver and child. This chapter has introduced a semistructured interview that may be helpful in assessing the proposed new criteria for caregiver–child relationship problems. Care must be taken to carefully assess the child's individual symptoms, the child's symptoms within each important caregiving relationship, and the overall functioning of the primary family when trying to understand fully how to treat a child's difficulties. It is possible for children to have a primary psychiatric diagnosis, for example, major depression or ADHD, as well as a caregiver–child relationship problem. In those situations, it is possible that outcomes of the

TABLE 16.3 Global Assessment of Relational Functioning (GARF) Scale

81–100 Overall: Relational unit is functioning satisfactorily from self-report of participants and from perspectives of observers.
61–80 Overall: Functioning of relational unit is somewhat unsatisfactory. Over a period of time, many but not all difficulties are resolved without complaints.
41–60 Overall: Relational unit has occasional times of satisfying and competent functioning together, but clearly dysfunctional, unsatisfying relationships tend to predominate.
21–40 Overall: Relational unit is obviously and seriously dysfunctional; forms and time periods of satisfactory relating are rare.
1–20 Overall: Relational unit has become too dysfunctional to retain continuity of contact and attachment.
0 Inadequate information.

TABLE 16.4 Parental Bonding Instrument—Brief Current Mother or Female Caregiver Version

Think about how your ***mother or female caregiver*** has treated you ***over the past 3 months***, and mark the appropriate column with an X.

	Never	Sometimes	Usually
1. My mother does not help me as much as I need.			
2. My mother lets me do those things I like doing.			
3. My mother seems emotionally cold to me.			
4. My mother understands my problems and worries.			
5. My mother likes me to make my own decisions.			
6. My mother tries to control everything I do.			
7. My mother treats me like a baby and tries to protect me from everything.			
8. My mother makes me feel better when I am upset.			

primary disorder may be moderated by the presence or absence of a parent–child problem as well. More careful assessment, using agreed upon and reliable criterion for caregiver–child relationship problem, will be an approach for the future to further clarify the role of these key relationships in moderating outcomes for other childhood disorders.

REFERENCES

Abidin, R. R., & Wilfong, E. (1989). Parenting stress and its relationship to child health care. *Children's Health Care, 18*(2), 114–116.

Angold, A., & Costello, E. J. (2000). The Child and Adolescent Psychiatric Assessment (CAPA). *Journal of the American Academy of Child & Adolescent Psychiatry, 39*(1), 39–48.

Baker, B. L., Heller, T. L., & Henker, B. (2000). Expressed emotion, parenting stress, and adjustment in mothers of young children with behavior problems. *Journal of Child Psychology & Psychiatry, 41*(7), 907–915.

Beach, S. R., Wamboldt, M. Z., Kaslow, N. J., Heyman, R. E., & Reiss, D. (2006). Describing relationship problems in DSM-V: Toward better guidance for research and clinical practice. *Journal of Family Psychology, 20*(3), 359–368.

Bor, W., Sanders, M. R., & Markie-Dadds, C. (2002). The effects of the Triple P-Positive Parenting Program on preschool children with co-occurring disruptive behavior and attentional/hyperactive difficulties. *Journal of Abnormal Child Psychology, 30*(6), 571–587.

Brown, G. W., Birley, J. L., & Wing, J. K. (1972). Influence of family life on the course of schizophrenic disorders: A replication. *British Journal of Psychiatry, 121*(562), 241–258.

Dausch, B. M., Miklowitz, D. J., & Richards, J. A. (1996). Global assessment of relational functioning scale (GARF): II. Reliability and validity in a sample of families of bipolar patients. *Family Process, 35*(2), 175–189.

Denton, W. H., Nakonezny, P. A., & Burwell, S. R. (2010). Reliability and validity of the global assessment of relational functioning (GARF) in a psychiatric family therapy clinic. *Journal of Marital & Family Therapy, 36*(3), 376–387.

Ganiban, J. M., Ulbricht, J., Saudino, K. J., Reiss, D., & Neiderhiser, J. M. (2010). Understanding child-based effects on parenting: Temperament as a moderator of genetic and environmental contributions to parenting. *Developmental Psychology, 47*(3), 676–692.

García-Lopez, L. J., Muela, J. M., Espinosa-Fernandez, L., & Diaz-Castela, M. (2009). Exploring the relevance of expressed emotion to the treatment of social anxiety disorder in adolescence. *Journal of Adolescence, 32*(6), 1371–1376.

Group for the Advancement of Psychiatry Committee on the Family. (1996). Global Assessment of Relational Functioning scale (GARF): I. Background and rationale. *Family Process, 35*(2), 155–172.

Hooley, J. M., Miklowitz, D. J., & Beach, S. R. H. (2007). Expressed emotion and the DSM-V. In S. R. H. Beach, M. Z. Wamboldt, N. Kaslow, R. E. Heyman, M. B. First, L. G. Underwood, & D. Reiss (Eds.), *Relational processes and DSM-V: Neuroscience, assessment, prevention and intervention.* Washington, DC: American Psychiatric Association.

Hooley, J. M., & Parker, H. A. (2006). Measuring expressed emotion: An evaluation of the shortcuts. *Journal of Family Psychology, 20*(3), 386–396.

Hooley, J. M., & Teasdale, J. D. (1989). Predictors of relapse in unipolar depressives: Expressed emotion, marital distress, and perceived criticism. *Journal of Abnormal Psychology, 98*(3), 229–235.

Klimidis, S., Minas, I. H., & Ata, A. W. (1992a). The PBI-BC: A brief current form of the Parental Bonding Instrument for adolescent research. *Comprehensive Psychiatry, 33*(6), 374–377.

Klimidis, S., Minas, I. H., Ata, A. W., & Stuart, G. W. (1992b). Construct validation in adolescents of the brief current form of the Parental Bonding Instrument. *Comprehensive Psychiatry, 33*(6), 378–383.

Luijk, M. P., Tharner, A., Bakermans-Kranenburg, M. J., van Ijzendoorn, M. H., Jaddoe, V. W., Hofman, A., Tiemeier, H. (2011). The association between parenting and attachment security is moderated by a polymorphism in the mineralocorticoid receptor gene: Evidence for differential susceptibility. *Biological Psychology, 88*(1), 37–40.

Magana, A. B., Goldstein, J. M., Karno, M., Miklowitz, D. J., Jenkins, J., & Falloon, I. R. (1986). A brief method for assessing expressed emotion in relatives of psychiatric patients. *Psychiatry Research, 17*(3), 203–212.

McGuire, J. B., & Earls, F. (1994). The test-retest stability of the five minute speech sample in parents of disadvantaged, minority children. *Journal of Child Psychology & Psychiatry, 35*(5), 971–979.

Mello, A. F., Blay, S. L., & Kohn, R. (2007). Global Assessment of Relational Functioning Scale (GARF): A validity study in patients with recurrent major depression in Brazil. *Transcultural Psychiatry, 44*(1), 55–64.

Miklowitz, D. J., Axelson, D. A., George, E. L., Taylor, D. O., Schneck, C. D., Sullivan, A. E.,…, Birmaher, B. (2009). Expressed emotion moderates the effects of family-focused treatment for bipolar adolescents. *Journal of American Academy of Child & Adolescence Psychiatry, 48*(6), 643–651.

Miklowitz, D. J., Wisniewski, S. R., Miyahara, S., Otto, M. W., & Sachs, G. S. (2005). Perceived criticism from family members as a predictor of the one-year course of bipolar disorder. *Psychiatry Research, 136*(2–3), 101–111.

Narusyte, J., Neiderhiser, J. M., Andershed, A. K., D'Onofrio, B. M., Reiss, D., Spotts, E.,…, Lichtenstein, P. (2011). Parental criticism and externalizing behavior problems in adolescents: The role of environment and genotype–environment correlation. *Journal of Abnormal Psychology, 120*(2), 365–376.

Oztop, D., & Uslu, R. (2007). Behavioral, interactional and developmental symptomatology in toddlers of depressed mothers: A preliminary clinical study within the DC: 0–3 framework. *Turkish Journal of Pediatrics, 49*(2), 171–178.

Sanders, M. R. (2012). Development, evaluation, and multinational dissemination of the Triple P-Positive Parenting Program. *Annual Review of Clinical Psychology, 8*, 345–378.

Schechter, D. S., Willheim, E., Hinojosa, C., Scholfield-Kleinman, K., Turner, J. B., McCaw, J.,…, Myers, M. M. (2010). Subjective and objective measures of parent–child relationship dysfunction, child separation distress, and joint attention. *Psychiatry, 73*(2), 130–144.

Shimodera, S., Mino, Y., Inoue, S., Izumoto, Y., Kishi, Y., & Tanaka, S. (1999). Validity of a Five-Minute Speech Sample in measuring expressed emotion in the families of patients with schizophrenia in Japan. *Comprehensive Psychiatry, 40*(5), 372–376.

Skovgaard, A. M., Houmann, T., Christiansen, E., Landorph, S., Jorgensen, T., Olsen, E. M.,…, Lichtenberg, A. (2007). The prevalence of mental health problems in children 1(1/2) years of age—the Copenhagen Child Cohort 2000. *Journal of Child Psychology & Psychiatry, 48*(1), 62–70.

Skovgaard, A. M., Olsen, E. M., Christiansen, E., Houmann, T., Landorph, S. L., & Jorgensen, T. (2008). Predictors (0–10 months) of psychopathology at age 11/2 years—a general population study in the Copenhagen Child Cohort CCC 2000. *Journal of Child Psychology & Psychiatry, 49*(5), 553–562.

Sonuga-Barke, E. J., Lasky-Su, J., Neale, B. M., Oades, R., Chen, W., Franke, B.,…, Faraone, S. V. (2008). Does parental expressed emotion moderate genetic effects in ADHD? An exploration using a genome wide association scan. *American Journal of Medical Genetics Neuropsychiatric Genetics, 147B*(8), 1359–1368.

Sroufe, L. A. (1985). Attachment classification from the perspective of infant–caregiver relationships and infant temperament. *Child Development, 56*(1), 1–14.

Stein, M. B., Hilsenroth, M., Pinsker-Aspen, J. H., & Primavera, L. (2009). Validity of *DSM-IV* axis V global assessment of relational functioning scale: A multimethod assessment. *Journal of Nervous & Mental Disease, 197*(1), 50–55.

Uehara, T., Yokoyama, T., Goto, M., Nakano, Y., Kawashima, Y., & Someya, T. (1999). Reliability of the 5-min speech sample for assessing expressed emotion in Japanese patients. *Psychiatry & Clinical Neurosciences, 53*(4), 511–514.

Wamboldt, F. S., Wamboldt, M. Z., Gavin, L. A., Roesler, T. A., & Brugman, S. M. (1995). Parental criticism and treatment outcome in adolescents hospitalized for severe, chronic asthma. *Journal of Psychosomatic Research, 39*(8), 995–1005.

Wamboldt, M. Z., Wamboldt, F. S., Gavin, L., & McTaggart, A. S. (2001). A parent–child relationship scale derived from the child and adolescent psychiatric assessment (CAPA). *Journal of American Academy of Child & Adolescent Psychiatry, 40*(8), 945–953.

Zero to Three. (2005). *Diagnostic Classification of Mental Health and Developmental Disorders of Infancy and Early Childhood, Revised (DC: 0–3R).* Washington, DC: ZERO TO THREE: National Center for Infants, Toddlers and Families.

PART V: CURRENT STATE OF PUBLIC HEALTH RESPONSE AND FUTURE DIRECTIONS

17

Prevention and Reduction of Parent–Child Relationship Difficulties

Ron Prinz

CONTEXTS FOR PARENTING INTERVENTIONS

Parenting is critical to many facets of child development and family well-being. Parenting and parent–child variables are implicated either directly or as contributing factors in a wide variety of child/adolescent outcomes and societal problems, such as childhood aggression and oppositional defiant disorder, conduct disorder and delinquency, attention deficit hyperactivity disorder, inadequate readiness for school, academic failure and school dropout, youth substance abuse, teen pregnancy, youth depression, and child maltreatment (Biglan, Brennan, Foster, & Holder, 2004; Collins, Maccoby, Steinberg, Hetherington, & Bornstein, 2000; Hawkins, Catalano, & Miller, 1992; Jones & Prinz, 2005; Patterson, Reid, & Dishion, 1992). Similarly, parenting also contributes to positive development and outcomes (Farah et al., 2008; Komro, Flay, Biglan, Prinz, & PNRC, 2011).

A large body of evidence in support of parenting interventions has accumulated over multiple decades (Barrett & Ollendick, 2004; Biglan et al., 2004; Donovan & Spence, 2000; Essau, 2003; Lochman & van den Steenhoven, 2002; Petrie, Bunn, & Byrne, 2007; Prinz & Dumas, 2004; Prinz & Jones, 2003; Sutton, 2007). Aspects of parenting strategies and practices associated with positive child adjustment and healthy parent–child relationships are known and form the basis for viable parenting interventions (Hart & Risley, 1995; Prinz, 2009; Taylor & Biglan, 1998).

Parenting interventions are applicable to the domains of prevention (including universal, selected, and indicated prevention), early intervention, and treatment. In practice, evidence-based parenting interventions share more similarities than differences across these domains. Whether in a prevention or treatment context, evidence-based interventions aim to reduce reliance on coercive or ineffective discipline practices, to increase the use of parenting strategies that emphasize frequent positive interactions, to promote a positive learning environment in the home, and to reduce or prevent child adjustment problems.

There are many evidence-based parenting interventions, too numerous to list here. Readers are referred to identification of evidence-supported interventions by respected policy sources such as the National Institute of Clinical Excellence (NICE, 2006), the World Health Organization (World Health Organization, 2009), Blueprints for Violence Prevention (2011), and the California Evidence-Based Clearinghouse for Child Welfare (2011). Without respect to any single intervention, there are several attributes that many of the current evidence-based parenting interventions share in common above and beyond more subtle variations in emphasis and format.

SHARED ATTRIBUTES OF EVIDENCE-BASED PARENTING INTERVENTIONS

Despite some differences in approach, most of the evidence-based parenting interventions in the field nonetheless share several attributes in common. A distillation of common elements is outlined below.

Theoretically Driven

One or more theoretical conceptualizations drive the various evidence-based parenting interventions. Social learning and social-interactional theory speaks to the complex role that family environment plays in shaping child behavior, and has led to strategies for altering problematic patterns of parent–child interaction. A related theoretical approach, applied behavior analysis, provides parents and professionals with practical ways to analyze and modify child behavior. Cognitive-behavioral principles underlie the observation that parental cognitions and beliefs can influence parent–child interactions and in some instances interfere with effective parenting. Many of the practical strategies for specific child-rearing strategies derive from developmental research on parenting in everyday situations. Other theoretical contributions to parenting interventions come from research on attribution theory, developmental psychopathology and resilience, public health, family systems, communication theory, and attachment theory.

Adoption of a Positive Frame

Parenting interventions typically adopt a positive frame in multiple ways. Interventionists take a nonblaming stance toward parents, looking to build on their assets and insights. A key goal is to help parents adopt a positive approach to their children, even when there are serious and challenging behavior problems. Program tasks, such as ones that increase parental recognition of positive child behaviors, are intended to build on modeling of a positive approach by the interventionist who encourages the parent and reinforces parental attempts to achieve parenting goals.

Action Focused

Intervention developers have come to the realization that talking with parents and presenting abstract ideas about family life are not sufficient to be helpful. Evidence-based parenting interventions are action focused. Parents actually do things during the programs, rather than simply engage in conversation with the interventionist. An action focus not only meets parental expectations, it also increases the likelihood of positive behavior changes in children.

Problem-Solving Oriented

Successful parenting interventions are problem-solving focused. That is, parent and interventionist address specific challenges and solving child-related problems. Such an orientation does not preclude building on the assets and strengths of child and family. However, focusing on assets alone does not solve the problems that parents are facing and want to resolve. Parents want to find solutions to challenges they are facing in child-rearing on a regular basis. For example, if a child is prone to explosive tantrums in public places, such as the grocery store or a restaurant, then the parent is looking for effective ways to reduce this stressful problem. Effective parenting interventions assist parents in generating action plans that have a reasonable probability of solving the problem at hand.

Specific Parenting Strategies

Being action focused and problem-solving oriented are necessary but not sufficient for successful parenting intervention. Parents need and want specific, concrete, and practical parenting strategies. Most evidence-based programs offer a menu of previously validated and specific parenting strategies so that parents can find the best fit for the personal preferences to address the particular child issue at hand. Instead of vague platitudes such as "Show your child a lot of love" or "Be consistent," parents benefit more from specific ways to build closer or more affectionate parent–child relationships, to address child-rearing challenges, and to promote positive child development. From specific examples, more general principles can be induced over time so that parents are able to conquer future challenges. For more complex child situations (i.e., beyond the more common and straightforward behavioral challenges), interventions can help parents step by step to develop and implement a set of strategies.

Collaborative Goal Setting

Sometimes the general public and the media have the mistaken impression that parenting programs are about telling parents what to do. The notion of a "parenting class" has the connotation of passive participants (i.e., the parents) receiving instruction in how to parent. In reality, evidence-based parenting programs typically involve collaborative efforts between parent and interventionist. Interventions seem to work best if parents set specific goals for themselves and their children. The professional serves a facilitative role in asking guiding questions and helping the parent to articulate practical and specific goals. The parent's role in this collaborative process is critical. Parenting interventions usually involve identification and honing of specific goals that the parents want to achieve with their children. Attending to parental preferences during goal setting is an important way not only to tailor programming to meet individual family needs but also to reflect variations across cultural groups.

Consultative Rather Than Prescriptive

Building on the emphasis on collaborative goal setting, evidence-based parenting interventions are typically implemented in a consultative rather than prescriptive manner. That is, interventionists try to facilitate the parents' efforts rather than tell them what to do. Interventions provide menu options, answer parents' questions, and use facilitative interactions to gently influence parenting.

PUBLIC HEALTH APPROACH

The Centers for Disease Control and Prevention identified 10 great public health achievements in the United States, including motor vehicle safety, safer workplaces, control of infectious diseases, fewer coronary/stroke deaths, safer and healthier foods, healthier mothers and babies, family planning, fluoridation of drinking water, tobacco use as health hazard, and vaccination. Conspicuously absent from this list is the improvement of parenting, which could also involve the prevention of child maltreatment. The field of parenting intervention is slowly beginning to consider the adoption of a public health approach.

The Center for Global Development identified five core characteristics of successful public health interventions: (a) implemented on a significant scale (e.g., county, state, national, regional, or global); (b) addressed problems of major public health significance; (c) lasted at least 5 consecutive years; (d) proven to be cost-effective; and, (e) documented evidence of a clear and measurable effect on health outcomes. All of these criteria are pertinent to the development of a public health approach to parenting intervention. However, these might not be sufficient; there are additional considerations, noted below, which are specific to the parenting intervention area and which might prove essential to success.

Addressing Multiple Goals

As noted earlier, parenting is central to many areas of healthy and problem development of children and adolescents. A public health approach to improvement of parenting at a population level needs to coalesce around multiple goals with the same parenting intervention. For example, some parenting intervention efforts have focused on prevention of child maltreatment, while others have focused on reducing or preventing child behavioral problems at school entry, and still others on reducing early childhood family risk factors for later problems such as substance abuse or delinquency. In actuality all three of these applications can be served by the same type of parenting intervention. Combining goals addressed by implementation of the same parenting intervention creates efficiencies (cost and otherwise), which makes a population-wide public health approach more viable.

Promoting Broad Reach

By definition, a public health approach to strengthening parenting requires interventions that achieve broad reach. There are several ways to promote reach:

1. The intervention should be readily accessible to parents. This is accomplished mainly by making the intervention program available in many different settings, agencies, and organizations. Traditionally, parenting programs are often offered by one or perhaps two agencies in single settings, such as a mental health center, a school, or a social services agency. To optimize a public health approach, parents need to be able to access parenting and family support in many different venues, including health care centers, community centers, and specific agency centers (mental health, social services).
2. Service workers from several disciplinary backgrounds should deliver the parenting interventions. Parents want to be able to select not only the delivery setting but also the person with whom they feel most comfortable to provide parenting support. The array of workers can be broad and include traditional disciplines, such as psychology, social work, and counseling, as well as nurses and other primary health care staff, parent educators in school settings, child development specialists, and even clergy.
3. Parenting interventions should minimize stigma. If parents perceive that a parenting program stigmatizes them in some manner or is only intended for parents with a serious problem or dysfunctional family, this could be a major barrier to uptake and participation. For example, parents might be reluctant to participate in a prevention program on parenting that is delivered by an organization with "child abuse" in its name. A public health approach to parenting intervention can minimize potential stigma by appealing to all parents, by including content and examples that are universally relevant to all parents (even though some parents might need the intervention more than others), and by messaging via program description and media communications in a way that does not trigger pejorative or restrictive connotations.

Multiple Intensity Levels and Delivery Formats

Some parents need more intensive programming but most do not. If a parenting intervention relies on one intensity level for all families, this strategy is not easily adapted to a public health approach, particularly if the intensity level is relatively high (e.g., 10 contact sessions per family). A more public-health-compatible strategy is to have a range of program intensities varying from one to many contacts, based on family need and parental preference. Similarly, a parenting intervention is more flexible and public-health friendly when it has multiple delivery formats, such as group meetings, individual consultation, home visitation, a self-directed format, and media communication.

EXAMPLE OF A PUBLIC HEALTH APPROACH: THE TRIPLE P SYSTEM

The aforementioned criteria and considerations relevant to the pursuit of a public health approach to parenting intervention are not purely hypothetical. An example of a public-health-oriented approach to parenting and family support is presented here to demonstrate what is attainable and where the field is headed.

Triple P—Positive Parenting Program

A system of parenting interventions called the Triple P—Positive Parenting Program was developed by Sanders and colleagues at the University of Queensland and has evolved based on 30-plus years of research and refinement (Sanders, 1999, 2008, 2012). The broad goal of Triple P is to prevent and reduce severe behavioral, emotional, and developmental problems in children and adolescents by strengthening the quality of parenting in the population. Triple P is a multilevel system involving five levels of parenting intervention on a tiered continuum of increasing strength. To match parental preferences and organizational needs, Triple P is delivered using a wide variety of formats, including individual consultation (brief and extended), small group programming, large parenting seminars, offline and online self-directed modalities, and broad media. The five intensity levels include: Universal Triple P (Level 1) involving media and communications strategies at a community or population level, Selected Triple P (Level 2) involving brief parenting intervention (one to two occasions), Primary Care Triple P (Level 3) involving relatively brief intervention (up to four occasions), including active skills training, Standard Triple P (Level 4) involving more extended intervention to address problems of greater intensity or number, and Enhanced Triple P (Level 5), which augments Level 4 for families with additional risk factors or needs (e.g., family conflict, risk for child maltreatment, childhood obesity, divorcing families).

All of the Triple P interventions are based on a core set of principles for positive parenting: providing a safe and engaging environment, constructing a positive learning environment, employing assertive discipline, adopting realistic expectations, and attending to parental self-care. These principles of positive parenting have been translated into 40 specific and core parenting skills clustering into eight categories: encouraging desirable behavior, teaching new skills and behaviors, managing misbehavior, parent–child relationship enhancement skills, anticipating and planning, self-regulation skills, mood and coping skills, and partner support skills. Triple P implementation makes use of several ways of conveying parenting information and conducting active skills training and support, such as media and other audiovisual depiction of realistic possible solutions to commonly encountered parenting situations (e.g., bedtime, mealtime, behavior in public places), live modeling, rehearsal, professional feedback, and between-session activities.

Over 30+ years but especially in the past 10 years, Triple P has been systematically evaluated in close to 200 published studies, including efficacy and effectiveness randomized trials and involving almost 300 investigators. The evidence base spans development from infancy to adolescence, with accrued findings being strongest for the toddler, preschool, and elementary school ages. Triple P has been shown to be effective in both prevention and treatment contexts, with a variety of families from several countries and cultures, across a wide range of outcomes related to parenting, parental confidence and self-efficacy, parent–child relations, child adjustment, and family functioning.

Every Family Project

The first of two population-based outcomes studies was the Every Family project (Sanders et al., 2008). Using a quasi-experimental design involving 20 catchment areas in Brisbane and Sydney, Every Family targeted parents of all 4- to 7-year-old children. All five levels of the Triple P system were implemented and made broadly available to all parents in 10 of the 20 catchment areas for a 2-year period. Triple P implementation included a media and communication strategy, parenting seminars, individually administered programming, and parenting groups. A total of 375 practitioners delivered Triple P, including physicians, child health nurses, school nurses, mental health services staff, and family intervention specialists. Population-level outcomes were assessed via household telephone surveys of parents. The Triple P catchment areas reflected greater reductions in child behavioral and emotional problems, coercive parenting, and parental depression and stress. This study demonstrated that population-level change in parenting practices and child mental health outcomes can be achieved through a public health model like Triple P.

U.S. Triple P System Population Trial

The U.S. Triple P System Population Trial tested the proposition that dissemination of evidence-based parenting and family support community-wide would reduce population indicators related to child maltreatment (Prinz, Sanders, Shapiro, Whitaker, & Lutzker, 2009). All levels of the Triple P system, including media strategies, were implemented in a controlled trial.

The research strategy for this population trial was a place randomization design, with county as the unit of randomization. This trial is apparently the only place randomization study, to date, on the prevention of child maltreatment. The strategy involved random assignment of counties to intervention versus no intervention, the training the existing multidisciplinary workforce of service-delivery providers to create many access points for parents, and then determination of the impact on prevalence indicators related to child maltreatment. A total of 18 mid-size counties with populations between 50,000 and 175,000 in South Carolina were included in the study. The counties were picked geographically rather than recruited in any manner, and none had any prior exposure to Triple P. After matching for poverty rates, child maltreatment rates, and population size, the 18 counties were randomly assigned to either Triple P dissemination or usual-services comparison.

During the population trial, over 600 service-delivery providers located in the nine Triple P (intervention) counties received professional Triple P training. All of the individuals receiving Triple P training were members of the existing workforce that included, preschool and day care directors, public-health center staff, personnel in elementary schools (e.g., counsellors, parent educators, kindergarten teachers), workers in the social service and mental health systems, staff in various community and nongovernmental organizations serving families, and clergy with counseling backgrounds. Several media strategies constituting Universal (Level 1) Triple P were initiated and maintained throughout the study, making use of radio, local newspapers, newsletters at schools, mass mailings to family households, presence at community events, and website information, to convey positive parenting information, provide modeling of parental success stories, normalize parenting support, and empower parents to solve child-rearing issues.

All professionals who received Triple P training were followed longitudinally. Based on data provided by these program-delivery staff, it was determined that approximately 13% of the 85,000 households with one or more children under 8 years of age participated in face-to-face delivery (i.e., Levels 2–5) Triple P in the Triple P counties.

For the purpose of examining impact on the prevention of child maltreatment, the population of interest was all children from birth to age 8 years. Three indicators for the population trial were derived from three separate reporting systems: (a) child out-of-home placements reported by the foster care system; (b) hospital-treated child maltreatment injuries (emergency room or inpatient hospitalization) reported by the health care system; and, (c) founded child maltreatment cases reported by the child protective services system. Preliminary analyses determined that the two sets of counties were comparable on all three indicators prior to formal initiation of the population trial. That is, none of the three indicators produced significant baseline differences between the two sets of counties or a significant county-set by time interaction for the 5-year prestudy period, verifying that preexisting baseline differences or diverging trends could not account for the observed outcomes.

The findings for all three population indicators supported the hypothesis that community-wide implementation of the Triple P system positively impacted the problem of child maltreatment. Controlling for baseline and after 2½ years of Triple P programming, the result was significantly fewer out-of-home placements (foster care), hospital-treated maltreatment injuries, and founded child maltreatment cases in the nine Triple P counties compared with the nine control counties.

The results of this population trial demonstrated that a public-health approach to parenting intervention, in the form of the multilevel Triple P system, can favorably alter rates of foster care placements and hospital-treated injuries from child maltreatment. These promising findings on prevalence reduction for child maltreatment indicators need to be interpreted in light of the many controlled outcome studies showing reliable effects of Triple P assessed at the family level (e.g., reduced reliance on coercive parenting practices, improved child functioning; Nowak & Heinrichs, 2008; Sanders, 2012). Collectively, all of the Triple P studies support its viability as a population-based approach (a) to the prevention of child maltreatment that includes reduction of potentially detrimental parenting practices that do not necessarily get picked up by the child protective services system, and (b) to the promotion of effective parenting more generally to impact child development in beneficial ways.

CONCLUSION

Parenting is a critical part of child development and major contributor to many adverse and positive outcomes affecting individuals and society. This chapter outlined the rationale and elements of a public health approach to intervention aimed at parenting and the reduction or prevention of parent–child difficulties. A public health approach to parenting intervention, as illustrated by the Triple P system, is a departure from the traditional work in this area but nonetheless builds on the high-quality research by many parenting intervention experts contributing over a 50-year period. Triple P demonstrated the feasibility and potential of such a strategy but also represents a paradigm shift in how policy makers and community leaders think about the improvement of parenting population-wide for the well-being of children and society.

REFERENCES

Barrett, P. M., & Ollendick, T. H. (Eds.). (2004). *Handbook of interventions that work with children and adolescents: Prevention and treatment*. London, UK: Wiley.

Biglan, A., Brennan, P. A., Foster, S. L., & Holder, H. D. (2004). *Helping adolescents at risk: Prevention of multiple problem behaviors*. New York, NY: Guilford Press.

Blueprints for Violence Prevention. (2011). Retrieved from www.colorado.edu/cspv/blueprints

California Evidence-Based Clearinghouse for Child Welfare. (2011). Retrieved from www.cebc4cw.org

Collins, W. A., Maccoby, E. E., Steinberg, L., Hetherington, E. M., & Bornstein, M. H. (2000). Contemporary research on parenting: The case for nature and nurture. *American Psychologist, 55*, 218–232.

Donovan, C. L., & Spence, S. H. (2000). Prevention of childhood anxiety disorders. *Clinical Psychology Review, 20*, 509–531.

Essau, C. A. (Ed.). (2003). *Conduct and oppositional defiant disorders: Epidemiology, risk factors, and treatment*. Mahwah, NJ: Lawrence Erlbaum.

Farah, M. J., Betancourt, L., Shera, D. M., Savage, J. H., Giannetta, J. M., Brodsky, N. L.,..., Hurt, H. (2008). Environmental stimulation, parental nurturance and cognitive development in humans. *Developmental Science, 11*(5), 793–801.

Hart, B., & Risley, T. R. (1995). *Meaningful differences in the everyday experience of young American children*. Baltimore, MD: Paul H. Brookes.

Hawkins, J. D., Catalano, R. F., & Miller, J. Y. (1992). Risk and protective factors for alcohol and other drug problems in adolescence and early adulthood: Implications for substance abuse prevention. *Psychological Bulletin, 112*, 64–105.

Jones, T. L., & Prinz, R. J. (2005). Potential roles of parental self-efficacy in parent and child adjustment: A review. *Clinical Psychology Review, 25*(3), 341–363.

Komro, K. A., Flay, B. R., Biglan, A., Prinz, R. J., & PNRC. (2011). Creating nurturing environments: A science-based framework for promoting child health and development within high-poverty neighborhoods. *Cliical Child and Family Psychology Review, 14*, 111–134.

Lochman, J. E., & van den Steenhoven, A. (2002). Family-based approaches to substance abuse prevention. *Journal of Primary Prevention, 23*, 49–114.

NICE. (2006). *Parent-training/education programmes in the management of children with conduct disorders*. London, UK: National Institute of Clinical Excellence.

Nowak, C., & Heinrichs, N. (2008). A comprehensive meta-analysis of Triple P-Positive Parenting Program using hierarchical linear modeling: Effectiveness and moderating variables. *Clinical Child and Family Psychology Review, 11*(3), 114–144.

Patterson, G. R., Reid, J. B., & Dishion, T. J. (1992). *Antisocial boys*. Eugene, OR: Castalia.
Petrie, J., Bunn, F., & Byrne, G. (2007). Parenting programmes for preventing tobacco, alcohol or drug misuse in children under 18: A systematic review. *Health Education Research, 22*, 177–191.
Prinz, R. J. (2009). Behavioral parent training. In H. Reis & S. Sprecher (Eds.), *Encyclopedia of human relationships* (pp. 154–158). Thousand Oaks, CA: Sage.
Prinz, R. J., & Dumas, J. E. (2004). Prevention of oppositional defiant disorder and conduct disorder in children and adolescents. In P. M. Barrett & T. H. Ollendick (Eds.), *Handbook of interventions that work with children and adolescents* (pp. 475–488). Chichester, UK: Wiley.
Prinz, R. J., & Jones, T. L. (2003). Family-based interventions. In C. A. Essau (Ed.), *Conduct and oppositional defiant disorders: Epidemiology, risk factors, and treatment* (pp. 279–298). Mahwah, NJ: Lawrence Erlbaum.
Prinz, R. J., Sanders, M. R., Shapiro, C. J., Whitaker, D. J., & Lutzker, J. R. (2009). Population-based prevention of child maltreatment: The U.S. triple P system population trial. *Prevention Science, 10*(1), 1–12.
Sanders, M. R. (1999). Triple P-Positive Parenting Program: Towards an empirically validated multilevel parenting and family support strategy for the prevention of behavior and emotional problems in children. *Clinical Child and Family Psychology Review, 2*(2), 71–90.
Sanders, M. R. (2008). Triple P-Positive Parenting Program as a public health approach to strengthening parenting. *Journal of Family Psychology, 22*(4), 506–517.
Sanders, M. R. (2012). Development, evaluation, and multinational dissemination of the Triple P-Positive Parenting Program. *Annual Review of Clinical Psychology, 8*, 11.11–11.35.
Sanders, M. R., Ralph, A., Sofronoff, K., Gardiner, P., Thompson, R., Dwyer, S., & Bidwell, K. (2008). Every family: A population approach to reducing behavioral and emotional problems in children making the transition to school. *The Journal of Primary Prevention, 29*(3), 197–222.
Sutton, J. M. (2007). Prevention of depression in youth: A qualitative review and future suggestions. *Clinical Psychology Review, 27*, 552–571.
Taylor, T. K., & Biglan, A. (1998). Behavioral family interventions: A review for clinicians and policymakers. *Cliical Child and Family Psychology Review, 1*, 4–60.
World Health Organization. (2009). *Preventing violence through the development of safe, stable and nurturing relationships between children and their parents and caregivers*. Geneva, Switzerland: Author.

18

Current State of the Global Public Health Response to Child Maltreatment and Intimate Partner Violence

Christopher Mikton and Alexander Butchart

It is only in the past 30 years that public health has begun to address child maltreatment and intimate partner violence and only in the past 15 years has it done so at the global level (Dahlberg & Mercy, 2009). This is a much shorter period of time than public health has been tackling other health problems of comparable magnitude and with similarly severe life-long consequences. The issues of definition, classification, and measurement addressed in this book have played a prominent part in the global public health response from the start.

The global public health response to interpersonal violence began in earnest in the mid-1990s. In 1996, the World Health Assembly adopted Resolution WHO49.25, which declared violence "a leading worldwide public health problem" and requested that the World Health Organization (WHO) initiate public health activities to (a) document and characterize the burden of violence, (b) assess the effectiveness of programs, with particular attention to women and children and community-based initiatives, and (c) promote activities to tackle the problem at the international and national levels. WHO's initial response to this resolution was to create the Department of Violence and Injury Prevention and Disability and to publish the *World Report on Violence and Health* (2002).

The case for the public health sector addressing interpersonal violence, including child maltreatment and intimate partner violence, rests on at least four arguments (Prothrow-Stith, 2004; WHO, 2002). First, the significant amount of time health care professionals dedicate to caring for victims and perpetrators of violence has made them familiar with the problem and has led many, particularly in emergency departments, to mobilize to address it. The information, resources, and infrastructures the health care sector has at its disposal are an important asset for research and prevention work. Second, the magnitude of the problem and its potentially severe life-long consequences and high costs to individuals and wider society call for population-level interventions typical of the public health approach. For instance, WHO estimates that between a quarter and a half of children are victims of child physical abuse and 20% of girls and 5% to 10% of boys are victims of child sexual abuse (WHO, 2010a). In a WHO multi-country study, rates of physical and/or sexual violence against women by an intimate partner ranged from 15% in Japan to approximately 70% in Ethiopia and Peru (WHO, 2005a). Third, the criminal justice approach, the other main approach to addressing violence, has traditionally been more geared toward violence that occurs between male youths and adults in the street and other public places—which makes up the bulk of homicides in most countries—than toward violence occurring in private settings, such as child maltreatment, intimate partner violence, and elder abuse—which makes up the largest share of nonfatal violence. Fourth, evidence is beginning to accumulate that a science-based public health approach is effective at preventing interpersonal violence, including child maltreatment and intimate partner violence (McMillan et al., 2009; WHO, 2009, 2010c).

The "global public health response" described in this chapter will be largely confined to WHO's response to child maltreatment and intimate partner violence. WHO is the directing and coordinating authority for global health and public health within the United Nations (UN) system. Where relevant, the chapter will also mention some of the other major global initiatives to address these forms of violence to which WHO has contributed. However, before describing WHO's response, the strategy developed to respond to these two forms of violence by WHO's Prevention of Violence Unit will be presented. The strategy emphasizes the primary prevention of child maltreatment and intimate partner violence: because of the high prevalence and serious consequences of these forms of violence, even the best-resourced countries can only provide quality secondary and tertiary services to a fraction of victims. The strategy focuses in particular on low- and middle-income countries where over 80% of the world's population lives, where rates of these forms of violence often appear to be higher (Reza, Breiding, Mercy, Blanton, & Mthethwa, 2009; Runyan, 2008; Runyan & Eckenrode, 2004; WHO, 2005a), and where resources to address them are scarce. After describing WHO's response, this chapter will briefly evaluate the state of the wider global public health response before concluding by exploring the implications of the issues of definition, classification, and measurement addressed in this book for the global public health response.

THE STRATEGY

WHO's strategy presented here was first formulated at the time the *World Report on Violence and Health* (2002) was published, drawing on its recommendations, and is closely related to WHO's core functions. This strategy has evolved over time, drawing on different sources such as Morris, Gogill, Uavy, & Group (2008), Shiffman and Smith (2007), and work currently under way to assess the resources and readiness of countries to implement large-scale child maltreatment prevention programs (Mikton et al., 2011). The centerpiece and ultimate

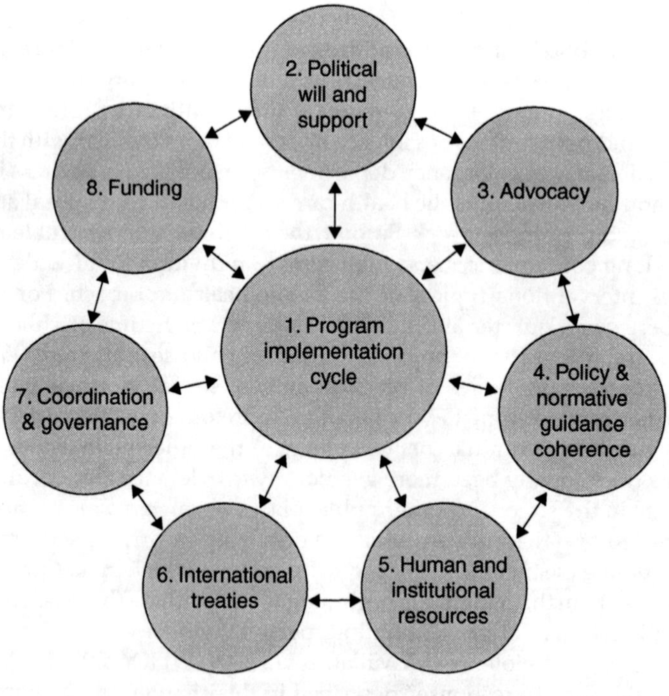

FIGURE 18.1 Strategy for World Health Organization's global response to child maltreatment and intimate partner violence.

aim of the strategy is to implement on a large-scale evidence-based program to prevent child maltreatment and intimate partner violence and mitigate their consequences, nationally or even regionally. This strategy is made up of the following eight components with the program implementation cycle component at its heart (Figure 18.1).

1. **Implement effective population-level prevention programs based on a four-step cycle:** This four-step cycle aims to generate scientific knowledge and data about child maltreatment and intimate partner violence and how to prevent them and then implement effective programs on a large scale (WHO, 2002).

   Step 1: Defining the problem by describing its nature, the characteristics of those affected, its magnitude, distribution, and consequences through the systematic collection of data. It is in this step that issues of definition, classification, and measurement of child maltreatment and intimate partner violence arise.

   Step 2: Investigating why violence occurs by conducting research into risk and protective factors for child maltreatment and intimate partner and sexual violence, causes and correlates, and factors that might be modifiable through intervention.

   Step 3: Exploring ways to prevent violence, drawing on the information from Steps 1 and 2, by designing, implementing, and monitoring programs and rigorously evaluating them using randomized controlled or high-quality quasi-experimental research designs.

   Step 4: Scaling up those programs that have been proven effective and widely disseminating information on the effectiveness of the programs. This step also includes adapting programs to local contexts and rigorously reevaluating them and determining the cost and cost-effectiveness of the programs. The cycle begins again as new data and knowledge are produced, leading to more effective and cost-effective programs.

Key characteristics of the public health approach underlying the program implementation cycle are that it emphasizes primary prevention; that it is population-based, interdisciplinary, and adopts a life-course perspective; and that it is based on the ecological model which considers that violence, rather than being the result of any single factor, is the outcome of multiple risk factors and causes, interacting at four levels of a nested hierarchy (individual, close relationship/family, community, and wider society). The ecological model is used to organize risk factors in Step 2 and guide interventions in Steps 3 and 4 (WHO, 2002). An additional important characteristic of the public health approach is that it is multisectoral; cooperative efforts from such diverse sectors as health, education, social welfare, and criminal justice are often necessary to solve what are usually assumed to be purely "medical" or "criminal" problems.

While at the heart of the strategy, the program implementation cycle alone is unlikely to achieve the aim of preventing child maltreatment and intimate partner violence through a population-level program. Other conditions also have to be met. These make up the other seven components of the WHO's strategy for a global response to child maltreatment and intimate partner violence.

2. **Mobilize political will and support:** This component refers to the existence of political leaders or actors who express sustained concern for the issue, enact measures to address it in a proactive way, and mobilize resources to tackle it that are commensurate with its severity (Shiffman & Smith, 2007). These political leaders or actors include organizations and agencies such as UN agencies, international and regional development banks, bilateral aid agencies, international nongovernmental agencies, major universities and research centers, and private foundations.
3. **Intensify advocacy:** Advocacy denotes activities, including effective communications strategies, designed to place child maltreatment and intimate partner violence prevention high on the political, health, and development agenda; foster political will; increase

financial and other resources on a sustainable basis; and hold authorities accountable to ensure that pledges are fulfilled and results achieved (WHO, 2006a).

4. **Ensure coherence in policy and normative guidance:** The prevention of child maltreatment and intimate partner violence at the international level, involves numerous different sectors and organizations. Each of these sectors—for example, criminal justice, human rights, public health, development sectors—brings its own perspectives, policy recommendations, and normative guidance for addressing the problem. Without a measure of convergence, such diversity can result in ineffective action.
5. **Develop human and institutional resources:** While much of capacity building must take place at country level, international actors can make an important contribution to building up human and institutional resources. For instance, they can help develop training materials and support universities and research institutions in high-income countries who offer training in child maltreatment and intimate partner violence to focus more on low- and middle-income countries.
6. **Promote and monitor adherence to international and regional treatises, conventions, and consensus-building documents relevant to child maltreatment:** These aim to set standards for national legislation and establish norms and limits for behavior relevant to child maltreatment and intimate partner violence (WHO, 2002).
7. **Ensure effective international coordination and governance:** An effective global response to child maltreatment and intimate partner violence is likely to be enhanced by the existence of a global governance or coordinating body mandated to act at the international level. Its role might include, for instance, leading and coordinating, setting priorities, devising long-term plans, harnessing other global change processes (e.g., the millennium development goals), and anticipating future trends.
8. **Raise funds:** This component refers to the money raised, pooled, and invested by the international organizations, agencies, and other actors to address child maltreatment and intimate partner violence.

As indicated in Figure 18.1, there are complex two-way interactions between the program implementation cycle and the other components of the strategy. For instance, mobilizing political will and support, advocating for change, and raising funds for child maltreatment and intimate partner prevention—Components 2, 3, and 8—will require that the severity of the problem has been convincingly demonstrated by accurately describing its magnitude and consequences and that effective and cost-effective interventions are available to address it—parts of Component 1. At the same time, conducting the multicountry studies necessary to demonstrate the severity of these problems and the large outcome evaluations to prove that prevention programs are effective and cost-effective requires some preexisting political will and support, advocacy efforts, and funds at the global level. Furthermore, as suggested in Figure 18.1, components of this strategy overlap to varying extents and influence and depend on each other in complex ways.

WHO'S GLOBAL PUBLIC HEALTH RESPONSE TO CHILD MALTREATMENT AND INTIMATE PARTNER VIOLENCE

A fundamental part of WHO's global response to child maltreatment and intimate partner violence are several publications that constitute important tools with which to implement the different components of its strategy.

The most important of these is the *World Report on Violence and Health* (2002), on which WHO's violence prevention activities are based, and which includes chapters on child maltreatment and intimate partner violence structured according to the four steps of the program implementation cycle. The *World Report* describes the magnitude and impact of these and all other main types of violence throughout the world; identifies key risk factors; gives an account of the types of intervention and policy responses that have been tried and summarizes what is known about their effectiveness; and makes recommendations for action at local, national, and international levels. Its goals are to raise awareness about the problem of violence globally, and to make the case that violence is preventable and that public health has a crucial role to play in addressing its causes and consequences. The *World Report on Violence and Health* (2002) was the result of a broad-based consultative process with over 200 academics, public health experts, and advocates around the world.

In 2006, WHO and the International Society for the Prevention of Child Abuse and Neglect (ISPCAN) published *Preventing Child Maltreatment: A Guide to Taking Action and Generating Evidence*. This is a practical guide, based on the four steps of the program implementation cycle, to help countries to prevent child maltreatment. Directed at professionals working in governments, research institutes, and nongovernmental organizations (NGOs), it provides advice on how to measure the extent of child maltreatment and its consequences and how to design, implement, and evaluate prevention programs.

To help address intimate partner and sexual violence, WHO, in partnership with the London School of Hygiene and Tropical Medicine and with input from a globally representative panel of experts, published *Preventing Intimate Partner and Sexual Violence Against Women: Taking Action and Generating Evidence* in 2010. This manual, structured according to the four steps of the program implementation cycle, aims to provide sufficient information for policy makers, program planners, and funding bodies in public health and related sectors to develop evidence-based programs and policies.

The *UN Secretary-General's Study on Violence Against Children* was published in 2006, based upon technical input from three lead UN agencies (Office for the High Commissioner for Human Rights, UNICEF, and WHO). Unique in integrating a human rights perspective with public health tools for prevention and victim services, it provides an in-depth global picture of violence against children in five settings (the home and family, institutions, schools, workplace, and the community). Also in 2006, the *UN Secretary-General's In-Depth Study on All Forms of Violence Against Women* was released. This study aims to highlight the persistence and unacceptability of all forms of violence against women, strengthen the political commitment to prevent them; and identify ways to ensure more sustained and effective implementation of state obligations to address them, and to increase state accountability. WHO's response to child maltreatment and intimate partner violence, in terms of the eight-component strategy outlined above, has been as follows:

1. *Program implementation cycle:* WHO has contributed to the program implementation cycle for child maltreatment and intimate partner violence prevention through its own activities and by contributing to those of partners.

The *World Report on Violence and Health* (2002), *Preventing Child Maltreatment: A Guide to Taking Action and Generating Evidence* (2006b), *Preventing Intimate Partner and Sexual Violence Against Women: Taking Action and Generating Evidence* (2010c), and the *WHO Multi-Country Study on Women's Health and Domestic Violence Against Women* (2005a) put forward what have become authoritative definitions of violence, child maltreatment, and intimate partner violence. The latter three publications address issues of operationalization of definitions at some length.

WHO, in collaboration with UNICEF, has been working on developing a small number of data collection instruments and indicators for violence against children that are scientifically credible and appropriate for low-resource settings.

The WHO current Global Burden of Disease estimates include measures of mortality and morbidity broken down by sex and age groups that are relevant to child maltreatment and intimate partner violence (WHO, 2008a). An update to these estimates in late 2012 will provide new estimates based on a systematic review of all existing data on child maltreatment and intimate partner, including estimates of prevalence and of population attributable risk for a number of diseases and other outcomes related to these forms of violence.

WHO has been involved in carrying out studies on Adverse Childhood Experiences and their long-term consequences in the Philippines (Ramiro, Madrid, & Brown, 2010), the Former Yugoslav Republic of Macedonia, and Lithuania. WHO has also been contributing to the Clinton Global Initiative's Together for Girls, which is tackling sexual violence with a focus on girls using three linked strategies: national surveys and the use of data to inform and mobilize government leaders, NGOs, civil society, and donors; facilitating the development and implementation of a policies and programs; and strengthening communications and public awareness. National surveys have been completed in Swaziland (Reza et al., 2009), Kenya, Tanzania, and Zimbabwe, and are planned in several countries in Africa and Southeast Asia.

In 2005, WHO's Department of Reproductive Health and Research published its landmark study the *WHO Multi-Country Study on Women's Health and Domestic Violence Against Women* documenting the high prevalence of violence against women by their intimate partners in many low- and middle-income countries (WHO, 2005a). The main report presented evidence collected from over 24,000 women in 15 sites across 10 countries: Bangladesh, Brazil, Ethiopia, Japan, Peru, Namibia, Samoa, Serbia and Montenegro, Thailand, and the United Republic of Tanzania. It also issued 15 recommendations to strengthen national commitment and action on violence against women. The methodology used in the multi-country study has since been used to conduct studies in the Maldives, New Zealand, Samoa, the Solomon Islands (SPC, 2009), and Kiribati (SPC, 2010) and a study is under way in Vietnam. Alongside the study, WHO has also published *Researching Violence Against Women: A Practical Guide for Researchers and Activists* (2005b) and *Putting Women First: Ethical and Safety Recommendations for Research on Domestic Violence Against Women* (2001).

Relevant to Step 4 of the program implementation cycle is the tool WHO and U.S. Centers for Disease Control and Prevention (CDC) released to help countries calculate the costs of violence, the *Manual for Estimating the Economic Cost of Injuries Due to Interpersonal and Self-Directed Violence* (2008b). It provides a standardized set of recommendations to estimate the direct and indirect economic costs of interpersonal and self-directed violence—including child maltreatment and intimate partner violence. The manual has been implemented in a number of East African Countries including Kenya and Uganda.

Several publications in the WHO series *Violence Prevention: The Evidence* (2009), which summarized the evidence for the effectiveness of seven main strategies for violence prevention, address the effectiveness of child maltreatment and intimate partner prevention programs—in particular Preventing Violence Through the Development of Safe, Stable, and Nurturing Relationships Between Children and Their Caregivers; Promoting Gender Equality to Prevent Violence Against Women; and Changing Cultural Norms That Support Violence. As has been repeatedly highlighted in these publications and other reviews of the evidence for the effectiveness of child maltreatment and intimate partner prevention programs produced by WHO (Mikton & Burchart, 2009; WHO, 2002, 2010c), outcome evaluations of child maltreatment and intimate partner violence prevention programs in, low- and middle-income countries have been, to date, exceedingly rare.

To fill this gap, WHO's Prevention of Violence unit and other partners have been supporting the development and evaluation of a number of prevention programs. The Nucleo de Estudos dâ Violencia (NEV) at the University of Sao Paulo is developing and evaluating a program to prevent child maltreatment by targeting young mothers in socially deprived neighborhoods in Brazil. It is made up of both a home visiting component, delivered by trained para-professionals, and a center-based group component. In Malawi and South Africa, WHO is in the process of conducting studies on the acceptability and feasibility of implementing several different child maltreatment programs. In the Philippines, WHO and local partners are exploring the possibility of population-level implementation and evaluation of a parenting education program.

In addition, WHO's Department of Reproductive Health and Research is initiating a study on addressing violence against women among those attending antenatal care in Mozambique and South Africa. The Department of Reproductive Health and Research is also currently in the process of developing guidelines for the health care response to intimate partner and sexual violence. These are based on expert consultations as well as available evidence compiled from systematic reviews of evaluated intervention studies. It also recently published *Addressing Violence Against Women and HIV/AIDS: What Works?* (2010b).

WHO has been engaged in evaluating the resources and readiness of countries to implement population-level child maltreatment prevention programs with a view to increasing them. Initial assessments of resources and readiness were conducted in Mozambique, Malawi, the Philippines, and South Africa. Since 2009, WHO has been developing, testing, and implementing a more rigorous method, based on an instrument with sound psychometric properties, to assess child maltreatment prevention resources and readiness in low- and middle-income countries. This method, which assesses child maltreatment prevention readiness along 10 dimensions, has been implemented in Brazil, China, Malaysia, the former Yugoslav Republic of Macedonia, Saudi Arabia, and South Africa.

2. *Political will and support:* Some 10 resolutions of the World Health Assembly, WHO's Executive Board, and WHO Regional Committees have provided political support for violence prevention, often with a specific focus on child maltreatment and intimate partner violence (WHO, 2011a). The first of these was the 1996 World Health Assembly Resolution WHO49.25 described at the beginning of this chapter.

Since the early 1990s, the UN has appointed a series of Special Representatives and Rapporteurs on topics directly relevant to child maltreatment and intimate partner violence. For instance, a Special Rapporteur on Violence Against Women was appointed in 1994 for the first time. The Special Rapporteur collects and analyzes data on violence against women in order to recommend measures to be taken at the international, regional, and national levels. In 2009, a Special Representative on Violence Against Children was appointed to implement the recommendations of the Secretary-General's Study on Violence Against Children and more recently, in 2010, a Special Representative on Sexual Violence in Conflicts was appointed.

3. *Advocacy:* The first component of WHO's advocacy strategy is the Global Campaign for the Prevention of Violence, established in 2002, shortly after the launch of the *World report on Violence and Health* (2002). Central to this campaign are the Milestones of a Global Campaign for Violence Prevention meeting series. Meetings take place every 2 years, convene between 200 and 300 participants and take stock of progress in the field and make plans for the future. The 2011 Fifth Milestones Meeting's theme was *Joining forces—Empowering prevention* and will partly focus on highlighting the links between child maltreatment, youth violence, and intimate partner and sexual violence.

The second component of WHO's advocacy strategy is the Violence Prevention Alliance (VPA). The VPA is a network of some 50 international, governmental, NGO, and research organizations and private foundations committed to preventing interpersonal violence using a public health and multisectoral approach. VPA participants include, for instance, the U.S. CDC, the United Nations Development Programme, UNICEF, the United Nations Office on Drugs and Crime, and the World Bank. The majority of participant organizations focus either partly or wholly on the prevention of child maltreatment and/or intimate partner violence.

The network of officially appointed focal persons for injury and violence prevention in over 100 Ministries of Health in the world is the third component of the advocacy strategy. Their role is to advocate for increased efforts to address violence and injury prevention—including child maltreatment and intimate partner violence prevention—and to coordinate and facilitate national efforts (see WHO, 2007).

4. *Policy and Normative Guidance Coherence:* The publication *Developing Policies to Prevent Injuries and Violence: Guidelines for Policy Makers and Planners* (WHO, 2006c) is intended to enhance policy coherence by assisting those wishing to develop national policies to prevent injuries and violence—including child maltreatment and intimate partner violence—based on a public health approach.

WHO has issued its own normative guidance for a public health response to child maltreatment and intimate partner violence in the widely disseminated *Preventing Child Maltreatment: A Guide to Taking Action and Generating Evidence* and *Preventing Intimate Partner and Sexual Violence Against Women: Taking Action and Generating Evidence*. These guides aim to assist governments, NGOs, and international agencies to develop sound programs and policies to address these forms of violence drawing on the evidence base. For example, Chapter 4 of *Preventing Intimate Partner and Sexual Violence Against Women: Taking Action and Generating Evidence* (WHO, 2010c) presents a six-step framework for implementing prevention policies and programs.

While WHO is committed to the public health approach in its work on child maltreatment and intimate partner violence prevention, it sees this approach as overlapping with, and largely complementary to, other approaches such as the human rights and criminal justice approaches and the gender perspective on which other international agencies base their work.

5. *Human and institutional resources:* WHO's main contribution to developing human and institutional resources has occurred through a comprehensive violence and injury capacity development program. In the areas of human resources, WHO has identified training and skills development as two priority needs. To address training, WHO has collaborated with a global network of experts to develop a modular violence and injury prevention and control curriculum, applicable for a wide variety of settings, known as TEACH-Violence and Injury Prevention (VIP; WHO, 2011c). The latest edition covers both child maltreatment and intimate partner violence. TEACH-VIP has been disseminated worldwide and has been incorporated into the curriculum of many schools of public health. TEACH-VIP e-learning is a self-administered, self-paced online training resource that has been adapted from TEACH-VIP. WHO also hosts a series of webinars addressing violence prevention topics. Finally, WHO has developed short courses to be delivered over 3 or 4 days on child maltreatment and intimate partner violence prevention, complete with presentations, detailed facilitators' notes, student handouts, etc. To address skills development, WHO runs a global mentoring program for violence and injury prevention known as MENTOR-VIP. It aims to provide a low-cost model for mentoring and, therefore, mentoring takes place primarily online and by phone.

To strengthen institutional resources to address violence prevention, WHO created in 2000 the Department of Violence and Injury Prevention and disability and shortly afterwards, the Prevention of Violence Unit within it. The department has a network of violence and injury prevention advisers in each of the six main regions of the world. Child maltreatment and intimate partner violence have been priorities of the Prevention of Violence Unit from the start. The Departments of Gender, Women, and Health and of Reproductive Health and Research, starting in the mid-1990s recognized the need for sound data on violence against women and subsequently initiated the *WHO Multi-Country Study on Women's Health and Domestic Violence Against Women* (WHO, 2005a). These departments have played a key role both within WHO and outside of it in establishing violence against women as a public health issue and pushing it higher up the health agenda.

To develop networks and partnerships, WHO's Department of Violence and Injury Prevention and Disability has established some 20 official WHO Collaborating Centres and leads the VPA, described above. These 20 WHO Collaborating Centers, many of which focus on the prevention of child maltreatment and intimate partner violence, are research institutes and university departments that are designated to provide strategic support to the Department, implement programs, and strengthen institutional capacity in regions and countries. The VPA's Training Project Group serves as a resource to the VPA and the violence prevention field in general for information on training and related activities.

The instrument that has been developed and implemented to assess child maltreatment prevention readiness, described above, includes two detailed scales that evaluate human and institutional resources. Based on previous work in Malawi, Mozambique, the Philippines, and South Africa in 2008 to 2009 and findings from the administration of the instrument in Brazil, China, the Former Yugoslav Republic of Macedonia, Malaysia, Saudi Arabia, and

South Africa, human and institutional resources appear to be extremely limited in most of these countries.

6. *International and regional treaties, conventions, and consensus-building documents:* One of the nine recommendations of the *World Report on Violence and Health* (2002) is to "promote and monitor adherence to international treaties, laws, and other mechanisms to protect human rights." The single most important international convention in the area of child maltreatment prevention is the 1989 UN Convention on the Rights of the Child. The Convention on the Rights of the Child is the most widely accepted human rights treaty—of all the UN member states, only the United States and Somalia have not ratified it. Article 19 of the Convention concerns the right of the child to freedom from all forms of violence and the first paragraph asserts that "States Parties shall take all appropriate legislative, administrative, social and educational measures to protect the child from all forms of physical or mental violence, injury or abuse, neglect or negligent treatment, maltreatment or exploitation, including sexual abuse, while in the care of parent(s), legal guardian(s) or any other person who has the care of the child." WHO, along with a number of other organizations, is currently a member of the Implementation Steering Committee for General Comment 13 on Article 19 of the UN Convention on the Rights of the Child. The General Comments will act as a guide for the implementation of Article 19 for the Committee on the Rights of the Child, which monitors countries' compliance with the convention.

The most important international legislation and human-rights instruments relevant to intimate partner violence are:

- Convention on the Elimination of All Forms of Discrimination Against Women (1979)
- The Declaration on the Elimination of Violence Against Women (1993)
- The Beijing Declaration and Platform for Action (1995)
- The Millennium Declaration (2000) and
- The Inter-American Convention on the Prevention, Punishment and Eradication of Violence Against Women (Convention of Belem do Para, 1994).

7. *Coordination and governance:* Currently there is no officially appointed coordination or governance mechanism or lead agency for child maltreatment or intimate partner violence prevention at the global level comparable to, for instance, the United Nations Road Safety Collaboration (led by WHO's Department of Violence and Injury Prevention and Disability). Yet a plethora of UN agencies and international and local NGOs are involved in child maltreatment and intimate partner violence prevention, often duplicating each others' activities and sometimes pulling in opposite directions. They include, for example, the International Labour Organization, the Office for the High Commissioner for Human Rights, UNICEF, the United Nations Population, the United Nations Development Programme, the recently created UN Women, the World Bank, WHO, Plan International, and Save the Children.

8. *Funding:* There is no single source of global funding for the prevention of violence, child maltreatment, or intimate partner violence comparable to the global funding mechanism available for other important public health problems, such as the *Global Fund to Fight AIDS, Tuberculosis, and Malaria*. Yet the global burden of mortality and morbidity due to violence exceeds those due to either tuberculosis or malaria (WHO, 2008a). Current sources of funding for the global public health response for prevention of child maltreatment and intimate partner violence are limited and piecemeal. They include, for instance, funding from governments of a handful of high-income countries and private foundations.

EVALUATING THE GLOBAL PUBLIC HEALTH RESPONSE TO CHILD MALTREATMENT AND INTIMATE PARTNER VIOLENCE

As the description of WHO's global public health response to child maltreatment and intimate partner violence by WHO indicates, significant progress has been made. A dozen years ago, it was nonexistent and today it is firmly established. WHO has contributed to the rapid growth in the science base underlying the program implementation cycle. For instance, the magnitude of child maltreatment and intimate partner violence is beginning to be delineated more accurately in several low- and middle-income countries thanks to population-based surveys such as the *WHO Multi-Country Study on Women's Health and Domestic Violence Against Women* (2005a) or the recent national surveys on child maltreatment being conducted by UNICEF, the U.S. CDC, and the Clinton Global Initiative's Together for Girls. WHO has contributed to reviewing and disseminating the evidence base for the effectiveness of prevention programs for these two types of violence and has also begun to invest in strengthening the evidence base. An important recent development, for which WHO has acted as an adviser, is the creation of the Evaluation Challenge Fund by the Bernard van Leer, UBS Optimus, and Oak Foundations. The aim of the fund is to support quality evaluations of programs to prevent violence against children. These evaluations will expand the evidence base and help create better violence prevention and protection programs and policies for children.

Political will and support for child maltreatment and intimate partner violence prevention at the global level, wholly absent less than 20 years ago, has begun to mobilize. In parallel, WHO's advocacy and communication efforts have intensified, partly through the Global Campaign for the Prevention of Violence and the Violence Prevention Alliance. Since it was created, WHO's Prevention of Violence Unit has made a concerted effort to issue clear and evidence-based normative and policy guidance and to influence other international organizations and agencies to harmonize their guidance. WHO has prioritized sustained efforts to develop human and institutional resources for child maltreatment and intimate partner violence prevention. In addition to establishing the Prevention of Violence Unit within WHO with its network of regional advisers, collaborating centers, and Ministry of Health focal points, institutional resources have been strengthened by the creation of the Violence Prevention Alliance. Funding has begun to be stepped up with the number of governmental and private donors gradually increasing.

Other organizations, besides WHO, have contributed to the global public response to child maltreatment and intimate partner violence. Perhaps most prominent among these is the U.S. CDC through its support for WHO and through its own international child maltreatment and intimate partner violence prevention activities. Although, beyond the scope of this chapter, many more organizations have contributed to the global response to child maltreatment and intimate partner violence adopting approaches other than a public health approach, such as human rights, social welfare, or criminal justice approaches. Yet, there is a consensus among most of them that major gaps remain and the global response to child maltreatment and intimate partner violence is still very much in its infancy.

Significant gaps remain in all four steps of the program implementation cycle, particularly in low- and middle-income countries. For most low- and middle-income countries in the world, the exact magnitude and consequences of child maltreatment and intimate partner violence are unknown country-specific risk factors have not been identified, and outcome evaluations are nonexistent. A dozen high-quality and large-scale outcome evaluation studies from low- and middle-income countries demonstrating that child maltreatment and intimate partner violence prevention programs work would represent a sea change in the evidence base. It would take these fields a long way forward in convincing policy makers and funders of the preventability of these types of violence in settings where their prevalence is greatest.

The gradually increasing political will and support for child maltreatment and intimate partner violence, notwithstanding, they remain lower down the list of global public health priorities than their prevalence and consequences warrant. A source of political support that could be strengthened is that from development agencies. Increasing the political priority of child maltreatment and intimate partner violence prevention will require intensified and more effective advocacy efforts.

More should be done to increase policy and normative guidance coherence. The diversity of approaches adopted by different agencies in the field is one of the strengths they bring to the challenge of child maltreatment and intimate partner violence prevention. It can, however, lead to fragmentary and uncoordinated—and sometimes contradictory—normative guidance, a lack of interorganization policy coherence, and a failure to harness potentially important synergies. For instance, the potential for the ethical framework provided by the human rights approach to inform the evidence-based public health approach still remains largely unrealized—as does the potential for the evidence-based strategies of the public health approach to help fulfill the ambitious aims of the human rights approach. Similarly, the evidence-based and more activist approaches to intimate partner violence prevention have largely developed in isolation from each other. This has resulted in the former having largely failed to benefit from the energy, dynamism, and advocacy skills of activists, while the latter has remained largely uninformed by the evidence base.

The urgent need to step up efforts to increase human and institutional resources is suggested by WHO's systematic assessment of readiness and resources in several low- and middle-income countries, its experience in implementing programs in low- and middle-income countries, and its work at the international level. Although most countries in the world have signed up to the main international and regional treatises, conventions, and consensus-building documents relevant to child maltreatment and intimate partner violence prevention, WHO's work on assessing the child maltreatment prevention readiness, indicates that many still fail to align their national legislation with them and, even when they have, fail to enforce the legislation adequately. A global coordinating structure with the mandate, resources, and capacity to begin to address these priorities in a coordinated fashion is sorely needed. Once in place, a global funding mechanism to mobilize adequate financial resources for the field should be considered.

Conclusions about the current state of the global response to child maltreatment similar to these have been reached independently by several international actors: for instance, regarding child maltreatment prevention, by the ISPCAN (2010) in its annual *World Perspectives on Child Abuse*, by those assessing the extent of the implementation of the Article 19 of the Convention of the Rights of the Child (e.g., Svevo-Cianci, Hart, & Rubinson, 2010), and by advocates for the need for a General Comment on Article 19 (e.g., Bennett, Hart, & Svevo-Cianci, 2009).

CONCLUSION: DEFINITION, CLASSIFICATION, AND MEASUREMENT AND THE GLOBAL PUBLIC HEALTH RESPONSE

This book's effort to arrive at consensual and operational definitions and to develop clinically validated assessments of family problems and family violence is to be welcomed. The clinical implications of this effort have been repeatedly pointed out in previous chapters. Inclusion of such definitions in the ICD-11 could significantly improve data collection on these two forms of violence given the influence of the ICD-11. ICD codes are widely used in health facility–based surveillance and WHO's *Guidelines for Conducting Community Surveys on Injuries and Violence* (2004) strongly recommends, for reasons of comparability, that ICD codes and classifications be used when developing survey instruments. No component of the global strategy for responding to these two forms of violence, however, is unaffected by these issues of definition, classification, and measurement.

Ascertaining the magnitude, distribution, and consequences of child maltreatment and intimate partner violence and the subsequent steps of the program implementation cycle are directly dependent on the definitions and measurement instruments. For instance, Finkelhor in his 1994 review of the international epidemiology of child sexual abuse lamented that the lack of consensus on these definitional and measurement issues prevented direct cross-country comparisons. A 2009 update of Finkelhor's 1994 review of the international epidemiology arrived at a similar conclusion: because of definitional, measurement, and other methodological issues, it remains "impossible to compare data" within and between countries (Pereda, Guilera, Forns, & Gomez-Benito, 2009). Moreover, valid and reliable measurement is a prerequisite for the elucidation of risk factors and causal pathways, without which effective interventions cannot be developed.

Given the two-way interactions between the program implementation cycle and the other components of WHO's strategy to respond to child maltreatment and intimate partner violence (Figure 18.1), poor measurement and its impact on subsequent steps of the program implementation cycle can also potentially undermine the overall strategy. Poor measurement can lead to advocacy efforts being seriously discredited as prevalence estimates fluctuate unaccountably (Andrews, Corry, Slade, Issakidis, & Swanston, 2004; Hart et al., 2011; Pereda et al., 2009), agreement on severity of consequences becomes elusive (Lilienfeld, 2002), and costs to individuals and society become difficult to determine with any accuracy. Poor measurement can conceivably lead to the political will to address the problem slackening, the necessary human and institutional resources not being developed, and the likelihood of establishing the required global coordinating and funding mechanism decreasing.

Nevertheless, it is critical to remain pragmatic and not lose sight of the fact that the ultimate aim is to implement programs on a large scale to prevent child maltreatment and intimate partner violence and mitigate its consequences—and not to pursue the development of the best possible definitions and measurement instruments as an end in themselves. Problems of definition and valid measurement will never be completely resolved. "Inevitably, then, validity is an evolving property and validation a continuing process" (Messick, 1989). Considerable energy has been expended in recent years discussing and trying to improve definitions and measurement of child maltreatment and intimate partner violence (e.g., Barnett, Manly, & Cicchetti, 1993; Leeb, Paulozzi, Melanson, & Arias, 2007; Manly, 2005; National Research Council, 1993; WHO, 2005a, 2006b; Wolfe & McIsaac, 2010; Wyatt & Peters, 1986). Yet important outstanding issues remain: for instance—concerning child maltreatment—distinguishing suboptimal, nonabusive parenting from maltreatment; disentangling neglect from the effects of poverty; developing cross-culturally valid measures; and measuring emotional maltreatment with reliability and validity, perhaps the most important type of maltreatment, which underlies the detrimental impact of the other main forms of abuse. From a research policy perspective, however, some thought should be given to determining (a) when existing definitions and measurement instruments can be considered good enough for the task at hand and (b) when to begin reallocating the energy and resources currently dedicated to improving definitions and measurement instruments to implementing effective large-scale prevention programs around the globe. Not quite yet, I suspect, but this book should help to bring this time closer.

NOTE

1. WHO's core functions are providing leadership on matters critical to health and engaging in partnerships where joint action is needed; shaping the research agenda and stimulating the generation, translation and dissemination of valuable knowledge; setting norms and standards and promoting and monitoring their implementation; articulating ethical and evidence-based policy options; providing technical support, catalyzing change, and building sustainable institutional capacity; and monitoring the health situation and assessing health trends (WHO, 2011b).

REFERENCES

Andrews, G., Corry, J., Slade, T., Issakidis, C., & Swanston, H. (2004). Child sexual abuse. In M. Ezzati, A. Lopez, A. Rodgers, & C. Murray (Eds.), *Comparative quantification of health risks: Global and regional burden of disease attributable to selected major risk factors* (vol. 2, pp. 1851–1940). Geneva: World Health Organization.

Barnett, D., Manly, J., & Cicchetti, D. (1993). Defining child maltreatment: The interface between policy and research. In D. Cicchetti & S. Toth (Eds.), *Child abuse, child development, and social policy* (pp. 7–73). Norwood, NJ: Ablex.

Bennett, S., Hart, S., & Svevo-Cianci, K. (2009). The need for a General Comment for Article 19 for the UN Convention on the Rights of the Child: Towards enlightenment and progress for child protection. *Child Abuse and Neglect, 33*, 783–790.

Dahlberg, L., & Mercy, J. (2009). History of violence as a public health issue. *AMA Virtual Mentor, 11*(2), 167–172.

Finkelhor, D. (1994). The international epidemiology of child sexual abuse. *Child Abuse and Neglect, 18*(5), 409–417.

Hart, S., Brassard, M., Davidson, H., Rivelis, E., Diaz-Thompson, V., & Binggeli, N. (2011). Psychological maltreatment. In J. Myers (Ed.), *APSAC handbook of child maltreatment* (3rd ed., pp. 125–144). Thousand Oaks: Sage.

International Society for Prevention of Child Abuse and Neglect (ISPCAN). (2010). *World perspectives on child abuse* (9th ed.). Carol Stream, IL: Author.

Leeb, R., Paulozzi, L., Melanson, C. T, T. S., & Arias, I. (2007). *Child maltreatment surveillance: Uniform definitions for public health and recommended data elements, Version 1.0*. Atlanta, GA: Centers for Disease Control and Prevention, National Center for Injury Prevention and Control.

Lilienfeld, S. (2002). When worlds collide: Social science, politics, and the Rind et al. child sexual abuse meta-analysis. *American Psychologist, 57*, 176–188.

MacMillan, H., Wathen, C., Barlow, J., Fergusson, D., Leventhal, J., & Taussig, H. (2009). Interventions to prevent child maltreatment and associated impairment. *The Lancet, 373*, 250–266.

Manly, J. (2005). Advances in research definitions of child maltreatment. *Child Abuse and Neglect, 29*, 425–439.

Messick, S. (1989). Validity. In R. Linn (Ed.), *Educational measurement* (3rd ed., pp. 13–103). New York, NY: Macmillan.

Mikton, C., & Butchart, A. (2009). Child maltreatment prevention: A systematic review of reviews. *Bulletin of the World Health Organization, 87*(5), 353–361.

Mikton, C., Mehra, R., Butchart, A., Addiss, D., Almuneef, M., Cardia, N.,…, Raleva, L. (2011). A multidimensional model for child maltreatment prevention readiness in low- and middle-income countries. *Journal of Community Psychology, 39*(7), 826–843.

Morris, S., Gogill, B., Uavy, R., & Group, C. U. S. (2008). Effective international action against undernutrition: Why has it proven so difficult and what can be done to accelerate progress? *The Lancet, 371*, 608–621.

National Research Council. (1993). *Understanding child abuse and neglect—Panel on research on child abuse and neglect*. Washington, DC: National Academy Press.

Organization of American States, *Inter-American Convention on the Prevention, Punishment and Eradication of Violence against Women ("Convention of Belem do Para")*, 9 June 1994, available at: http://www.unhcr.org/refworld/docid/3ae6b38b1c.html [accessed 4 July 2012]

Pereda, N., Guilera, G., Forns, M., & Gomez-Benito, J. (2009). The international epidemiology of child sexual abuse: A continuation of Finkelhor (1994). *Child Abuse and Neglect, 33*, 331–342.

Prothrow-Stith, D. (2004). Stengthening the collaboration between public health and criminal justice to prevent violence. *Journal of Law, Medicine, and Ethics, 32*, 82–88.

Ramiro, L., Madrid, B., & Brown, D. (2010). Adverse childhood experiences (ACE) and health-risk behaviors among adults in a developing country setting. *Child Abuse and Neglect, 34*, 842–855.

Reza, A., Breiding, M. J, J. G., Mercy, J., Blanton, C., & Mthethwa, Z. (2009). Sexual violence and its health consequences for female children in Swaziland: A cluster survey study. *The Lancet, 373*, 1966–1972.

Runyan, D. (2008). The challenges of assessing the incidence of inflicted traumatic brain injury. *American Journal of Preventive Medicine, 34*, S112–S115.

Runyan, D., & Eckenrode, J. (2004). International perspectives on the epidemiology of child neglect and abuse. *Annales Nestle, 62*(1), 1–12.

Shiffman, J., & Smith, S. (2007). Generation of political priority for global health initiatives: A framework and case study of maternal mortality. *The Lancet, 370*(9595), 1370–1379.

SPC, Secretariat of the Pacific. (2009). *Solomon Islands family health and safety study: A study on violence against women and children*. Solomon Islands: Secretariat of the Pacific Community for the Ministry of Women, Youth and Children's Affairs and National Statistics Office, Ministry of Finance and Treasury, National Reform and Planning.

SPC, Secretariat of the Pacific. (2010). *Kiribati family Health and Support study: A study on violence against women and children*. Republic of Kiribati, Noumean, New Caledonia: Secretariat of the Pacific Community for Ministry of Internal and Social Affairs and Statistics Division. Ministry of Finance and Economic Development.

Svevo-Cianci, K., Hart, S., & Rubinson, C. (2010). Protecting children from violence and maltreatment: A qualitative comparative analysis assessing the implementation of UN CRC Article 19. *Child Abuse and Neglect, 34*(1), 45–56.

Wolfe, D., & McIsaac, C. (2010). *Distinguishing between poor/dysfunctional parenting and child emotional maltreatment*: Prepared for the Family Violence Prevention Unit of the Public Health Agency of Canada. Unpublished report.

World Health Organization. (2001). *Putting women first: Ethical and safety recommendations for research on domestic violence against women*. Geneva, Switzerland: Author.

World Health Organization. (2002). *World report on violence and health*. Geneva, Switzerland: Author.

World Health Organization. (2004). *Guidelines for conducting community surveys on injuries and violence*. Geneva, Switzerland: World Health Organization.

World Health Organization. (2005a). *WHO multi-country study on women's health and domestic violence against women*. Geneva, Switzerland: Author.

World Health Organization. (2005b). *Researching violence against women: A practical guide for researchers and activists*. Geneva, Switzerland: Author.

World Health Organization. (2006a). *STOP the global epidemic of chronic disease: A practical guide to successful advocacy*. Geneva, Switzerland: Author.

World Health Organization. (2006b). *Preventing child maltreatment: A guide to taking action and generating evidence*. Geneva, Switzerland: Author.

World Health Organization. (2006c). *Developing policies to prevent injuries and violence: Guidelines for policy makers and planners*. Geneva, Switzerland: Author.

World Health Organization. (2007). *Preventing injuries and violence: A guide for ministries of health*. Geneva, Switzerland: Author.

World Health Organization. (2008a). *The global burden of disease: 2004 update*. Retrieved March, 2011, from www.who.int/healthinfo/global_burden_disease/2004_report_update/en/index.html

World Health Organization. (2008b). *Manual for estimating the economic cost of injuries due to interpersonal and self-directed violence*. Geneva, Switzerland: Author.

World Health Organization. (2009). *Violence prevention: The evidence*. Geneva, Switzerland: Author.

World Health Organization. (2010a). *Child maltreatment—Fact sheet No. 150*. Retrieved March 2011

World Health Organization. (2010b). *Addressing violence against women and HIV/AIDS: What works?* Geneva, Switzerland: Author.

World Health Organization. (2010c). *Preventing intimate partner and sexual violence against women: Taking action and generating evidence*. Geneva, Switzerland: Author.

World Health Organization. (2011a). *Capacity building*. Retrieved from www.who.int/violence_injury_prevention/capacitybuilding/en

World Health Organization. (2011b). *The role of WHO in public health*. Retrieved March 2011, from http://www.who.int/about/role/en/index.html

World Health Organization. (2011c). *Related resolutions*. Retrieved March 2011, from www.who.int/violence_injury_prevention/publications/violence/en/index.html

Wyatt, G., & Peters, S. (1986). Issues in the definition of child sexual abuse in prevalence research. *Child Abuse & Neglect, 10*, 231–240.

19

Relational Problems Co-Occurring With Medical Problems: The Conceptual Basis of Cross-Coding

David Reiss

Many chapters in the current volume have demonstrated the feasibility of reliable assessments of relational disorders. Drawing on a strong empirical base, clear-cut criteria have been developed and strong epidemiological evidence has been reviewed documenting the frequency with which these relational disorders are associated with serious problems of both child and adult behavioral and mood problems, as well as impaired adjustment to current challenges in work and social relationships. Some studies, using rigorous designs, suggest that the relational disorders appear to have a causal role in these adjustment problems. First, they precede them in time. Moreover, the problems in adjustment—such as adolescent and adult substance abuse and adult depression—are ameliorated following therapeutic interventions that improve relationships and relapse of these disorders is prevented. Previous chapters have suggested a broad range of these associated psychiatric disorders. These are summarized in Table 19.1, together with a few direct physical consequences of relational problems, such as sexually transmitted infections, that may be a consequence and conspicuous clinical sign of these problems. There is now ample evidence that patients with psychological difficulties summarized in this table would benefit greatly if their clinicians also assessed the status of their primary relationships. Thus, a clinically useful diagnostic manual should suggest to mental health clinicians who diagnose a patient with any of the disorders shown in Table 19.1 that they should also search for an associated relationship problem. In terms of diagnostic logic, the clinical situation is identical to a physician who after making a diagnosis of a patient's first myocardial infarction, also searches diligently for previously unrecognized diabetes.

Should health care workers, upon diagnosing a *medical* illness, also be encouraged to search for a relational disorder? Research is rapidly accumulating on the co-occurrence of relational disorders and medical disorders. These data alone provide justification for considering co-occurring relational problems upon the diagnosis of a broad range of medical disorders in children and in adults, as the relational problems often affect the outcome or management of the physical illness. However, the strongest argument for searching for co-occurring relational problems—one that should have a broad appeal in an international diagnostic manual—is that there is a *causal relationship* between relational problems and a range of medical disorders. Is there a sound empirical basis for this argument? This chapter addresses that question.

MECHANISMS UNDERLYING THE CO-OCCURRENCE OF RELATIONAL AND MEDICAL DISORDERS

In thinking about co-occurrence of relational problems and medical disorders, we draw heavily on the work of Krueger and Markon (2006) and Neale and Kendler (1995) on the comorbidity of psychiatric disorders. We distinguish in Figure 19.1 four different mechanisms that might account for the co-occurrence.

TABLE 19.1 Summary of Psychiatric Clinical Syndromes, and Closely Associated Physical Consequences, Associated With Relational Problems

Spouse or Partner Relational Problem
Anxiety, depression, substance use disorders, sexual dysfunction, somatization, chronic pain, exacerbation of health conditions not otherwise accounted for
Spouse or Partner Violence
Anxiety disorders, depression, substance use disorders, posttraumatic stress disorder (PTSD), physical injury, suicide, homicide, unwanted pregnancy, sexually transmitted infections (sexual abuse), bed sores (elderly), malnutrition (elderly), child behavior and emotional problems
Child Abuse and Neglect
Depression, insecure attachment, anxiety, PTSD, oppositional defiant disorder, conduct disorder, attentional problems, somatization and school phobia and enduring cognitive problems in severely neglected children, suicidal thoughts and behavior in adolescence and adulthood as well adult major depression, anxiety disorders, antisocial personality disorder, PTSDs, and substance abuse disorders. Child sexual abuse is associated with borderline personality disorders in adults as well as bulimia, dissociative disorders and risky sexual behavior, physical injury, including a broad range of fractures and burns, hemorrhage in the retina or elsewhere.
In sexual abuse: Genital/anal injuries, sexually transmitted infections and pregnancy
In neglect: Severe dental problems, malnourishment, repeated infections, and broad deficits in social, academic, and attachment processes
Caregiver Child Relational Problems
Insecure attachment, separation and withdrawal patterns in young children, failure to thrive physically/psychologically

No Causal Relationship

A health care worker may encounter a patient with a medical disorder, perhaps cataracts, who also is in a distressed marriage. However, no data exists, on the *population* level that these two disorders occur together more often than by chance alone. The health care worker might elect to treat both conditions, because the treatment of one may have an impact on the treatment for the other (e.g., someone who is not seeing well may be more irritable with spouse, or a controlling spouse may prohibit getting the patient the surgery they require), but the presence of one disorder is unlikely to have causal implications for the other. Following Krueger and Markon (2006), this is co-occurrence on the *individual* level.

Common Causal Influences

Medical and relational disorders can co-occur because they have a common etiology. For example, childhood abuse is associated with adult cardiovascular illness (Fuller-Thomson, Brennenstuhl, & Frank, 2010) as it is with disrupted marital functioning (Colman & Widom, 2004). Thus, the co-occurrence of a marital relational problem and cardiovascular disease might be attributed to the long-term effects of child abuse on both disorders. This common origin, not to the influence of either disorder on the incidence or prevalence of the other, accounts for their co-occurrence. Preliminary evidence suggests that the long-lasting effects of abuse may reflect different mechanisms. Marital disruption among victims of child abuse may reflect pervasive insecurity in relationships, caution and pessimism about relationships once they begin, and failure to attract a mate whose warmth and engagement could offset long-lasting effects of abuse. In contrast, the long-term effects of abuse on cardiovascular illness may reflect enduring abnormalities of the stress response system, in particular heightened and sustained cortisol responses to psychological distress.

In Figure 19.1, there is second possibility illustrated (see 2B) to account for how a medical and a relational disorder might arise from a common cause. As illustrated, it is possible that an etiological circumstance (or a set of closely related circumstances) may first lead to a serious relationship disorder and then, *as a consequence of that effect*, lead to the development of a medical disorder. In this instance one might advocate for treating a relational disorder both to alleviate the distress it engenders and to prevent the development of a subsequent medical disorder. Well-conducted prospective epidemiological studies suggest that, for example, marital distress precedes and may contribute to the cause of medical disorders such as metabolic syndrome (Whisman & Uebelacker, 2012), a range of chronic illnesses in mid-life (Hughes & Waite, 2009) and, for limited measures of marital interaction, cardiovascular disease (Eaker, Sullivan, Kelly-Hayes, D'Agostino, & Benjamin, 2007). However, there is—as yet—little evidence that marital distress *mediates* the relationship between an etiological agent (or closely related cluster of agents) and the evolution of serious medical disorder as implied by diagram 2B in Figure 19.1. To meet this criterion the etiological factor would have first to cause or strongly influence the relational disorder and, as a consequence, lead to the medical disorder.

The impact of both poverty and minority status are well-known risks for a broad range of health outcomes, but the evidence that relational problems mediate this causal connection is scant. For example, there is some evidence that highly restrictive parenting practices might mediate the effect of family ethnicity on gylcemic control in preadolescent diabetic children (Davis et al., 2001). However, the links between ethnicity or social stratification of parents or of children and the evolution of chronic illness are complex and highly conditioned by the varying quality of parent–child relationships within ethnic groups and economic strata (Singer & Ryff, 1999) and by stress responses characteristics of children (Boyce, 2004).

In sum, while there is scant evidence that relational problems mediate, in a straightforward way, the role of well-defined etiological factors on illness evolution, the important role of relational disorders themselves in the evolution of some medical disorders, even without meeting the formal criteria of 2B raises the possibility that treating these relational disorders may reduce the risk of subsequent disorders.

Version 2B might be conceptualized in reverse order: an etiological agent may lead first to a serious medical disorder and then, as a consequence, lead to a serious disorder

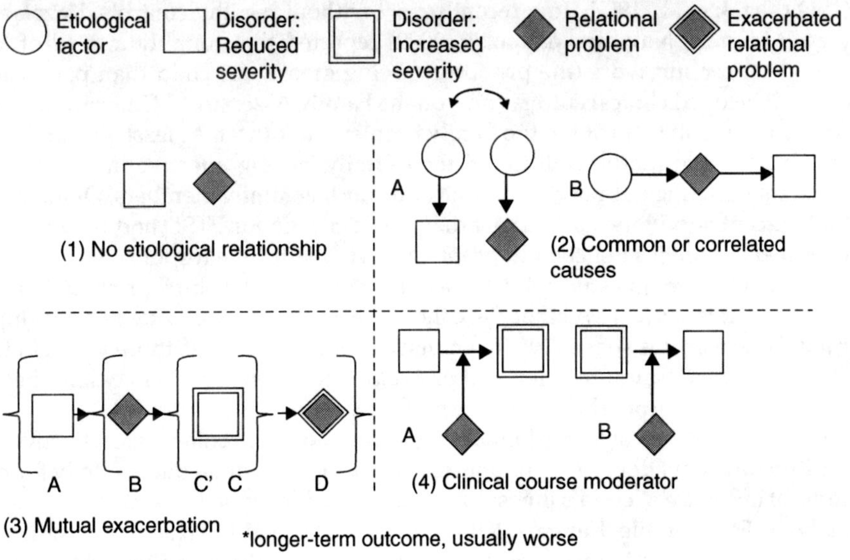

FIGURE 19.1 Mechanisms linking medical disorders and relational problems.

of parent–child or marital relationships. However, the literature on both parent–child and marital relationships does not, at this time, confirm straightforward effects of this kind. For example, in pediatric cancer it is clear that parents experience enduring levels of distress following the child's diagnosis and treatment, even some suffering diagnosable posttraumatic stress disorder (PTSD), but evidence to date does not clearly confirm a main effect of pediatric cancer in eliciting significant, sustained disorders of parent–child or marital relationships (see Pai et al., 2007, for a recent meta-analysis). More recent data, reviewed below, suggests the relationships within some families do suffer in response to pediatric cancer.

Mutual Exacerbation

A much broader range of studies support this mechanism of co-occurrence. The basic idea is that while there may not be a strong causal relationship between the incidence of relational problems and of medical disorders, each has the capacity to exacerbate the other. There are few, if any, studies that have examined the full cycle of events depicted in Figure 19.1. To do so, would require a multipanel design that spanned the initiation of a cycle of mutual exacerbation by a medical disorder (starting with bracket A) and ending with an exacerbated relational disorder (bracket D).

Diabetes and asthma are the most prevalent chronic illnesses in children. They have provided an opportunity to explore mutual exacerbation. Many studies take advantage of objective assessment of fluctuations in illness severity; in the case of diabetes using HbA1c which indexes glycemic control over an extended period and, in asthma, peak expiratory flow rate (PERF)—a measure of airway constriction—that measures current severity. For example, McQuaid et al. (2007) explored a mutual exacerbation effect spanning brackets B to D. They measured PERF in children, particularly their capacity to accurately estimate it, effective parental response to symptoms (such as administering medication or seeking medical advice), and asthma morbidity (severity of symptoms and functional impairment). Their cross-sectional data supported an idea that inaccurate symptom perception in the child, led to ineffective parental response, which in turn led to, increased asthma morbidity. More typical analyses focus on presumed impact of parent–child relational problems on illness severity such as HbA1c (Anderson et al., 2009) or on severe impact of illness on the family (Katz, Laffel, Perrin, & Kuhlthau, 2011). These impacts elevate stress level in the family, such as interfering with parental work routine and increasing economic hardship or even PTSD (Kazak et al., 1997). In a recent report without healthy controls, Kazak and her colleagues (Alderfer , Navsaria, & Kazak, 2009) reported that roughly a third of families of childhood cancer survivors (the proportion being greater for child than parent reports) exceed well-developed clinical cutoff scores on the Family Assessment Device although their design made it difficult to attribute the family problems to cancer. At least 40% of adolescent survivors, fathers, and mothers all found their family lacking affective involvement, with adolescents also singling out poor communication among family members. Of interest, 12 of the 144 adolescent survivors studied met diagnostic criteria for PTSD and they were differentially located in families deficient in problem solving, affective responsiveness, and affective involvement. Since this study did not assess family relationships prior to diagnosis of pediatric cancer, it is unclear whether the cancer exacerbated underlying relationship problems or not. However, it is suggestive that given a cancer experience, those youth in families with more concurrent communication and problem-solving difficulties may have been more likely to develop PTSD from the medical experience.

With the advent of new statistical modeling techniques, particularly growth curve analyses using structural equations, it is possible to examine longitudinal data directly for reciprocal patterns of influence of child's illness on parent adaptive capacities and the reverse, in the same analyses. For example, Kaugars, Klinnert, Robinson, and Ho (2008) were able to show in pediatric asthma a positive reciprocal relationship, across three waves of data, between a child's medication use and parental effective adaptation to the challenges of caring for a very young child with wheezing. Thus, their investigation spanned the full range from brackets A to D in diagram 2 in Figure 19.1. The average level of parent's successful adaptation was influenced by their own cognitive resources, whereas the increase of their adaptive strength overtime responded to the severity of their child's illness.

The same pattern of findings seems to hold for adult medical disorders. Here, the mutual exacerbation model has energized studies of both the impact of relational problems on worsening of illness, particularly chronic illness and the impact of chronic illness on relational problems. For example, in adults with chronic illness the study of the impact of relational problems can also include a very definite endpoint: mortality. A series of studies have suggested, for example, that patients with severe renal disease requiring dialysis might be quite sensitive to relational problems. Kimmel et al. (2000) showed, that in women, marital conflict predicted mortality, controlling for other risks for mortality in these patients. This seems like a more specific extension of previous findings that family-wide strain predicted mortality in renal patients on dialysis (Reiss, 1990; Reiss, Gonzalez, & Kramer, 1986; Turner-Musa et al., 1999). The role of marital relational problems in the evolution of cardiac illness has also been carefully documented. Particularly in women, marital relational problems predict shortened survival in patients with already established congestive heart failure (Rohrbaugh, Shoham, & Coyne, 2006). Of special interest are studies that document the prospective relationship between marital problems on intermediate risk factors for cardiovascular disease, such as the metabolic syndrome (Whisman & Uebelacker, 2012). Particularly striking is recent evidence of how early in development the cardiovascular system is sensitive to relational problems. For example, negative, nonsupportive parenting of kindergarten children predict elevated heart rate and blood pressure 4 to 6 years later (Bell & Belsky, 2008). These findings are consistent with a series of very long-term predictive studies of the impact of marital disruption on health and mortality (Friedman et al., 1995b; Hughes & Waite, 2009; Tucker, Friedman, Wingard, & Schwartz, 1996).

Conversely, chronic illness has a clear and sustained impact on marital and family systems although, as in the case of many other severe stresses on the family there is a wide range of response (Flaherty & O'Brien, 1992). The negative reciprocal cycles that fully characterize the mutual exacerbation cycle are probably true of an important subset of families facing chronic illness or its preliminary stages. For example, consider a long-term follow-up of the impact of very low birth weight children on parental burden and distress. This effect (Moore, Taylor, Klein, Minich, & Hack, 2006) continues, in some cases, through the child's early adolescence. Importantly, psychological distress in the parents, as measured by a symptom inventory, persisted only in economically disadvantaged families. A different pattern was true for the burden and worry that parents felt about the child's lingering disabilities. These persisted mostly in families with ample "resources" drawn from satisfaction in work, positive life events, and relationships with friends and extended family. The latter finding might be explained by the family's increased expectations for the child and hence, greater sensitivity to the child's limits. Thus, in the case of very low birth weight children we might expect negative cycles involving parental symptoms to be initiated in the subset of economically disadvantaged families. Negative cycles involving parents' experienced burden and concern might be initiated, primarily, in families drawing satisfaction from other aspects of their life.

In considering the mutual exacerbation cycles a word of caution is in order. Many of these studies of the impact of relational problems on medical disorders have used stringent controls for other confounding factors. However, many potentially confounding variables are not measured. For example, in the case of effects of marital problems on chronic illness no study has examined the role of genetic influences. Heritable aspects of temperament and personality often index these influences. Heritable and nonheritable aspects of personality play a major role in marital functioning (Bradbury & Karney, 2004; Jocklin, McGue, & Lykken, 1996; Spotts et al., 2004) as they do in the evolution of patterns of health and disease (Friedman et al., 1995a; Hampson, Goldberg, Vogt, & Dubanoski, 2006; Kern & Friedman,

2008). Unmeasured in all studies cited, these or other heritable traits may confound the observed relationship of relational problems with health and disease outcomes. We return to challenges in research design such as these in the final section of this chapter.

Clinical Course Moderator

This mechanism of co-occurrence is distinguished from mutual exacerbation because the relational disorder is not necessarily responsive to earlier phases of the disorder. Despite a modest or nonexistent association between early phases of the illness and subsequent relational problems, in this category are studies demonstrating that relational problems may accelerate the downward course of medical disorders. Many studies we have just cited, showing the impact of relational problems on the evolution of chronic medical disorders control for baseline levels of disorder, at the time relational problems are assessed. Thus, from these data we can say that relational problems predict exacerbation of medical disorders above and beyond the impact of baseline severity. Another way of putting this is that baseline relational disorders predict *change* in severity of medical disorders. In contrast, a clinical course moderator interacts with baseline levels of disease severity. The expected finding is that serious levels of disorder predict a downward course of illness *only in the presence of a relational problem.* It is possible for relational disorders to both mediate and moderate the course of illness. However, moderation is impossible to demonstrate where the presence of illness or illness severity is highly correlated with relational disorders. Diagram 4A (see Figure 19.1) reflects circumstances where the relational problem serves only as a moderator.

Evidence for the role of relational problems in moderating the evolution or course of medical illness comes primarily from two sources. First, are very long-term longitudinal studies where the temporal ordering of illness course and relational problem can be clarified, particularly where there is modest or no relationship between early risk factors or disease manifestations and relationship problems. Thus, in the study by Singer and Ryff (1999), already cited, the design focused on the long-term health risks of childhood economic adversity. Their endpoint was biomarkers of high allostatic load in adults, evidence that risk for a broad range of illness was advancing. Because the level and severity of relational problems varied strikingly, within economic strata, they could demonstrate that childhood economic adversity lead to evidence of high allostatic load *particularly in the presence of relation problems,* thus the presence of a relational problem moderated the impact of childhood economic adversity.

Portion B of the diagram illustrates circumstances where a favorable relationship may slow the progress of a medical disorder or contribute to full or partial recovery. While such a circumstance may occur naturalistically, diagram B (see Figure 19.1) is meant primarily to call attention to the sizable literature on family-based interventions that appear to lead to some amelioration in medical disorders. As we will detail in the next section of this chapter, portions A and B are not simply opposites. It is certainly the case that intervention studies directed at improving family relationships of medically ill patients offer the possibility for strong inferences about the role of relational problems in health and illness. This is especially true if two conditions are met. First, the study randomizes a sufficient number of parent–child dyads or couples to a treatment designed to improve their relationships or to a control group that is unlikely to affect the quality of relationships. Second, the study must use a valid measure of disease progression. With important qualifications, if a sufficient number of studies favor the relationship intervention over the control we may infer that relationship improvement plays a role in ameliorating the course of illness. The presumed advantage of the randomized controlled trial (RCT) is that it helps reduce or eliminate confounding variables that plague ordinary longitudinal studies. Even results from well-controlled longitudinal studies that estimate the impact of impaired parent–child or marital relationships on disease incidence, chronicity, or progression may reflect the effects of unmeasured biological or social variables rather than the relational problems under study. We have already pointed to the possible confounding effects of personality differences that may influence both relational problems and ill health; unmeasured they are unidentified confounds. In theory, randomization mutes or eliminates the effects of even unmeasured variables of this kind. In a sufficiently large sample we may presume that the treated group and the controls are equal in personality characteristics even if we have not measured them.

Indeed, there is a very sizable literature reporting RCTs of parent–child, marital or family interventions that include studies where outcome measures reflect the course of medical illness. To date at least five meta-analyses of studies that include this work have been published. We summarize them briefly here; the interested reader can consult these accessible reviews directly for more detail.

Four meta-analyses focus on interventions for adults with chronic medical illness. The first of these (Martire, Lustig, Schulz, Miller, & Helgeson, 2004) summarized the results of 70 studies published during or before 2002, most of these involving families of patients with dementia, heart disease, or frailty due to old age. A much smaller number of studies included patients with cancer, chronic pain, and stroke. Half the interventions focused specifically on improving relationships while the other half included a family member in an intervention focusing primarily on the patient. Patient mortality was the most direct measure of disease progression but was used in only nine of these studies with a small but reliable positive impact on patients without dementia but not on those with. Surprisingly this effect was achieved only in the seven studies where the intervention did not focus on family relationships although these may have been strengthened nonetheless. The largest effect in this meta-analysis was the moderate effect of marital interventions on patient depression. Surprisingly, there was no overall effect of these interventions on the patients' satisfaction with their primary family relationships in the five studies in which this was measured.

A more recent review, focusing just on couple interventions extended these findings in a meta-analysis of 25 studies of patients with cardiovascular disease, cancer, arthritis, and chronic pain (Martire, Schulz, Helgeson, Small, & Saghafi, 2010). The only indicator of disease progression was measure of pain that was obtained in 14 of the studies and this indicator of outcome, because of its subjective nature, may be regarded only as a weak proxy for disease severity. That said, couple interventions compared with treatment as usual had a small but significant effect on reducing pain. In contrast to the earlier review, the 18 studies in which marital functioning was the focus of the intervention show small but reliable effects of intervention when the comparison was either to treatment as usual or to a psychosocial treatment that was given only to the patient.

A more recent review of a broader range of family interventions for patients with chronic illness added a number of studies not included in any of the previous reviews (Hartmann, Bazner, Wild, Eisler, & Herzog, 2010). The review covered 52 randomized trials, but its index of medical outcomes was very broad and included patient's rating of their own physical health, patient autonomy versus dependency, and patient's competence in disease management. Thirty-nine of these studies—including patients with cardiovascular disease, cancer, and arthritis—showed small but reliable effects, primarily for cardiovascular disease. In contrast to earlier reviews, studies that focused on relationships showed notably larger effects than those that focused on family-oriented education about the illness and management. Moreover, the 17 interventions that focused on marriage achieved notably larger effects than interventions using other family members. Of special interest, this is the only one of the five meta-analyses cited here that examined the likelihood of publication bias, a plague endemic to both pharmacologic and psychotherapy outcome studies (Cuijpers, Smit, Bohlmeijer, Hollon, & Andersson, 2010). Using a funnel plot the review found no evidence of bias.

Finally, one meta-analysis focused on 13 studies of parent–child interventions with an emphasis on parent training in effective approaches to managing type 1 diabetes in their children (Armour, Norris, Jack, Zhang, & Fisher, 2005). A small positive effect was noted in the eight studies that measured glycated hemoglobin; this routine blood test indexes a combination of dietary and medication management across several weeks. The effect size was small but reliable.

Meta-analyses like these leave a number of issues murky. One of them is whether including a family member in an intervention is clearly superior to a well-crafted psychosocial intervention that involves only the patient. In an earlier review, Martire and her colleagues identified 12 randomized trials that specifically addressed this question (Martire, 2005). The number of studies was too small for a formal meta-analysis but the data reviewed suggest superiority of the family intervention for joint swelling in arthritic patients, blood pressure in patients with hypertension, and pain levels in patients suffering chronic pain. The more recent review of couple-focused interventions (Martire et al., 2010), cited above, also confirmed a small but reliable superiority of couple-focused interventions over interventions delivered to the patient alone.

Since the reviews we cite cover studies extending back several decades it is useful to ask whether we might weight more recent studies more heavily on the assumption that research designs have improved with time. We are unaware of any systematic study of this kind for family interventions. However, for trials of individual, psychodynamic psychotherapy Gerber et al. have shown, using strict criteria for the design of randomized trials of psychotherapy, a marked improvement especially in the past decade. On the assumption that the same may be true for randomized family-based interventions we can give special weight to more recent meta-analysis and the studies they evaluate.

We can draw five tentative conclusions from this work. First both adult and child studies show small but reliable effects of family interventions on ameliorating physical features of medical illness. Second, these interventions also improved quality of relationships. Third, family interventions show distinct superiority over psychosocial interventions that include only the patient. Fourth, in adults, the general tactics of family-level interventions seem widely applicable across a broad range of medical disorders including cardiovascular conditions, cancer, and arthritis. It must be noted that many of the interventions contain strategies that are tailored to the demands of the specific illness. However, it is possible that there are general principles for designing family-level interventions across a broad range of illness. This is particularly important because it may mean we do not have to evaluate the efficacy of family-level interventions for every child and adult disorder in the International Classification of Diseases (ICD), a task that is quite impossible for very rare conditions that may benefit from family-level interventions as much as common disorders. There is one potential caveat in the search for general principles: children and adults with severe cognitive deficits may pose a special challenge to family-level interventions. The 2004 Martire et al. review, cited above showed, quite specifically, the ineffectiveness of family-level interventions for the four studies of interventions for demented patients. This echoes a broad literature on illness and families. For example, in the study on the long-term impact on families of low birth weight infants already cited (Moore et al., 2006) it is likely that the cognitive deficits associated with low birth weight have the most prolonged effects on the family. Fifth, as this is an important caveat, the meta-analyses could not deal with a crucial question: Are the interventions indicated only for parent–child relationships or marital relationships that meet the clear threshold for a "problem" as defined elsewhere in this book. Alternatively, are they equally important to help all families under the assumption that severe illnesses place a psychological and relational burden on all families and all can, theoretically at least, benefit from an evidence-based, family-level intervention? A fundamental reason the meta-analysis could not answer this question is that there are no widely accepted criteria for a "problem level" in relationship distress.

THE INTERPLAY BETWEEN RESEARCH AND THE CLINICAL DIAGNOSIS OF CO-OCCURING MEDICAL DISORDERS AND RELATIONAL PROBLEMS

Needs for Revision in the Medical Diagnostic Process: Three Steps

Our review of the literature has been schematic: it has been designed to introduce and illustrate four processes that help explain co-occurrence between medical disorders and relational problems. However, even this limited review fully justifies encouraging medical diagnosticians to search for relational problems once they establish the diagnosis of a medical disorder. The evidence is abundant for the importance of this assessment in the two most prevalent chronic illnesses in childhood: asthma and diabetes, as it is for some of the most prevalent chronic illnesses in adults: cardiovascular conditions of many kinds and probably cancer, arthritis, and adult diabetes. All of these could be added to Table 19.1 based on a strong empirical foundation. However, it is the intent of this chapter to initiate a *process of increasing diagnostic precision and comprehensiveness in medical disorders* rather than compile a list of medical disorders where the possibility of relational disorders should be routinely considered. The latter would require an exhaustive, book-length review of an enormous corpus of clinical research—clearly beyond the scope of a single chapter.

What are needed now are three simple steps. First, ICD-11 must contain explicit criteria for the diagnosis of parent–child and marital problems, at a minimum. The major burden of this book is to present these criteria and their empirical basis. Without clear diagnostic criteria most clinicians, except in extreme cases, will be at loss in making a diagnosis of a relational problem and—even among clinicians who diligently search for relational problems—there will be an unacceptable lack of reliability across clinicians and across patients.

As we have already clarified one paradoxical advantage of these clear-cut criteria is to clarify where they are *not* important in clinical decision making for medical disorders or where an assessment of the presence or absence of well-defined relational disorder may be woefully incomplete. We have noted, for example, that some family-level interventions may be useful for all families facing the challenge of chronic illness whether or not any relationship meets criteria as a "problem." Although more evidence is crucial on this point, where this is true it would be a disservice to dismiss the clinical needs of families who fall below a diagnostic cutoff. Also, and this is particularly true in the area of severe, chronic, treatment-intensive medical illness, families may need help with challenges that are particularly relevant for the medical disorder to which they are responding. These same disease-specific demands are irrelevant to the more general categories of relationship problems that are intended to be generalizable across a very broad range of clinical settings. For example, in pediatric cancer or asthma, families must master their own roles in the treatment process—recognizing signs of impending trouble, knowing what treatment they can provide and when to seek urgent medical care. For sustained, treatment-intensive illness, families must manage a rearrangement of their own schedules and roles to balance the medical needs of the sick child against the needs of their well children, their own needs, and the demands of economic survival. It seems likely that most families need some help with these daunting tasks whether or not they have relational problems that preceded or follow from the medical disorder.

A second step for a diagnostic manual such as ICD-11, for selected medical disorders, is that it should contain specific recommendations to the diagnostician to search for a relational disorder; that is, the diagnostic manual should *improve the likelihood of making a co-occurring diagnosis* where evidence suggests that co-occurrence is likely and crucial in clinical decision making. However, such notations, in the sections on specific medical disorders should be written to prevent clinicians from simply dismissing the importance of the family if diagnostic criteria are not met.

A third step, and the most important of the three, is the *development of an open empirical system* encouraging the interplay of improved criteria of relational disorders and the highly productive and broad program of research on the causal relationships between relational problems and medical disorders. A crucial link in this process is improved clinically relevant methods for objectively assessing relational problems. Chapter 18 of this book describes, for example, a structured interview for assessing parent–child relational problems. In addition, family researchers have worked to provide their medical colleagues with well-developed instruments to appraise the marital, parent–child, and family-wide problems related to medical disorders (Alderfer et al., 2008; Holm, Wamboldt, & Reiss, 2008). Research on the causal links between relational problems and medical disorders will all benefit from improved research design. A brief set of recommendations follow, recommendations that are keyed to our classification of processes underlying co-occurrence that are summarized in Figure 19.1. We add one more consideration to this scheme: the importance of cultural variation.

AN OPEN EMPIRICAL SYSTEM: INCREASING OUR UNDERSTANDING OF THE CAUSAL LINKS BETWEEN RELATIONAL PROBLEMS AND MEDICAL DISORDERS

Common or Correlated Cause

Both family and medical researchers have rarely considered the possibility that relational disorders and medical disorders may have the same common origin. However, the importance of such common origins may be profound. Logically and clinically, to continue an example used at the outset of this chapter, it is the same circumstance as that facing a medical clinician who—in examining a patient with a recent myocardial infarction, a patient he has never seen—notes also early signs of vascular retinopathy. As soon as possible the clinician looks for diabetes as the most likely underlying cause of both disorders. We have already cited the example of early child abuse as a predisposing cause or risk factor for both adult relational problems and for heart disease. Clinicians are eager to identify underlying causes of multiple disorders because if these underlying conditions can be treated the therapeutic gains may be substantial. Of course, the immediate sequelae of abuse in childhood cannot be reversed but some of its longer-term effects might be aborted. In the case of depression as a sequel, this is a likely basis of why psychotherapy is a more effective treatment than antidepressant medication (Nemeroff et al., 2003). In a related area, recent studies suggest that fetal malnutrition is a common, very early cause of both psychiatric (Costello, Worthman, Erkanli, & Angold, 2007) and medical disorders (Godfrey, Gluckman, & Hanson, 2010). Findings such as these have broad implications for prevention: a single program of research aimed at maternal nutrition might reduce the incidence of both medical and behavioral problems much later in the life course. Beyond a few studies of child abuse, a major question is whether future research can identify common, early, and malleable risk factors common to both relational and medical disorders.

In this search, we will need innovative and stringent research designs. For example, in looking for early common physical or psychological risk factors designs will have to distinguish these factors from those that persist well into the life course. For example, in the case of child abuse and neglect this adverse circumstance rarely has a discrete end point. Toddlers who are severely abused or neglected by a parent are likely, if they remain with the abusive parent, to receive poor care across many years of their lives. Moreover, abusive care is tightly correlated with other adverse environmental circumstances—such as economic adversity and parental mental illness—whose adverse affects are difficult to tease apart from the abuse.

The same is true for improving our estimates of the long-term impact of severe illness on relational problems. We have cited, for example, a study of very low birth weight babies and their impact on parental stress and burden (Moore et al., 2006). The observed effect on parents extends well past the first decade of the child's life. However, it seems unlikely that this durable effect is a result only of the early traumatic experience of bearing a sick child and enduring the intensive care the child required. Rather, it is the child's continuing deficits and difficulties, most notably cognitive difficulties and their associated stigma, that persist long after the early parental trauma.

One powerful design to address many of these concerns is the adoption design: a child is exposed to severely adverse parental abuse or other environmental adversity at the start of life and then is adopted by a more supportive family. Rutter and his colleagues used this design to document the persistent effects on child cognitive abilities and attachment patterns of children of their exposure at the start of their life to the harsh conditions of Romanian adoption agencies. These children were adopted at various ages by competent adoptive families (Rutter & O'Connor, 2004). Rutter and his colleagues asked: Can effective rearing subsequent to early childhood adversity reverse the effects of early trauma? If so, then previous studies had overestimated these effects and underestimated the importance of adversity continuing past early childhood. In the case of autistic traits and attachment patterns they found that, for many children, rearing by competent adoptive families did not fully reverse the early effects of life in Romanian institutions. However, it is not necessary to go all the way to Romania. In Britain, for example, the majority of adopted children are placed several years after birth when many, but not all of them, have already experienced severe trauma. If the effects of this trauma persist, during the years the child lives with a more caring adoptive family, we may be more secure that it was the early trauma that was a contributory cause. Adoption designs have not been fully exploited to note the prolonged effects of early trauma, particularly the severe problems of child abuse and neglect, on the emergence of physical illness.

A second powerful design is drawn from behavioral genetics. For example, using twins several investigators have been able to show that some forms of psychopathology and medical disorders have common genetic roots. This is true for atopic illnesses and depression (Thomsen, Kyvik, & Backer, 2008; Wamboldt et al., 2000) and for depression and coronary artery disease (Kendler, Gardner, Fiske, & Gatz, 2009). In parents the quality of their relationship with their children is notably influenced by their own genes (Neiderhiser, Reiss, Lichtenstein, Spotts, & Ganiban, 2007; Neiderhiser et al., 2004) as well as by the child's genes (Reiss, Neiderhiser, Hetherington, & Plomin, 2000; Wamboldt et al., 2000). Likewise, the quality and durability of marriage is notably influenced by the genetic factors in both husbands and wives (Alfonso et al., 2004; Jocklin et al., 1996; Johnson, McGue, Krueger, & Bouchard, 2004; Lykken, 2002; Spotts et al., 2004; Spotts, Prescott, & Kendler, 2006). Thus, it is plausible that many of the genes that influence parenting or marriage may also influence the development of medical disorders. There is excellent precedent for hoping so. For example, the links between parenting and some forms of psychopathology in adolescents are *mostly* accounted for by genetic factors common to both (Reiss et al., 2000). Behavioral genetics models are poorly understood and have never been used in the study of links between relational problems and medical disorders. They have the capacity not only to distinguish genetic etiologies that may be common to both but also to suggest, if not identify, environmental factors common to both.

Mutual Exacerbation

We have cited above the Kaugars et al. (2008) study on the reciprocal relationship between medication use and favorable parental adjustment to early childhood wheezing. We cited this study to emphasize how essential a multipanel design is in exploring mechanisms of mutual exacerbation. The study also illustrated well the statistical models required for rigorously testing reciprocal effects. However, asking not just whether such reciprocal influences occur but how they occur will notably strengthen investigation of mutual exacerbation patterns.

For example, as cited, McQuaid et al. (2007) suggest that, in many cases, it is not the severity of asthma—as might be apparent to an outside observer—that triggers parental response but rather *the accuracy by which the patient perceives his or her own airway resistance* during an asthma episode. Inaccurate child observers evoke more maladaptive parental responses.

In the opposite direction, Wood, Miller, and their colleagues have explored the mechanisms by which adverse family climate (as directly observed and coded) influences the progression of childhood asthma. They showed two intermediate steps: adverse family environment leads to childhood depression and then, once children are depressed, vagal nerve mechanisms lead to increased airway constriction. They also have explored a parallel mechanism: decreased parental support leads to increased cortisol resistance and the inability of cortisol to exert its ordinary facilitation of immune responses (Miller, Gaudin, Zysk, & Chen, 2009).

Recently an increasing volume of studies explored the mechanisms that might link marital problems to impaired health. For example, Kiecolt-Glaser et al. (2011) has summarized a number of self-report and lab-based studies linking marital conflict to impaired immunological responses, patterns of impairment that other studies show increased risk for several medical disorders. Likewise, in a series of studies, Smith and his colleagues (Smith et al., 2009, 2011) have shown the impact of marital negativity on vagal self-regulation of heart rate, especially in women whose husbands are poor self-regulators. Other studies suggest this pattern of loss of self-regulation is a notable risk factor for several medical disorders.

These mechanistic studies are an important step forward but their value in understanding how relational problems exacerbate medical disorders, or the reverse, remains limited. The great majority of these mechanistic studies are done on healthy individuals with limited or no follow-up to explore the role of these mechanisms in the evolution of medical disorder in the *same subjects.* Other mechanistic studies, usually in laboratory conditions, are done with already ill patients who may simply be more sensitive to adverse relationships. Moreover, it is not enough to link two separate studies, the first showing contemporaneous mechanisms linking relational problems to biological risk factors and then, in a second study on another sample, to show these same biological risk factors predicting later onset of disease. What is crucial is to demonstrate directly that these mechanisms mediate the links between relational problems and medical disorders in the same subjects. This requires, in many instances, long-term follow-up. Though expensive and time consuming, these studies will be well worth the investment. If these mediational processes, such as accurate reports of airway constriction or immune responses or vagal self-regulation, are themselves malleable they become potential targets for intervention. For example, can one abort a negative asthma–parent response cycle by teaching children with asthma to be more accurate in their perceptions of their own airway constriction?

Clinical Course Moderator

As we have noted, convincing evidence for this role for relational problems can come from two sources. Longitudinal data allow for comparing the clinical course of illness where family relations are not troubled to the course when there are notable relational problems. Strong inferences about the role of the family, in studies of this kind, require research designs that are very difficult to achieve. In general, we need a multipanel design extending across a period when the ordinary course of the medical disorder is evolving. We also need to show that relational problems that are not a consequence of the disorder have an effect on its outcome. Thus, in the first panel we need to assess the medical disorder, in a second we need data on the relationship, and in a third we need to check again on the medical disorder. Even so, studies of this kind are plagued with both measurable and unmeasurable confounds: our two groups—those with relational problems and those without—are likely to differ in many characteristics that, in turn, might influence disease course.

It is not surprising, therefore, that the literature is sparse in this area. This is why the intervention studies loom so large in our understanding of the role of family relationships in the moderation of disease course. In this instance the investigator studies the effect of the relational disorder by purposely changing it (hopefully for the better). The use of a randomized, control design—if the sample is large enough—helps to rule out the effects of confounding variables. The meta-analyses of these interventions that we cited, particularly those that are focused on disease outcome such as patient survival or changes in the physical attributes of medical disorders, suggest that relational assessment and intervention should be a routine part of clinical care. The evidence seems particularly impressive for parent–child interventions in diabetes and marital or adult partner interventions in cardiovascular disease. However, as much as any work we have cited, this body of evidence calls out for clear criteria for relational problems, criteria spelled out elsewhere in this volume. We will want to know, in the next round of studies, whether these interventions are useful for all patients or whether they are indicated only where there are clear-cut and well-defined relational problems.

While the practical significance of the large number of randomized trials in this area is clear, we must be cautious about drawing inferences about mechanisms of effect. The trials indicate the clinical value of focusing on relational problems associated with specific disease states. In general, they are still mute on the underlying mechanisms. The meta-analyses do indicate that many of the trials showed that the intervention not only affected disease course but also improved the relationship that was the target of the intervention. What they did not show was that clinical improvement in the medical disorder was a *consequence* of the improved relationship.

As we have noted elsewhere (Howe, Reiss, & Yuh, 2002) the strongest inferences about etiological mechanisms can be drawn from intervention studies when they are linked, in a single design, with longitudinal studies. We need to do more than randomize patients to a relational intervention group or a control. As in good longitudinal studies we need to measure (perhaps at several time points) the status of the relationship itself and test whether the effect of the intervention is a consequence of change in the relationship. We need to rule out potential *mediational confounds*. That is, our intervention may have affected some other factor in the patient or the family that was responsible for its effect, a process other than *improvement in the relationship*.

A leading candidate for a mediational confound is the very general effect that well-conducted psychotherapies have on improving the relationship between the patient and the care provider. In individual psychotherapy for both adult (Martin, Garske, & Davis, 2000) and child (McLeod, 2011) psychological problems, the quality of the relationship between client and therapist has a small but reliable effect on psychological outcome across many different types of treatment. The concept of a therapeutic alliance has been successfully applied to families, although it is more complex since each member of a family has their own alliance with a care provider and may be influenced by their perception of other members' alliance (Pinsof & Catherall, 1986). Nonetheless, successful measures have been developed and a recent meta-analysis suggests the alliance between care provider and family is as crucial for the outcome of family-based treatment as it is for individually based treatment (Friedlander, Escudero, Heatherington, & Diamond, 2011). Most pertinent are recent studies that have applied this concept to medical patients (Aikens, Bingham, & Piette, 2005) and their families (Gavin, Wamboldt, Sorokin, Levy, & Wamboldt, 1999) in medical care settings. Thus, many of the interventions cited in the meta-analyses we have reviewed may have achieved their effects through enhancing the alliance of patient and family with the medical care team rather than enhancing relationships within the family. Thus, an important task ahead is for a partnership we advocate here: clear criteria for relational problems and interventions designed to address those relational problems and determine their role in mediating intervention effects.

Cultural Context

Data we have so far reviewed argues strongly for the importance of assessing relational problems in medically ill patients. However, one final word of caution is important, particularly as formal criteria for relational problems are being considered for an international classification of diseases. Cultural differences play a major role in how illnesses are experienced by patients and their families and the role families are expected to play in their care. A full discussion of this is beyond the scope of this chapter. However, a productive research partnership between improved relational assessment in medical settings and effective interventions must include relevant cultural factors in research designs. To illustrate, we mention briefly here only two of these: *stigmatization* and *familism*.

Most clinicians know about the stigmatization of mental illness, particularly the addictions although there is meaningful variation across cultures in these processes. Similarly, there is widespread stigmatization of sexually transmitted diseases. What is less widely appreciated is that a number of other medical conditions are stigmatized in many cultures. For example, obstetric fistulae occur often in countries with limited obstetric care, and are highly stigmatized. They preferentially affect poor, single women whose status alone would ordinarily stigmatize them (Bangser, 2006). Lung cancer is also stigmatized because, in many cultural settings, patients are blamed for smoking. A similar effect is now being recognized for cervical cancer. Paradoxically, this may be most severe in countries advancing the use of vaccines against the human papilloma virus (HPV), a sexually transmitted infection. Paradoxically, cervical cancer patients are being stigmatized because they are perceived to be at fault (Dyer, 2010).

Familism is a broad term used to distinguish among culturally supported beliefs and values on the importance of the family. High familism conceives the family is the main source of pride and support for its members. Individuals in "high familism" cultures feel a strong sense of pride in their families, strong obligations to help a family member in need, expectations that their family will help them when they need it, and strong connections between their own self-esteem and the successes and failures of the family. Paradoxically, familism can be a burden. For example, in long-term family caregivers of dementia patients the obligation component of this culturally endorsed value feels like a burden. This can reduce the care one family member gives to another (Sayegh & Knight, 2011).

When stigma and familism combine the mixture may be toxic; the entire family may feel stigmatized by illness. Relationships within the family may seem very problematic. Assessment focused just on relationship problems, using criteria described in this volume, may be misleading. Addressing these relational problems with an intervention insensitive to cultural processes may be ineffective or injurious.

SUMMARY

The advent of ICD-11 provides a welcome opportunity for improvements in nosology. Much of this book provides a rationale for one important improvement: criterion-based assessment of parent–child and partner relational problems. The current chapter is directed at an equally important opportunity: cross coding. An effective diagnostic manual should alert health professional about the possibility of important co-occurring disorders, particular those that may have a major impact on the course or treatment of the illness identified in the primary diagnosis. This chapter has presented data that argue that an evidence-based diagnostic manual should encourage medical clinicians to consider co-occurring relational problems. The evidence is now persuasive, for a number of medical illnesses, that this search for co-occurring relational problems should be standard practice.

REFERENCES

Aikens, J. E., Bingham, R., & Piette, J. D. (2005). Patient-provider communication and self-care behavior among type 2 diabetes patients. *Diabetes Education, 31*, 681–690.

Alderfer, M. A., Fiese, B. H., Gold, J. I., Cutuli, J. J., Holmbeck, G. N., Goldbeck, L.,..., Patterson, J. (2008). Evidence-based assessment in pediatric psychology: Family measures. *Journal of Pediatric Psychology, 33*, 1046–1061.

Alderfer, M. A., Navsaria, N., & Kazak, A. E. (2009). Family functioning and posttraumatic stress disorder in adolescent survivors of childhood cancer. *Journal of Family Psychology, 23*, 717–725.

Alfonso, J., Pollevick, G. D., Van Der Hart, M. G., Flügge, G., Fuchs, E., & Frasch, A. C. C. (2004). Identification of genes regulated by chronic psychosocial stress and antidepressant treatment in the hippocampus. *European Journal of Neuroscience, 19*, 659–666.

Anderson, B. J., Holmbeck, G., Iannotti, R. J., McKay, S. V., Lochrie, A., Volkening, L. K., & Laffel, L. (2009). Dyadic measures of the parent–child relationship during the transition to adolescence and glycemic control in children with type 1 diabetes. *Families, Systems, & Health, 27*, 141–152.

Armour, T. A., Norris, S. L., Jack, L., Jr., Zhang, X., & Fisher, L. (2005). The effectiveness of family interventions in people with diabetes mellitus: A systematic review. *Diabetic Medicine, 22*, 1295–1305.

Bangser, M. (2006). Obstetric fistula and stigma. *The Lancet, 367*, 535–536.

Bell, B. G., & Belsky, J. (2008). Parenting and children's cardiovascular functioning. *Child: Care, Health, & Development, 34,* 194–203.

Boyce, W. T. (2004). Social stratification, health, and violence in the very young. *Annals of New York Academy of Sciences, 1036,* 47–68.

Bradbury, T. N., & Karney, B. R. (2004). Understanding and altering the longitudinal course of marriage. *Journal of Marriage and Family, 66,* 862–879.

Colman, R. A., & Widom, C. S. (2004). Childhood abuse and neglect and adult intimate relationships: A prospective study. *Child Abuse & Neglect, 28,* 1133–1151.

Costello, E. J., Worthman, C., Erkanli, A., & Angold, A. (2007). Prediction from low birth weight to female adolescent depression: A test of competing hypotheses. *Archives of General Psychiatry, 64,* 343–350.

Cuijpers, P., Smit, F., Bohlmeijer, E., Hollon, S. D., & Andersson, G. (2010). Efficacy of cognitive-behavioural therapy and other psychological treatments for adult depression: Meta-analytic study of publication bias. *British Journal of Psychiatry, 196,* 173–178.

Davis, C. L., Delamater, A. M., Shaw, K. H., La Greca, A. M., Eidson, M. S., Perez-Rodriguez, J. E., & Nemery, R. (2001). Parenting styles, regimen adherence, and glycemic control in 4- to 10-year-old children with diabetes. *Journal of Pediatric Psychology, 26,* 123–129.

Dyer, K. E. (2010). From cancer to sexually transmitted infection explorations of social stigma among cervical cancer survivors. *Human Organization, 69,* 321–330.

Eaker, E. D., Sullivan, L. M., Kelly-Hayes, M., D'Agostino, R. B., & Benjamin, E. J. (2007). Marital status, marital strain, and risk of coronary heart disease or total mortality: The Framingham offspring study. *Psychosomatic Medicine, 69,* 509–513.

Flaherty, M. J., & O'Brien, M. E. (1992). Family styles of coping in end stage renal disease. *ANNA Journal, 19,* 345–349.

Friedlander, M. L., Escudero, V., Heatherington, L., & Diamond, G. M. (2011). Alliance in couple and family therapy. *Psychotherapy, 48,* 25–33.

Friedman, H. S., Tucker, J. S., Schwartz, J. E., Martin, L. R., Tomlinson-Keasey, C., Wingard, D. L., & Criqui, M. H. (1995a). Childhood conscientiousness and longevity: Health behaviors and cause of death. *Journal of Personality and Social Psychology, 68,* 696–703.

Friedman, H. S., Tucker, J. S., Schwartz, J. E., Tomlinson-Keasey, C., Martin, L. R., Wingard, D. L., & Criqui, M. H. (1995b). Psychosocial and behavioral predictors of longevity: The aging and death of the "Termites." *American Psychologist, 50,* 69–78.

Fuller-Thomson, E., Brennenstuhl, S., & Frank, J. (2010). The association between childhood physical abuse and heart disease in adulthood: Findings from a representative community sample. *Child Abuse & Neglect, 34,* 689–698.

Gavin, L. A., Wamboldt, M. Z., Sorokin, N., Levy, S. Y., & Wamboldt, F. S. (1999). Treatment alliance and its association with family functioning, adherence, and medical outcome in adolescents with severe, chronic asthma. *Journal of Pediatric Psychology, 24,* 355–365.

Gerber, A. J., Kocsis, J. H., Milrod, B. L., Roose, S. P., Barber, J. P., Thase, M. E., et al. (2011). A quality-based review of randomized controlled trials of psychodynamic psychotherapy. *The American Journal of Psychiatry, 168*(1), 19–28.

Godfrey, K. M., Gluckman, P. D., & Hanson, M. A. (2010). Developmental origins of metabolic disease: Life course and intergenerational perspectives. *Trends in Endocrinology and Metabolism, 21,* 199–205.

Hampson, S. E., Goldberg, L. R., Vogt, T. M., & Dubanoski, J. P. (2006). Forty years on: Teachers' assessments of children's personality traits predict self-reported health behaviors and outcomes at midlife. *Health Psychology, 25,* 57–64.

Hartmann, M., Bazner, E., Wild, B., Eisler, I., & Herzog, W. (2010). Effects of interventions involving the family in the treatment of adult patients with chronic physical diseases: A meta-analysis. *Psychotherapy and Psychosomatics, 79,* 136–148.

Holm, K. E., Wamboldt, F. S., & Reiss, D. (2008). Family risk factor measures. In A. J. Rush, M. B. First, & D. Blacker (Eds.), *Handbook of psychiatric measures* (2nd ed., pp. 211–235). Arlington, VA: American Psychiatric Publishing.

Howe, G. W., Reiss, D., & Yuh, J. (2002). Can prevention trials test theories of etiology? *Development and Psychopathology, 14,* 673–694.

Hughes, M. E., & Waite, L. J. (2009). Marital biography and health at mid-life. *Journal of Health and Social Behavior, 50,* 344–358.

Jocklin, V., McGue, M., & Lykken, D. T. (1996). Personality and divorce: A genetic analysis. *Journal of Personality & Social Psychology, 71*(2), 288–299.

Johnson, W., McGue, M., Krueger, R. F., & Bouchard, T. J., Jr. (2004). Marriage and personality: A genetic analysis. *Journal of Personality and Social Psychology, 86,* 285–294.

Katz, M. L., Laffel, L. M., Perrin, J. M., & Kuhlthau, K. (2011). Impact of type 1 diabetes mellitus on the family is reduced with the medical home, care coordination, and family-centered care. *Journal of Pediatrics*. Retrieved from www.ncbi.nlm.nih.gov/pubmed/22133424

Kaugars, A. S., Klinnert, M. D., Robinson, J., & Ho, M. (2008). Reciprocal influences in children's and families' adaptation to early childhood wheezing. *Health Psychology, 27,* 258–267.

Kazak, A. E., Barakat, L. P., Meeske, K., Christakis, D., Meadows, A. T., Casey, R., & Stuber, M. L. (1997). Posttraumatic stress, family functioning, and social support in survivors of childhood leukemia and their mothers and fathers. *Journal of Consulting & Clinical Psychology, 65*, 120–129.

Kendler, K. S., Gardner, C. O., Fiske, A., & Gatz, M. (2009). Major depression and coronary artery disease in the Swedish twin registry: Phenotypic, genetic, and environmental sources of comorbidity. *Archives of General Psychiatry, 66*, 857–863.

Kern, M. L., & Friedman, H. S. (2008). Do conscientious individuals live longer? A quantitative review. *Health Psychology, 27*, 505–512.

Kiecolt-Glaser, J. K., Gouin, J. P., Weng, N. P., Malarkey, W. B., Beversdorf, D. Q., & Glaser, R. (2011). Childhood adversity heightens the impact of later-life caregiving stress on telomere length and inflammation. *Psychosomatic Medicine, 73*, 16–22.

Kimmel, P. L., Peterson, R. A., Weihs, K. L., Shidler, N., Simmens, S. J., Alleyne, S.,..., Phillips, T. M. (2000). Dyadic relationship conflict, gender, and mortality in urban hemodialysis patients. *Journal of the American Society of Nephrology, 11*, 1518–1525.

Krueger, R. F., & Markon, K. E. (2006). Reinterpreting comorbidity: A model-based approach to understanding and classifying psychopathology. *Annual Review of Clinical Psychology, 2*, 111–133.

Lykken, D. T. (2002). How relationships begin and end: A genetic perspective. In Anita L. Vangelisti & H. T. Reis (Eds.), *Stability and change in relationships: Advances in personal relationships* (pp. 83–102). New York, NY: Cambridge University Press.

Martin, D. J., Garske, J. P., & Davis, M. (2000). Relation of the therapeutic alliance with outcome and other variables: A meta-analytic review. *Journal of Consulting and Clinical Psychology, 68*, 438–450.

Martire, L. M. (2005). The "relative" efficacy of involving family in psychosocial interventions for chronic illness: Are there added benefits to patients and family members? *Families, Systems, & Health, 23*, 312–328.

Martire, L. M., Lustig, A. P., Schulz, R., Miller, G. E., & Helgeson, V. S. (2004). Is it beneficial to involve a family member? A meta-analysis of psychosocial interventions for chronic illness. *Health Psychology, 23*, 599–611.

Martire, L. M., Schulz, R., Helgeson, V. S., Small, B. J., & Saghafi, E. M. (2010). Review and meta-analysis of couple-oriented interventions for chronic illness. *Annals of Behavioral Medicine, 40*, 325–342.

McLeod, B. D. (2011). Relation of the alliance with outcomes in youth psychotherapy: A meta-analysis. *Clinical Psychology Review, 31*, 603–616.

McQuaid, E. L., Koinis Mitchell, D., Walders, N., Nassau, J. H., Kopel, S. J., Klein, R. B.,..., Fritz, G. K. (2007). Pediatric asthma morbidity: The importance of symptom perception and family response to symptoms. *Journal of Pediatric Psychology, 32*, 167–177.

Miller, G. E., Gaudin, A., Zysk, E., & Chen, E. (2009). Parental support and cytokine activity in childhood asthma: The role of glucocorticoid sensitivity. *The Journal of Allergy & Clinical Immunology, 123*, 824–830.

Moore, M., Taylor, H. G., Klein, N., Minich, N., & Hack, M. (2006). Longitudinal changes in family outcomes of very low birth weight. *Journal of Pediatric Psychology, 31*, 1024–1035.

Neale, M. C., & Kendler, K. S. (1995). Models of comorbidity for multifactorial disorders. *American Journal of Human Genetics, 57*, 935–953.

Neiderhiser, J. M., Reiss, D., Lichtenstein, P., Spotts, E. L., & Ganiban, J. (2007). Father–adolescent relationships and the role of genotype–environment correlation. *Journal of Family Psychology, 21*, 560–571.

Neiderhiser, J. M., Reiss, D., Pedersen, N. L., Lichtenstein, P., Spotts, E. L., Hansson, K.,..., Ellhammer, O. (2004). Genetic and environmental influences on mothering of adolescents: A comparison of two samples. *Developmental Psychology, 40*, 335–351.

Nemeroff, C. B., Heim, C. M., Thase, M. E., Klein, D. N., Rush, A. J., Schatzberg, A. F.,..., Keller, M. B. (2003). Differential responses to psychotherapy versus pharmacotherapy in patients with chronic forms of major depression and childhood trauma. *Proceedings of the National Academy of Sciences, 100*, 14293–14296.

Pai, A. L., Greenley, R. N., Lewandowski, A., Drotar, D., Youngstrom, E., & Peterson, C. C. (2007). A meta-analytic review of the influence of pediatric cancer on parent and family functioning. *Journal of Family Psychology, 21*, 407–415.

Pinsof, W. M., & Catherall, D. R. (1986). The integrative psychotherapy alliance: Family, couple and individual therapy scales. *Journal of Marital and Family Therapy, 12*, 137–151.

Reiss, D. (1990). Patient, family, and staff responses to end-stage renal disease. *American Journal of Kidney Disease, 15*, 194–200.

Reiss, D., Gonzalez, S., & Kramer, N. (1986). Family process, chronic illness and death: On the weakness of strong bonds. *Archives of General Psychiatry, 43*, 795–804.

Reiss, D., Neiderhiser, J. M., Hetherington, E. M., & Plomin, R. (2000). *The relationship code: Deciphering genetic and social influences on adolescent development*. Cambridge, MA: Harvard University Press.

Rohrbaugh, M. J., Shoham, V., & Coyne, J. C. (2006). Effect of marital quality on eight-year survival of patients with heart failure. *American Journal of Cardiology, 98*, 1069–1072.

Rutter, M., & O'Connor, T. G. (2004). Are there biological programming effects for psychological development? Findings from a study of Romanian adoptees. *Developmental Psychology, 40*, 81–94.

Sayegh, P., & Knight, B. G. (2011). The effects of familism and cultural justification on the mental and physical health of family caregivers. *The Journals of Gerontology: Series B: Psychological Sciences and Social Sciences, 1*, 3–14.

Singer, B., & Ryff, C. D. (1999). Hierarchies of life histories and associated health risks. *Annals of New York Academy of Sciences, 896*, 96–115.

Smith, T. W., Cribbet, M. R., Nealey-Moore, J. B., Uchino, B. N., Williams, P. G., Mackenzie, J., & Thayer, J. F. (2011). Matters of the variable heart: Respiratory sinus arrhythmia response to marital interaction and associations with marital quality. *Journal of Personality and Social Psychology, 100*, 103–119.

Smith, T. W., Uchino, B. N., Berg, C. A., Florsheim, P., Pearce, G., Hawkins, M.,..., Olsen-Cerny, C. (2009). Conflict and collaboration in middle-aged and older couples: II. Cardiovascular reactivity during marital interaction. *Psychology and Aging, 24*, 274–286.

Spotts, E. L., Neiderhiser, J. M., Towers, H., Hansson, K., Lichtenstein, P., Cederblad, M.,..., Reiss, D. (2004). Genetic and Environmental Influences on Marital Relationships. *Journal of Family Psychology, 18*, 107–119.

Spotts, E. L., Prescott, C., & Kendler, K. (2006). Examining the origins of gender differences in marital quality: A behavior genetic analysis. *Journal of Family Psychology, 20*, 605–613.

Thomsen, S. F., Kyvik, K. O., & Backer, V. (2008). Etiological relationships in atopy: A review of twin studies. *Twin Research and Human Genetics, 11*, 112–120.

Tucker, J. S., Friedman, H. S., Wingard, D. L., & Schwartz, J. E. (1996). Marital history at midlife as a predictor of longevity: Alternative explanations to the protective effect of marriage. *Health Psychology, 15*, 94–101.

Turner-Musa, J., Leidner, D., Simmens, S., Reiss, D., Kimmel, P. L., & Holder, B. (1999). Family structure and patient survival in an African-American end-stage renal disease population: A preliminary investigation. *Social Science and Medicine, 48*, 1333–1340.

Wamboldt, M. Z., Hewitt, J. K., Schmitz, S., Wamboldt, F. S., Rasanen, M., Koskenvuo, M.,..., Kaprio, J. (2000). Familial association between allergic disorders and depression in adult Finnish twins. *American Journal of Medical Genetics, 96*, 146–153.

Whisman, M. A., & Uebelacker, L. A. (2012). A longitudinal investigation of marital adjustment as a risk factor for metabolic syndrome. *Health Psychology, 1*, 80–86.

20

Future Directions for Science and Public Health

Steven R. H. Beach, Nadine J. Kaslow, Heather M. Foran, Richard E. Heyman, and Claudia García-Moreno

This book takes several steps toward enhancing surveillance and clinical assessment of family problems. The chapters that are focused on impact in each of the sections document an important role for family processes in the emergence of physical and mental health problems. They also highlight the costs and burden of maladaptive family processes and violence for those in low-, middle-, and high-income countries. As the data suggest, the connections between health outcomes and family processes involving distress, violence, or abuse are multifaceted, sometimes direct and sometimes indirect. Family relationships often change as a function of psychological and physical health problems (Wamboldt & Wamboldt, 2000) and, in some cases, interpersonal difficulties are an integral part of a psychological disorder (e.g., Reid, Patterson, & Snyder, 2002). Distressing relationships in the family also can affect the burden associated with psychological impairment (see Whisman & Ubelaker, 2006), as well as the long-term course of some mental disorders (see Hooley, Miklowitz, & Beach, 2006). These findings suggest that tracking such relationships can provide invaluable information about future costs and the total financial burden likely to be imposed by mental health problems. Maltreatment in parent–child relationships and violence in partner relationships can lead directly to injury. Further, maltreatment and conflict in family relationships can negatively impact endocrinological and immunological systems (Kiecolt-Glaser, McGuire, Robles, & Glaser, 2002), further increasing the degree of functional impairment produced by a disorder. Likewise, disturbances in primary relationships early in life can change neural systems that control emotional resilience (Suomi, 1999), and so create long-term changes in vulnerability to mental disorders (Gallo, Troxel, Matthews, & Kuller, 2003), or influence inflammatory and other regulatory mechanisms setting the stage for increased physical health problems in adulthood (Miller, Chen, & Parker, 2011), enhancing the perpetuation of disorder from one generation to the next. For each of these reasons, enhanced surveillance of family problems, during early childhood and beyond, can provide an essential window and perhaps an early warning indicator of broader secular changes in psychological and physical health.

In considering the set of relationships that may be most relevant to track, two types of family relationships emerge as being of particular importance. Problems in the relationship with the spouse or partner and problems in the parenting relationship have strong associations with psychopathology and a range of health outcomes. Indeed, it has been suggested that human beings are "hard-wired" to respond to events occurring in primary attachment relationships (Insel & Young, 2001; Young, Francis, & Insel, 2003), suggesting that these close family relationships require special attention in surveillance and treatment. Likewise, practical considerations point to the likely value of special attention to family relationships, as these often are the primary focus of preventive efforts and clinical intervention.

Thus, family stressors and problems have a substantial impact on both mental and physical health outcomes. By refining criteria and measurement conventions, we anticipate that the field will be ready to move to the next generation of research on the circumstances under which family problems result in particular health outcomes, the protective factors that may enhance resilience, and the genetic and biological processes that are key elements of the progression from family problems and violence to mental and physical health outcomes.

GETTING STARTED

A first step toward reducing the mental and physical health burden imposed by family violence and other relational problems is to develop a common language about these patterns that will allow the sharing of information across national boundaries. This has been a primary goal of this book. Enhanced, cross-national surveillance will allow policy makers to identify the role of family relationship problems, including domestic violence, in the development of both mental and physical health problems in their own countries and to share information and strategies for prevention and intervention.

For each of the proposed categories there is a substantial body of research, across multiple contexts, suggesting that family problems occur frequently and have potent effects on individual outcomes. This suggests that enhanced systematic surveillance will better document worldwide prevalence, costs, and risk and protective factors, providing a firmer foundation for policy and decision making. Heretofore, categories in the International Classification of Diseases, Tenth Edition (ICD-10) for coding these problem areas did not provide a firm foundation for reliable and valid assessment, nor did they facilitate easy communication across national boundaries. Furthermore, the complexity of the categories in the ICD-10 limited the clinical utility of the categories, especially in low-resource settings. By simultaneously (a) simplifying the coding of relational categories in the ICD-11, (b) improving the clarity of the criteria, and (c) providing clear measurement tools, the proposed categories have potential to have more clinical utility across the array of health care settings in which family problems and family violence are detected (e.g., primary care settings, mental health clinics, and emergency rooms).

It is therefore timely to focus on enhancing the reliability and validity of our assessments of family violence and other relational problems, and to take steps to ensure that researchers and surveillance systems utilize similar definitions. This is one reason this book goes beyond new consensus category definitions and provides more detailed assessment guidelines designed to enhance reliability and validity. Enhanced reliability is of critical importance for future advances in the scientific understanding of family processes and their connection to the etiology of mental and physical health, as well as for advances in knowledge about the maintenance of particular mental and physical health problems (e.g., Heyman et al., 2009). Without reliable, shared definitions of key family problems, there can be no cumulative progress toward a shared understanding of the role family processes play in the etiology and maintenance of a broad array of health and mental health difficulties.

NEXT STEPS FOR POLICY MAKERS

The mere presence of a shared definition that can be reliably applied by individuals operating in different contexts is a step forward, allowing researchers, clinicians, and policy makers to communicate efficiently, and to accumulate a foundation of replicable, cross-national results. Incorporation of these common definitions into public health surveillance systems will provide continuous, systematic collection and analysis of health-related family processes, and so set the stage for planning, implementation, and evaluation of public health practice in this area. This has the potential to lead to both new insights regarding the role of family processes in health outcomes and to potentially powerful points of preventive intervention. In key family domains, such as maltreatment/violence or severe distress in parenting or marital/couple subsystems, enhanced surveillance can notify policy makers when there is substantial change in problematic family functioning in a given region or subgroup, serving as an early warning system in some cases of additional impending public health problems. In particular, a sudden increase in family problems may provide early indicators of widespread breakdown in other support systems and the emergence of broader social problems. Ongoing surveillance also will allow policy makers to examine documented effects of interventions and track progress toward specified public health goals.

For policy researchers, enhanced surveillance with shared, reliable categories will facilitate comparison of prevention programs as a function of context and variation in implementation strategies, further enhancing our understanding of how best to intervene in support of developing nurturing and healthy relationships and families around the world. Perhaps most significantly, enhanced surveillance will allow policy makers and researchers to clarify the epidemiology of various forms of family violence and other relational problems worldwide and allow for better characterization of the true scope of health implications of family problems, providing a better foundation for public health policy and strategies related to the family.

FUTURE DIRECTIONS FOR POLICY REGARDING HEALTHY FAMILIES

In addition to the importance of family problems for mental and physical health outcomes already noted, causes of death and morbidity in low-, middle-, and high-income countries are shifting toward problems with substantial lifestyle and behavioral components. Family problems, including child abuse and partner violence, are associated significantly with many of the leading contributors to lifestyle and behavior problems, including strong links to depression, substance use, risky sexual behaviors, and unwanted pregnancies among other major health problems worldwide (see Chapters 3, 7, 11, and 15 in this book). As a result, issues related to behavior change, lifestyle choices, and the management of chronic problems increasingly are on the forefront of public health concerns worldwide. In the context of public health concern for management of chronic conditions, increased attention to family stressors and problems is long overdue.

Family relationships also are strongly related to other aspects of physical health (Burman & Margolin, 1992; Kiecolt-Glaser & Newton, 2001), creating other opportunities to use enhanced family health surveillance to better understand and influence a range of physical health outcomes. For example, it appears that married individuals are physically healthier than are single, divorced or separated, and widowed individuals, even after controlling for income and age (Verbrugge, 1979). Further, marital status predicts mortality for several chronic and acute conditions (Johnson, Backlund, Sorlie, & Loveless, 2000; Verbrugge, 1979). Similarly, family relations appear to be particularly useful in predicting autonomic, endocrine, and immunological outcomes (Uchino, Cacioppo, & Kiecolt-Glaser, 1996), suggesting great potential for increased understanding and better managing physical health outcomes through surveillance of family relationships. Although healthier individuals are more likely to marry and to stay married, the association between physical health and marriage remains after controlling for selection effects (Wu, Penning, Pollard, & Hart, 2003) and effects on coping and health behaviors (e.g., diet, sleep, exercise, and medication compliance). Accordingly, available evidence suggests that there are likely to be direct and important payoffs in terms of enhanced physical health that result from greater attention to the role of family processes, with the caveat that the impact of these processes may vary in important ways as a function of gender and social context.

NEXT STEPS FOR BASIC, PREVENTIVE, AND SERVICE DELIVERY RESEARCH

At a basic level, shared definitions are necessary for scientific progress because they allow for the accumulation of data. As we move forward with increasingly sophisticated measurement of genetic, epigenetic, and biological processes and biopsychosocial outcomes, it is appropriate that the precision of definitions of family violence and other family processes keep pace. As has been noted in the preceding literature reviews, currently researchers have no internally accepted, reliable set of standard definitions upon which they can rely when summarizing evidence and accumulating data on the impact of key family processes. This leads to different researchers using the same language to refer to different things—or equally problematic, using different language to refer to the same thing. The net result is decreased capacity to integrate findings across studies and even more difficulty integrating findings across language and national barriers. Integration across national boundaries will be particularly important as researchers and policy makers attempt to better understand the way social context influences family violence and other family processes and their impact on mental and physical health outcomes.

The improved ICD codes in the ICD-11 for key family processes will encourage greater inquiry into basic etiology and the role of family in mental and physical illnesses and create opportunities for advances in applied research. For example, considerable evidence suggests that serious marital dissatisfaction predicts increased risk for a major depressive episode (Whisman & Bruce, 1999) or comorbidity, and both couple conflict and physical abuse predict subsequent increases in psychological distress, depressive symptoms, and suicidality among women (Beach, Kim, Cercone-Keeney, & Brody, 2004; Cano & O'Leary, 2000; Kendler, Hettema, Butera, Gardner, & Prescott, 2003; Leiner, Compton, Houry, & Kaslow, 2008). Accordingly, disturbance in intimate adult relationships is key for understanding the etiology of depressive symptoms for many individuals and has the potential to supplement genetically based models (Caspi et al., 2003). The enhanced definitions resulting from the ICD-11 process will allow for the impact of these relationships to be examined in cultural context to see how the processes change depending on different national and regional patterns. This has the potential to lead to substantial advances in our understanding of basic etiological processes, as well as the limits of generalization from affluent contexts to less wealthy contexts or from Western contexts to non-Western contexts.

A similar opportunity exists with regard to parenting relationships. Some forms of conflict between offspring and parents may have lasting effects. For example, women who were adopted soon after birth and who were at high genetic risk for depression showed no evidence of the disorder if reared by adoptive parents without psychopathology or couple difficulties (Cadoret et al., 1996), suggesting that some parenting environments may be necessary to observe a genetic effect. Similarly, adoptees with a genetic risk for schizophrenia and exposure to specific communication styles in their adopted families were more likely to develop the disorder than were genetically susceptible persons raised by families with more clear communication and clear roles (Tienari et al., 1994), again highlighting the possibly key role of parenting environment in the transmission of illness. These data suggest that an interaction between the relationship environment and particular genetic diatheses may be critical to the etiology of certain major mental disorders (Caspi et al., 2003). As investigators have more, high-quality surveillance data on specific problematic family patterns, such relationships should be apparent in national and international data sets as well. Again, this has the potential to lead to substantial advances in understanding of basic etiological processes.

Uniform definitions also will allow us to determine how the burden of risk is distributed and how family risk factors favor or impair care in different cultural contexts. This will facilitate examination of health care delivery systems and the role of the family in a more contextually appropriate manner. As noted in several of the preceding chapters, there is a substantial impact of family violence and other family problems on the delivery of interventions. These impacts have been observed in higher income regions and are likely to be as strong or stronger in less affluent areas. By using the same standardized questions and protocols, all countries can contribute to and benefit from the monitoring of within-country trends as well as benefit from comparisons of experiences across countries. A uniform surveillance approach encourages the collection of small amounts of useful information on a regular and continuing basis. With standard definitions that are widely shared, there is increasing potential to identify the role of family problems in optimal treatment planning and in prevention programs. This also increases the potential for enhanced outcomes because obstacles that might otherwise have been overlooked can be identified and addressed. More reliable definitions will allow the ICD system to better capture a broad array of research on the social determinants of health.

In the context of advances already being implemented by the World Health Organization (WHO), the addition of improved definitions of family processes will provide higher quality statistics, readily accessible to researchers and policy makers, allowing them to access data on the worldwide implications of family problems and processes. This will enhance the ability of all interested parties to readily contribute to the discussion of how best to support and strengthen healthier, safer, and more resilient families, decreasing the public health burden of key problematic family processes.

OTHER FUTURE DIRECTIONS

For the treatment of severe mental illness, as well as for alcohol and drug abuse, there is strong evidence that relational processes are pivotal for both short-term and long-term outcomes (Beach, 2001; Miklowitz, 2004). However, there is currently relatively little empirical evidence detailing the extent to which well-specified relational variables predict treatment response and maintenance of treatment gains. As a result, almost no guidance is available with regard to specific family relationship indicators that can identify when family interventions are optimal or essential for effective treatment or prevention, and conversely when they may be unhelpful (e.g., relying on the spouse when couple violence co-occurs with a suicide attempt). Given the importance of disrupted relationships as a source of distress, morbidity, and mortality, better surveillance should provide rapid gains in understanding predictors of response to existing treatments as well as an increased understanding of the true impact of different treatments on overall family burden.

Research also is needed to identify effective methods for engaging partners and family members in relational treatments where they are indicated and to better outline the contexts in which relational treatments are appropriate. This line of inquiry should pay particular attention to varying cultural and subcultural barriers to participation. The barriers to participation in an adequate course of treatment, even for highly motivated couples and family members, should be taken seriously (e.g., Sullivan, Pasch, Cornelius, & Cirigliano, 2004). However, problems associated with implementation of relational interventions currently are compounded by poorly understood variations related to cultural expectations. At a minimum, family interventions that require both or all involved parties to attend sessions may face competing demands in the form of work and childcare requirements, and may at times be unhelpful. The result is that focused research is necessary to identify practical methods of delivering relational interventions across a range of disorders and relationship circumstances. In addition, research aimed at marketing relational interventions in a culturally appropriate manner will also be of considerable value.

Of particular importance for long-term progress in the integration of family preventive and intervention strategies with widely utilized biological interventions is better understanding of the biological mechanisms linking family processes to outcomes over time. Research that documents the effect of relational interventions on biomarkers of stress, brain activity pre-post intervention, and impact on gene expression may help elucidate these key mechanisms. Likewise, it will be illuminating if research on interventions with early family environment examines biochemical effects of intervention and the extent to which such changes account for their effect on long-term positive outcomes.

SUMMARY AND CONCLUSIONS

The adoption of the new definitions for the identification of key family problems in the ICD-11 represents a significant step forward. To the extent that these new criteria are included in surveillance systems and steps are taken to ensure reliable application of the categories across settings, the new system will allow new discoveries in basic science, applied science, and health policy.

ACKNOWLEDGMENT

This chapter was made possible by a grant from the Fetzer Institute awarded to the first author.

REFERENCES

Beach, S. R. H. (2001). *Marital and family processes in depression: A scientific foundation for clinical practice.* Washington, DC: American Psychological Association Press.

Beach, S. R. H., Kim, S., Cercone-Keeney, J., & Brody, G. (2004). Physical aggression and depression: Gender asymmetry in effects? *Journal of Social and Personal Relationships, 21,* 341–360.

Burman, B., & Margolin, G. (1992). Analysis of the association between marital relationships and health problems: An interactional perspective. *Psychological Bulletin, 112,* 39–63.

Cadoret, R. J., Winokur, G., Langbehn, D., Troughton, E., Yates, W. R., & Stewart, M. A. (1996). Depression spectrum disease, I: The role of gene–environment interaction. *American Journal of Psychiatry, 153*(7), 892–899.

Cano, A., & O'Leary, K. D. (2000). Infidelity and separations precipitate major depressive episodes and symptoms of nonspecific depression and anxiety. *Journal of Consulting and Clinical Psychology, 68*(5), 774–781.

Caspi, A., Sugden, K., Moffitt, T. E., Taylor, A., Craig, I. W., Harrington, H.,..., Poulton, R. (2003). Influence of life stress on depression: Moderation by a polymorphism in the 5-HTT gene. *Science, 301*(5631), 386–399.

Gallo, L. C., Troxel, W. M., Matthews, K. A., & Kuller, L. H. (2003). Marital status and quality in middle-aged women: Associations with levels and trajectories of cardiovascular risk factors. *Health Psychology, 22*(5), 453–463.

Heyman R. E., Slep, A. M. S., Beach, S. R. H., Wamboldt, M., Kaslow, N. J., & Reiss, D. (2009). Relationship problems and the DSM: Needed improvements and suggested solutions. *World Psychiatry, 8,* 7–14.

Hooley, J. M., Miklowitz, D. J., & Beach, S. R. H. (2006). Expressed emotion and the *DSM-V*. In S. R. H. Beach, M. Wamboldt, N. Kaslow, R. E. Heyman, M. B. First, L. G. Underwood, & D. Reiss (Eds.), *Relational processes and DSM-V: Neuroscience, assessment, prevention and intervention.* Washington, DC: American Psychiatric Association Press.

Insel, T. R., & Young, L. J. (2001). The neurobiology of attachment. *Nature Reviews Neuroscience,* 2(2), 129–136.

Johnson, N. J., Backlund, E., Sorlie, P. D., & Loveless, C. A. (2000). *Marital* status and mortality: The National Longitudinal Mortality Study. *Annals of Epidemiology, 10,* 224–238.

Kendler, K. S., Hettema, J. M., Butera, F., Gardner, C. O., & Prescott, C. A. (2003). Life event dimensions of loss, humiliation, entrapment, and danger in the prediction of onsets of major depression and generalized anxiety. *Archives of General Psychiatry, 60*(8), 789–796.

Kiecolt-Glaser, J. K., McGuire, L., Robles, T. R., & Glaser, R. (2002). Emotions, morbidity, and mortality: New perspectives from psychoneuroimmunology. *Annual Review of Psychology, 53,* 83–107.

Kiecolt-Glaser J. K., & Newton T. L. (2001). Marriage and health: His and hers. *Psychological Bulletin, 127,* 472–503.

Leiner, A. S., Compton, M. T., Houry, D., & Kaslow, N. J. (2008). Intimate partner violence, psychological distress, and suicidality: A path model using data from African American women seeking care in an urban emergency department. *Journal of Family Violence, 28,* 473–481.

Miklowitz, D. J. (2004). The role of family systems in severe and recurrent psychiatric disorders: A developmental psychopathology view. *Development and Psychopathology, 16,* 667–688.

Miller, G. E., Chen, E., & Parker, K. J. (2011). Psychological stress in childhood and susceptibility to the chronic diseases of aging: Moving toward a model of behavioral and biological mechanisms. *Psychological Bulletin, 137,* 959–997. doi:10.1037/a0024768

Reid, J. B., Patterson, G. R., & Snyder, J. (2002). *Antisocial behavior in children and adolescents: A developmental analysis and model for intervention.* Washington, DC: American Psychological Association.

Sullivan, K.T., Pasch, L.A., Cornelius, T., & Cirigliano, E. (2004). Predicting participation in premarital prevention programs—The health belief model and social norms. *Family Process, 43,* 175–193.

Suomi, S. J. (1999). Developmental trajectories, early experiences, and community consequences: Lessons from studies with rhesus monkeys. In D. P. H. Keating & Clyde (Eds.), *Developmental health and the wealth of nations: Social, biological, and educational dynamics* (pp. 185–200). New York, NY: Guilford Press.

Tienari, P., Wynne, L. C., Moring, J., Lathi, I., Naarala, M., Sorri, A.,..., Kaleva, M. (1994). The Finnish adoptive family study of schizophrenia: Implications for family research. *British Journal of Psychiatry, 164*(Suppl. 23), 20–26.

Uchino, B. N., Cacioppo, J. T., & Kiecolt-Glaser, J. K. (*1996*). The relationship between social support and physiological processes: A review with emphasis on underlying mechanisms and implications for health. *Psychological Bulletin, 119*(3), 488–531.

Verbrugge, L. M. (1979). Marital status and health. *Journal of Marriage and Family*, *41*, 267–285.
Wamboldt, M. Z., & Wamboldt, F. S. (2000). Role of the family in the onset and outcome of childhood disorders: Selected research findings. *Journal of the American Academy of Child and Adolescent Psychiatry*, *39*(10), 1212–1219.
Whisman, M. A., & Bruce, M. L. (1999). Marital dissatisfaction and incidence of major depressive episode in a community sample. *Journal of Abnormal Psychology*, *108*, 674–678.
Whisman, M. A., & Uebelacker, L. A. (2006). Impairment and distress associated with relationship discord in a national sample of married or cohabiting adults. *Journal of Family Psychology*, *20*, 369–377. doi: 10.1037/0893-3200.20.3.369
Wu, Z., Penning, M. J., Pollard, M. S., & Hart, R. (2003). In sickness and in health: Does cohabitation count. *Journal of Family Issues*, *24*, 811–838.
Young, L. J., Francis, D. D., & Insel, T. R. (2003). *The biochemistry of family commitment and youth competence: Lessons from furry mammals* (Working Paper No. 76–18). New York, NY: Institute for American Values.

Index